ECONOMICS

THE COMPLETION OF THE "DISPUTE OF TWO CAMBRIDGES"

VLADIMIR S. GRODSKY

MONOGRAPH

ACADEMUS
Publishing

Academus Publishing
2021

ACADEMUS
Publishing

Academus Publishing, Inc.

1999 S, Bascom Avenue, Suite 700 Campbell CA 95008
Website: www.academuspublishing.com
E-mail: info@academuspub.com

The right of Vladimir S. Grodsky, Doctor of Economics.
For e-mail correspondence: omega2017@bk.ru

ISBN 10: 1 4946 0024 2
ISBN 13: 978 1 4946 0024 2
DOI 10.31519/0024-2

The monograph for the first time comprehensively investigates two main areas of modern economics — mainstream and 'neo-Ricardianism', which are in a state of the so-called 'dispute of two Cambridges'. The theoretical advantages and disadvantages of the directions are shown, as well as specific proposals for their synthesis. The author's interpretations of many issues of economic theory are presented, aimed at increasing its consistency, logical persistence and predictability of further development.

Addressed to researchers, graduate students and teachers, specializing in the field of economics.

Table of contents

Foreword

The town of Cambridge near Boston, Massachusetts, USA, where the Massachusetts Institute of Technology and Harvard University are located since the 1930s of the last century turned out to be closely connected with the city of the same name located not far from London, famous for its ancient university: at that time, between the English and American scientists of these research centers, discussions began on some issues of economic theory that have entered modern history of this science as the 'dispute of two Cambridges'.

After the publication of the book of the professor of the English Cambridge University of Italian origin Piero Sraffa (1898-1983)[1] (*Production of Goods by Means of Goods. Prelude to the Criticism of Economic Theory*, 1960)[2], which addressed the unsolved Ricardian problems of political economy, the 'controversy' acquired acute character and turned into a confrontation between the newly formed direction – 'neo-Ricardianism' – and the well-established theory of the mainstream in the form of 'post-Keynesianism'. Theorists of other areas of economics were also involved in the controversy.

At present, the intensity of the 'dispute of two Cambridges' has somewhat subsided in view of the main representatives of the directions who have passed away, but the fundamental problems of economics have not been resolved. They have remained that way to this day.

In the economic literature, references to the Cambridge problems are constantly found, but there is no thorough scientific study of the dispute and its prospects, while the controversy between neo-Ricardians and post-Keynesians expresses the contradiction of modern economics, is connected with its main issue – the issue of product value – and affects almost all of its sections. In the monograph offered to the readers' attention, for the first time, an attempt is made to analyze the history, reasons, essence, possibilities of exhausting the 'dispute of two Cambridges'.

The content of Sraffa's small book can be considered a really serious "prelude to criticism of economic theory", and over the past 60 years, many 'claims' have accumulated not only to the mainstream, but also to 'neo-Ricardianism'. Their comparison and systemic constructive criticism are contained in our work.

The monograph shows that the statements of representatives of both the mainstream and 'neo-Ricardianism' about the reproductive approach to mod-

---

[1] Hereinafter, in the main text of the monograph, the well-known full names (in some cases, only with the initials found) and the years of life of the personalities are given only at the first mention of them.

[2] The titles of the works in the main text of the monograph are given without quotes in italics, indicating, if necessary, the dates of their first publication (writing).

eling economic equilibrium are in fact declarative in nature, and their models need to be improved, it is shown that the responsibility for creating a single truly reproductive theory of value lies mainly in modern economics. But the modified research results of neo-Ricardians are also used in solving this main problem of modern economics. In monograph, from the standpoint of consistently marginal methodology and the duality of the reproduction process, prerequisites have been developed for the convergence of the theories of mainstream and 'neo-Ricardianism', their synthesis, as well as giving the synthesis economics as a whole a greater practical orientation.

The monograph consists of three chapters devoted to the problems of the end of the 'dispute of two Cambridges', as well as an important conclusion, which examines the long-term trends in the development of economic practice and theory.

The mathematical paraphernalia of modern economics is presented in the monograph in the minimum required volume, it does not contain lemmas and theorems, and the emphasis is placed on graphic illustrations of certain issues and the logic of the development of the research subject. The long-term, short-term and multivariate analysis existing in the economic literature often leads to the simultaneous representation of many functions, some of which are also so-called 'shock' functions, that is, associated with the action of the second , third and other factors, which makes it extremely difficult to perceive the models of even an individual firm, not to mention the models of the economy as a whole. The figure, which we borrowed

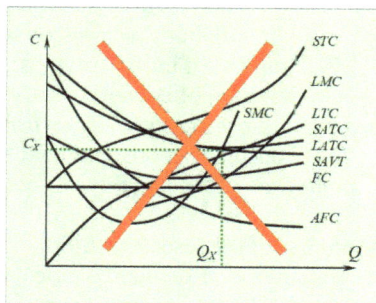

from one modern textbook [26, v. 1, p. 330] and reproduced here with a prohibitive cross, a typical 'mixture' of functions, also called complex abbreviations of the corresponding English terms, is depicted. The reader will not come across such graphs and their complex names in our monograph. We tried to carefully select the most simplified illustrations and often, instead of hard-to-perceive shock functions, we depicted more visual volumetric figures.

For a better understanding of market phenomena, we have developed and used "marketrons" – complete, double integral-differential, market models. Since the main tasks of the monograph are the analysis of the problems of economics and the search for a unified general economic equilibrium (GEE) scheme, our material also contains several new complex multi-quadrant equilibrium schemes.

The monograph uses symbols that exclude complex abbreviations of foreign terms that make it difficult to understand mathematical formulas and equations. To reduce the number of characters, many homogeneous indicators are designated by us with letters with lower indexing in the form of certain abbreviated Russian words and expressions. The letters marked with the upper stroke represent the derivatives of the corresponding functions.

The book uses the following conventions:

a) Latin alphabet:

A – flow of nominal income, income function (profitability); function of constant income (isoquant); a – coefficient or any term; AB – contract amount, contract function and its limitation (isocost);

B – flow of nominal expenses, function of expenses (expense), function of fixed expenses (constant expense, "isospenda"), depreciation; b – coefficient or any term;

C – annuity, material costs, or reimbursement fund in real terms; const – the sign of a constant value; cos – the sign of the trigonometric cosine of the angle;

D – the function of equilibrium preferred economic growth ("preference"); d – sign of an infinitely small increment of a variable; ∂ – sign of a particular infinitesimal increment of a variable;

E – capital-labor ratio; e – the base of the natural log-rhyme;

F – nominal of money savings; f – a sign of a mathematical function;

G – criterion of economic activity, profitability of capital or profitability of production; g – the share of the firm in the total volume of market sales;

H – consumer goods, nominal consumption fund, consumption function; h – an indicator of the quality of economic growth;

I – nominal investment flow or accumulation fund, investment function; i – number of the research object;

J – the level of technological-institutional culture of production; j – the number of the research object;

K – stock of capital goods, number of jobs, monetary value of capital goods; k – the coefficient of proportionality or the norm of the indicator;

L – human labor force, total labor force, number of employed personnel (labor resources), 'human capital'; demand for money in the IS-LM model; l – fundamental economic constant; ln – the sign of the natural logarithm;

M – profit stream; money supply in the IS-LM model; max – the sign of the maximum of the variable, min – the sign of the minimum of the variable;

N – reserves of natural resources, monetary value of natural resources (land); n – the number of research objects;

P – the level of development of production technology; p – the level of monetization of total income;

Q – volume of production in physical or real money terms, the country's production potential; q – an indicator of the level of Tobin's mono-polyism;

R – the efficiency of production or any factor thereof, the economic potential (efficiency of the economy) of the country; r – the velocity of money circulation;

S – the level of development of institutions ("sociology") of production; money savings in *IS-LM* and *IS* models; sin – the sign of the trigonometric sine of the angle; $\int$ – the sign of the integral of a variable;

T – the population size; t – time, calendar years and dates, the term of the loan or lease of goods; time of 'maturation' of investments; tg – sign of the trigonometric tangent of the angle;

U – the level of utility of the good, function and amount of utility;

V – the flow of wages in real money terms;

W – monetary value of the resource potential (national wealth) of the country;

X – unit price of goods, price index; x – unknown equation;

Y – national product (income); y – conditional spatial index;

Z – the nominal sum of money-stock ('cash balances'), money-flow, monetary aggregate or capital-credit; z – the entropy;

b) Greek alphabet:

α – the elasticity of a variable;

β – substitutability of one good for another;

γ – complementarity of goods;

Δ – the sign of the increment of a variable over a period of time;

δ – the share of sectoral costs in total costs, the share of sectoral (individual) capital in total capital;

ε – amplitude of fluctuations of variable magnitude;

η – the share of investments in the total product;

θ – an indicator of the reproductive equilibrium of the economy;

ϑ – equilibrium point (intersection or touch of functions);

λ – the growth rate of the variable;

μ – the share of taxes in the total product, tax rate;

ν – the depreciation rate of the value of durable goods;

Π – sign of multiplication of values;

π – the efficiency of investments; π_{di} – discount factor;

ρ – the Keynes multiplier;

Σ – sign of summation of values;

σ – the frequency of fluctuations of a variable value;

τ – the service life (exhaustion) of the good;

φ – generalized indicator of competition;

ψ – the person's age;

ω – the rate of growth or reproduction of a variable.

Please send your comments on the content of the monograph to omega2017@bk.ru.

Chapter I
Patterns of origin and evolution in the economics of the 'dispute of two Cambridges'

1. Mainstream and 'neo-Ricardianism' economics as sides 'Dispute of two Cambridges'

Modern economic theory is distinguished by an extraordinary variety of scientific directions, schools and concepts. And this phenomenon has objective reasons: the complication of the social market economy itself – the traditional object of the theory, the expansion of its subject beyond the scope of purely economic relations, as well as the development of new research tools. In the economic theory of the past century, the problems of analysis, rather than synthesis, were successfully solved, which led to an increasingly complex differentiation of its subject. Thus, a set of weakly interacting, rather amorphous and contradictory structures of economic knowledge was formed. The correct interpretation and further development of this 'information conglomerate' without establishing a new internal order in it are problematic. Let's try to divide modern economics into enlarged components on the basis of a fundamental contradiction, which consists in using in it both the classical one-factor and neoclassical three-factor theories of the value of goods.

English Cambridge after the publication of the *General Theory of Employment, Interest and Money* (1936) by John Maynard Keynes (1883-1946) turned out to be the source of this contradiction. In the scientific center, a motley 'post-Keynesianism' with a dominant neoclassical[1] methodology and orthodox 'neo-Ricardianism', which preserved the traditions of 'Ricardianism' and 'Marxism', now exists in a fairly formalized form.

Let us turn, first of all, to the characterization of 'post-Keynesianism' as the more well-known and dominant trend (mainstream).

In the literature, one can encounter an extremely large variety in the names of 'post-Keynesianism' and its components [24, v. 5. p. 556]. We, in order to avoid confusion, only all the "equilibrium" economic theories of the second half of the XX century we call 'post-Keynesianism'. It includes three doctrines, one after the other: 'monetarism', 'new classical macroeconomics'[2]

---

[1] The first to use the name 'neoclassical economic theory' was the American institutionalist economist Torten Veblen (1857-1929) (*Theory of the Leisure Class. The Economic Study of Institutions*, 1899).

[2] The term 'macroeconomics' appeared before the term 'microeconomics', was first used in the article *Macroeconomics and the Theory of Rational Behavior* (1946) by the American economist Lawrence Klein (1920-2013) after the expression "microeconomic

and 'new Keynesianism'.

To the monetarists ('Chicago school'), we include the Americans Milton Friedman (1912-2006) – the head of the doctrine, Karl Brunner (1916-1989), Phillip Keygan (1927-2012) and Alan Meltzer (1913-1980). 'Monetarism' as a whole is critical not so much of Keynesian theory as of 'Keynesianism', considers imbalance in the economy as a result of Keynesian intervention in it, considers it necessary to restore the classical principle of laissez-faire and require 'clearing' the market. 'Monetarism' took from Keynes the position on the importance of money, confirms its non-neutrality, the impact on money income and other quantitative indicators of the economy, calls for a 'minimum state', which is reduced to the control of money emission.

Representatives of the 'new classical macroeconomics' who are in solidarity with monetarists on the issue of the effectiveness of the laissez-faire principle are a kind of successors of 'Monetarism', the developers of the 'supply theory ("seplicers")' and 'the theory of rational expectations'[1]. New classics include include Americans John Moot (1930-2005), Robert Lucas (b. 1939), Martin Feldstein (1939-2019), Arthur Laffer (b. 1940), Edward Prescott (b. 1940), and the Norwegian Finn Kydland (b. 1943). Seplisiders as well as monetarists substantiate the necessity of 'clearing the markets' and the reason for the stagnation is considered to be excessive Keynesian taxation, which, according to the 'Laffer function', should be minimal, ensuring high economic growth.

Lucas brought Friedman's skepticism about the regulation of the economy to its logical end, considering it impossible for the adaptive actions of agents who know the market mechanism, who always have rational expectations, in which regulation becomes useless. But the models of Lucas, Kidland-Prescott and other theorists of 'dynamic stochastic general equilibrium' (DSGE-models) are too mathematized, are formal-econometric and are not always unreasonable logically[2]. Israeli economists Daniel Kahneman (b. 1934) and Amos Tversky (1931-1996) (*Theory of Prospects: Analysis of Risk-Based Decisions*, 1979) showed that human expectations and behavior are highly irrational.

Representatives of the 'new Keynesianism', criticizing the 'old' 'Keynesianism' as distorting Keynes's teachings on many issues, are engaged in 'clearing' and a certain development of this doctrine itself. New

---

interpretation" used in the article *Elasticity Demand by Income, a Macroeconomic Interpretation* (1941) by another American, P. de Wolff.

[1] The American economist James Tobin (1918-2002) proposed the division of monetarism into types I and II, understanding the latter as 'the theory of rational expectations'.

[2] Keynes, in his early work *Treatise on Probability* (1921), rejected the effectiveness of econometric research methods because of their inability to identify logical connections between phenomena.

Keynesians also consider Keynes's doctrine to be weakly microeconomic and offer different options for its foundation. At the same time, many concepts of 'new Keynesianism' contain positive assessments of a certain return to the laissez-faire principle, an emphasis on the monetary policy of monetarists and, instead of actively regulating the economy, a transition to its stabilization. We include the Americans Sydney Weintraub (1914-1983), Edmond Malinvo (1923-2015), Robert Clauer (1926-2011), Axel Leyonhufwood (b. 1930), Stanley Fischer (b. 1943), Robert Barrot (b. 1944), Olivier Blanchard (b. 1948), Gregory Manqui (1958) and David Rohmer (b. 1958).

In general, 'post-Keynesianism' as a modern mainstream is characterized by a macroeconomic approach, rehabilitation of the laissez-faire principle and continued use of marginal instruments in research.

Next, we will consider how, simultaneously with the mainstream, another economic trend of modernity developed – 'neo-Ricardianism', which was originally perceived simply as a kind of 'left Keynesianism', which arose among Keynes's employees in Cambridge, but in a developed form became a serious alternative to the rest of macroeconomics.

Many economists of the time believed that the classical theory of value was forever forgotten. The American economist Joseph Schumpeter (1883-1950) (*Capitalism, Socialism and Democracy*, 1942) considered her "dead and buried" [130, p. 59], but the classics were revived in 'neo-Ricardianism', which in the history of economic thought is symmetrical to classical 'Ricardianism' and opposite to the current mainstream.

We refer to the neoricardians as the English economists Joan Robinson (1903-1983), Sraffa, Nicholas Kaldor (1908-1986), Jeffrey Harcourt (b. 1931), the German Heinz Kurz (b. 1946), the Italian Luigi Pasinetti (b. 1930), representatives of the so-called 'analytical Marxism', left-radical economists, Americans Paul Sweezy (1910-2007), Paul Baran (1910-1964) and John Romer (b. 1945), as well as developers of the so-called "system of optimal functioning of the economy" (SOFE) in the USSR Vasily Nemchinov (1894-1964), Alexander Lurie (1903-1970) and Nikolai Fedorenko (1917-2006).

Initially, the direction was associated with the name of the representative of the English Cambridge and 'first wave' marginalism Robinson. She became famous thanks to the models of monopoly and monopsony she created (*Economics of Imperfect Competition*, 1933), which should be seen as a development of the price scissors model of her English teacher Alfred Marshall (1842-1924). But later, Robinson, having made a sharp turn in her work towards criticism of neoclassicism, turned from an orthodox into a heretic of doctrine. Robinson has published a number of anti-marginalist works. It literally fell on the macroeconomic aggregate production function proposed by the Americans, the economist Paul Douglas (1892-1976) and the mathematician Charles Cobb (1875-1949) (*Theory of Production*, 1928). In the article *Production function and the theory of capital* (1953), Robinson called this function "a powerful tool of false enlightenment" [151, p. 81]. Robinson considered the alleged impossibility of the existence of an aggregate measure of the amount of capital goods as a serious reason for rejection of the function. Later, she began to deny the correctness of the marginal distribution of the value created in production on factor income, and in the book *Capital Accumulation* (1956), she methodically tried, according to the figurative expression of Schumpeter, to 'Keynesize' the teachings of the German philosopher and economist Karl Marxs (1818-1883) and 'Marxize' Keynes [129, v. 3, p. 1168]. Robinson, considering 'Keynesianism', formed after Keynes, "illegitimate" [149, p. 90], tried to systematically express her Left Keynesian views on industrial economics.

Robinson's radicalism and non-constructive criticism of the mainstream provoked a stream of publications by followers of the current, mainly the theoreticians of American Cambridge, and the emergence of a protracted 'dispute of two Cambridges' on fundamental issues of modern macroeconomics. The most active and participants in the dispute on the part of 'post-Keynesianism' are the Americans Paul Samuelson (1915-2009), Robert Solow (b. 1924), Franco Modigliani (1918-2003), Joseph Stiglitz (b. 1943) and the Englishman Frank Hahn (1925-2013), who defended their theoretical positions not always effectively.

Samuelson in the article *Parabola and Realism in Capital Theory. The surrogate production function* (1962) proposed a solution to the 'problem of measuring capital', but then admitted in the article *Summing up* (1966) the fallacy of its design. The ambiguity of the positions of Samuelson and other post-Keynesians in their 'justifying theories' greatly confused the solution to the problem posed by Robinson, which is quite easily solved if one consistently adheres to the differentiation of macroindicators into stocks and flows[1].

In English Cambridge with Robinson and her supporters[2], Sraffa worked, whose work was consonant with the views of his colleagues and, at the same time, more radically. If the left Keynesians did not recognize the existing concept of capital, then Sraffa generally excluded this factor of production from the study, switched to the position of the classical one-factor labor theory of value and tackled the problem of the "invariable measure of value" posed by the English political economist David Riccardo (1772-1823). The seriousness of Sraffa's work made him the actual creator of an alternative mainstream macroeconomic trend, collectively called 'neo-Ricardianism',

---

[1] The solution to the 'capital problem' is presented in section 7 of the monograph.
[2] Among the supporters of Robinson's views in English Cambridge, the most famous were Michal Kaletsky (1899-1970) (*Essays on the Theory of Conjuncture*, 1933) and Kaldor (*What's Wrong with Economic Theory?*, 1975).

which was able to compete with 'post-Keynesianism' in the 'dispute of two Cambridges'.

Sraffa was a deeper theorist than the ambitious Robinson. Back in 1926, he published an article *Laws of Return in Competitive Conditions*, which is anti-marginal in nature and proves that perfect competition is possible only in the case of constant capital return and falling marginal income.

Subsequently, Sraffa worked for a long time to publish eleven volumes of the *Works and Correspondence of David Ricardo*, published in 1951-1973, and only in 1960 published his main work *Production of goods by means of goods. Prelude to the criticism of economic theory*, in which he presented an original macroeconomic model built using mathematical models of the input-output balance of the Russian researcher Vladimir Dmitriev (1868-1913) and the American economist Vasily Leontiev (1906-2001), but representing land and capital as "by-products" of production[1]. Sraffa's book caused a great response and heated discussions that continue to this day.

Samuelson wrote that Sraffa's theory is revisionist and moves "in a direction opposite to the mainstream of neoclassical economics after 1870" [156, p. 106]. In economic theory, as in science as a whole, returns to past or long-standing unresolved issues are natural, but the movement of the whole direction in the opposite direction is impossible. Therefore, historically, 'neo-Ricardianism' is a rather powerful developing direction, 'arguing' with the mainstream, replenished by new researchers and turned to the future. However, it is characterized by the preservation of the erroneous upholding of the classical labor theory of value and the need to regulate its state distribution according to social-class criteria.

Many theorists argue about the regulation of the economy, but among them there are those who study its regulators themselves, that is, those rules, norms and legal laws by which the regulation process is carried out. We are talking about institutionalists looking for objective laws of formation, action, evolution, reform and abolition of institutions that regulate the activities of business entities. Despite the fact that the 'old institutionalism', like the 'historicism' that preceded it, developed, as it were, independently of the other cross-cutting directions of economic theory that we considered above, the 'new institutionalism' noticeably intensified its interaction with 'post-Keynesianism' and 'neo-Ricardianism', became equal with them in the use of mathematical tools.

But usually in the literature, 'new institutionalism' is viewed by inertia as a secondary direction of economics, is often simply ignored and even discredited. For example, Blaug mentioned him in his authoritative book

---

[1] Dutch economist Mark Blaug (1927-2011) on this occasion jokingly suggested another title for Sraffa's book – "Production of goods without anything called capital" [14, p. 125].

Economic Thought in Retrospect (1962) only in passing only in a short *Methodological Postscript* [14, p. 656]. Blaug argued this approach with the "sterility" of 'institutionalism' and deduced morality: "in order to defeat the old theory, it is not enough to subject its premises to destructive criticism or to gather new facts – it is necessary to propose a new theory" [Ibid, p. 125]. But 'neoinstitutionalism' turned out to be just the most diverse and productive scientific macroeconomic direction, which had already proposed a concept that could bring itself, 'post-Keynesianism' and 'neo-Ricardianism' closer to synthesis. Therefore, let us take a closer look at the evolution of the newest theory of institutions, which is characterized by both a sharp expansion and unification of the subject of research.

The above description of the subject of initial 'institutionalism', in view of the innovations that took place in it, which allowed us to propose the name "sociological direction", needs to be expanded. The current subject of the direction is the study of the rules of human behavior in different, historically changing social media – economic, legal, political and cultural. Therefore, today the direction includes the following teachings (in the order of their chronological appearance): 1) The theory of property rights; 2) Economics law; 3) New economic history; 4) Evolutionary economics; 5) Economics of the state; 6) The theory of public choice.

'Theory of property rights' was founded by the American economist Ronald Coase (1910-2013) (*The Problem of Social Costs*, 1960), who can be considered the ancestor of the renewal of 'institutionalism'. He suggested turning the external effects of economic activity, the so-called 'externalities,' into a marketable commodity, fully realized through the state with a corresponding expansion of traditional property rights and low 'transaction costs'. Coase's concept turned out to be programmatic, and in the face of a fiasco of various recipes for market regulation, the economy returns to the classical principles of self-organization of the economy and laissez-faire.

The most famous representative of 'Economics law' is the American Richard Posner (b. 1939) (*Economic Analysis of Law. In 2 volumes*, 1973), who considers the question of the mutual economic profitability of not only the unjudicial purchase and sale of externalities, but all court transactions, and applying a neoclassical market approach to the study of all sections of modern law. Some works of the American Gary Becker (1930-2014) (*Human Capital: Theoretical and Empirical Analysis*, 1964), who applied the marginal market approach in the study criminal behavior of business entities. Becker began to use the standard neoclassical 'Marshall cross' in the analysis of not only the deviant behavior of subjects, but also various other social structures – the 'marriage market', family, household and state, discovering, thus, the path to the universalization of microeconomic tools.

The most famous scientists who began to apply the institutional approach in explaining specific historical phenomena, and only they should be considered the theorists of the 'New Economic History', are Americans Douglas North (1920-2015) (*Structure and Changes in Economic History*, 1981), Robert Vogel (1926-2013) (*Without consent and contract: the rise and fall of slavery in America*, 1989), etc. They viewed the institutions of society as social and technological products that are simply created, implemented, reformed, exported and imported as regular goods. The theorists of 'Evolutionary economics' adhere to the school of new economic historians. Americans Richard Nelson (b. 1930) and Sidney Winter (b. 1935) (*The Evolutionary Theory of Economic Change*, 1982) are recognized as the founders of this doctrine, since they began to directly refer to all elements in the study of the interactions of business entities. the concept of "struggle for existence" by the English evolutionary biologist Charles Darwin (1809-1882) (*On the Origin of Species by Natural Selection*, 1859). Representatives of the Evolutionary Economy have developed the key concept of 'routine', which denotes a certain standard for conducting any business affairs, which is stable and, as a genetic material, is passed on to a new generation of entrepreneurs in the process of the evolution of their community, while competition they see it as 'selection' in the struggle for survival and efficiency.

In modern 'institutionalism', the 'Economics of the state' also appeared, exploring the origin and development of government as a result of a rationally acting 'dictator' constantly comparing the costs and benefits of current and institutional decisions made by him. The founder of this theory, the American economist Mansur Olson (1932-1998) (*The Logic of Collective Action: Public Goods and Group Theory*, 1965), rejecting all existing contractual concepts of the state, developed his own theory of becoming modern democracy based on the concept of 'violence', inherent in any power, initially not much different from the predatory power of the 'dictator'.

American economist James Buchanan (1919-2013) (*Calculus of Consent*, together with G. Tullock, 1962; *Limits of Freedom: Between Anarchy and Leviathan*, 1975), deeply analyzing the essence of the functioning of a democratic state, recreated the 'theory of public choice', he believes, owned by the Swedish economist Knut Wicksell (1851-1926). Buchanan himself writes about this as follows: "Wicksell deserves universal recognition as the founder of modern theory of public choice, because in his 1896 dissertation (*Research on the theory of finance – the author*) there were three important elements on which this theory is based : methodological individualism, the concept of 'economic man' (homo oeconomicus) and the concept of politics as exchange" [19, p.18]. The interpretation of 'politics as exchange' is a key element of public choice theory, since it allows the state to be considered a producer of public goods, the choice of which, according to Buchanan, differs from the usual private market choice only by roundabout democratic voting procedures on the state budget. A variety of benefits can be considered as public: from the most essential services for a person, for example, in health care, or pensions, to the benefits of general public use – the law enforcement system, the system of mass information and communication, sustainable functioning and development of the economy, etc.

The pioneers of 'institutionalism' simply promoted an interdisciplinary approach in every possible way, simply believing that "the economy is larger than the market," and put forward a rather banal proposition that the state, as an institution for organizing society, should regulate the market economy according to social criteria and parameters. Therefore, for example, the Swedish economist Gunnar Myrdal (1898-1987) (*The role of the political factor in the development of economic theory*, 1929) proposed the use of political, legal and sociological methods in economic analysis. As it evolved and built up a rather dense content in itself, the 'new institutionalism' became more ambitious, and its representatives boldly declare the primary role of the organization of society in the functioning and development of the economy, while theorists of the mainstream and 'neo-Ricardianism', by inertia, adhere to the opposite determinism.

But, with all the initial polarity of mutual rejection of the views of the representatives of the three directions of the current economics [126], their interaction has changed, in the economic literature there has been a certain convergence of the points of view of theorists [131]. And this is explained by the fact that the so-called social-class factors in the distribution of the product and income, taken into account by the neo-Ricardians, are an expression of the new institutional structures of society.

The phenomenon of 'economic imperialism' in theory, which means the use of standard tools for market research in the study of supra-economic structures of society, allows not only the factors previously treated in economics as exogenous for the market to be transformed into a whole endogenous complex, amenable to market description and balancing, but also to include in this complex the results of purely state affairs in the form of public goods. For example, the spheres of monetary and fiscal regulation lend themselves to quasi-market balancing, which makes it possible to transfer significant volumes of discretionary administration, that is, regulation at the discretion of the state, to the mode of 'built-in regulator', which is more compact, transparent and efficient.

2. Unified positive-normative study methodology economics and assessment of its results

Usually the term 'methodology' (from the Greek words 'way' and 'word') is defined as the doctrine of methods, ways of researching something. That is, only the cognitive side of the methodology is indicated. Therefore, in relation to economic theory, it has long been said about its subject and method. This is the construction of the fundamental essay *On the definition of the subject of political economy and on the method of research inherent in it* (1836) by the English economist James Mill (1806-1873), an important book by his compatriot John Neville Keynes (1859 -1949) (*The Subject and Method of Political Economy*, 1891)[1] and many other more modern publications on the methodology of economic theory and methodology in general.

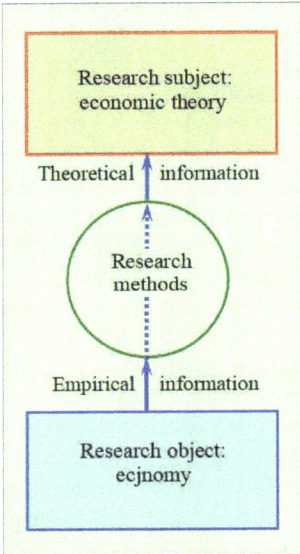

Fig. I.1

It should be noted that the two-element definition of the concept of methodology is quite sufficient for 'objectless' sciences, for example, philosophy or mathematics, which are the instrumental basis for other, 'object' sciences, for example, physics or biology. But, since the economic theory is an object science, then its methodology should provide for the characteristics of the economy itself. The absence of this element entails not only methodological errors in the study of economic phenomena, but also a serious lack of economic theory as a whole – the absence of a full-fledged section on the very object of this science. In textbooks, at best, you can meet a scanty topic under the approximate title 'Historical forms of economic management'[2].

But we are not talking about an independent and important 'Economic History', but about a new section of modern economics devoted to the laws of development, reform and all other changes in social production.

Thus, it seems to us that an effective methodology of economic theory is, in a first approximation, a certain system of interactions between economics – the object of research, their methods and the subject – economic theory (Fig. 1.1). This methodological triad has a number of features, which we will consider in the appropriate sequence.

According to the widespread modern definition, the economy as an object of research is a sphere in which "a society with limited resources decides what, how and for whom to produce" [120, p. 781]. This definition was first

---

[1] J.N. Keynes is the father of the renowned English economist J.M. Keynes.
[2] Sometimes it is said "about the coordination of choice in various economic systems" (see, for example, the textbook: [61]), which, in our opinion, is completely insufficient.

16

given by Samuelson (*Economics: An Introduction to Analysis*, 1948) in order to show the existing differences in the forms of organization of production, highlighting, however, from history only the market, command and mixed economies [96, p. 50]. They supposedly differ from each other in how society solved and solves these three problems. Samuelson's definition is analogous to the well-known Marxist interpretation of economics as a "set of production relations" corresponding to a given stage of development of the productive forces of society, for in both cases business is considered only in a specific organizational form. Of course, the economy is always qualitatively determined, but, nevertheless, it contains a certain universal essence that remains unchanged under all possible organizational metamorphoses. In addition, the historical forms of economics are established not simply as a result of the coordinated solution of these three tasks by people, but in a more complex way, objectively and naturally.

It does not express the essence of the economy and its typical definition as a sphere of society's struggle with the scarcity of goods, as a sphere of "use of rare resources for the production of valuable goods and their distribution among people" [Ibid, p. 48], since the concept of 'scarcity of goods' does not explain the root causes of human production activity, and the product of labor does not always take the form of a commodity, but in reality, benefits are abundant. When characterizing the economy, it is important to show that the surrounding world does not satisfy a person and he changes, remakes him by his actions.

The philosophy of economics is as follows. Self-developing matter as a whole takes on various forms of its motion, arising in a certain sequence and coexisting in a certain combination with each other. This is how mechanical, chemical, biological and social forms of movement are distinguished. Society is the highest, most complex form of motion of matter. And if 'life' is "a way of existence of protein bodies" [69, p. 48], then, paraphrasing this well-known definition of the biota of the German theorist Friedrich Engels (1820-1895) (*Dialectics of Nature*, 1925), we can say that production is a way of existence of society. Therefore, the essence of human production activity consists in the creation of material and spiritual goods, which are of a certain value and satisfy his needs.

The appearance in human nature can be represented as dividing it into many subjects and objects. People become active intelligent, economic entities, and objects and processes of the surrounding world become objects of ordering influence and cognition. In this regard, all existing processes, phenomena and objects can also be divided into natural and socially natural, associated with purposeful human production activities. The goods created by people, or artifacts, form the nature that is being mastered and appropriated by society – an artificial material environment, a structure that we call economics. Since society is the most complex, intelligent form of organization of matter, there are no other material forms and forces in nature that a person could not cognize and which he could not master in principle. There are only natural elements that are already involved and not yet involved in the economy. Nature as a whole is not only a condition, a natural environment for existence, but also an absolute resource for the development of society.

In view of the above, the object 'economy' must first be defined as a sphere of production, transforming the nature of human activity.

Further, it is important to show that the production activity of people is not only useful, but also more and more beneficial for them. Derived from 'economics', the word 'economy' literally means saving, benefit. Therefore, business practice is an efficient, benefit-maximizing activity.

The growth of the efficiency of the economy is associated, first of all, with the division of social labor, that is, quantitative differentiation, the division of the aggregate labor activity of people into more or less independent, separate production processes. Each worker does not have the ability for any kind of work, a fully universal workforce in an increasingly diverse and complex work is ineffective. Therefore, the deepening of the division of social labor and the specialization of individuals – the concentration of their activities on performing more and more simple work, which took place in the history of the economy – were rational, contributed to the growth of savings in the total time spent on the production of goods. The flip side, the inevitable consequence of the division of labor, was the strengthening of cooperation, interdependence, cooperation of people in production.

Thus, production is always dual, isolated and generalized at the same time. The deeper the division of labor in society, the wider and more intensive its cooperation becomes. The division and cooperation of labor are in a relationship of unity and opposition.

It should be noted that the division and cooperation of human labor are implemented in accordance with the rules developed in society, moral norms and legal laws – unofficial and official institutions of society, regulating the interaction of people in the process of their life. The original meaning of the word 'economy' is normative, institutional, associated with the reproduction of life – the daily renewal of the process of production of goods according to certain rules.

The benefits necessary for a person are very diverse, these are internal benefits – positive qualities of an individual – satiety, health, ability to work (possession of labor), education, culture, 'confidence in the future', etc. – and external benefits – a favorable natural environment, food, clothing, housing, family, work, economic and political stability, growth of welfare and individual rights, etc. Among the external benefits of a person, an important place is occupied by the benefits of various communication, cooperation and exchange of his activities with other individuals – the institutions of society.

Economic benefits are also usually divided into: a) resource (land, capital goods and human labor, information and money) and produced with the help of these resources; b) renewable and non-renewable; c) means of production and consumer goods; d) material and spiritual; e) individual, group and public.

Thus, if we combine the considered aspects of production, then we can give the following already quite complete definition of the object of research: the economy, or economy, is a sphere of joint, institutionalized and repetitive, transforming the nature of human activity on the creation and consumption of various goods.

In the historical conditions of limited economic benefits and the rise of human needs in society, private ownership of the means and results of production arose, and the cooperation of people was supplemented by relations of their rivalry, competition, which meant the transition to commodity production and a market economy ... Its reproduction has become a very complex process, including the phases of production, exchange, distribution, consumption and accumulation of goods.

The market economy also continued to develop along the lines of sophistication and diversity. In modern conditions there are markets: 1) perpetual markets, where there is an exchange and change of owners of goods and money, and fixed-term (rental) markets, where goods are sold only for temporary use; 2) ordinary private goods and public goods, the choice of which is carried out using the mechanisms of political voting of citizens; 3) internal and external, associated with the export and import of goods. Science today raises the question of the existence of political, marriage, criminal and other social markets.

Due to the multifactorial nature and complexity of the process of the progressive evolution of the economy, the impression of complete arbitrariness in its directions and forms is created. However, for all the 'elasticity' and stochasticity of the course of development of society, it still obeys the action of objective laws. Knowing them makes it possible to foresee the development of economic life. When comparing different economic theories that satisfactorily explain the current state of the economy, preference should be given to the theory that gives a more accurate and long-term forecast, achieved by identifying its historical trend.

It is important to emphasize that the economic forecast is based not only on the theory of the existing structure of the economy and trends in its further development, but also on the study of the most important past events. The wider the retrospective of the moment is, the more opportunities are created for its broad perspective. That is, it is necessary to know equally the mechanisms of both functioning and evolution of the economy. Therefore, the modern economics needs a de-ideologized and advanced section 'meta-conomics'[1], which, unlike the standard sections microeconomics and macroeconomics, would contain modern models of historical forms of economic management and a non-equilibrium synergetic theory of interformational transitions.

Too rhetorical for economic practice and scientific definition of the object 'economy' the above questions "What, how and for whom to produce?" are better suited for our definition of the methodology of economic cognition, the description of its triad – the object, methods and subject, for here the questions really arise: what does economic theory study, how scientific research is carried out and for whom it is intended? Therefore, the really existing economy, to which the cognitive activity of a scientist is directed, is an object, the means by which the processing and use of data on economic activity are methods, and systematized corresponding knowledge is the subject of economic research (Fig. 1.1) .

The starting point of the study of the economy should be considered empirical information about its state in the current period. But, since it is in continuous change, the scientist is interested not only in the current, but also in its past and future states. Moreover, it is possible to accurately characterize the existing object only in the historical context. Therefore, economic theory, or economics, is essentially a historical science. At the same time, economics, which is at the foundation of the system of economic sciences, does not consider all aspects of an object, but only those that make it possible to reveal the laws of its functioning and development. For this reason, the subject of economics is the characteristics of the most essential sides, properties and structures of the economy.

The formation of the subject of economics is carried out using research methods, which are a combination of scientific principles, tools and specific techniques for translating empirical economic information into a harmonious system of knowledge. The starting points here are: 1) the principle of objectivity of the economy, that is, the principle of its existence regardless of the consciousness and desires of a person; 2) the principle of recognizability of the economy, excluding agnosticism in any form; 3) the principle of determinism, interconnection and causality of economic phenomena; 4) the principle of simplicity ("Occam's blade", first described by the English philosopher William of Ockham (1285-1349), who developed the rule "do not complicate an explanation beyond measure," for "a simple explanation is better than a complex one," according to which of several interpretations of one and the same phenomenon should be chosen the simplest. Departure from these scientific principles of economic research leads to subjectivity and

---

[1] The prefix 'meta' in this name means something changing, developing or reformed. For the first time 'Metaeconomics' as a section of modern economics was presented in our work: [38].

distortion of the picture of reality. Subjectivism is inevitably accompanied by a withdrawal to the analysis of secondary, superficial, insignificant aspects of economic efficiency (sophistry), placing the essential and inessential "on the same level," or substituting one for the other (eclecticism).

The receipt, processing and systematization of economic information are presented in Fig. 1.1 line with arrows, ascending from 'Object' to 'Subject' through 'Research Methods'. Means of purposeful perception of the phenomena of economic life (observation) provide primary empirical knowledge, which is exposed to the logical tools of abstract thinking. At this stage of cognition, the similarities and differences of economic phenomena are clarified (they are compared), assumptions are made about the causes of the phenomena (hypotheses). With the help of the mental division of the object of knowledge into separate parts (analysis), the transition from the general to the particular (induction) and from the particular to the general (deduction), from quantity to quality, from the logical to the historical and vice versa, as well as the mental connection of parts into a single whole (synthesis) a certain system of knowledge about the studied

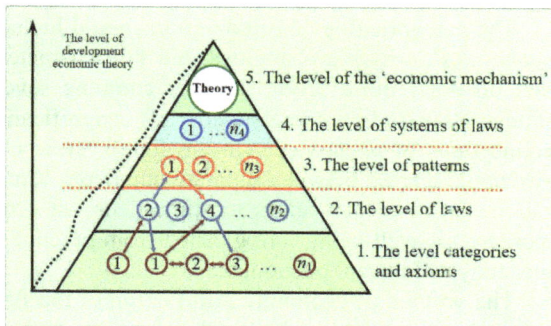

Fig. I.2

economic object is formed. The receipt, processing and systematization of economic information are presented in Fig. I.1 line with arrows ascending from 'Object' to 'Subject' through 'Research Methods'. The means for the purpose of the directed perception of the phenomena of economic life (observation) give the primary empirical knowledge, which is exposed to the influence of the logical tools of abstract thinking. At this stage of cognition, the similarities and differences of economic phenomena are clarified (they are compared), assumptions are made about the causes of the phenomena (hypotheses). With the help of the mental division of the object of knowledge into separate parts (analysis), the transition from the general to the particular (induction) and from the particular to the general (deduction), from quantity to quality, from logical to historical and vice versa, as well as mental By combining parts into a single whole (synthesis), a certain system of knowledge about the studied economic object is formed.

The process of transformation of possibly scattered and incomplete, fragmentary information about an object in economic theory can be represented as a kind of 'pyramid of knowledge' (Fig. 1.2). The general direction and degree of maturity of the theory is indicated by the coordinate 'Level of development of economic theory' directed upwards. It consists of a number of separate levels of knowledge of the economy, in our model there are five of them. The scheme narrows towards the top, which indicates a phased 'collapse' of information, its becoming more compact, formalized and systematized.

Initial cognition of an object is carried out at the 'Level of categories and axioms', here the 'word' of economics is formed, consisting of concepts that name and briefly characterize economic phenomena. Such concepts are economic categories. Any economic term that has a scientific interpretation and, possibly, a statistical assessment is included in this level of knowledge. Economic categories are the nodal points of cognition, the initial moments of penetration of thinking into the essence of phenomena.

The categorical level of cognition should include the so-called 'axioms of economics', which are obvious, but key characteristics of economic reality that do not require proof. Axioms combine several categories into certain statements based on some superficial, insignificant, but practically important connections of phenomena (in the figure, these connections are depicted by horizontal arrows between separate numbered 'Categories'). For example, the statements 'a person reacts to stimuli' or 'an economic individual seeks to increase his well-being' are gleaned from practice and how the axioms guide the study of relevant phenomena.

The volume of economic information of the first 'Level of categories and axioms' (n_1) increases with the development of the object itself, as well as the subject of research. So new concepts and terms are included in the scientific community due to the emergence of either the very certain economic phenomena in reality, or specific analytical and synthesis developments within the subject. Thus, the subject of economic research changes as a whole in accordance with the development of the economy, but the independent development of economics intensively increases its complexity, which approaches the complexity of the object itself.

The next stage of economic cognition should be considered the 'Level of laws', at which the theory becomes more rigorous, since each economic law reflects a repetitive and essential cause-and-effect relationship of phenomena (categories). In Fig. 1.2 these connections are depicted by arrows passing to the 'level of laws' from the first, purely descriptive, verbal, level.

Individual laws are considered as acting in real or imaginary conditions of immutability of all other phenomena of the object. This abstraction of the simplest studied subject is called for brevity by the Latin expression ceteris paribus, meaning 'other equal'. The research premise of ceteris paribus in economics is important and widespread.

Since laws unite categories, the total number of laws (n_2) is less than the number of categories, and with the transition to the second level of cognition, economic information becomes more compact and ordered. At the third level of development of economic theory and cognition of economics, called the 'Level of regularities' (the total number of regularities – n_3, $n_3 < n_2 < n_1$), further 'densification' of knowledge occurs, since some stable causal relationships between the laws themselves. Such connections, as a rule, are more elastic and ambiguous, take the form of 'law-tendencies' or even mathematical correlations. However, this level of knowledge is especially important, since it is on it that the possibility of obtaining quantitative characteristics of the formulated laws, as well as dividing all economic knowledge into descriptive and mathematized, appears.

An even higher fourth level of the study of economics contains whole 'Systems of economic laws' and even more 'curtailed' economic knowledge. For example, systems of laws of processes of production, distribution, exchange, consumption and accumulation, systems of laws of functioning and laws of development of economics, etc. are formed here. Several sublevels can be distinguished here, falling on the study of these different systems of laws. The total number of systems of laws of the fourth level is indicated on the diagram as n_4, in the general inequality it is presented as follows: $n_4 < n_3 < n_2 < n_1$.

The concept of 'Economic mechanism' of the highest, in our 'pyramid' of the fifth level, combines the knowledge of both substances, systems of objective laws of the economy, and the system of instances, institutions of society, directly or indirectly used in the functioning and development of the economy, a kind of its design. This difficult-to-achieve level should correspond to economic theory in the full sense of the word as a highly organized unified system of fundamental knowledge about economics (n_5), which corresponds to an extended line of inequalities: $n_5 < n_4 < n_3 < n_2 < n_1$.

It is important to note that the subject of research is always only an informational display of the object. The subject of economics is made up of primary statistics and other factual material about economics, processed, model, information in the form of categories, axioms, laws, concepts and theories. In addition to these ordered scientific forms, the subject usually contains all possible 'paradoxes', 'dilemmas', 'dichotomies', 'dogmas', 'logical apoments' and other 'intermediate' research products, which disappear as the cognition of the object deepens.

By the aforementioned quantitative knowledge, we mean not just formalized knowledge, but knowledge that contains calculations and specific recommendations for their implementation that are important for more efficient economic practice. Only the establishment of links between laws allows one to obtain such knowledge. Depending on whether the economic theory has reached the level of regularities or not, one can judge its overall quality and ability to perform not only cognitive, but also practical functions.

Fig. I.3 clearly shows the mechanism of the rise of theory from descriptive to quantitative knowledge of economic reality. The figure in the form of a closed contour conventionally represents the economy – the object of research, and the segments tangent to it are separate laws of the theory. As you know, the main economic contradiction between the limitlessness of needs and, in general, the limitedness of benefits, business entities always resolve through savings and savings. One might even say that economic theory is the science of economics in the literal sense of the word. Therefore, we will show how the accumulation law is obtained in the theory of a quantitative characteristic.

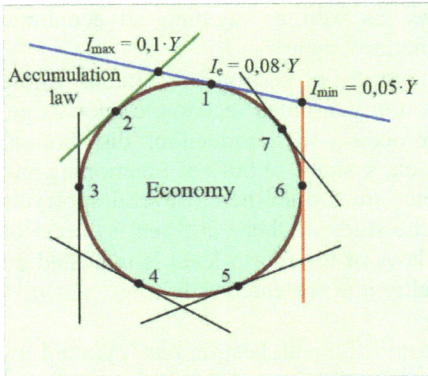

Fig. I.3

If, for example, we consider the law of accumulation separately from other laws, then its formulation only states the objective need to convert part of the national income (Y) into investment (I), providing improvement of technology, achievement of certain levels of employment and economic growth. Even the formalization of this causal relationship does not allow us to give it a quantitative characteristic, because it will only be a symbolic image of the verbal definition of the law. But as soon as the research proceeds to establishing the links of this law with other related laws, it becomes possible to obtain quantitative data. Let us assume that these are the laws of growth in the efficiency of production and population. The first of them will already determine the upper limit of investments ($I_{max} = 0,1 \cdot Y$), and the second – their minimum volume, providing employment for the population ($I_{min} = 0,05 \cdot Y$). A certain range of accumulation appears, due to the operation of three economic laws. If the number of laws studied jointly increases, then the range of accumulation narrows, up to the appearance of its equilibrium value ($I_e = 0,08 \cdot Y$). Moreover, the balancing of the economy cannot be local, referring only to accumulation. Here the concept of 'equilibrium' has a systemic, emergent character and applies to all 'joints', 'intersections' of laws (in Fig. I.3 these are points 1, 2, 3, 4, 5, 6, 7). In this ideal case, the theoretical display of the object will be complete, and the 'polyhedron' of economic laws will merge with the closed loop 'Economy'.

Formalization of descriptive material in economic theory is a great achievement and is important for the subsequent filling of models with specific calculations. Economics as a social object is difficult to lend itself to even a simplified mathematized display. It is due to the special nature of economic ties that their rigorous models contain not only functional dependencies usual for natural sciences, but also average and marginal (marginal) indicators, as well as 'elasticities' (the ratio of marginal and average indicators factors), 'multipliers' (scale factors for the transition of the system from one state of equilibrium to another due to the action of destabilizing factors) and multifactorial (matrix) characteristics.

The multifactorial nature of economic phenomena forces us to resort in theory to the indicated 'abstraction', the premise of ceteris paribus and the subsequent 'concretization'. Due to the still rather weak quantitative economic theory and its limited experimental capabilities, modern economics mainly uses rather abstract mathematical modeling and purely illustrative graphical tools.

In connection with the issue of complex economic knowledge, it should be noted that in the literature only its cognitive, educational, methodological and practical functions are usually indicated. But it seems to us that a special allocation of the prognostic function is necessary. It is important for all sciences, but for economic sciences it is one of the main functions, since knowledge of the prospects for the development of society is of special value for a person. The full implementation of the predictive function in economics, especially in connection with the development of the 'metaeconomics' section in it, will become an indicator of its high level of development.

Methodology is not exhausted by the formation of an economic system of knowledge, since it has a feedback line between theory and practice. To clearly demonstrate this

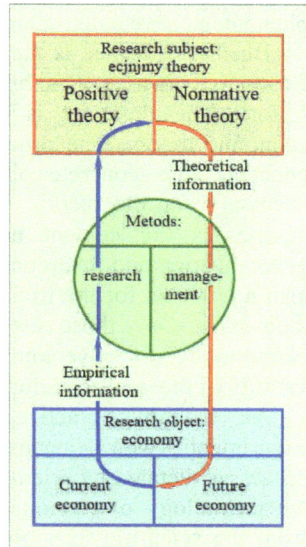

Fig. I.4

connection, we will divide all three elements of the above model of economic research methodology into two parts (Fig. 1.4). This allows us to show, firstly, the transformation of a positive theory into a normative theory, secondly, the use of the latter various methods of management, that is, with all management tools at different levels, and, thirdly, the implementation of theoretical developments Current and recommendations in the economy. Thus, the expanded model of methodology and the above 'pyramid' of economic knowledge demonstrates the whole closed circle of expanded reproduction of economic information, its production, distribution over five levels, exchange in the process of rationing, consumption and accumulation. The accumulation of scientific information occurs at all levels of the 'pyramid' intensively in the form of a deeper knowledge of the economy of the current period and extensively as a result of the transition of the economy to a higher and more complex level of development (in Fig. I.2, this is the dotted line)

Analysis of a single methodological reproduction cycle shows that theoretical research methods should bring hypotheses in line with the facts, and practical methods of management, on the contrary, should bring the actual parameters of the economy in line with the developed norms. Thus, the methods of research and management become adequate to each other, and the disproportions between them mean the manifestation of either dogmatism – an orientation only towards economic theory, which turns into a dogma, or pragmatism – an orientation only towards economic practice. Both phenomena have a detrimental effect on the development of society.

Business practice is the starting and ending point of economic research. Economic practice in a broad sense, as the experience of mankind in its historical development, is in unity with the cognitive activity of man, with economic theory. The processes of cognition and action transform abstract concepts into concrete objectivity. Practice, giving the factual material necessary for the theory, forms the subject of cognitive activity himself, determines the content and direction of his thinking, the method of generalization and theoretical processing of empirical information. Practice is also a criterion for the truth of economic knowledge, serves as a measure of their value. Only those research results that have been tested by practice can claim to be objective knowledge, since economic activity determines the validity of the goals developed by science.

An economic practice is associated with the concept of 'economic experiment', which means a certain change in the course of economic processes dictated by scientific goals. Although the experiment is foreseen by the technology of economic research, which in principle should not differ from the scientific technologies of natural science, but as a social science, economic theory in this part has limitations associated with with the prevention of any negative consequences for people. Therefore, when they talk about an economic experiment, they mean local microeconomic (sectoral or regional) testing of innovations, which is temporary in nature and does not entail social damage. Experimentation in economic theory is mainly associated with modeling, that is, with a virtual imitation of economic phenomena.

To determine the place of economics in the modern system of sciences, it is advisable to first select natural science from all sciences, the data of which are used by economic sciences, and social science, in which economics

26

functions in direct interaction with other humanities (Fig. I.5). There are also universal sciences that do not have their own research objects (see the arrow directed from the block 'Science as a whole'). These are philosophy, logic, mathematics, cybernetics and a relatively new science – synergetics. Philosophy equips economics with a general scientific toolkit of cognition, logic allows, with the help of strict rules for the formation of concepts, judgments, inferences and definitions, to draw the necessary conclusions and generalizations, proofs and refutation of certain scientific provisions. Mathematical techniques make it possible to concretize and formalize economic research. Since the economy is a complex self-organizing, controlled and dynamic system, cybernetics and synergetics provide very fruitful methods for modeling its functioning and development.

In economic research, object natural sciences are also used, the data of their technological directions, data of applied natural science are generalized. The value is represented by information about highly efficient means and organization of

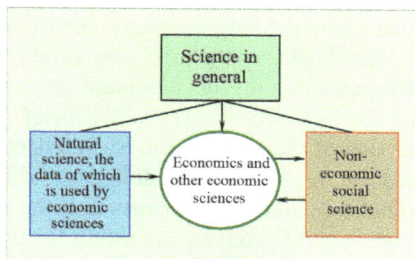

Fig. I.5

production. Since ekonomix studies anthropogenic effects, ecology and its data on the interaction of society and nature are of great importance for it.

Social science as a ramified system of sciences consists of history, economics, political science, law, theology, ethics and cultural studies, and economics performs the system-forming function here, which, thanks to the study of the economic foundations of human life, Combines the listed sciences into one whole. Economics is the core of social consciousness, it not only coordinates its constituent industries, but also receives data from them for generalizations.

Social science does not have a clear border with natural science, and the sciences at the junction often turn out to be important for the economy. For example, anthropology as a branch of natural science can successfully solve its question of anthropogenesis, in our opinion, only with the help of an analysis of human economic activity, and this, in turn, makes it possible to strengthen the axiomatic foundations of the economy itself. Frontier economic cybernetics is extremely important to economies. It uses divisions of cybernetics such as systems analysis, praxeology, operations research, optimal control theory, mathematical programming, and game theory. These branches of science allow to optimize economic models and the economy itself.

3. 'Dispute of two Cambridge' and the development of a new model history of economic thought

The model presented above of the universal positive-normative methodology of expanded reproduction of economic knowledge should incorporate all the various achievements in the toolkit for researching social production throughout its history. We do not intend to review these advances as the literature provides a good overview of the *History of Economic Methodology* in Blaug's book *Methodology of Economics, or How Economists Explain* (1980). We will limit ourselves only to a general remark that the changes in research paradigms have always occurred as a result of radical changes in the very economic life of people.

Our task is to clarify the essence, prerequisites for the emergence and prospects for the development of the modern 'dispute of two Cambridge', which has already received a brief and superficial description in the first section of the monograph. Such a deeper analysis of the 'dispute' requires not just an appeal to the standard 'History of Economic Doctrines', which contains a simple enumeration of the facts of cognition of phenomena and, at best, several grouped according to formational or some other characteristics. We need a special science that solves the problems of the existence of regularity and patterns of development of economic thought as a whole, the evolution of the internal content of individual research paradigms and in replacing one with another.

We call this science 'retroeconomics'[1], which can represent the solution of these issues in a strict model form and represent a special section economics. The term 'retroeconomics' is consistent with the above-mentioned title of another section 'metaeconomics' that we are proposing, as well as with the existing names of other standard sections of economic theory: microeconomics, macroeconomics and megaeconomics. The rise to a retroeconomic mix will contribute to theoretical homogeneity, logical harmony of economies, and, consequently, the entire system of economic knowledge.

The modern transition to 'retroeconomics' is predetermined by the entire course of the historical development of economic theory, which is no more than two hundred years old.

The authors of the first systematized textbooks on the History of Political Economy were the theoretical economists themselves: the Englishman John McCulloch (1789-1864) (*Historical sketch of the emergence of the science of political economy*, 1826), the French Alban Villeneuve-Bargemont (1784-1850) (*History of Political Economy, or Historical, Philosophical and*

---

[1] See: [38, 36].

Religious Studies on the Political Economy of Ancient and Modern Peoples, 1841) and Adolphe Blanqui (1798-1854) (*History of Political Economy in Europe*, 1841). Marginal economic theory was first reflected in the *History of Political Economy* (1878) by the American John Ingram (1823-1907) and the *History of Economic Doctrines* (1909) by the French Charles Gide (1847-1932) and Charles Rist (1874-1955). The well-known and rather perfect *History of Economic Thought* (1938) was written by the professional historian Englishman Eric Roll (1907-2005). A special event in the development of the theory of this science was the extensive and deep *History of economic analysis* (1954) by Schumpeter.

In the second half of the XX century publications appeared that could stimulate research on the history of economic thought: excerpts from the three-volume *Theory of Surplus Value* by Marx published in English in 1951, the ten-volume *Proceedings and Correspondence of David Ricardo*, prepared by Sraffa and the American Marxist Maurice Dobb (1900-1976), thirty-volume *Collected Works of J.M. Keynes* and seven-volume *Collected Works and Correspondence of Adam Smith*.

However, by that time, the attitude towards the history of economic thought was divided.

On the one hand, in the conditions of the formation of economics, works appeared in which an operationalist (mathematized) view of the entire previous theory was carried out. These are, first of all, the books by Blaug, *Economic Theory in Retrospect* (1962), The *Cambridge Revolution: Success or Failure?* (1974) and the Japanese researcher Takashi Negishi (b. 1933) *History of Economic Theory* (1987), in which an attempt was made to marginalize the teachings of the past, which seem to resonate with the modern mainstream. Such studies, in spite of a certain rationalization (modernization) and imparting science to the 'History of economic doctrines', did not raise the level of its scientific level. We consider already counterproductive not only the existing superficial chronologies of scientific events, but also the data. widespread interpretations of theories of the past from the standpoint of their contribution to modern science. If, in the first case, the regularities of the process elude the researcher, then in the second case, judgments about the prehistory look too arrogant.

On the other hand, in the last thirty years, profound works have been published, advancing science towards 'retroeconomics'. First of all, Dobb's book *Theories of Value and Distribution after Adam Smith* (1973) should be noted, which outlined two opposing lines of the theory of value of the XIX century, arising from Smith's *Study on the Nature and Causes of the Wealth of Nations* (1776). Dobb believed that the division of the views of scientists occurred under the influence of ideology (hence the subtitle of the book *Ideology and Economic Theory*), which is more characteristic of the third direction of development of the theory – 'institutionalism'. Also important for the theorization of the 'History of Economic Doctrines' was a series of works by the Englishmen Samuel Hollander (b. 1937): about the classics – *Economics of Adam Smith* (1973), *Economics of David Ricardo* (1979), *Economics of John Stuart Mill. In 2 volumes* (1985), The *Economics of Thomas Robert Malthus* (1997), The *Economics of Karl Marx: Analysis and Application* (2008) and *Classical Economics* (1987), and The *Early Economic Works of Alfred Marshall, 1867-1890* (1975) and *Keynesian Economics: The Quest for Initial Principles* (1983) by Alan Coddington (1941-1982).

In this series of publications, of interest is the book *Man in the Mirror of Economic Theory (Essay on the History of Western Economic Thought* (1993) by the Russian economist Vladimir Avtonomov (b. 1955), who believes that 'the phenomenology of man' is the basis for modeling the history of economic theory. In the rest of the economic literature in the USSR and Russia, the search for patterns in the development of world economic thought is so far reduced to an in-depth analysis of only its individual stages [4, 107, 79, 128].

The most correct seems to be a strict retroeconomic modeling of the sequence of the entire process of the evolution of knowledge, considering it as a complex interaction of broad, cross-cutting, directions. The scientific groundwork available in the literature for 'retroeconomics' needs to be generalized and developed. But progress and trends in the most modern economy also make it possible to more accurately characterize not only its past and present, but also its future state. The formation of a full-fledged 'retroeconomics' makes it possible to clarify and connect between them the characteristics of the creativity of economists, schools and entire periods in theoretical history.

One of the signs of the emergence of 'retroeconomics' can be considered the addition of the external binding of its subject to the known stages of development of social production, which is characteristic of the 'History of Economic Doctrines', with a description of the process of internal self-development of science. The qualitative state of any economic theory is actually determined by a complex of circumstances, both internal and external. But the division of the history of economic doctrines on the Marxist formational criterion that still exists in literature cannot be flawless, since, even abstracting from the groundlessness of the 'five-member' and, despite the general historical adherence of theoretical thought to the development of economic practice, between the latter often large time gaps are formed. The theory sometimes anticipates real events, and sometimes it takes a long time to solve problems, the practical relevance of which has already disappeared. These phenomena prove that science develops primarily according to its internal laws, which are always conditioned by the special and complex interaction of broad, 'cross-cutting' directions that coexisted not only at every historical moment, but also in previous and subsequent times.

Retroeconomic analysis of systems of economic knowledge requires the disclosure of their internal fundamental theoretical contradictions. Accuracy in this matter is of fundamental importance, because it allows you to objectively evaluate the work of a wide range of economists. In this regard, the article *Political Economy* of the *Modern Russian Economic Encyclopedia* (1999), typical of the historical and economic approach, reads: "As a generalizing economist of manufacturing capitalism, Smith simultaneously applied two different research methods: descriptive and abstract – and as a result formed the beginnings of two actually different theoretical systems, still closely intertwined in his economic doctrine. One of them reflected external, directly perceived properties and dependencies of economics, while the other explored its internal, essential laws" [133, p. 986].

In general, the attempt made in the article to isolate from the general historical flow of economic research information conflicting scientific directions should be assessed as positive. Indeed, throughout the development of political economy, there has been a dispute between the classics and neoclassics over the value of goods. However, the characteristics of the directions in the article are based on the opposition of the essence and phenomenon attributed to them, respectively, which, in our opinion, is erroneous. Analysis of the development of economic knowledge, going beyond the 'period of political economy' in the field of its prehistory and modernity, shows that the classical and neoclassical concepts of value are complementary parts of the theory of the market, consisting of equal producers and consumers of goods.

A scientifically grounded dialectical view of things makes it possible, firstly, to interpret the schools of political economy under consideration as segments of larger directions extending throughout the history of economic thought, and secondly, not to build hopes on "reconciliation" nie schools in the future [Ibid, p. 990], but to look for the foundations of the synthesis concept in already existing economic theories and, thirdly, as already noted, to move from the 'history', which registers only the scientific events that have taken place, to the 'theory' that conducts research not only of the past science, but also its prospects.

The retro approach to modeling the development of economic theory[1] allows us to assert that the foundations of the synthesis concept of value were already laid by Marshall (*Principles of Economics*, 1890). His model of market equilibrium includes both production and consumer pricing. The first is built on the classical principle of production costs, and the second – on the neoclassical principle of scarcity of goods. And these principles are in the

---

[1] See: [32, 37, 40].

31

model not in the relationship between essence and phenomenon, but as equivalent. At the same time, it is important to emphasize that the 'Marshall cross' itself can be considered both in the essential and the phenomenal aspects. Let us note that it is precisely the insufficient knowledge of the essence of the 'cross' that determines the opposition of the concepts of value and value of goods, embedded in the modern theories of mainstream and 'neo-Ricardianism', respectively.

Due to the noted false priority of the classical approach to interpretations of history and the content of economic theory, the latter turn out to be strongly distorted. So, the reason for the change in the name of science by Marshall in the mentioned article is declared not to be an objective implementation in market economic practice of the principle of non-interference of the state in private entrepreneurial activity (according to Smith – "the system of natural freedom" [109, p. 647], the principle of laissez-faire of physiocrats), and the author's subjective desire to create a "politically neutral economic discipline" [137, p. 988]. The introduction of non-economic reasons into the analysis of the market behavior of buyers-consumers of goods by neoclassicists in the article is explained not by the multifactorial and individuality of their choice, but by the desire of marginalists to consider only the "superficial cut of economic laws, their own its kind is the laws of the economic form" [Ibid].

Proceeding from the same incorrect interpretation of the contradictions of the classics, the article under consideration does not even mention the division of marginalism into cardinalism and ordinalism, which is important for the nature of the further development of the entire economic theory of the XX century, and the work of the American economist John Clark (1847-1938) (*Distribution of Wealth*, 1899), which extended the marginal cardinalist approach to the study of production and thereby created the conditions for the formation of a complete and final theory of the value of economic benefits.

The erroneous division of economic knowledge into 'essential' and 'phenomenal' ('substantial' and 'formal', 'vulgar') adopted in the dictionary entry throughout its historical development did not allow the authors to understand modern economic theory, which is mentioned only partially and in passing, only in connection with the development of economic policy. Meanwhile, it is the second half of the XX century, as we have shown above, that opens a new scientific stage in history, without a detailed structuring of which it is impossible to carry out its accurate scientific assessment and reliable forecast of the development of economic knowledge. The predictive function economics can begin to be effective only with the appearance of 'retroeconomix' in it, built on the separation from the historical stream of ideas, concepts and schools of the system of extremely generalized, externally and internally contradictory scientific directions.

It is important to note separately that the noted erroneous asymmetric approach to the development of knowledge about the market does not allow one to correctly interpret the use of mathematical tools in economic research. In the mentioned article, this historical regularity is associated with the transfer of the emphasis of representatives of the neoclassical direction to the study of superficial economic phenomena. However, the tendency to mathematize economic theory has an independent and systemic meaning, not associated only with any of its individual directions, and cannot be considered only as an increase in the formalization of knowledge. Mathematical modeling provides fundamental possibilities for determining economic proportions of different levels, both deep and superficial, and as a result obtain quantitative knowledge necessary for economic policy and practice[1]. 'Retroeconomics' of the modern economics can be presented in a rather formalized form and thus becomes closer to its other, already mathematized sections.

Returning to the question of studying the essence and its phenomena, it is important to emphasize that this dialectical dualism in the development of economic theory corresponds, first of all, to the unity and opposition of substantial and institutional research. The latter is considered to be a theoretical innovation, but in fact they were observed throughout the development of economic knowledge. In particular, elements of institutional reasoning are seen in antiquity, 'mercantilism' and the 'historical school'. Moreover, it makes sense that it is 'institutionalism', and not economics, to be regarded as not only an independent, but even an axial 'general mainstream', since it permeates the entire history of economic thought and connects all its scientific formations into a consistent chain.

The components of modern economic theory considered above – 'post-Keynesmianism' and 'neo-Ricardianism' – also have, although not yet very clear, but very broad retrospective, which, as a rule, unreasonably escapes the attention of the History of Economic Teachings. In the following sections of the monograph and its Conclusion, we have made an attempt to fill this gap in science and present a graphical retroeconomic model.

The choice of the initial time point of the analysis is of great importance for the adequate reproduction of the historical process of economic research and finding the appropriate regularities. But the problem of the origins and lower boundaries of economic thinking is very complex and controversial. In the literature on this score, there are different models: from the 'short' one, in which the presentation of the issue begins with the characteristics of the period of completion of the formation of the actual economic theory, political

---

[1] It is necessary to distinguish between mathematized and quantitative knowledge. If the first can be a symbolic designation of phenomena and their causal-effect relationships – graphs of dependencies, formulas and equations, then the second always involves numerical calculations.

economy, at the end of the XVIII century [5], to the 'long', in which the authors try to find out the nature of the economic thinking of primitive people by psychoanalytic deciphering of ancient mythology [77, 121] on the basis of the assumption that, as a rule, behind each any economic scene is hidden by the mythological plot.

Obviously, the question of including or not including in 'retroeconomics' 'paleoeconomics' ('paleo' – translated from Greek means 'ancient') does not exist, since the content of the subject cannot be approached from the point of view of the amount of available surviving material that reflects economic knowledge of people. It is always necessary to take into account the facts of the indissolubility of the historical process, the principles of balance and completeness (but not necessarily the details) of the presentation, which make it possible to show the sources of systematized economic knowledge.

In the development of a retroeconomic model, the actually existing symmetry and recurrence of many phenomena of the historical process should also be taken into account. The corresponding approach will make it possible to reconstruct the insufficiently studied initial period of creative evolution and more accurately predict future scientific events that are symmetrical to the past. The deeper the retroeconomic analysis penetrates into history, the broader its forecast becomes.

'Retroeconomics' should better than 'History of Economic Studies' meet the general universal requirements for any science. First, it is necessary to confirm the concept of the development of sciences as a change in the research programs of the English historian of science Imre Lakatos (1922-1974) (*Evidence and refutation*, 1964; *Falsification and methodology of scientific research programs*, 1970) [64]. Taking into account the development of research on the institutional design of historical landmark production technologies can serve as an illustration of the concept of the existence in economic theories of a stable "hard core" and a changeable "protective shell" of Lakatos.

Secondly, the identification in 'retroeconomics' of qualitative changes in the theoretical concepts of scientists as the main scientific events makes it possible to demonstrate the criterion for changing one conceptual scheme of formulating and solving scientific problems (paradigm) to another, developed in 1963 by the American representative of the "philosophy of science" Thomas Kuhn (1922-1996) (*The structure of scientific revolutions*, 1962) [60]. And, thirdly, since the truth of the model of the historical development of economic thought as a product of a certain scientific simplification of reality can always be "falsified" (refuted) according to the criterion of the Austrian philosopher Karl Popper (1902-1994) (*Logic and the growth of scientific knowledge*, 1935; *Objective knowledge. Evolutionary approach*, 1972) [84], and verification of the retroeconomic model by direct verification (empirical verification) is difficult to implement, then it makes sense to use the principle of symmetry (equivalence) between the forecast and an explanation of what has already happened, which is regarded as a backward prediction.

Therefore, to confirm the correctness of the retroeconomic model, a satisfactory explanation of the known historical facts, ordered by cause-and-effect relationships, is sufficient. For better structuring of a huge amount of accumulated material on the history of economic thought, in the monograph we will mainly use a visual graphical modeling method, which is already found in the relevant literature[1].

Our retroeconomic interpretation of the history of economic is directly related to the above-repeatedly considered universal reproduction approach in various studies.

It is important for us to show that the functioning of the modern economy repeats its history. Everyday reproductive practice, which consists in the periodic alternation of the processes of production, distribution, exchange, consumption and accumulation of goods, underlying the momentary, logical, structuring of developed economic knowledge, has its historical equivalent – a change in the theory chicheskikh paradigms, a chain of qualitative forms of economic knowledge. This objective phenomenon is observed due to the action in society of the 'sociogenetic law', which is analogous to the well-known physicists 'ergodic law' and biologists 'biogenetic law'. We believe that the 'economic-genetic law' is subject to the development of not only the total knowledge obtained by the community of theoretical economists, but also the creativity of its individual representatives who reproduce and promote already existing science.

The philosophical basis of these laws is the heuristic, cognitive, equivalence of 'logical and historical' – a pair from a well-known set of dual research methods, which in the literature is sometimes called 'synchronous-diachronic', 'moment-time' method of analysis. In the literature there are also several interpretations of the concepts 'logical' and 'historical'. So, in the *Philosophical Encyclopedic Glossary* it is noted that these concepts characterize "the relationship between historically developing objective reality and its reflection in theoretical knowledge. Logical is a theoretical reproduction of a developed and developing object in all its essential, lega connections and relations" [119, p. 23]. Another *Encyclopedia* gives a different definition. 'Logical' in it is interpreted as a short reproduction of the historical, further, logical analysis is associated with a mature object, and the historical method – with the development, formation of an object, and, finally, logical means a general, abstract line of differentiation. the twist of the object,

---

[1] See, for example: [5, 96].

and under the historical – the concrete expression of the logical in all the variety of its special and individual manifestations [16, v. 14. p. 607].

Comparing these definitions, first of all, it should be noted that the comparison of the logical and the historical as the theoretical and the practical is hardly legitimate, since the logical and the historical are present both in theory and in practice. The second and third given characteristics, as will be shown below, are closest to the essence of the methods under consideration.

As for the last interpretation of categories, it goes back to the works of Marx. It is known that he contrasted the logical and historical methods of research. In particular, he wrote that "it would be impracticable and erroneous to interpret economic phenomena in the sequence in which they historically played a decisive role. On the contrary, their sequence is determined by the relationship in which they are to each other in modern ... society, and this relationship is directly opposite to that which seems natural or corresponds to the sequence of historical development" [69, v. 46 , part II, p. 44, 45].

Engels, the co-author of some of Marx's works, put a different content into the correlation of methods: "From where history begins, the train of thought should begin with the same, and its further movement will be nothing more than a reflection of the historical process in an abstract and theoretically consistent form, the reflection is corrected, but corrected in accordance with the laws that the actual historical process itself gives" [Ibid, v. 13, p. 497]. Engels believed that the logical method is "the same historical method, only freed from historical forms and from interfering accidents" [Ibid].

Such a simplified understanding of the historical, which supposedly differs from the logical only in greater detail ('concretization'), is encountered by many contemporary authors. But the logical method of researching economics is to determine the momentary structure of social production, while the historical (diachronic) method presupposes the analysis of economic processes, that is, phenomena occurring in time (on this basis, economic laws can be divided into the laws of development and the laws of functioning, reproduction of the investigated object). The momentary structure of an object, being a synchronous display of the relations of the system's elements, can be rationally described only by a certain coherent sequence of separate moments, that is, a reproductive, circular sequence.

The reproduction of the essence (structure) of a specific socio-economic organism can be investigated when it reaches the maturity phase, which is characterized by a balance between the factors of its formation and modification. This is how the logical method was implemented by Marx in his fundamental work *Capital: A Critique of Political Economy. T. 1. The Process of Capital Production* (1867). The work is built on the principle of reproduction and is devoted to the analysis of developed capitalism. "... In our study," noted Marx, "we are dealing with an already established bourgeois society moving on its own basis" [47, p. 138].

The most important aspect of the relationship between logical and historical research methods is, as noted above, their heuristic equivalence. This refers to the fact that the process of functioning of an object always continuously describes its history in such a way that the phases of reproduction correspond to the phases of the historical development of the object. "History ... is played out daily in our eyes" [69, v. 23. p. 157] – wrote the German philosopher Georg Hegel (1770-1831). This property of integral systems has a universal character, known in physics by the equality of the time-averaged values of the parameters of an object to their statistical average, in biology as a short and rapid repetition in the individual development of an individual (ontogeny) of the most important stages of the evolution of a species (phylogeny), fair and for the economy of society.

So, in the logic of *Capital*, "the history of capitalism and the analysis of the concepts that summarize it" are concluded in a 'removed', transformed form [Ibid, v. 29, p. 30]. The property of brief repetition, 'recapitulation', the philosophical interpretation of which was given by Hegel[1] and Engels[2], is in essence associated with the coincidence of ontology (dialectics), logic and epistemology of cognition.

The principle of equivalence of temporal and momentary research methods was actually widely used by Marx in Capital, when he wrote: "What we previously considered as changes that occur with the same capital, consistently in time, now we are expanding we see as simultaneously existing differences between capitalist enterprises operating one side by side in various spheres of production" [69, v. 25, part I, p. 156]. But Marx did not focus on the cognitive equivalence of the logical and the historical, Engels only mentioned this, for Hegel, this equivalence was one of the fundamental elements of his philosophy.

Thus, the logical and historical research methods are opposite in form, but the same in content, they express duality, an internal contradiction between the stability (reproducibility) and variability (development) of the phenomena of reality.

It is indisputable that Marx's analysis of specific economies and the generalization of the orders of different countries into one systemic concept of

---

[1] "... An individual in the course of ontogeny of his cognition goes through once again in a very abbreviated form the phylogenesis of cognition of the whole society" [27, v. 4. p. 130]; "In pedagogical successes, we learn sketched, as in a condensed sketch, the history of education of the whole world" [Ibid, v. 14. p. 15].

[2] "... This can be called a parallel of individual embryology and paleontology of the spirit, a reflection of individual consciousness at various stages of its development, considered as an abbreviated reproduction of the steps historically traversed by human consciousness" ([69, v. 21, p. 278]).

'social formation' made it possible, thus common for natural science, the requirement of repeatability of an experiment, which is to the study of the structure of reproduction and the corresponding structuring of the historical process. In this sense, the reproducibility of the economy acts as the reproducibility of experience, and economic theory is not inferior to experimental sciences in the possibility of obtaining empirical material. Moreover, the economic theory has a cognitive advantage, since the reproduction process carries information not only about the past, but also about the future of the object under study. The predictive function of the logical method is important from both theoretical and practical points of view, because it allows you to find the most general laws of development of the economy and use them.

Historical and logical methods, considered and applied separately, have shortcomings. 'Historicism' in its pure form suffers from empiricism, descriptiveness, superficial phenomenolism, while 'structuralism' is characterized by a priori, speculative theoretical constructions. So, for example, the 'historical school' in political economy presented the development of public production only in a descriptive form. On the contrary, in Marx's *Capital*, historical qualitative transformations of social production, saturated with events, are reduced only to logical contradictions and paradoxes, poor content. If the transition to the capitalist system here corresponds in the reproductive aspect to the elementary market act of converting money into capital and the logical contradiction of its 'general formula' in terms of the emergence of 'surplus value' ("that formula of circulation, in which The second money doll turns into capital, contradicts all previously developed (in Capital – the author) laws regarding the nature of goods..." [Ibid, v. 23, p. 166]), then the technological transition to machines production corresponds to the transformation of the aggregate of individual capitals into 'total social capital' and, again, to the logical contradiction of the "general capital formula," but already in terms of realizing the "surplus value" Shown by the German economist Rosa Luxemburg (1870-1919) (*Capital Accumulation*, 1913). Her analysis of Marx's reproduction schemes proved the impossibility of realizing the national surplus product without exporting it to the world market space.

The need for a complete resolution of these logical contradictions and answers to the inevitably arising questions "Where did the free labor force come from in simple commodity production?" and "How was the technological integrity of the 'aggregate social capital' formed?," without going beyond the reproductive analysis, forced Marx to formally 'tie' the study of the process of initial accumulation of capital, that is, the process of expropriation of the bulk of simple commodity producers, to the study of 'secondary', reproductive accumulation of capital (while the initial accumulation was inevitably interpreted in a 'removed' (transformed) and, consequently, distorted form; within the framework of the "general law of capitalist accumulation" expropriation of commodity producers becomes a form of "impoverishment" of capital producers), and the mechanism of cross-sectoral overflow of capital, equalization of the rate of profit and formation, thereby, the national economy is considered separately in the third volume of *Capital*. This caused the emergence of the well-known concept of 'contradictions between the first and third volumes of Capital' among critics of Marx. Such 'strains' of the logical method and its extreme absolutization, as well as the aforementioned shortcomings of a purely historical approach to research, violate the harmony and consistency of the dialectical theory.

The model of the historical development of the economy, which consists in the logical shell of the 'functioning of capital', can be realized not by formal, but by a real synthesis of historical and logical research methods. The data of the instant analysis of the reproduction of the economy contain information about its historical past and future, which is sufficient for constructing a generalized model of economic development in 'metaeconomics'.

At the same time, it will be fair to say that the reproductive structure of economies as a whole is equivalent to the reproductive structure of its historical development. Therefore, the division of economics into theories of production, distribution, exchange, consumption and accumulation of goods corresponds to the division of the history of the subject into the same periods of creation of theories of the same name by different economists-theorists.

In our opinion, these are the British Smith, Ricardo, Marshall and Keynes. Their work is characterized by the most important achievements in the history of economic thought and, at the same time, must correspond to the sequence of sections of the current economy. Let us show this in the retroeconomic model we have developed.

4. Contradiction of 'Classical political economy' – source the cambridge problems of modern economics

A fully retroeconomic model will be described in the Conclusion of the monograph. In this section, its main part is considered, showing the main discoveries in absolute coordinates 'The level of development of economic theory – Years' (Fig. I.6).

The model contains a diagonal axial direction, sections of which correspond to the 'historical school' and 'institutionalism', following one after another and having a common property – the descriptive nature of knowledge. This highway, around which various other scientific concepts and paradigms have developed in interaction, we call the "sociological direction", taking into account, firstly, the fact that in modern conditions in economics there are models, descriptions not only the economy, but also other spheres of society, and, secondly, that the tasks of economics began to be charged with the development of recipes for solving a complex of social problems. Circle and semicircles in our model designate three most important formations of the development of science: 'Classical political economy', 'Neoclassical

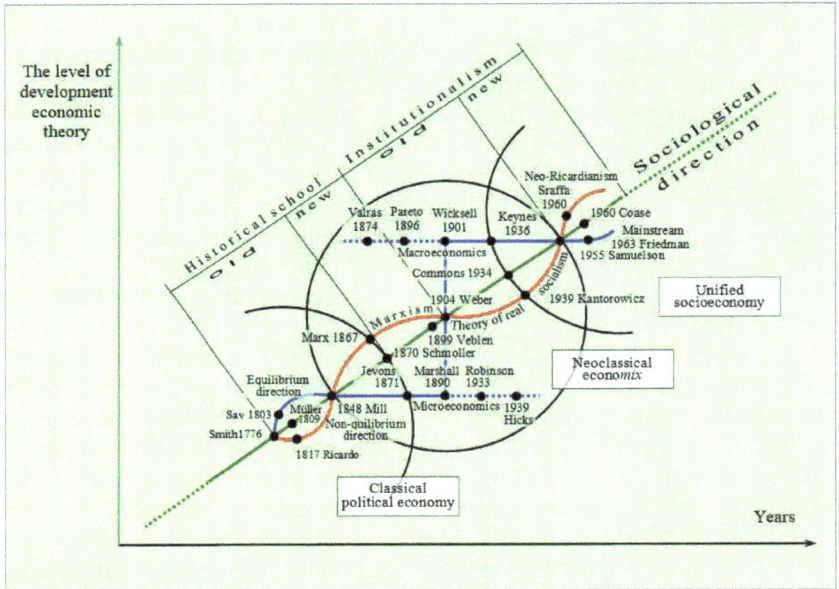

Fig. I.6

economix' and modern 'Unified socioeconomy' ('Novoclassics'). Economics instead of the name 'political economy' was established after the publication of *Principles of Economics* (1990) Marshall. Our name 'economix' (from the English word 'to mix'), consonant with economics, emphasizes that the vast scientific formation is a mixture of two main heterogeneous systems of knowledge – microeconomics and macroeconomics – with other teachings. The name of the third formation is connected with the fact that the theory of 'social markets' and practical recommendations for solving social problems appear in it, and it is generally of a new classical nature due to the revival and rethinking of the classical principle of laissez-faire.

This part of the complete retroeconomic model summarizes the main figures in the entire history of economic thought. Other authors are only mentioned here, and the work of many of them is considered in other sections of the monograph.

The starting point of the model is the *Study of the Nature and Causes of the Wealth of Nations* (1776) by Smith – the central figure of 'Classical Political Economy'. Of all the numerous scientific achievements contained in his book, we single out the following: 1. An attempt to synthesize the previous directions of the emerging classics: utopia, 'mercantilism' and 'physiocracy'; 2. Emphasis on the analysis of the production process; 3. Creation of an advanced labor theory of value; 3. Justification of the laissez-faire principle; 4. Interpretation of the division of labor as the main factor in the development of a market economy; 5. Putting forward the postu lata on the growth of public welfare on the basis of private benefit due to the action of some "invisible hand", that is, competition. Basically, these advances indicate the systemic, micro-macroeconomic nature of Smith's theory.

The contradiction in Smith's interpretation of the process of value creation as one-factor, and the process of its distribution as three-factor, was the reason for the division of 'Classical political economy' into two streams and its subsequent rapid development.

The first trend was represented by the three-factor theory of production and distribution of the French economist Jean Say (1767-1832) (*Treatise on Political Economy. A Study of How Wealth is Produced, Distributed and Consumed*, 1803), free from Smith's contradiction. Say was the first to consider the science of production, distribution and consumption of goods, which allows us to consider his teaching as reproductive. Say's accentuated attention to the production process, like all the classics, was expressed in the so-called 'Say's law of markets', according to which "sales for products are created by production itself" [114, p. 43].

Say was the founder of the school, which we call the 'equilibrium direction' since she saw in economics only harmony, proportionality, justice, and preached the principle of laissez-faire. The direction included, in addition to Say, the French Frederic Bastiat (1801-1850), the British McCulloch, William Senior (1790-1864), Richard Cobden (1804-1865) and John Bright (1811-1889), as well as the American Henry Carey (1793-1879), who in their works gradually reduced the actions of Smith's 'invisible hand' of the market to its objective laws.

Smith's one-factor theory of value formed the basis of an alternative to Sey's "nonequilibrium direction" of the classics, the founder of which was Ricardo (*On the principles of political economy and taxation*, 1817). He pointed to the class contradictions and injustice of the market economy, aggravated with the transition from manufacturing to industrial economy, proposed an active redistribution of national income using the state budget and, accordingly, reduced the subject of political economy to the problem of distribution of income and benefits. At the end of his work, Ricardo was fascinated by the important, from his point of view, the problem of "invariable measure of value", but he did not manage to solve it, without completing the composition *Absolute value and exchange value* (1951).

We include compatriots Ricardo Thomas Malthus (1766-1834) and Robert Torrens (1780-1864), Swiss Semond De Sismondi (1773-1842), utopians of the 2nd half of the XIX century in the line of the non-equilibrium line of research of the classics. the French Saint-Simon (Henri de Rouvroix) (1760-1825) and Francois Fourier (1772-1837), the Englishman Robert Owen (1771-1858), the English Ricardian socialists Thomas Godskin (1787-1869), William Thompson (1785-1833), John Gray (1798-1850) and John Bray (1809-1895), as well as the left Hegelians of the Germans Wilhelm Weighling (1808-1871) and Karl Rodbertus-Yagetsov (1806-1875), French Pierre

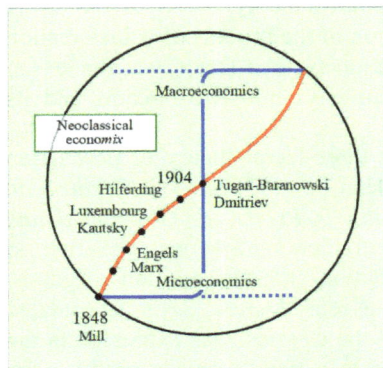

Fig. I.7

Proudhon (1809-1865). All these economists were distinguished by the originality of creativity, they generally adhered to critical views of the market economy and offered various recipes for its improvement in terms of income and product distribution.

One of the earliest critics of the laissez-faire principle was the English economist James Lauderdale (1759-1839), author of the *Study on the Nature and Origins of Social Wealth* (1804), in which he clearly distinguished between public and private households. Later, the public (national, national) economy became the subject of the so-called old German 'historical school', which in our model is a fragment of the diagonal 'Sociological trend' that belongs to the classics. The original science for the historicists was 'cameralistics' as a theory of state management. To this school we include, first of all, Adam Müller (1779-1829), Friedrich Liszt (1798-1846), Bruno Hildenbrand (1812-1878) and Wilhelm Roscher (1817-1894). Müller (*Elements of Sovereign Art*, 1809) criticized Smith's teaching, called it "cosmopoliteconomy" and pointed out the importance of "spiritual values of the people," which expanded the subject of science beyond macroeconomics. Economists-historians, by virtue of the descriptive nature of their research, were between the arguing theorists of the equilibrium and unequal directions, accumulating empirical data about society.

The final phase of the simultaneous development of the equilibrium, unequal and 'historical schools' of 'Classical political economy' is associated with the name of the English economist John Mill (1806-1873) (*Principles of political economy with some of their applications to social philosophy*, 1848). He undertook another attempt to synthesize those formed by the middle of the

XIX century specified directions. Successful in logic, Mill tried to restore order in political economy, for the first time applying the strict axiomatic method of its construction. The structure and content of the *Principles* indicate the reproductive nature of Mill's teachings, despite the fact that he did not consider the process of consumption of goods separately.

Mill's figure in our model occupies a special place, since he was the finalizer of the classics and at the same time the founder of the 'Neoclassical econo*mix*'. We regard this next scientific formation as the culmination in the development of the economic theory of the market. In the formation, the Ricardian unequal and Sey equilibrium directions had continued. The first – in the form of objective-dialectical 'Marxism', which absolutized Smith's labor production theory of value and the disequilibrium of the economy, and the second – in the form of subjective-marginal[1] neoclassical microeconomics, which absolutized the equilibrium three-factor theory of the formation and distribution of Say's value. In addition, post-synthesis 'historicism' has 'opened up a second wind' in the form of a 'new historical school' (see Fig. I.6).

Marx (*Capital: a Criticism of Political Economy. In 4 volumes*, 1867-1935) used in his reproduction research of already clearly contradictory market capitalism a new, adequate and subtle instrument – dialectics, which allowed him to create a unique nonequilibrium economic theory and to develop a model of the formational division of the history of public production, which has not lost its scientific value until now[2].

In addition to Marx, we include the German scientists Engels, Karl Kautsky (1854-1938), Luxembourg, Rudolf Hilferding (1877-1914) among the main representatives of the non-equilibrium Marxist direction of political economy (Fig. I.7), who are mainly from a dialectical standpoint, they studied the monopolistic stage of development of the world market, as well as the Russians Mikhail Tugan-Baranovsky (1873-1939) and Dmitriev, who tried to synthesize the theories of value and utility in their own way.

A direct continuation of 'Marxism' was also the non-equilibrium 'theory of real socialism', which, despite its ideologized character, had scientific and practical significance. To the main theorists of real socialism (Fig. I.8), we include the Soviet political and statesmen Vladimir Lenin (1870-1924) and Leon Trotsky (1879-1940), the economists Nikolai Bukharin (1888-1938), Stanislav Strumilin (1877-1974), Leonid Yurovsky (1884-1938), Grigory

---

[1] The name 'marginalism' was introduced into scientific circulation by the English economist John Hobson (1858-1940) in the book *The Industrial System* (1909).
[2] We turn to Marx's theory in the *Conclusion* of the monograph. Note that modern dialectics as a science of development has acquired a rigorous mathematical toolkit of synergetics, which studies open nonequilibrium self-organizing systems, which include society (see: [91, 45, 39]).

Feldman (1884-1958), Nikolai Kondratyev (1892-1938), Leonid Kantorovich (1912-1986) and the Pole Oskar Lange (1904-1965).

The founder of the direction, Lenin (*Imperialism, as the Latest Stage of Capitalism (Popular Essay)*, 1917), as a supporter of the economic theory of Marx, supplemented it with the concepts of imperialism and socialism. He also substantiated the connection of the plan and the market with the help of the so-called 'business accounting'. This theoretical and practical symbiosis allowed to systematically overcome economic contradictions, stabilized the economy of the USSR, accelerated its pre-industrialization as a single complex and significantly increased the well-being of the people.

In the 'new historical school', which stems from the 'diagonal' classics, there was less criticism of classical political economy, attempts were made to develop an overarching economic history, explaining many aspects of human activation of economic activity. The most famous representatives of the 'new historical school' were (Fig. I.9) Gustav Schmoller (1838-1917), Lujo Brentano (1844-1931), Karl Knis (1821-1897), Karl Bücher 1847-1930), Werner Sombart (1863- 1941) and Max Weber (1864-1920).

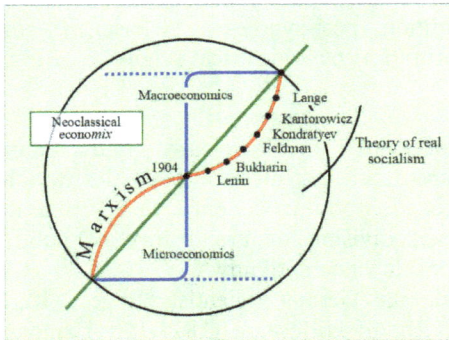

Fig. I.8

The head of the Schmoller school (*History of German Small Industry in the XIX Century*, 1870) argued with the Austrian economist Karl Menger (1840-1921) on methodological issues, criticized the laissez-faire principle of the classics and considered political economy a normative science, including into psychology, sociology and geography. Weber (*Protestant Ethics and the Spirit of Capitalism*, 1904) was the finisher of the 'historical school' and the creator of the concept of "ideal types of farming" – some schemes reminiscent of the Marxist structuring of society, but suggesting the reverse determination of its development – from institutions to market technology. Thus, being an opponent of Marx's theory, Weber actually made it more realistic (see the intersection of the diagonal and the wave line of 'Marxism' in Fig. I.9).

In the final phase of its development, the 'historical school' passed on its broad and descriptive subject as a baton to institutionalists who studied the advanced corporate-industrial economy of 'mass production', which needed legislative registration of the system of redistribution of benefits by the state. Therefore, they recognized the contradictions of society, rejected the classical principle of laissez-faire and used an interdisciplinary approach in the

44

development of institutions that regulate the economy.

To institutionalists (Fig. I.9), we include the Americans Veblen, who is the founder of the direction, William Mitchell (1874-1948), John Commons (1862-1945), who gave the name to the direction, John Galbraith (1908-2006), Schumpeter and partly Samuelson, Hobson, Russian Alexander Bogdanov (1873-1928), German Walter Euken (1891-1950), Frenchman Francois Perroux (1903-1987).

The above-mentioned subjective-marginal microeconomics 'Neo-classical econo*mix*' arose as a result of the transition of the positivist-axiomatics Mill from the classical essential production theory of value to the study of the observed phenomena of supply and demand of market exchange.

Mature marginalism (Fig. I.10), which widely used indicators in infinitely small increments, characterizing the rational behavior of homo oeconomicus, is the work of prominent economists: the English Stanley Jevons (1835-1882), Marshall, Francis Edgeworth (1845-1926), Philip Wickstead (1844-1932), Robinson and John Hicks (1904-1983), representatives of the Austrian school of Menger, Eigen von Boehm-Bawerk (1851-1914) and Friedrich von Wieser (1851-1926), Americans Clark and Edward Chamberlin (1899-1967).

Jevons (*Theory of Political Economy*, 1871), Menger and other

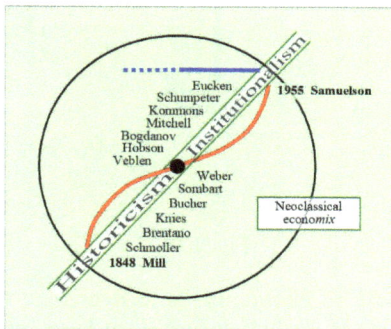

Fig. I.9

marginalists developed the concept of consumer utility value, and the representative of the English Cambridge Marshall combined it with the classical theory of production cost value in one exchange-pricing model. Clarke (*Distribution of Wealth*, 1899), based on the identity of production and consumption, was the first to use marginal tools to describe the production of goods.

After Marshall created a synthesis model of exchange, it was detailed by the orthodox microeconomics, but this mainstream of 'Neoclassical econo*mix*' quickly rose to a higher level and became micro-macroeconomic (see Fig. I.10), based on the work of representatives of the 'Lausanne school' by the Frenchman Leon Walras (1834-1910) and the Italian Vilfredo Pareto (1848-1923), the developments of the representatives of the 'Swedish school' Wicksell, Karl Kassel (1866-1945), Erik Lindahl (1891-1960), Myrdal and Bertil Ulin (1899-1979), the Americans Irving Fisher (1867-1947) and Samuelson, as well as the Englishmen Arthur Pigou (1877-1959), Keynes and partly Hicks.

The founder of the Lausanne school of Walras (*Elements of Pure Political Economy, or The Theory of Social Wealth*, 1874-1877), developed the theory of general economic equilibrium, and Pareto (*Course of Political Economy*, 1896-1899) linked it to the problems of efficiency economy and public welfare, thereby reviving the subject of political economy of Smith's theory. Viksel (*Lectures on National Economy, Based on the Principle of Limit. In 2 volumes*, 1901, 1906), was the first to attempt to combine micro- and macroeconomics into one system of knowledge. Creativity of the creator of modern macroeconomics Keynes (*General Theory of Employment, Interest and Money*, 1936) falls on the final phase of 'Neoclassical econo*mix*' and, at the same time, the beginning of the next scientific formation, which we called 'Unified Socioeconomy' ('new classics'). The essence of the *General Theory*, devoted mainly to the study of the fourth phase of reproduction – the consumption of goods, consists in the following provisions: 1. The need for widespread use of aggregate economic indicators and their combination with psychological characteristics of a person, his "inclinations"; 2. The main task of ekonomiks is to overcome not rarity, but, on the contrary, surplus of goods, including surplus of labor, capital and money; 3. In the economy, there are defects in the form of immobility (rigidity) of labor prices and forced unemployment, which require the use of the principle of non-laissez-faire, active state fiscal and monetary regulation of employment; 4. Money is not neutral, and market players often show a "preference for liquidity", which creates an additional demand for money; 5. The uncertainty of the future of the industrial economy makes it difficult to take into account the expectations of business entities in its modeling. The publication of the *General Theory* gave rise to scientific controversy and various teachings of 'Keynesianism' that exist to this day[1].

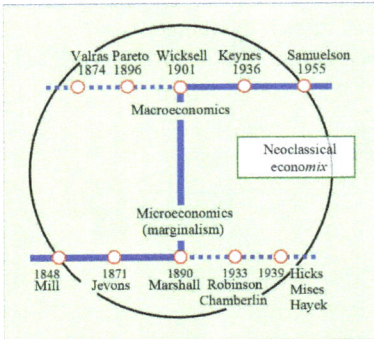

Fig. I.10

At the end of the centennial development of 'Neoclassical econo*mix*' Samuelson (*Economics: an Introduction to Analysis. 3rd edition*, 1955) made an attempt to synthesize the directions contained in it – macroeconomics, the 'theory of real socialism' and 'institutionalism' – in the form of his concepts

---

[1] American economists Paul Davidson (b. 1930) and Weintraub in 1978 founded the specialized *Journal of Post-Keynesian Economics*.

of 'neoclassical synthesis'[1] and 'mixed economy'[2]. The constructive idea of the first concept was that after the elimination of forced unemployment by the state according to Keynesian recipes, the economy can again function and develop according to the laissez-faire principle.

But Samuelson's theoretical synthesis turned out to be contradictory, he mechanistically combined the 'methodological individualism' of marginalists and the 'methodological holism' of Keynes. If Samuelson concluded that the classical principle of laissez-faire should once again become the basis for the functioning of the economy, then involuntarily the question arises about the designation of a significant public sector in it, provided for by his concept of a 'mixed economy'. Is it really only in order to intervene in the market mechanism at the right time and achieve its acceptable social parameters?

The answer to this question is connected with many other related issues of economics included in the subject of our monograph, but in the context of this section of it, we set the task of clarifying the structure of modern economics, the structure just outlined in the first section of the monograph. And the display in the retro model of certain patterns of development of economic thought allows you to solve this problem. So the symmetry in the arrangement of historical scientific formations-paradigms shows that all their synthetic works contained internal contradictions, thanks to which new research guidelines arose in the future, demonstrating, at the same time, continuity with pre-synthesis directions, that is, their repeated passage of the phases of divergence, opposition and convergence.

The natural nature of the spread of large, end-to-end 'waves' of economic thought shows that the fate of Samuelson's teachings repeated the history of synthesized works of the past – it broke up into three new directions, which we briefly discussed above: 'post-Keynesianism' (mainstream), 'neo-Ricardianism' and 'neoinstitutionalism' (Fig. I.11). These directions represent the initial phase of the modern, not yet fully formed, scientific formation 'Unified socioeconomy'. The formation is, according to many signs, symmetrical 'Classical political economy', but based on the general circular

---

[1] For the first time, a kind of 'neoclassical synthesis' was carried out by Hicks (*Mr. Keynes and the 'Classics'. The Proposed Interpretation*, 1947), followed by the synthesis of Samuelson, who owns the term: "Over the past years, 90% of American economists have ceased to classify themselves as 'Kensianzam' or 'anti-Kensians'. Instead, they try to synthesize everything of value that was in the old and modern economic theories of determining the level of income. The result was a theory that could be called neoclassical synthesis. In general, it was accepted by almost all economists, with the exception of about 5% of the most ardent representatives of the right and left wing" [154, p. 212].

[2] The idea of a 'mixed economy' was put forward at the end of the 19th century. German economists Albert Scheffle (1831-1903), Adolf Wagner (1835-1917) and Sombart. In addition to Samuelson, in the second half of the XX century the theory of 'mixed economy' was developed by the Americans John Maurice Clarke (1884-1963) Alvin Hansen (1887-1975) and Stuart Chase (1888-1975).

logic of the development of economic knowledge shown above, the fifth phase of reproduction – the accumulation of benefits – becomes the subject of research in the formation.

The retroeconomic model points not only to the closest source of discrepancies between 'neo-Ricardianism' and the mainstream – the contradiction of Samuelson's economics – but also to their common historical reason – the contradiction between the provisions on one-factor production and three-factor distribution of the value of goods contained in Smith's *Wealth of Nations*.

The retroeconomic model also shows that the neoinstitutional theory, wedged between the mainstream (new classics-1) and 'neo-Ricardianism' (new classics-2), qualitatively changes the situation in modern economics and moves it towards a synthesis of directions. The maturing synthesis, first of all, will make it possible to finally resolve the historical disputes about the laissez-faire principle discussed above. If Smith interpreted this principle as a kind of favorable external condition for the production of goods and only as a thesis, and Keynes adhered to the non-leis-sez-faire antithesis, then mathematizing 'institutionalism' ("new classics 3") can fully justify the gradual inclusion of state activity, regardless of its scale and functions in ordinary commercial production. This will be facilitated by the neoclassical character of the neighboring mentioned directions. In the shortest form, the historical development of the laissez-faire principle can be represented as a dialectical scheme: thesis – antithesis – synthesis.

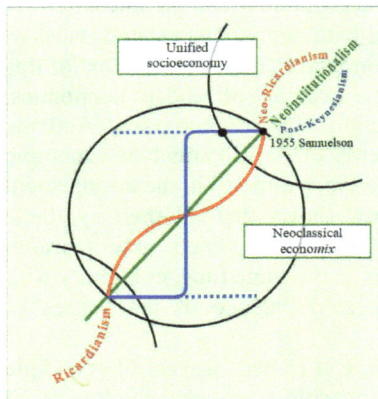

Fig. I.11

Of course, the advancement of economics to a new synthesis will require some intellectual efforts dictated by the ambitions of 'economic imperialism' and insufficient knowledge of the laws of functioning and development of society. The first priority is to solve the problem of improving the mainstream marginal 'Marshall cross', which is necessary both for the successful synthesis of 'post-Keynesianism' and 'neo-Ricardianism', and for its use in the study of complex spheres of society. The existing neoclassical model of market equilibrium is the weakest component of the theory, which for a hundred years has not been able to concretize the archaic and abstract concept of 'utility of a good', although the prerequisites for this in the theory were and are now. The modernized 'Marshall cross' can become a truly unified

48

research tool, capable of modeling both micro- and macroeconomic and supra-economic social objects from a single marginal position.

The question arises as to which of the three areas should be tackled by this modernization. 'Neo-Ricardianism' made a challenge to the marginal theory of the mainstream and thanks to the "Sraffian revolution" [110, p. 250] has in its arsenal a fully working linear multivariate model of macroeconomics. However, 'neoinstitutionalism', which does not have operational traditions, but considers practically the entire society as a set of markets for social goods, is unable to improve the research tool borrowed from marginalists. It is these circumstances that impute the solution of the problem under consideration to skeinsianism. The conceptual completeness of the marginal theory of value will allow the direction, firstly, to strengthen its position in the dispute with 'neo-Ricardianism', turning the linear model of the so-called 'total cost of production' by Sraffa into an extreme case of a nonlinear complete 'Marshall cross' and, secondly, to overcome mechanism Samuelson's 'neoclassical synthesis', carrying out a more 'organic' 'Keynesian-neoclassical synthesis' and, thus, to show the true form of Keynes's theory. The *Companion to Contemporary Economic Thought* (1991) [80] notes the inevitability of a 'neo-Keynesian synthesis' [81, v. 1, p. 178]. On this occasion, the American economist James Tobin (1918-2002) wrote: "Keynesian ideas will survive the counter-revolution. The synthesis that arises under their influence will, I think, be more acceptable theoretically than the previous 'neoclassical synthesis'" [147, v. 1, p. 178], "in a new intellectual synthesis, which, in my opinion, will replace the current contention and chaotic debate regarding macroeconomic policy, Keynesian ideas will take their place of honor" [138, p. 6]. But Keynes's authentic economic model is important, first of all, because it itself can have a microeconomic justification and does not need any external funding. A careful reading of the General Theory shows that it already contains the idea of a direct connection of 'micro- and macroeconomics[1], which must be fully implemented.

5. Opposition, active interaction and synthesis 'neo-Ricardianism' and mainstream

Our analysis of the laws of the historical development of economic thought, presented above, showed that 'neo-Ricardianism' and the mainstream for a certain time existed, as it were, independently of each other. But this divergence of directions has inevitably been replaced in modern conditions by the stage of their active interaction. Sraffa, after his anti-marginalist articles,

---

[1] This is discussed in more detail in sections 14 and 16 of the monograph, as well as in our work: [34].

abstracted himself from the mainstream, and 'neo-Ricardianism' as a whole was removed from it. But the directions have reached maturity, which makes it possible to compare the main elements of already two systems of views on the economy.

Sraffa's book *Production of Goods by Means of Goods. The Prelude to the Criticism of Economic Theory* looks concise and abundantly mathematized, without the necessary explanations in certain places. For example, the author does not indicate why he applies the one-factor labor theory of value, while it was possible to develop an alternative marginalism, but a three-factor theory of pricing. Sraffa's work as a whole laid the foundations of 'neo-Ricardianism', but he never gave a systemic criticism of the mainstream and a sufficiently detailed presentation of his theory. The emerging direction developed for a long time without breakthrough work. Only in 1995 did Kurz's fundamental work (*Theory of Production: A Long Period Analysis*, together with N. Salvadori, 1995) appear, which presented 'neo-Ricardianism' in a somewhat expanded manner, but, again, with excessive mathematics and without comparisons with the mainstream in economics.

It should be noted that over the past time 'neo-Ricardianism' has become more and more abstract, and the mainstream theory, on the contrary, has consistently approached reality, freeing itself from its original conventions. Therefore, the concepts of 'neo-Ricardianism', as an 'objective' teaching based on the classics, and of neoclassicism as a 'subjective' teaching, preserved in the literature, are outdated.

Let's try to conduct a comparative analysis of the conflicting trends and, above all, their methodological attitudes.

Ricardo's continued quest for an 'invariable measure of value' by neo-Ricardians turned out to be, in fact, an alternative to the fundamental research premise ceteris paribus mainstream. In his last manuscript *Absolute Value and Exchange Value* (1823), published in 1951, Ricardo noted that in addition to labor costs, the cost of a product is influenced by the costs of other factors, which creates the impression of price uncertainty. The same impression is left by the neoclassicists' use of the presupposition 'with other unnamed'. Sraffa's equilibrium theory, which contains a model of the economy disaggregated by industry, means his rejection of the ceteris paribus principle and the need to move to the macro level in research. But, the same transition is possible in the mainstream theory. The possibility of determining the absolute prices of goods with the help of marginal models is hardly considered in the economic literature. It is only known that Marshall also raised the issue of absolute measures, but not prices, but utilities, tried to understand the value of money for different people and, fearing to fall, as he put it, into the "scholastic realm" of theory, quickly refused the question. The forms of realization of the prerequisite ceteris paribus and the possibility of a multifactor marginal determination of the absolute prices of goods in the economy will be shown in sections 6 and 8 of the monograph, respectively.

Ricardo wrote about the existence of accurate measurements in the natural sciences[1] and regretted the absence of such in political economy. Even in the third edition of the book *On the Principles of Political Economy and Taxation*, he inserted in the first chapter *Section VI. About the Invariable Measure of Value*, in which he noted: "If the relative cost of goods changes, then it is desirable to have a way to determine which goods have increased and for which their actual cost has fallen. This can be done only by consistently comparing them with some unchanging standard measure of cost, which itself would undergo none of the fluctuations that other goods experience" [86, p. 105, 106]. Ricardo came to the conclusion that having a standard measure of cost "is impossible, because there is no product whose cost would not undergo the same changes as the value of other items that we want to measure" [Ibid, p. 106]. But Sraffa did not agree with this conclusion and believed that the very conditional model of cost created by him after very lengthy research solves the issue. Subsequent neo-Ricardian studies of the 'accurate' cost meter turned out to be more and more complex and divorced from the real economy.

In our opinion, the problem of measuring value and the inevitability of building 'monster models' far from practice arises only because the classics and neo-Ricardians, while recognizing prices, mistakenly believed that their basis was a one-factor 'cost'. The neoclassicists, however, abandoned this duality, pointing to the real existence of only prices, which was rational, simple and practical. Thus, a good was found that fulfills the function of an absolute measure of value – money. The problem of 'unchanging measure of value' existed only among the classics, Marx, and exists among the neo-Ricardians. They cannot directly measure value through labor. In this regard, one cannot agree with the English economist John Itwell (b. 1945) when he writes: "*The Production of Goods by Means of the Goods* of Sraffa opens the way to the further development of analysis based on the theory of additions. no value" [50, p. 169]. The labor theory of surplus value is far from market reality.

'Neo-Ricardianism', which is trying to revive the classics, cannot but be 'neo-Marxism', since the band of 'Marxism' enters the general end-to-end non-equilibrium direction in the development of economic thought, combines 'Ricardianism' with 'neo-Ricardianism' and is largely embodied in the latter. However, Sraffa, in contrast to the critics of Marx's teaching on the relationship between value and prices, approached constructively and made significant progress in solving it.

---

[1] This statement by Ricardo is wrong. In natural sciences, all measures are relative.

Boehm-Bawerk was the first to talk about the "two systems of measurement" of value that exist in Marx's *Capital*: 'value' and "production price". Subsequently, a number of economists proposed to abandon one of the two theories, others, in particular, the Russian economist Vladislav Bortkevich (1868-1931) and the Japanese economist Michio Morishima (1923-2004), considered it necessary to complete the analysis of the transformation of cost into the price of production, the third, the Englishman Ian Steadman (b. 1941), John Romer and others, considered the 'cost' unnecessary, and Samuelson called the theory transformation "pseudo-problem."

The so-called 'analytical Marxism' has also developed a two-system, but somewhat different from the first, approach to the value of goods: 1) the 'value' system, which claims to cognize a substance, in fact, to cognize production relations; 2) the system of 'prices', focused on the knowledge of the instance, that is, on the knowledge of the institutions of pricing. For Marx himself, value, like all other concepts, is only objective 'production relations' between people. This is their interaction, joint activity, work. From the point of view of specific rules and institutions that Marx did not investigate, this work appears as costs, profits, prices and other observable market phenomena. Therefore, value is an essence, not an expanded synonym, but price is a phenomenon, concreteness.

The work of Marx is constructed dialectically, that is, with a combination of the historical and the logical. It is useless to look for formal logic from him, as many theoreticians do, since dialectics shows contradictions in all the objects under study, and this contradiction is also manifested in the presentation of individual issues. Therefore, we can say that Marx studies separately, as such, value-essence and price-phenomenon (in the form of the so-called "converted" form of 'production price') in the first and third volumes of Capital, respectively, without showing himself the process of moving from one to another. The book Production of goods by means of Sraffa's goods is structured formally and logically. Therefore, he, who generally recognizes 'value', does not consider its contradiction, but immediately takes the 'production price' as the basis for modeling.

Capital as a special scientific work leaves an imprint not only on Sraffa's work, but also on the subsequent development of 'neo-Ricardianism' and all other areas of economics. Therefore, in modern conditions of the development of science as a whole, the existing verbal presentation of dialectics needs to be combined with a very mathematized synergetics, which is instrumental in the closest to dialectics and successfully studies non-equilibrium systems. Sraffa, following Marx, made a fundamental mistake in constructing his model of 'production prices', using the concept of 'single rate of profit', which is equivalent to our concept of 'profitability of production' (G_e). In real competitive market activity, there cannot be a single profitability of production ($G_{pr} = M/(C + V)$, where M, C, and V – total profit, costs of constant capital and costs of variable capital, respectively), but there is only a single 'Profitability of capital', or 'Profitability' ($G_P = M/K$).

Marx, and then the neo-Ricardians, confuse the concepts of economic stocks and flows. The term 'capital', which has existed for a long time in economic theory and was first used by the Englishman Nicolas Barbon (1640-1698) (*Discourses on Trade*, 1690), subsequently acquired not only a double meaning – the momentary stock of capital goods and the periodic flow of credit value, but also the third meaning in the Marxist comparison of two flows – profit and costs – in terms of the 'rate of return'. Below in the monograph, we criticize 'Marxism' and 'neo-Ricardianism' on this issue, and also distinguish between supposedly identical indicators.

The fallacy of the labor theory of value and the indicated incorrectness in the construction of indicators of the price of production led political economy to the concept of the "average structure of capital" by Marx [69, v. 25, part I, p. 190]. He was wrong when he wrote that "the price of production of a commodity is equal to its production costs plus the average profit" [70, v. III, p. 196]. Accordingly, his formula for the price of production $X_i = B_i + B_i \cdot G_{ge}$, where B_i – the costs of a separate production, and G_{ge} – the "general rate of profit" [Ibid, p. 204], or $X_i = B_i(1 + G_{ge})$, $X_i = \lambda_K \cdot B_i$, where λ_K – the 'total' growth rate of 'capital'). The formula should be such that the rate of profit in it is determined in proportion to total capital assets (K) used in a separate production, and not as an average profit, proportional to costs. That is, the formula should not contain 'total', but the average profit. Marx gives a numerical example – "the price of production $X_i = B_i + B_i \cdot G_{ge} = 300 + 300 \times$ $\times (15/100)$" [Ibid], but strictly it should be like this: $300 + 300 \times 300/2000$, where 2000 – the total costs in the economy, 300 – the total profit, and $300/2000$ – the share of the costs of individual production in the total costs. Marx's statements about the price of production contradict each other: the verbal definition of the price formula does not correspond to its calculation. In the first case, the average profit should be added to the costs, and in the second, this profit depends on the costs.

However, Marx's formula ($X_i = \lambda_K \cdot B_i$) is true only for the total output (Q): $Q = \lambda_K \cdot B$, where B – the total production costs (costs). Kurz writes: "If X_i is the price of the i-th commodity, and C_i and V_i are the corresponding constant and variable capitals, then ... we have, following Marx, $X_i = (1 + G_{ge})(C_i + V_i)$, $i – 1, 2,..., n$, where n is the number of goods" [62, p. 44] (our notation – *the author*). And this conclusion is erroneous, since in the formula for the production price of an individual product there must be a coefficient of the share of industry costs in total costs (δ_c), which determines the industry 'surplus value' (Mi): $X_i = (C_i + V_i) + [M/(C + V)] \cdot (C_i + V_i) = B_i + \delta_c \cdot M$.

It is important to show that: 1) the profit of a separate production is determined as a share in the total profit: $M_i = \delta \cdot M$, where δ – the share of a separate (individual) capital (K_i) in the total capital K; 2) M_i, like M, is formed regardless of production costs. Therefore, the Marx formula should be written as follows: $X_i = B_i + \delta \cdot M$. According to Marx's hypothesis, the price of production and the value coincide only where there is an average "organic composition of capital", in other sectors there is a discrepancy between these values. But for the entire aggregate output, its price and value supposedly coincide again. It turns out that deviations from average prices exactly compensate each other, which in the general case is unlikely.

Another question arises, why does Marx, illustrating his formula for the price of production, consider five identical 'capital-costs'? After all, the real capitals of individual industries can be of different sizes, and then the error of Marx's formula for the price of production becomes obvious.

The industries differ not only in capital, but also in technology. This explains the mismatch of the Marxist indicators in them. Commentaries of Marx's work indicate that the formation of a single profitability of capital requires its single "technical structure"[1] But this is impossible to realize. The technological structure can be averaged over the entire economy, but in industries it is, of course, differentiated. And competition cannot bring this indicator closer or make it the same. But the same profitability across all industries is real. Cross-sectoral capital redistributions equalize only the rate of return as a criterion result of entrepreneurial activity. In the formula for the price of a separate product $X_i = B_i + M_i$, only M_i is unknown, depending on the total profit M.

Marx, using the concept of "general rate of profit", identifies 'general' and 'average' rates. But the average value indicates only the mathematical operation of averaging, and the concept 'general' reflects a complex relationship, the interaction of capitals.

For brevity and unambiguity of interpretation, we will use the term 'single profit', which characterizes the completion of the process of equalizing the profitability of capital. Here we will show how the formula for the Marxist price of production can be explained logically and in a short time. Marx and Sraffa deduced a formula based on the equality of profitability of the branches of the economy. This thesis of Sraff, unlike Marx, did not prove in any way. Marx, simplistically assuming that during the production cycle capital goods are completely worn out, and their cost is fully included in the costs of production, and only in a short note did you describe the mechanism equalizing the profitability of capital, moreover, it did it with the help of the market model 'supply-demand', at the same time calling it a confusion [70, v.

---

[1] See, for example: [3, p. 471, 472].

III, p. 229], he himself introduced into his theory the concept of "market value" which was impossible in his methodology.

But the equalization of the profitability of capital can be shown independently of the Marxist concepts of 'value', 'surplus value', 'organic structure of capital', etc. Let us consider this process in more detail in conventional market terms, that is, with the help of universal concepts of 'competition', 'demand' and 'supply'.

For simplicity, let's first present a market economy, which consists of two sectors: industry and agriculture. Suppose also that the economy has a trade, payments and migration external balance, and the profitability of industry (G_1) turns out to be somewhat higher than the profitability of agriculture (G_2) (Fig. I.12, *a*). Under these fairly realistic conditions, the economy, which is 'overheated' in one of its parts, will observe the phenomena of multiple intersectoral overflow of capital (ΔK), overproduction of industrial and underproduction of agriculture. production and vice versa, as well as changes in the ratio of the profitability of industries. After the completion of the oscillatory process of redistribution of investments, a situation of equal and middle

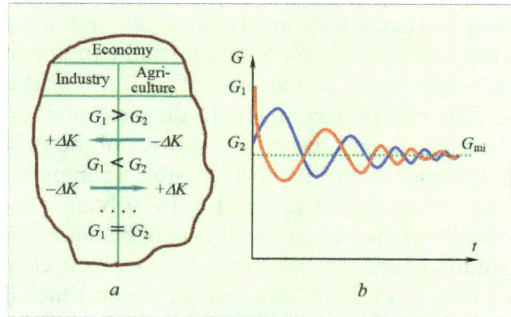

Fig. I.12

profitability (G_{mi}) will be achieved, that is, the profitability of all sectors of the economy at the level of the bank interest rate (G_b): $G_1 = G_2 = G_i = G_{mi} = \Sigma M_i / \Sigma K_i = G_b$ (Fig. I.12, *b*). The inevitable diffusion of capital transforms the locally 'overheated' economy into an equilibrium intersectoral complex, which, in addition to the 'agro-industry', will include construction, transport, trade, banking, and etc. In such an equilibrium, the prices of individual goods become dependent on the profitability of the economy as a whole, and the formula for the branch price $X_i = B_i + M_i$ takes the form: $X_i = B_i + G_b \cdot K_i$. At the macro level, the formula looks exactly the same, the value of the nominal aggregate product, its 'production price' will be equal to: $Q = B + G_b \cdot K$. Equal profitability of the spheres of capital application testifies to the completion of the process of formation of a harmoniously developed national economy, the technological basis of which is the aggregate capital closely intertwined in industries.

On the whole, the following should be noted. If we transform the Marx price formula $X_i = B_i + M_{mi}$ into the formula $X_i = B_i + \delta \cdot M$, then in theory everything falls into place. Therefore, the model of profitability of Sraffa's economy, modified by us, can bring 'neo-Ricardianism' on this issue closer to the mainstream theory.

We showed above that Sraffa and Walras were both macroeconomists. But Sraffa, not recognizing marginalism, replaced the Walrasian GEE scheme as a system of supply and demand interacting in time with a model of an intersectoral GEE, a momentary "photograph of the production structure of the economy" [89, p. 527], which is of a technological nature, in which the costs of capital goods in the creation of each product were declared as labor costs in the industry producing these capital goods. Such a technique was borrowed by Sraffa from Dmitriev, who was the first to introduce into the study the concepts of "direct" and "indirect" labor.

Important in such 'Ricardianism' is the question of the simultaneous determination of the rate of profit of production and the price of goods. Walras (*Lesson 40* of his *Elements of Pure Political Economy*, 1874-1877) criticized Ricardo for trying to find two unknowns in one equation: the price of a commodity and the rate of profit. In market practice, as you know, first of all, the rate of accumulation, the maximum possible self-growth of capital is determined, and secondly, the price of the goods. Neoricardians, starting with Bortkevich, considered it possible to simultaneously determine profitability and production prices simply by solving a system of equations. Sraffa also noted that the rate of profit cannot be determined without the prices of goods, but prices are also indefinite without their element – profitability [111, p. 35], that is, it must be done at the same time. But Steadman, in our opinion, correctly believes that "the cost can be calculated only after the rate of profit has been calculated (in the non-Ricardian understanding of the content of this indicator – the author)" [157, p. 65]. In fact, Sraffa found the profitability of production, like Ricardo in natural ("wheat" [111, p. 36]) terms, based on the technological intersectoral balance, compiled using linear algebra. And only then this value G was substituted into the formulas for the prices of goods. It turned out that the search for a Ricardian constant natural measure of value led to finding an independent measure of the profitability of production. And since then, the G indicator has split into natural and monetary ones.

Sraffa created a system of equations, meticulously balancing their number with the number of unknown quantities. But at the same time, everything 'converged' thanks to the exogenous introduction into the system of equations not of wages, the amount of which, according to Ricardo's 'iron law', should reflect the costs of living labor, but its standard. Considering that the national product was taken as the final aggregate product by Sraffa, the calculation of all unknowns in the model was quite simple. One way or another, such a model of the equilibrium of the economy combined natural indicators with cost indicators.

However, the mainstream theory, opposing 'neo-Ricardianism', basically operates in monetary indicators, and its natural indicators of equilibrium quantities of goods sold on the market, which are absent in 'neo-Ricardianism', are easily and really at the same time determined with with the help of the 'Marshall cross'. Sraffian, and then the subsequent non-Ricardian modeling, led to an incredible complication of models, which turned out to be very far from the economy itself. This gap occurred because the actual sectoral differences in the technological structure of production and the orientation towards the orthodox one-factor theory of pricing forced the authors to obtain unambiguity in the relative prices of goods in to include in the analysis an unrealistic premise about the coincidence of the structure of factors of production ('organic structure of capital') with the structure of its costs ("organic structure of production"). Only under such a premise, which Sraffa called the "standard system", did Marx's production price formula (with G equal to $M/(C + V)$) become equivalent to the actual price formula (with G equal to M/K).

Itwell [50, p. 167] considers Sraffa's concept of a "standard product" to be a more developed form of Marx's concept of an average industry. But this can be considered with great stretch, since Marx's division of production into the first and second subdivisions of the economy, which respectively produce means of production and consumer goods, is more specific than the Sraffian division of goods into "basic" and "non-basic", which only mask the three-factor nature of production. It is also obvious that Marx's "middle industry" is quite real, and Sraffa's 'standard system' is completely untrue.

Sraffa could not deny the three-factor value of a commodity, but, proceeding from classical traditions, he tried to create a model of the economy in which labor remained a factor of production, and capital and land became its 'by-products'. Moreover, land was not only excluded from the process of value formation, but was also considered a non-basic product. However, this perverse explanation of the formation of value turned out to be more complex than it is done by marginalists.

Kurtz, returning us to the contrived neo-Ricardian problem of measuring the volume of capital goods, initiated by Robinson, writes that "the rate of profit and the cost of capital, that is, the denominator in the expression that determines the rate of return, can only be determined simultaneously" [63, p. 31] that they are not independent. But this is a misconception. In section 7 of the monograph, we will prove the possibility of an independent assessment of both the physical and the value of the amount of capital goods. Sraffa, without touching on the problem of assessing capital goods, in his book tried to show not only a close connection between the amount of these goods and profits, but also to explain the nature of the latter in a new way. In this regard, he briefly analyzed the depreciation mechanism for reproducing the value and use value of fixed capital and pointed out the possibility of using depreciation funds for accumulation. Considering a specific example, he wrote that "in the case of the construction of several plants in a row over a number of years, the annual depreciation rates of the first units put into operation are available to finance subsequent units and ... as a result ... the total net investments will be the more, the higher the profit rate" [111, p. 112, 113]. And he quickly raised the issue of the depreciation fund as a source of invested profit.

For a complete answer to the questions raised by Sraffa, let us consider the process of spending the moment value-stock of capital goods. Since these benefits physically and morally wear out, are reimbursed and reproduced, the existence of a special economic mechanism of depreciation makes it possible to implement the law of preservation of the value of this factor of production[1]. All possible schemes for depreciation of capital goods (K) are shown in Fig. I.13.

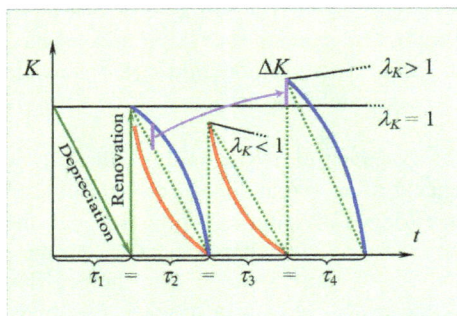

Fig. I.13

In the simplest case of the invariability of the value of K (the rate of its growth λ_K in this case is equal to one) and a complete one-time replacement, renovation, without losses (in Fig. I.13, this is a vertical arrow), uniform linear depreciation over a period of time called the averaged com service object (τ_1) (diagonal arrow), will mean the same annual write-off of value in the price of manufactured products. In the conditions of technical progress, which determines the early replacement of capital goods due to their moral depreciation, it is advisable to nonlinear amortization (concave line of the period τ_2), which reduces or even prevents loss of value. Such accelerated depreciation occurs regardless of the ongoing technical policy with a decreasing mass of capital goods ($\lambda_K < 1$ period τ_3) due to their 'aging', that is, an increase in the share of long-used assets. If the early replacement of capital goods during the service life is not expected, then it is advisable to use a delayed depreciation scheme (convex line of the period τ_2), which more accurately reflects the real rate of physical wear and tear of durables – its

---

[1] Depreciation is often misinterpreted in the economic literature. *Macmillan's Dictionary of Modern Economics*, for example, indicates that depreciation is "a decrease in the value of assets, usually as a result of depreciation" [104, p. 125]. But, strictly speaking, this process means the transformation of the value of an asset into a special monetary fund intended for complete replacement, renovation, good. The meaning of the Latin word 'amortization' – 'compensation'. Therefore, we should talk about the preservation of the value contained in the good in a different form.

slower nature at the accelerated loss of functional qualities by the end of the period. It is this kind of wear, according to Sraffa, that allows you to direct some of the released depreciation funds to the accumulation of capital goods (line with an arrow to Δ_K), and their mass increasing in this case ($\lambda_K > 1$ period τ_4), due to its 'rejuvenation', that is, an increase in the share of new assets in it, makes the self-growth of the value-stock a natural, regular and stable process.

However, in Sraffa's model, capital productivity is a constant value, which means that the annual depreciation costs are equal, which are not included in the cost of the product due to the fact that only labor[1] costs are taken into account in it, but are the source of net profit. These depreciation deductions Sraffa as financial 'innuities', including interest, and represent an increase in capital goods. It turns out that, on the one hand, depreciation in the model is charged only linearly, and, on the other hand, this depreciation is shifted to the slowed-down depreciation curve, covering the increase in capital goods, which determines the 'rejuvenation' of funds and the curvature of the function of their disposal.

Thus, the question of the origin of the profitability of the use of capital goods is, as it were, resolved: depreciation is charged as the consumption of the stock of capital goods, but includes funds sufficient not only for their compensation, but also for a certain accumulation in the amount of profit. If this is the case, then all other arguments of Sraffa about the interindustry technological predetermination of profits should be depreciated at once. True, Sraff in the further description of his model not only points to the amortization origin of net profit-investments, but also, following Ricardo, tries to regulate its share in the national income based on the correlation of "class forces" in society. If we accept the considered mechanism of self-expansion of stocks acting in the reproduction of not only capital goods, but also other factors of production – land and labor, then the profit of rent and the profit of wages in the form of workers' savings should be formed in the same way. However, such constructions are extremely contradictory and cannot be accepted in economic theory.

In section 16 of the monograph, we will show that the amount of profit and savings should be determined in a different way, that is, according to a whole complex of socio-economic factors (employment, scientific and technological progress, demographic circumstances, etc.), the action that is necessary take into account in the institutions of society. The multifactorial nature of profitability is manifested not only at the level of the entire

---

[1] Sraffa in the book *Production of Goods by Goods. The Prelude to the Critique of Economic Theory* (1961) briefly examined land use and reduced it, like the use of capital goods, to the production of a "non-basic," by-product. But the theory of the land as a real factor of production is much more complex and multifaceted.

economy, but also at the micro level, because the equality of profitability of capital in all sectors $M/K = M_i/K_i$ turns into the formula for the profit of a separate production $M_i = \delta \cdot M$. Clarification of the complex mechanism for optimizing the profitability of the economy will bring economics closer to the synthesis of 'neo-Ricardianism', the mainstream and 'neoinstitutionalism', to the end of the 'dispute of two Cambridges'.

We noted above that supporters and commentators of Sraffa's theory argue that he created a reproductive model of the equilibrium of the economy. But Sraffa never writes about this in the main text of his book. Only in the appendix *Literature references* does he criticize for the lack of a reproducible approach in mainstream theory and calls it a "one-way road leading from 'factors of production' to 'consumer goods'" [Ibid, p. 134][1]. Some authors argue that the very title of Sraffa's book indicates the reproductive nature of his model of equilibrium. However, this title looks universal, it is quite suitable for the research of marginalists, since they have long created the theory of prices of factors of production, the 'road' to which from the prices of 'results of production' has been paved. So the name *Production of Goods by Means of Goods* is only a guarantee of the synthesis of directions. What is the reproductive approach to the study of economic equilibrium as a whole, and does Sraffa have it?

Economic theory has answered the first part of the question for a long historical time. If the basis of Quesnay's reproductive modeling was statistics, and Marx's only numerical examples, then it was the neoclassicists who dotted almost all the i's in this matter. They created a fairly complete model of the economy, taking into account the phases of production, exchange, distribution, consumption and accumulation of goods. But a complete reproductive model of markets for goods should consider these goods as factor products that obey the universal laws of supply and demand. There is no such model in economic theory yet. Sraffa, on the other hand, made abstract mathematized constructions, according to which it was impossible to calculate anything, and they were based on a production approach. This is evidenced by the characteristics of Sraffa's research, given by the Italian economist Alessandro Roncaglia: "Value is not ... associated with utility ... The value of goods reflects the relationship between industries ..." [89 , p. 525, 526]. Thus, in general, Sraffa cannot be considered the creator of the reproductive theory of value, but we note that the modern theory of the mainstream also needs improvement in this direction.

---

[1] In the economic literature, there is a false statement that neoclassicism has developed a theory of pricing only in the markets of consumer goods (see, for example: [44, p. 17]). After Clarke, neoclassicism could model any production. But the corresponding theory has not yet been brought to the required completeness and universality.

One of the most important features of the new synthesis economic theory should be its expanded approach to reproduction. Above, we have shown the effectiveness of the reproductive representation of the methodology and history of economic research, but the main problems of the approach await us in a more detailed comparison and improvement of competing areas of economics. On the one hand, the reproduction approach undoubtedly exists in Sraffa's macroeconomic model of the 'production price', but this 'price' should become in the synthesis an explicit 'reproduction cost' of the economy. On the other hand, a very visual model of the 'circulation of goods and payment', which has long been available in neoclassicism, is not fully implemented in the theory of marginal pricing in the markets of factors and products of production, the theory of GEE. Now the GEE scheme in the mainstream, having lost the prerequisites for ceteris paribus, is failing, its functions become linear, which makes the equilibrium in it undefined. In solving this problem, marginalism can help 'neo-Ricardianism'. In general, the outline of the reproductive approach in modern economics should be based on the model implementation of all five phases of this process.

More. The price of the aggregate output of Sraffa consists of the sum of the aggregate wage fund and the normative aggregate profit, regulated by the criterion of the results of the "class struggle." For neoclassicists, this price includes total factor costs and maximum profit. The task of the unified theory is to develop such a concept of reproduction price, which would contain not the maximum possible, but also the normalized profit, but determined, as noted above, in an iterative, multi-step manner according to socio-economic criteria. A certain combination of positive knowledge and normative calculation would be very clever here. Modern economics, having satisfactory theories of production, distribution, exchange and consumption of goods, should focus on solving the problems of the theory of accumulation of goods, which is relevant in both 'post-Keinsianism' and Sraffa wrote that in neoclassicism "there is one obscure place that violates the harmony of the whole. It is represented by the supply curve based on the laws of increasing and decreasing profitability" [111, p. 138]. Indeed, Marshall's analysis did not clarify, but only complicated the theory of the market supply function. Apparently, this ambiguity of marginalism forced Sraffa not to get involved in the discussion and to accept the concept of the absence of a scale effect, which allowed him to operate only with simple linear functions.

Accordingly, there has long been a debate in the economics literature about the assumption of constant returns in Sraffa's model. Sraffa himself claimed that in his work "there is no such assumption", but contains "a study of those properties of the economic system that do not depend on changes in the scale of production or the proportion of 'factors'" [Ibid, p. 22]. How to combine these statements? It turns out that in the 'economy of Sraffa' as in reality, economies of scale can be observed, but his model is free from them. But the fact is that Sraffa's model is macroeconomic, conditionally all-factor, as if cleared of the premise of ceteris paribus, and therefore, linear and with a constant return to the factor of labor. So the controversy about the properties of Sraffa's model could have been significantly reduced if he had immediately declared the absence of the ceteris paribus prerequisite in his construction. But in real macroeconomics, in addition to scale effects, there are, for example, the effects of externalities and emergence, which Sraffa does not mention at all. One way or another, Sraffa, apparently, after his article in 1926, *Laws of Return in Pperfect Competition*, chose for further non-marginal research a simple concept of constant return of the labor force factor. But in reality, all causal relationships are not linear, which favorably distinguishes the mainstream theory adequate to this from the neo-Ricardian theory, which is replete with conventions.

In fairness, it should be noted that Sraffa's book contains an analysis of the distribution of the product, but it is rather weak and distorted, since the author applied an arbitrary, exogenous, rationing of wages. At the same time, it has the equilibrium of the economy and its profitability is endogenously determined by technological intersectoral flows of goods, and the total wages are thus easily determined by a simple deduction from the cost of the national product of total profit. At the same time, its disproportionately wide and complex variations in wages look incomprehensible. In our opinion, this is due to three reasons: 1) Sraffa's belonging to the followers of Ricardo, Marx and the theoreticians of real socialism, who considered it necessary to class redistribution of primary factor income (for all neoricadian rent, salary and profit are variables of the normative distribution, and not neoclassical prices of land, labor and capital, respectively); 2) the need for Sraffa, in the context of his fundamental rejection of the marginal model 'supply-demand', to determine the equilibrium volume of the national product as a substitute for aggregate demand in the form wage rates.

Thus, it can be stated that the mainstream theory has an objective picture of the market mechanism of income distribution, which depends on a combination of factors in production. Sraffa, having abandoned the marginal substance and moved to the class instance, did not begin to understand the substance of the classics, developed by its other orthodoxes. For example, the American Marxist John Romer notes that "if we want to preserve the fundamental relationship between exploitation and class status, then there is no other way but to make value dependent on price" [152, p. 99]. However, there is another way out to reality, which is to reject the one-factor labor theory of value.

At first Sraffa, following the classics, in the ninth paragraph of the book Production of goods by means of goods included the standard of wages in the advanced capital, but then in other sections of the book he spoke without any explanation about wages as paid Post factum in the distribution of national income. It seems that this was done by Sraffa deliberately. The fact is that the dependence between labor and capital, as well as between the corresponding cash costs in production, according to the neoclassical principle of decreasing efficiency of factors, is nonlinear, hyperbolic. Sraffa, in every possible way dissociating himself from marginalism and in spite of the production functions of Wickstead and Cobb-Dooglas already known at that time, translated the problem of rationing wages beyond the limits of production, into the distribution the sphere, where its dependence on profit becomes linear. He introduced into scientific circulation the corresponding inverse proportional

dependence (we call it the 'Sraffa function'), in which the argument is not wages, but the rate of profit (G_{pr}) (Fig. I.14, $V_1 = f(G_{pr})$). It should be noted that this function can also be considered a marginal function, similar to the well-known isocost, which Sraffa is silent about.

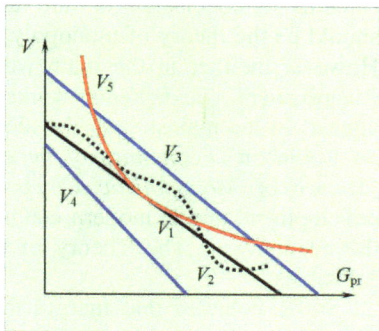

Fig. I.14

Let us turn to the problems of the so-called 'technology switching' considered by Sraffa and discussed in the 'dispute of two Cambridges'. Robinson was the first to analyze this model manipulation, called it a "deviant attitude" (*Capital Accumulation*, 1956) and considered the corresponding chapter of Sraffa's book unsuccessful and even canceling out all his positive scientific innovations. It is difficult to disagree with this, since Sraffa demonstrates the extreme helplessness of his research methodology when describing the usual process of technological development of economics. First, it abandons its function and introduces an additional nonlinear function (V_2), the intersections of which with the linear function V_1 should supposedly force manufacturers to 'switch technologies'. But since in this case the Sraffa function in the model is canceled, then there can be no switchings in it. Secondly, technological changes should simply shift the linear Sraffa function to larger (V_3) or smaller (V_4) volumes of the national product, but he did not show this. Thirdly, the non-linearity of additional arbitrary functions should have forced Sraff to normalize the profitability indicator again in the analysis of the production sphere, where the marginal law of diminishing efficiency is in effect. factors (in Fig. I.14 this is the marginal isoquant V_5), but he did not do this either, thereby showing non-sequencing in his model constructions. Fourth, the nonlinearity of the Sraffa function means the need to introduce a marginal assumption ceteris parubus, which contradicts the assumptions accepted in the model.

All this indicates at least a weak elaboration of the corresponding chapter of his book by Sraffa. It is characteristic that after 1960 in 'neo-Ricardianism' the problem of "switching technologies" has not been clarified, which already speaks of certain defects in all models built on the basis of the action of only the labor factor. The opinion of the Italian economist Pierangelo Garanani (1930-2011) [141, p. 4078-4136] that Sraffe was able to develop 'non-marginal' demand curves for capital looks unconvincing. It is important to note that, in mainstream theory, the shift in technology is simply fixed by a new proportion of capital and labor in the production function.

Back in an article in 1926, criticizing the neoclassicism of that time, Sraffa came to the conclusion that the rational beginning of the study of economics should be the theory of monopoly, which is closest to the real market reality. However, neither in the main work of Sraffa, nor in the subsequent 'neo-Ricardianism', fundamental works on monopoly economic structures did not appear. In the mainstream, the ideas embodied in the works of this direction by Robinson (*Economics of Imperfect Competition*, 1933) and Chamberlin (*Theory of Monopolistic Competition*, 1933) received further successful development, and in modern conditions a whole new industry has emerged in the economy – 'The Theory of Market Organization', based on marginal principles.

Sraffa believed that margin theory 'cannot be improved and should be discarded'. In the history of economic science, similar radical views have already been met by Mill, Marx, Jevons, and others) and have been successfully refuted by life. In our opinion, the mainstream theory can and should be improved, enriched with developments in other areas of modern economics, including 'neo-Ricardianism', despite the fact that they are perceived as antipodes of marginalists.

Sraffa in his book spoke very sparingly about the shortcomings of marginalism. Therefore, when moving towards a new synthesis, we will have to not only defend the mainstream theory, but also consider a wider range of its errors, problems and shortcomings than those found by neoricardians and representatives of other areas of economics.

The idea of the incompatibility of the two theories under consideration cannot be considered convincing, even if we compare their fundamental fundamental differences. For example. the classic "one-factor cost" can be easily interpreted in a marginal spirit. The well-known averaging of incremental "socially necessary labor costs" (SNLC) (B', $B' = \Delta B / \Delta Q$) of individual manufacturers of products of the industry (Q) (Fig. I.15, *a*, dotted line), which forms the value of the goods, with the arrangement of these costs in an ascending order (Fig. I.15, *b*) gives us a margin upward function offers and the price of this product.

But while advancing economics to a new synthesis, it is not necessary to marginalize the theory of neoricardians, but to use in the mainstream their few real discoveries concerning the theory of 'production prices'. In this regard, it is necessary to generally solve the well-known issue of dividing research into long-term and short-term. Kurz and Salvadori state that "Adam Smith is responsible for the development of a clear formulation of the method ... of long-term conditions, based on the concept of a single rate of return" [62, p. 26] and on this basis they ascribe long-term durability to the whole classics and 'neo-Ricardianism', specifically giving the subtitle *Long-term Analysis* to their book. But the long-term was declared by the classics only to justify the full use of production factors that they expected, which was not there in the entire history of the market. Equilibrium has always been established with unemployed workers, capital goods and lands. Therefore, any practical pricing model should only take into account the time required for the current market balancing. The model of interindustry equilibrium and the

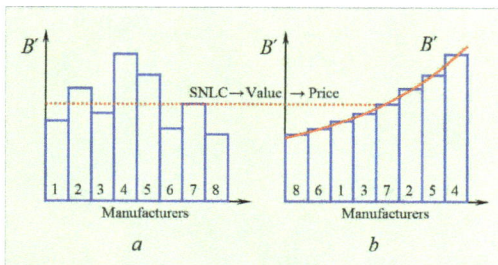

Fig. I.15

formation of a single rate of return by Sraffa is not long-term, just like the mainstream market equilibrium theory is not short-term, and may be compatible with the latter in this regard.

When developing a new synthesis economics, it is necessary to determine the place of Keynes's theory in it, which is the main one in the mainstream macroeconomics, but, at the same time, gave rise to 'left Keynesianism' and the 'dispute of two Cambridges'. However, our analysis of the concepts of Keynes' aggregated macroequilibrium[1] and Sraffa's interindustry equilibrium shows that they still coincide only on the need for active government regulation of the ratio of consumption funds and accumulation of national income. But only a proper accurate interpretation of Keynes's theory, from our point of view, will significantly bring the areas under consideration closer together. And the overdue complex correction of Keynes's theory removes the disputes in 'Keynesianism' and the 'dispute of two Cambridges' in economics from the agenda.

We raise the question of the synthesis of 'neo-Ricardianism' and the mainstream so far only on the basis of the laws of symmetry and repetition shown above, which are valid in the history of economic thought of some of

---

[1] See our work: [34].

the arguments in this section of the monograph. If the synthetic economic theories of the recent past – Marshall and Samuelson – turned out to be rather mechanistic and largely incomplete, then the maturing synthesis in the current 'Unified Socioeconomy' should be more successful. Such confidence is given to us by the update of the marginal micro- and macroeconomics, presented below in chapters II and III of the monograph.

CHAPTER II
SOLUTION OF MICROECONOMIC PROBLEM
THE 'DISPUTE OF TWO CAMBRIDGES'

6. Completion of a completely competitive price model produced goods

In section 4 of the monograph, we gave a brief positive assessment of the synthesis of the 'Marshall cross'. But Marshall was the creator of not only a model of equilibrium prices[1], but also the developer of the concepts of "representative firm", "consumer surplus", "elasticity", "organizational factor" of production and "quasi rent", which we also consider below. An undoubted scientific merit should be considered the preservation of their continuity in the development of economic theory, which, with its deployment in the second half of the XIX century. the so-called 'marginal revolution' was under threat. In the *Preface* to the first edition of *Principles of Economics*, he wrote that "when ... new studies fall into place over time, and their critical acuteness is removed, then it turns out that in reality they by no means violate the continuity of the process of the development of science. New doctrines only supplement the old ones, expand, sometimes correct them, often give them a different tone, highlight accents in a new way, but very rarely subvert them" [71, p. 47]. It was because of Marshall's apparent desire to adapt the classical theory of value to more modern knowledge that Veblen (*Presuppositions of Economic Science*, 1900) called him 'the first non-classical'.

In an essay by *Alfred Marshall, 1842-1924* (1925) Keynes noted: "... The contradiction in the interpretation of the role of demand and cost of production, respectively, in determining value was finally resolved. After Marshall's analysis of this problem, there was nothing more to add" [Ibid, p. 34]. But it seems to us that Keynes was too hasty in evaluating the price scissors model, which had drawbacks: the lack of links between its marginal functions and integral functions and the use of the non-rational archaic concept of 'utility'.

---

[1] In fairness, it should be noted that before the Marshall synthesis in the economic literature there were some similar developments on the theory of the market. The model of the crosshair of supply and demand functions has already been published by the Englishman Fleming Jenkin (1833-1885) (*Graphical Representation of the Laws of Supply and Demand*, 1870), although before Jenkin the 'cross' was used by German economists Karl Rau (1792-1870) (*Textbook of Political Economy. In 3 Volumes*, 1826-1837) and Hans von Mangoldt (1824-1868) (*Fundamentals of Economic Science*, 1863). But Marshall stubbornly did not give references to the sources of his model, even in all the numerous reprints of his *Principles of Economics*. But the expression 'Marshall cross' should be considered correct in view of its greatest contribution to the analysis of market equilibrium.

The model has become a paradigm of economics, but the indicated main and other shortcomings have survived to this day, so it needs updating.

If the theory of 'neo-Ricardianism' is to be cleared, as we have found, of such artificial elements as the 'standard system', 'basic and non-basic goods', 'dated labor', 'by-products of production' and 'technology switching', then more Marshall's early theory, on the contrary, needs completion, after which it can become a universal tool for studying the equilibria of various markets, traditional – commodity, factor, money, and new – externalities, votes, institutions, etc.

As you know, economics refers to nonlinear dynamic systems, and the theory of the analysis of such systems provides for the selection and formalization of their elements, sufficient to carry out an effective subsequent synthesis of systems, that is, to give them the given properties. Therefore, updating the model of local, sectoral equilibrium is important for the formation of modern macroeconomics.

Marshall, in the very first chapter of the *Graduation of Consumer Demand* for his work, introduces a coordinate system 'the amount of the consumed good – the price of the good', designed to illustrate the 'law of demand'. The available explanation of the graph by the author turns out to be rather contradictory. On the one hand, Marshall was the first to denote the quantity of the good on the abscissa, and the price on the ordinate, which corresponded to the theory of rarity and the rules of mathematics, but, on the other hand, in the question of what is a dependent and what is an independent variable, he was extremely not consistent. As a marginalist, he considered the price to be a derivative of the total utility, but considered it, now as a function, now as an argument. For example, he noted: "Our law, therefore, can be stated as follows: the more a person possesses a thing, the less ... will be the price that he is willing to pay for a small additional its quantity ..." [Ibid, p. 142]. But next to him he wrote the opposite: "... The general law of demand, ... the quantity of goods for which demand is presented, increases with a decrease in prices and decreases with an increase in prices" [Ibid, p. 146].

In microeconomics, 'price' is the central category and the desired quantity, which, moreover, depends on the quantity of not only one, but the entire set of goods. Therefore, before performing these scientific procedures, it is not permissible to vary the price in the model. Introducing price analysis as a premise is not logical and contradicts the marginal theory of scarcity. The methodological position on the value of a good, determined by its quantity, is fundamental, permeates not only micro-, but also macroeconomics. The theory does not deny, but practice confirms the existence of the inverse effect of the price on the quantity of a good, and to study this in the mathematical tools there are so-called inverse functions, but methodologically and didactically corresponding material should be derived from the main thing.

Marshall was a professional mathematician, but his most logically constructed statements and graphs were placed in footnotes. The same Keynes noted in this regard that for any economist it would be much wiser to read the footnotes and omit the main text than vice versa [123, p. 263].

Marshall described in detail the marginal characteristics of the process of consuming goods, but nowhere did he analyze or depict integral utility functions. He also repeatedly spoke on the issue of integrating the marginal utility function (restoring the general utility function), which was first raised by the Italian economist Giovanni Antonelli before him (*The Mathematical Theory of Political Economy*, 1886). Later, the American economist mathematician Hendrik Houtacker (1924-2008) (*Revealed Preference and Utility Function*, 1950) showed that models with many benefits do not satisfy the integrability conditions.

About his credo, he writes the following: "... I began to attach great importance to the fact that our ideas about nature – both moral and its material spheres – refer not so much to the aggregate of quantities as to increments quantities ..." [71, p. 50, 51]. Marginal functions with market research are necessary, but they are derived from integral functions. In this regard, Blaug [14, p. 315-320], and after him some other authors, the proof of the negative slope of the demand curve is attributed to Marshall. But Marshall did not make such logical constructions, in the main text of the *Principles of Economics* he only referred to the existence of the "law of diminishing utility" [71, p. 140] and in the *Mathematical Appendix* to the book he simply noted that "d^2U/dQ^2 always has a negative value" [Ibid, p. 792] (our notation – *the author*)[1], Marshall has nothing more than this statement. If he investigated jointly integral and differential dependencies, then inconsistencies in his constructions would be obvious.

The author of a complete analysis of the laws of consumption, based on psychological assessments of goods, their rarity, general and marginal utility, should be considered the representative of early marginalism, the German economist Hermann Gossen (1810-1858) (*Development of the Laws of Social Exchange and the Resulting Rules of Human Activity*, 1854), whose work has not yet been appreciated. In a somewhat archaic form, he formulates the so-called '1st Gossen's law' as follows, which would be more correctly called simply "Gossen's law of utility": the marginal "value of one and the same pleasure is steadily decreasing in in the event that we continuously continue to consume the good that provides this pleasure, until, finally, saturation occurs" [28, v. 2. p. 121]. This position in modern economics states: as the amount of consumed good Q increases, the function of its total utility U will slowly in-

---

[1] In the quote, d^2U/dQ^2 – the second derivative of the utility function (U), $U = f(Q)$, where Q – the amount of good consumed.

crease, it reaches the saturation point Umax, and the marginal utility function U', equal to dU/dQ, which is In essence, 'at the cost of a unit of utility', it decreases monotonically, becomes zero, measuring the equilibrium volume of the good Q_e, and then takes negative values (Fig. II.1). In full integro-differential form, the law automatically determines the decreasing nature of the marginal utility function.

Marshall was the first to apply the ceteris paribus assumption – the condition of the constancy of the quantities of all factors, except for the one under consideration. The assumption made it possible to simplify the study of local equilibrium and to reveal the fundamental laws of pricing. Marshall himself wrote about the essence of the premise: "... The forces with which one has to deal are so numerous that it is best to consider them as separate ... We exclude the influence of all other factors by the clause 'with other things being equal', although we do not consider them inert, but only temporarily ignore their action" [71, p. 53, 54].

It is important to emphasize that the premise of ceteris paribus is not an abstraction, not just a scientific device, it corresponds to a certain objective reality. The premise is not virtual, but can be realized in practice in the same way as, for example, isothermal or isobaric processes are realized in physical objects. The demand function is only a slice, one of the aspects of real reality. The ceteris paribus condition actually forces us to consider a complicated economic process, since it includes additional mechanisms that ensure a constant amount of all other benefits and nonlinearity of mathematical functions. And if the so-called 'latent heat' is observed in the named physical processes, then in the case of an economic process there is a 'latent value' associated with the intensification of the transfer of value from the form of a stock to the form of a stream with a constant quantity of $n - 1$ goods. The descending non-linear demand function can be considered an exact reflection of the phenomenon of the economy, observed in its study in real conditions ceteris paribus.

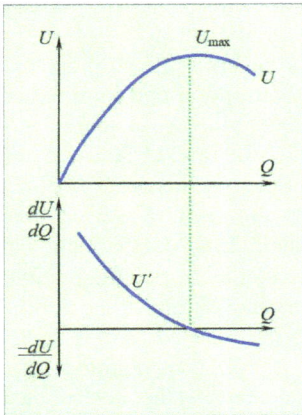

Fig. II.1

Other explanations for this type of demand function, which are abundant in the economic literature, are not required. The marginal utility indicator and the demand function characterize the efficiency of the process of consumption of the goods under consideration, say, by an individual, and if they decrease, this means, first of all, a drop in the efficiency of the process associated with saturation of a person, the inevitability of imbalances in his body, his home economy, social infrastructure and economy. Thus, ceteris paribus is a violation of the existing technology, the emergence of imbalances in the reproduction process as a whole.

Marshall put different meanings into the premise ceteris paribus – permanence: habits, fashion, disposable quantity and purchasing power of money, prices, qualities and quantities of competing goods, and so on. In each individual case or their combination, the nature of the corresponding functions was special. Marshall began to consciously adopt this approach to accomplish the task that he outlined in the *Preface* of his book *Principles of Economics* – to explain the phenomena observed in economics. But this circumstance was the reason for Marshall's own mistakes, since the 'observed phenomena' are multifactorial. In addition, considering the action of the above factors, he violated the very univariate premise of ceteris paribus, which excludes the 'shift' of functions. These errors were the cause of numerous disputes and misunderstandings that arose in economic theory after the publication of the book.

Big problems and inconsistencies are visible in Marshall's interpretation and use in research of the concept of utility of goods, which has long attracted the attention of theoretical economists.

The French mathematician Antoine Cournot (1801-1877) denied the relationship between demand and utility. Menger and Walras did not consider the problem of measuring utility at all. Jevons believed that the theory of pricing does not require a solution to the issue of utility operationality and it can only be raised in the theory of welfare. Marshall, on the other hand, made a certain breakthrough in the theory of utility, translating it into the language of prices, but he did this without proper explanations and details. He actually got away from solving the problem of any concretization of the concept of utility. After the fiasco of cardinalist research on the issue of utility, Kassel (*Theory of Social Economics*, 1918) proposed to abandon the clarification of the relationship between utility and the amount of good and simply use the demand function in theory.

Hicks (*Value and Capital*, 1939) argued that "cardinalism has outlived its usefulness" [143, p. 15] that "the quantitative concept of utility is not needed to explain the phenomena of the market. Therefore ... it is better to do without it ... These values are immeasurable in the context of this problem and their presence can significantly complicate its study" [144, p. 20, 21][1]. According to Hicks, the 'marginal utility'[2] indicator can be successfully replaced by the 'marginal substitutability' indicator of one good for another. However, it is

---

[1] We present our own translation of this passage, since in the Russian edition [124, p. 111] he sounds less categorical.
[2] The term 'marginal utility' was first used by Wieser (*On the Origin and Basic Laws of Economic Value*, 1884), but the more general term 'marginal gain' belongs to the German Johann von Thünen (1783-1850) (*An Isolated State in its Relation to Agriculture and National Economy. In 3 Volumes*, 1819-1863).

impossible to agree with these views of the authoritative theorist, since the ordinalist method of determining the demand function using Hicks's 'substitution of goods' is indirect, unnecessarily complicated and, moreover, not applicable when considering the usefulness of an individual good. Unfortunately, Hicks's concept contributed to filling the microeconomic mix with pseudoscientific effects of 'income', 'price', 'scale' and other derivatives and minor models that only distracted the theory from solving the issue of pricing.

The substitution of the concept of "revealed preferences" for the solution of this question was made by Samuelson[1]. If Marshall intuitively preferred the limiting characteristics, then Samuelson, known for his desire to pass any question that had not yet been properly understood through his 'mathematical meat grinder', formal analysis of utility absolutized and sought to "cleanse the theory of demand from all traces of the concept utility" [155, p. 71]. He wrote: "The choice of a specific indicator of utility has absolutely no effect on the observed price behavior" [97, p. 103]. Samuelson proposed to build a microeconomic mix using the concept of 'revealed preferences', that is, on the basis of a rigorous mathematical analysis of empirical data on consumer choice. But this idea remained unrealized, although it is necessarily understood in advanced textbooks on economics.

The remaining abstract concept of utility has not been recognized by some economists, with whose arguments it is difficult to disagree. For example, the American E. Downey writes about the "scientific futility of the theory of utility", expressing this pun even in the title of his article – The Futility of Marginal Utility (1910), since the word futility is translated as 'emptiness', and his compatriot Frank Knight (1885-1972) (Normal Price and Distribution, 1917) believed that the concept of utility even damaged economic theory.

In modern economics, the theory of utility, due to its methodological weakness, has been 'overgrown' with many axioms and theorems. It needs a return to its origins and, above all, a thorough study and use of Gossen's concept. But this author is often not mentioned at all in the mathematized economic literature. As a joke, we will say that, for example, in the textbook Advanced Microeconomic Theory (2001) by Jeffrey Jayley and Philip Reni, the 'Hesse matrix' [42, p. 709] is considered in detail in ten places, but the State sen, although the textbook contains a section on the history of utility theory. The authors call utility 'a certain substance' [Ibid, p. 15], which, due to un-

---

[1] In the textbook on microeconomics [42, p. 118] does not quite accurately indicate that Samuelson's 'revealed preference' approach was proposed in his Foundations of Economic Analysis (1947). In fact, the theory of this issue was presented by him in his article Remark on the Pure Theory of Consumer Behavior (1938), in the Foundations Samuelson did not yet call it the theory of 'revealed preferences' and spoke about "identifying the properties of the preference field necessary for maximum utility" [97, p. 115] and only in the 1948 article Theory of Consumption in Terms of Revealed Preference appeared the corresponding name.

certainty, is replaced by six axioms of consumer preference for goods, and from these dubious assumptions, unconvincing attempts are made to explain many other economic phenomena.

One can agree with Blaug, who noted that "the long and painful history of utility theory is a bleak picture. Few of the supporters of utility took the trouble to verify the conclusions of this theory, and it turned out that the theory of utility did not become a fruitful source of hypotheses characterizing real consumer demand" [14, p. 331].

Let us return, however, to Gossen, his Elaboration of the Laws of Public Exchange. Analyzing his graph of the "atom of pleasure," he formulated, in addition to the above, one more important provision on the consumer value of the good: "... The first measure of a thing ... has the highest value, each subsequent one ... has a lesser value ... and the whole a triangle ... gives in a generalized form a geometric reflection of value" [28, v. 2. p. 126]. This provision should be called "Gossen's law of value", since in it he reasonably identifies the usefulness of a good with its value. For him, for the first time, the area under the marginal utility curve on the ordinate of the integral part of the utility model represents the absolute monetary indicator.

Marshall, refusing to measure utility, also moved to money, but in a peculiar way. "It should be strongly emphasized," he writes, "that it is impossible or even inconceivable to directly measure the desires themselves or the satisfaction received from their fulfillment" [71, p. 140], "utility ... can be measured not directly, but only indirectly, through external manifestations ...", through the price "which a person is willing to pay for the fulfillment or satisfaction of his desire" [Ibid, p. 139, 140]. And further Marshall stated that "it cannot be argued that the price measures marginal utility in general, since the needs and material situation of different people are different" [Ibid, p. 146], and did not use the key category 'absolute utility' at all. These contradictory statements of Marshall, in our opinion, led him to a number of theoretical errors.

If we talk about price as an economic phenomenon, then its definition lies on the surface: the price of a unit of any good is a monetary expression of its value. But what is the essence of price? The answer of representatives of the consumer theory of value has also been known for a long time – this is the marginal utility of a good. Therefore, utility must be measured in money. But, realizing this, Marshall easily declared, "Now let's translate the law of diminishing utility into the language of prices" [Ibid, p. 157] and using a specific example of quantitative manipulations with tea, he already considered the price of a good as a variable factor, thereby narrowing and inverting the wording of the law: "... The quantity of goods for which demand is presented increases with a decrease in price and decreases with an increase in price" [Ibid, p. 163]. But at the same time, Marshall was forced to consider the problem of "marginal utility of money, or general purchasing power" [Ibid, p. 158] (U_A). The difficulty of solving this problem made him notice that "the richer a person becomes, the less the marginal utility of money for him" [Ibid, p. 142], that the question goes "far beyond the boundaries of economic science" [Ibid, p. 139] and it would be unsubstantiated to assume that U_A "constitutes a fixed value" [Ibid, p. 142] and therefore the prices of goods "are among themselves in the same relation as the usefulness of these two goods" [Ibid][1].

In Marshall's terminology, one might think that by U_A he means the price of money, but analysis of the corresponding formulas in the *Mathematical Appendix* to his *Principles* shows that we are not talking about the stock of money in real terms, but about the flow rate of the consumer's monetary income. Further, Marshall, assuming the immutability of U_A ($U_A = k$ = const), although he determined the utility "up to a constant multiplier" [14, p. 310] ($U = k \cdot X$), but was forced to assume the constancy of the consumer's income (A, $A = X \cdot Q$ = const), since only in this case a descending demand function is formed in the form of a hyperbole, which he depicts many times in the book. But with all this pile-up of conditions, the model of the consumption of goods becomes unrealistic

Marshall wrote that "money ... is considered as the main goal of human activity ..., they serve as the only suitable means of measuring the motives of human activity ..." [71, p. 75], but did not fully implement this correct position in his work.

Meanwhile, the integration of the price function gives us the monetary function of income. This alone forces us to seek as a result of the consumption of goods not the notorious 'utility, but a specific 'income'. The homogeneity of a possible 'monetary' integro-differential model of consumption would eliminate all the problems we have considered. In this regard, it is interesting that formal transformations above the above equation $U = k \cdot X$ lead to the following: $U = U_A \cdot X$, $U/U_A = X$, $(dU/dQ)/(dU/dA) = X$, $dA/dQ = X$. That is, if instead of utility we take monetary profitability, then the problem is solved absolutely. Without the intermediary factor U_A, the indicators of total and marginal utility are referred to as 'income from the consumption of the good' and 'the price of demand for the good', respectively. Let's try to substantiate the need for such substitutions in modeling the consumption of goods.

---

[1] The problem of the 'usefulness of money' is associated with the subjectivity of assessments of the utility of goods by individuals in general, which before Marshall was studied by the Swiss mathematician Daniel Bernoulli (1700-1782) (*Experience of the New Theory of Measuring the Lot*, 1738) and after Marshall by American mathematicians John von Neumann (1903-1957) and Oscar Morgenstern (1902-1977), and in our time Kahneman and Tversky (*Prospect Theory: Analysis of Risk-Based Decisions*, 1979). But these studies do not have sufficient results for a satisfactory solution of the problems of demand theory, but only develop and strengthen the idea of the subjectivity of utility assessments given by a person.

The possibility of such a justification is associated with the idea of John Clarke (*Distribution of Wealth*, 1899) to identify the processes of production and consumption of goods, which makes the marginal toolkit universal. In connection with the understanding that production is the consumption of its factors, and the consumption of goods is the production of factors, in fact, the concept of an 'economic entity' (Fig. II.2), which allows to describe the functioning of firms, households, the state and the economy as a whole from a single cardinalist-marginal position, as well as to give an accurate and modern interpretation of laws, from covered by Gossen. But Clarke did not make such generalizations and they are not in theory until now.

If we turn to the scheme of commodity-money circulation, depicted in any textbook on economics (Fig. II.3), it becomes obvious that the result of the process of consumption of the good Q created by the firm is not an abstract 'utility', but a con-

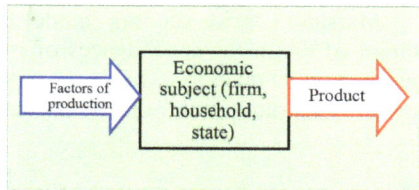

Fig. II.2

crete the labor force reproduced in the household (L), the expenditure of which (labor), measured in monetary form (wages) A, is a regressively increasing function of the amount of goods consumed: $A = f(Q)$. The first derivative of this function is the decreasing 'demand price function' (X_d): $A' = X_d$, $X_d = f(Q)$. The scheme of the circulation of benefits and incomes when interpreting utility as the final non-economic result of the consumption of a bug actually becomes open after the block 'household'. For the real joining of all elements of the model of economic circulation, according to their actual reproduction, a production interpretation of the process of consumption of goods is necessary. In this case, the good consumed itself becomes a factor of production, and the dependence of the 'law of utility of Gossen' acts as a 'production function', the first derivative of which (the marginal profitability of the good) is a function of the demand for the good, the price its consumer.

Such a 'neo-cardinalist' solution to the problems of the theory of consumption allows us to show that any process in the economy is a consumption-production and it can always be characterized by quantitative streaming indicators at the 'input' and 'output' of an object, which the constructive possibilities of the Clarke production margin research, which were mentioned above, can be realized.

Considering 'neo-Ricardianism' in section 5 of monographs, we noted that Sraffa did not consider neoclassicism as a reproductive theory. But it is the representation of households as 'producers of labor' that allows us to confirm the realism of the model of continuous double, commodity-money circulation in the economy.

Due to the more subjective nature of the consumption process than the production process, Marshall in the *Principles of Economics* had to consider many economic and non-economic factors of demand, which, when modeling pricing, turned out to be required. But Marshall devoted five times more space to analysis of supply than analysis of demand. As a result, he presented the issue of equilibrium between supply and demand incorrectly, in an 'asymmetric' form with various details of the process of production of goods. But to solve the main issue of microeconomics – the issue of local equilibrium – all these multifactorial details are not required, because at this level, with the premise of ceteris paribus, they are leveled.

Marshall's 'price scissors' model is generally based on the marginal principles of nonlinear dependences of production costs and the usefulness of a product on its quantity. Therefore, reproaches to Marshall for the static nature of his constructions should be considered unfair, since the very movement along the points of the corresponding functions of the models involves the cost of time. In this regard, Clarke (*Distribution of Wealth*, 1890), characterizing the labor market, noted: "The consistent introduction of people into work is a piece of imaginary dynamics ..." [56, p. 188][1].

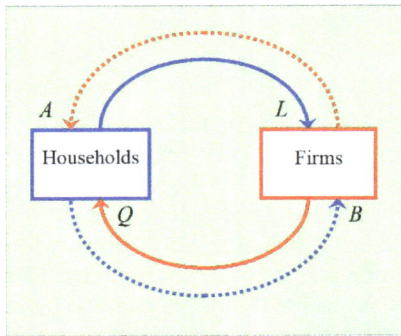

Fig. II.3

Marshall was the first to take into account the factor of time in the analysis of markets and introduced the concepts of short, medium and long term. But it so happened that his manner of accounting for the time of passage of economic processes came into conflict with his synthesis, with his principle of 'price scissors', which, again, led to certain misunderstandings, confusion and errors in mainstream theory. Marshall researched in great detail not only the numerous factors of production of goods, but also its organizational and technological changes in the current, short and long-term, as well as a wide historical period. He began to describe in detail the qualitative transformations of production. But it is known that comparative statics considers only the initial and final states of an object without clarifying the very transient process in it and its constituent parts.

Therefore, Marshall's analysis turned out to be unjustifiably asymmetric, one-sided and in terms of time. His extensive reasoning about the multi-factoriality and diversity of the supply of goods actually led him to three possible

---

[1] A certain equivalence of dynamics and comparative statics was proved in the form of the "principle of correspondence" by Samuelson (*Foundations of Economic Analysis*, 1947).

76

options for the functions of total and marginal costs of production of goods (Q) (Fig. II.4), which characterize decreasing (B_1 and B_1'), increasing (B_2 and B_2') and constant (B_3 and B_3') production efficiency.

But the concavity of the function of supplying a product, as well as the function of demand for it, is more logical to explain simply by the action of the premise ceteris paribus, which does not mean the absence of all other goods, but only their invariable quantity. Therefore, when in these conditions we increase the production of an individual product, then there is a purely intensive use of all other benefits and a corresponding progressive increase in costs.

It seems to us that the multiplicity of the form of the supply function in Marshall partly caused Sraffa's rejection of his theory. The non-linear variants of the function also did not correspond to the macro-approach in the Sraffa equilibrium model, which excluded the ceteris paribus premise, therefore, he could choose for it only a function with a constant return, the derivative of which gives horizontal product offerings.

Marshall, in his *Principles*, constantly changed the object of research and the reader often does not understand what is at stake – an individual, a firm, or the economy as a whole. Hence the incredible confusion that has arisen in theory and contributes to the appearance in it of the concepts we have mentioned that distract it from satisfactory solutions to pricing problems.

The 'methodological individualism' advocated by Marshall and all marginalists of the 'first wave' also played a bad role in the development of the structure of the *Principles of Economics*. Its application in the

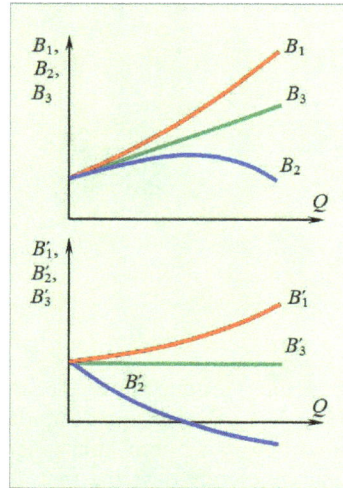

Fig. II.4

study of pricing-formation 'dissolves' all structures of the economy and presents it as homogeneous, 'atomic', supposedly consisting only of competing individuals. Such an extremely simplified approach gave certain results in the past of economic theory, but now it is no longer effective, since in the real economy there are no individuals who operate, and associations of individuals. Therefore, in our opinion, the sectoral approach improves the diversity of production units well and makes it possible to clarify the pricing mechanism.

The sectoral level of microeconomic analysis is important not only for its objectivity, but also for the fact that it synchronously meets and exchanges commodity and cash flows. The above scheme of the commodity-money circulation between one firm and one household for realism should be supplemented by the 'Market' block (Fig. II.5), mediating links between all households with firms in the industry.

Marshall wrote in his book: "We could equally reasonably argue about whether the value is regulated by utility or production costs, as well as about whether a piece of paper is cut by the upper or lower blade of the scissors" [71, p. 357], and further noted that the observed market mechanism is the action of "one universal law of supply and demand, each of them can be compared with one of the blades of scissors" [Ibid, p. 775]. But the unity and essence of the pricing process should be associated not with the 'law of supply and demand', but with the law of diminishing efficiency of the growing variable, acting in the same way under the premise of ceteris paribus both on factors and and on products of production.

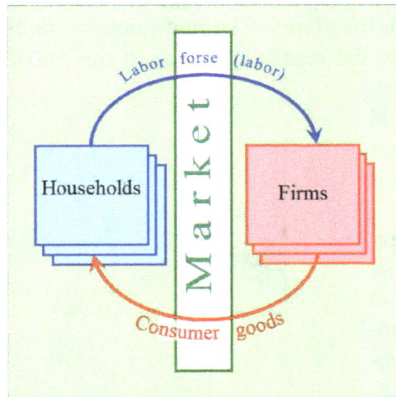

Fig. II.5

The representation of firms and households as consumers-producers of goods determines the division of the reproduction scheme of the turnover of values into two pricing models – in the markets of consumer goods ($X_Q = f(Q)$) and labor (L) ($X_L = f(L)$[1]). Each model is complete, that is, it contains integral and differential functions, includes a description of the market itself for a particular product in aggregate with all its producers and consumers (Fig. II.6). We call this type of model a 'marketron', which can become a universal instrument of micro- and macroeconomics, which makes it possible to fully and concretely describe the mechanism for balancing any market. In this regard, it would be most correct to consider firms and households as initial, and the industry in such an expanded form as the main objects of microeconomics.

A few more words about terminology. In many places in the *Principles of Economics*, Marshall uses different concepts to describe markets, which has created a certain terminological confusion in economics. He writes: "In the course of research ... we will often have to use the terms *production costs (cost)*, production waste (expenses) ..." [Ibid, p. 349]. But, the English words cited by the author in brackets should be replaced by places, since *cost* – the 'cost' in the market, that is, the cost of buying goods, hence the modern con-

---

[1] We will consider the analysis of this and other marketrons of factors of production in section 7 of the monograph.

cept of 'isocosta', first introduced into the economic theory by the Italian economist Enrico Barone (1859-1924) *(Essay on the Coordination of the Laws of Distribution*, 1894), and expenses – 'production costs', But it is better for this case to use the word 'spend' – 'use up', 'deplete', that is, spend the factors of production. We are introducing the word 'isospenda' into scientific circulation instead of the longer names used in economics 'curve of production opportunities' 'curve of transformation', 'curve of production opportunities' and 'border production capabilities'. In the general case, we will use the term 'expense', which is consonant with 'profitability'.

In Fig. II.7 presents the marketron of a perfectly competitive consumer goods market. It consists of integral and differential parts, which depict the dependences of the indicators B, B', A and A' on the quantity of goods Q, as well as the function of selling the good, or the contract function (AB), which expresses the profitability of the producers of the good. and at the same time the consumption of its consumers[1]. The value of B_{au} represents the so-called 'autonomous costs' of production, that is, the minimum costs of the industry with zero output.

Since, in perfect competition, all market participants are 'recipients' of the equilibrium price (X_e), the first ray of the contract function appears in the marketron (the contract amount is equal to $X_e \cdot Q$), then the concave function of the production cost B of the goods, followed by the convex profitability function A of its consumption. In the same order, we draw the first derivatives of the functions.

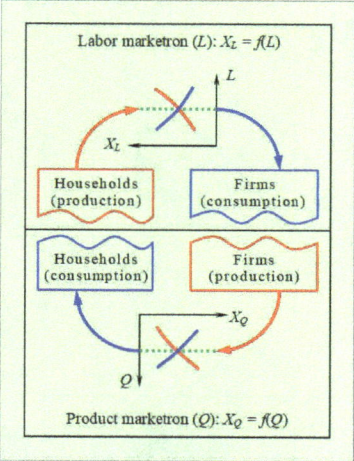

Fig. II.6

The marketron under consideration has a production-consumption profitability zone, located between Q_{min} and Q_{max}, in which the total profitability exceeds the total consumption, and two extreme zones of unprofitableness of the industry. In the lower, differential part of the model, the 'Marshall cross' is presented – the functions A, B and AB in the values of the first derivative $A' = dA/dQ$, $B' = dB/dQ$, $AB' = dAB/dQ$), which characterize the marginal market itself goods. Here, at the point of intersection of the functions, there are equal quantities for both groups of counterparties of the volume (Q_e) and the

---

[1] Cournot was the first to consider an integral-differential model of a monopolized industry with a graph of the demand function. Such modeling was essentially developed by the American economist Jacob Weiner (1892-1970) (*Cost Curves and Supply Curves*, 1931).

selling price X_e of the goods. The exponents A and B are equal to the integrals of the curves A' and B' (the areas under them): $A = \int A'(Q) \cdot dQ$, $B = \int B'(Q) \cdot dQ$.

It is important to point out that the theoretical justification of the 'Marshall cross' as an equilibrium of the limiting values of utility and costs was given by Gossen, who wrote: "To ensure the maximum amount of pleasure ... a person must distribute his time and effort ... in such a way that for each good the value of the atom, created by the latter, is equal to the amount of effort that would have to be applied ..." [28, v. 2, p. 127]. For all the archaic nature, this statement was historically the first and it should be considered the formulation "Gossen's law of price."

The total market profit in the integral part of the marketron is equal to the difference between A and B, and in its marginal part it corresponds to the area

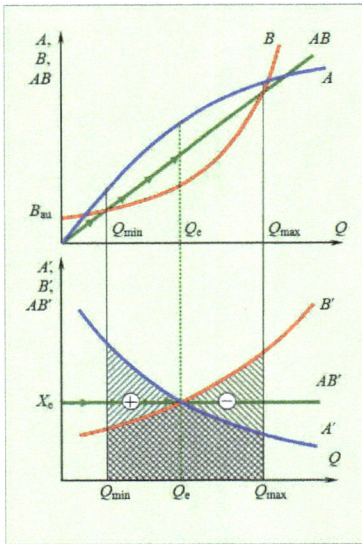

Fig. II.7

of the triangular area as the difference between the areas under the functions A' and B' on the output interval from Q_{min} to Q_e (on the interval of release from Q_{min} to Q_{max} this difference is zeroed). The contract function (price function) AB' divides the total profit into two parts – the profit of the manufacturer and the profit of the consumer of the goods, at the equilibrium point these profits reach the target maximum value. It is noteworthy that in the question of the profitability of the realization of the good, priority belongs to Gossen, since he wrote back in 1854 that "the pleasure obtained from what was created as a result of work is estimated higher than hardships associated with work ..." [Ibid]. Therefore, it would be fair to speak of "Gossen's law of surplus."

The considered new model shows the equilibrium of the market for consumer goods, but the market of any goods sold between firms, as well as the national market as a whole, can be presented in the form of a marketron.

Household profit in the literature is usually considered at the level of individuals and is called 'consumer surplus'. The term introduced into scientific circulation by the French engineer and economist Jules Dupuis (1804-1866) (*On the Usefulness of Civil Structures*, 1844) has been interpreted inaccurately and rather speculatively since the time of Marshall. In the *Principles of Economics*, we find the following definition: "The difference between the price that the buyer would be willing to pay, just not to do without this thing, and the price that he actually pays, is the economic a measure of its added useful-ness. You can call it a consumer surplus" [71, p. 166]. But, firstly, Marshall does not take into account that we are talking not just about a 'thing', but about a certain amount of a thing. Secondly, at the price level, the surplus can only be the area, but not the 'difference'. And, thirdly, the recipients of the consumer surplus can be consumers not only of the final product – individu-als, or households, but of an intermediate product, a firm.

After Marshall, the interpretation of consumer surplus, while remaining abstract, changed. So Clark, attributed the surplus to the factor of production fixed by the premise ceteris paribus. The attitude to the concept of surplus as a theoretical tool also changed. Samuelson, for example, was against its use. In the *Foundations of Economic Analysis* (1947) there is a section under the caustic title *Why the Consumer's Surplus Turns out to be Superfluous*, but the author did not give any arguments for such a position. The American historian of economic thought Benjamin Seligman (1912-1970) (*Main Trends in Mod-ern Economics: Economic Thought after 1870*, 1962) wrote perplexedly about surplus: "Marshall believed that if the total utility is equal to the area of the individual the demand curve (from zero to the purchased quantity), then the consumer's benefit is obviously the difference between the entire area and the area under the price line ... Despite the fact that the product is completely ab-sorbed by the sum of payments to the factors of production in the limit, each factor gets some other benefit" [100, p. 304]. The author, like many other economists, discerns a contradiction on this issue from Marshall, which has not yet been resolved. But one must understand that consumer surplus is sav-ings, savings. Firms and households save some of their income and invest it in the development of their activities. The function of the equilibrium price of the goods X_e and the corresponding integral contractual function AB, depend-ing on the ratio of market forces of supply and demand, divide the total profit of the marketron between the producers and consumers of the goods in a cer-tain proportion.

Consumer profit of individuals and households has the same essence as production profit. Therefore, there is a mutual benefit of the realization of the good in the market. Individuals are the same entrepreneurs seeking profit. They buy consumer goods, reproduce labor and sell labor at a profit. An indi-vidual's profit is an element of his wages and represents a real-life phenome-non, concrete and measurable. Mutual profitability, profitability, market coun-teragents allows them to proportionally increase their welfare. In this mecha-nism lies the solution to the operation of the 'invisible hand' of the Smith market (*Study on the Nature and Causes of the Wealth of Peoples*, 1776), proof of his thesis about the welfare of society on the basis of private benefit.

The equilibrium price of the good X_e includes the profit of both the producer and the consumer of this good. In Fig. II.8, depicting the marginal part of the marketron of product Q, the 'triangle' of consumer surplus is combined with the 'triangle' of producer surplus, but is included in the costs of B for the production of the equilibrium output of goods $Q_{1(e)}$, since they are already contain in themselves the full amount of wages, which in the form of income of workers A is spent on the purchase of goods, according to the balance of the circulation of payments in the industry. Thus, marginal sectoral prices provide expanded reproduction of firms and households in the economy.

If there are not enough economic benefits in society, then in this case they are normalized (rationed), for example, in the amount indicated by the vertical dashed line $Q_{2(e)}$ in Fig. II.8. And Gossen wrote about such an option of equilibrium in terms of "pleasure" and "atom of money": "A person provides himself with maximum pleasure ... if he distributes all the money he earned for the acquisition of various incentives. in such a way that ... the last atom of money spent, respectively, on each of these pleasures, provides an equal amount of pleasure" [71, p. 130]. This theoretical proposition should be called "Gossen's law of rationing."

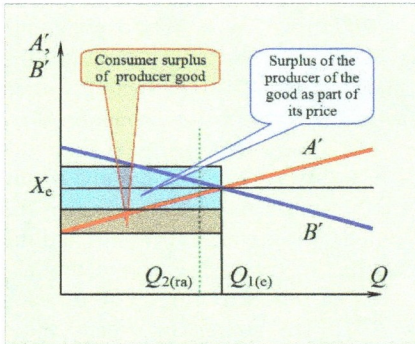

Fig. II.8

Marshall studied in detail the question of an indicator characterizing the degree of slope of a function and called it elasticity. But he was not the first discoverer of the indicator. Something similar was used by the mercantilist Thomas Man (1571-1641) (*The Wealth of England in Foreign Trade*, 1664), the idea of elasticity is also contained in Cournot, although he did not use this term. Marshall defines the indicator as follows: "... The degree of elasticity (or speed of response) of demand in the market depends on the extent to which its volume increases with a given price decrease or decreases with a given price increase" [Ibid, p. 148]. That is, he considered the price in the indicator as an independent variable, and the quantity of goods as a dependent variable: ($\alpha = (dQ/Q)/(dX/X)$. But, consistently adhering to the principle In the case of marginalism, we should represent this relationship in the opposite way, ($\alpha = (dX/X)/(dQ/Q)$, and the names 'elasticity of demand' and 'elasticity of supply' by Marshall should be replaced by 'elasticity demand prices' and 'supply price elasticity'.

The above proposed refinements and improvements to Marshall's theory of local equilibrium can somewhat rehabilitate the mainstream in the eyes of neoricardians and bring the directions closer to synthesis. At the same time, a complete model of 'price scissors' in the form of a marketron will serve as a theoretical basis for the creation of effective macroeconomics.

The monographs proposed in this section of clarification and improvement of the theory of the 'Marshall cross' can somewhat rehabilitate the mainstream in the eyes of neoricardians and bring the directions closer to synthesis.

7. Revision of the theory of pricing in the sale and purchase or lease of factors of production

For further more efficient generalized modeling of pricing processes in various markets, it is advisable to divide them into structural and infrastructural. The concept of 'structure' characterizes stable connections and the ratio of the main constituent parts of any system, its basic structure, while 'infrastructure' is usually called auxiliary connections that support the normal stable state of the structure of this system. In the economy, structural ties are provided by the functioning of markets for factors and results of production, and infrastructural ties – by the work of markets of numerous service industries.

The construction and principles of modeling the structural market of manufactured products were discussed above. Can we talk about factor markets? Despite the obvious positive answer, Samuelson did not agree with this and in his *Foundations of Economic Analysis* noted: "I believe it is worth avoiding the expression 'factor of production' at all ... I propose to directly include in the production function only 'resources' (inputs) and limit this term so that it describes only quantitatively measurable economic goods and services" [97, p. 84]. As for the need to measure the quantity of goods, Samuelson's remark is correct, but the term 'factors of production' in terms of the content is already the term 'resources', so both of them should be preserved in theory, while the words 'factor' and 'resurs' are completely interchangeable without prejudice to the meaning of the context.

Let us turn to the theory of prices of natural resources, capital goods and labor power. These markets are more complex than markets for consumer goods, their rental mechanisms of functioning in the economy are closely intertwined, and natural and capital goods are objects not only for rent, but also for ordinary sale and purchase, in which one has to take into account the physical and obsolescence of these durable objects.

The volume of scientific material on the natural resource market in standard economics is incomparably less than that which covers the coverage of the theory of other factors of production. Obviously, this indicates a low level of development of the research subject. In our opinion, even the initial precise definition of the very concept of 'natural resources' is important here. In the literature, it is ambiguous. So, Oxford dictionaries give completely banal concepts: natural resources – "factors of production, represented by nature" [15, p. 500], "the production factor, which, in order to become productive, usually has to combine with labor and capital" [10, p. 351]. Another definition is "natural resources – free material phenomena of nature available for human use" [105, p. 349] – too abstract. Also, the definition does not reflect the specifics of natural resources, according to which they are "one of the main factors of production; everything that can be used in production in its natural state, without processing ..." [22, p. 235]. And the first distinctive feature of natural resources is diversity in terms of their natural reproducibility. Therefore, natural resources (or simply land) are air, water and earth (area, fertile soil and subsoil) space, as well as flora and fauna used in the life of people (N).

An equally important feature of natural resources and, above all, purely natural agricultural land is their duality, the use of both tools and objects of labor at the same time. A complex of physical, chemical, geological, biological and other processes takes place in the earth, which determine its productivity, that is, its tool qualities. Man, however, only creates the most favorable conditions for these processes, controls and modifies their flow in the direction necessary for himself (in this sense, the use of land is much wider, more diverse than the use in the production of machines). The production process of agriculture consists in cultivating the land to maintain or increase its fertility, and here the land is already a subject of labor. Mineral resources, other objects and substances of the environment are also products of natural reproductive processes of different periods, the harvesting of these natural benefits also requires a certain human impact on them and the corresponding costs.

Taking into account the duality of natural resources makes it easier to explain many of the phenomena of nature management, in particular, the existence of two forms of fertility in agriculture – the main and the additional[1]. The land conditionally, based on practice, refers to natural resources that cannot be reproduced by labor. Hence the natural scarcity of land in general and suitable for agricultural use in particular. In addition, since the land is spatially, again conditionally, not relocatable (it is real estate), its natural fertility depends on a whole complex of geographic, climatic and other natural factors. Therefore, the use of land as an instrument of labor ('natural machine') leads to very different economic results. The result, due to the natural fertility of the land, as well as its location in relation to the markets that supply agricultural

---

[1] The Marxist terms 'differential rent I' and 'differential rent II', immediately indicating a complex form of land use and emphasizing the difference in its profitability, as well as the controversial term from the point of view of the modern theory of value, the term 'absolute rent', we are in modeling pricing we do not use it in the natural resources market.

production with everything necessary, we call the main fertility of the land. The result, associated with the use of land as a subject of labor, improvement of technology, land cultivation technology, the introduction of fertilizers into the soil, the development of science, culture and the organization of agriculture, other opportunities for the growth of production and requiring investment, will be called additional the fertility of the earth.

The relationship between the main and additional fertility of the earth is clearly shown in Fig. II.9, which gives the land distribution functions (dN/dR_N) by basic fertility (R_N). As can be seen from the graphs, investments in land increase not only the middle fertility $(R_{N(mi)}, R_{N(mi, 2)} > R_{N(mi, 1)})$, but also the total amount of land suitable for agricultural production (N) , that is, the area under the function increases: $\int (dN/dR_N)dR_N = N$ (the initial amount of land is the darkened area under the curve). Both forms of land fertility are interrelated, since, on the one hand, its additional fertility as a rule acquires the character of an ordinary natural property, develops into the main fertility and increases the general cultural condition of the land. On the other hand, an additional, intensive, increase in the fertility of the land is tantamount to, equivalent to the corresponding extensive expansion of useful land resources. With the development of nature management, with the growth of investments in land, its total price as a form of wealth rises.

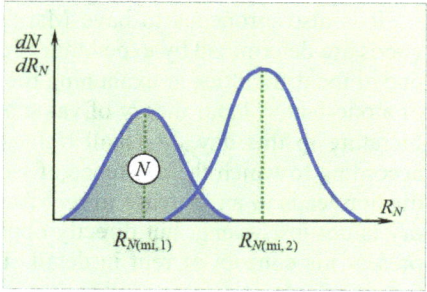

Fig. II.9

The specified division of the production result applies to the use of natural resources in general.

The provision on the original contradictory duality of the land allows you to clarify the terminology and get rid of a number of illusions in the theory of land use.

Strictly speaking, the term 'rent' by etymology and content is associated only with the lease of land, that is, with an agreement on the transfer by the landowner of it for temporary use to the lessee. However, since the structure of land factor income should theoretically not depend on the form of land ownership, and the term 'rent' has been preserved in the economic literature, we use it to denote the entire income of a natural resource. Taking into account the above two methods of increasing the productivity of the land, it is necessary to distinguish between primary and additional rent. Marshall's term 'quasirent', meaning a specific increased income from the temporary competitive advantage of an economic entity in the use of any factor of production, is not advisable in modern theory, since it is because of the prefix 'quasi', which gives the term meaning 'fake rent', 'like a rent', is not suitable for describing the use of natural resources. To display the effect of competitive advantage for each factor of production, it is better to use a separate terminology, for land – this is 'over-rent', for capital goods – 'over-profit', and labor – 'over-earnings'.

The high and largely fixed differentiation of land fertility and, in general, the productivity of nature management determines the typical Marxist idea that this area does not participate in the process of intersectoral capital inflow, and also maintains a stable difference in the level of profitability in the sectors of active nature management. In reality, a single profitability also exists here, and it is established both through the mechanisms of capital transfer, its organizational and technological implementation and fluctuations in product prices, and the mechanism of price changes for the land itself. As a result, more profitable land assets become more expensive and vice versa. Thus, the use of natural resources, like other sectors of the economy, participates in the national economic pricing. In this case, 'profitability' becomes a form of 'interest on capital' as a more general criterion for entrepreneurship in a developed market economy.

It is also erroneous to have Marx's idea that in agriculture the prices of goods are determined by expenditures on the least fertile land. This view arose due to the difficulties in explaining the origin of land rent from the standpoint of a one-factor, labor theory of value and has been preserved in the economic literature to this day. Marshall rightly criticized the Marxist theory of rent, according to which the existence of worse land or other worse factors of production leads to an increase in rent from better factors, he noted that this theory is not just wrong, but directly opposite to the truth. But Marshall did not present his concept of rent in detail. The arguments of the supporters of the theory of 'closing costs', indicating a high demand for agricultural products and the involvement in the production of all suitable land, looks unconvincing. The market economy is characterized by incomplete use of production factors, including land resources. In the agricultural sector, as in any other branch of the economy, the price of a product is determined not only by demand, but also by its supply; in addition, the market is not able to orient itself to the worst conditions of environmental management, since they are indefinable. Pricing in general involves the summation of volumes and marginal averaging of the conditions for the production and consumption of goods. These arguments apply to all nature management.

Remains in modern economic theory and the erroneous idea that there is a relative and absolute lag of agriculture from other sectors of the economy, allegedly associated with a lower level of capital-labor ratio in it than in industry. However, one should not forget that in the value of agricultural assets, which are of a dual nature, the overwhelming share falls on the land itself. Therefore, the monetary value of the land and the corresponding technical means per worker, or otherwise the cost of a job in agriculture, turns out to be much higher than in industry as a whole. But archaic forms of organization of agricultural production – the system of lease and sublease of land, absintheism of landowners, or incomplete ownership of agricultural assets in collective farms – are a real brake on the development of the sector. It is known that the struggle for the terms and rates of land lease between its owners and tenants, as well as the low capitalization of rent on the part of the rentier, leads to a lag in the development of the industry. But the transition to a competitive economy and free inter-sectoral capital flow ensures a more even development of all its sectors.

The Malthusian idea of a possible only linear increase in the production of natural resources in the presence of a geometric progression of population growth is also not confirmed by practice. It is based on the law of 'diminishing land fertility', which actually works, but only under the condition of a constant number of other factors of production used. History, however, does not know the prerequisites ceteris paribus and also shows an exponential growth in agricultural production at a rate that is still higher than the rate of demographic growth. In connection with this fact, ideas about three effective ways of developing agriculture are becoming obsolete: British with a specialization in animal husbandry, German with a specialization in crop production and American with balanced farming. In modern conditions, the global 'green revolution' is becoming relevant, implying a transition to industrial production on artificial soils, with constant irrigation and lighting. 'Revolutions' are also taking place in other branches of nature management.

Turning to the theory of land prices, it is necessary to note the duality of its market, the existence of not only the prices of units of stock, but also the prices of units of consumption of natural resources. In the first case, it is a moment indicator, the price of a square kilometer or hectare of land area, a cubic meter of gas, a ton of oil, a carat of diamonds, etc., and in the second, a period indicator corresponding to an income stream in the form of rent. In the economic literature, the issue of pricing in the use of natural resources is reduced only to the theory of rent, that is, to the analysis of a relatively complex form of market turnover of the corresponding goods. In this case, as a rule, a combination is made in one model of the land market of moment and period indicators, which is not an error, but requires an explanation of the reasons for the incorrectness. We must adhere to the principles of completeness of research and the transition in it 'from simple to complex', that is, to consider, first of all, the market for direct purchase and sale of land.

The confusion of land and land lease markets, the substitution of their parameters cause the existence of an indirect determination of the value (N) of land through its profitability (G_N, $G_N = A_N/N$, where A_N – 'absolute rent'): $N = A_N/G_N$. Moreover, instead of the very profitability of the land G_e, the calculations use the bank interest rate, that is, the indicator, although related, is of a different branch of the economy.

For the same reasons, the theory of rent recommends the so-called 'Hotelling's rule' proposed by the American mathematician Harold Hotelling (1895-1973) (*Economics of Exhaustible Resources*, 1931). The 'rule', unfortunately, "to this day remains central in the economic theory of natural resources" [105, p. 223], says: the optimal extraction of the resource is provided provided that the price of a unit of the resource remaining in the ground grows at a rate equal to the bank interest rate. The reason for this equality is the dilemma of the owner of the goods: either extract a unit of the good and invest the proceeds from its sale at the current interest rate, or leave it in the ground. One way or another, this rule reflects some objective regularity of rational nature management, but also connects the price of natural goods with the bank interest and therefore can be considered only as an indirect method of pricing.

The price of land as a stock is formed as a result of the interaction between the supply of land and the demand for it. In the economic literature, the land supply function is usually depicted as a fixed, strictly vertical. This emphasizes the limited and full involvement of natural goods in the economic turnover.

But in a market economy, as you know, there are always surplus factors of production, including ready-to-use natural resources. In addition, even in the short-term and especially in the long-term, due to additional costs, investments, in improving the land, its supply can be further increased. It is also worth remembering that the model of any immediate market is only the marginal part of the complete pricing model – the marketron. Therefore, the noted verticality should also be in the integral function of the cost of selling land, and this indicates infinitely high costs for the 'production' of the resource under consideration.

Indeed, it may be a conditionally non-renewable natural good, but in general this does not mean that its supply cannot be increased. The costs of the relevant market will increase non-linearly and may include the costs of scientific research in the field of economic use of a natural resource, the development of its cadastre, improvement of quality and preparation for direct sale. All prices of a good – the prices of its supply and the prices of demand for it – will be normal-elastic.

Land is a complex and multifunctional good with crop, livestock, industrial, construction, transport and recreational purposes, as well as more specific purposes. Therefore, the image in textbooks on the economic theory of 'multilayer' functions of demand for land and one single function of its supply should be recognized as erroneous, since, firstly, the multifunctionality of the earth requires consideration of a set of not only demand curves, but also supply curves, and, secondly, because of the inevitable unequal elasticity of these functions, they cannot be 'bundles' of mutually parallel lines. The functions of the model should represent the averaged model characteristics of the market for a particular natural resource.

Taking into account the foregoing, we conclude that the marketron of the buy-or-sale market of a particular natural resource is becoming quite standard (Fig. II.10). Its integral part contains the functions of the profitability of the production operation (A) of the resource and the consumption of its preparation for sale (B), the difference between which in the form of profit is divided by the linear contractual function (AB) into the maximum values of the user's net profit and net rent of the 'producer' of the resource[1]. The differential part of the marketron has the functions of the prices of the buyer (A'), seller (B') and the purchase and sale of a unit (AB', X_N) of the resource, as well as an indicator of its equilibrium quantity (N_e).

Modeling of pricing in the fixed-term, lease, land market, which provides for the determination of a lease price equal to the rent-lease payment, requires the use of an adequate, streaming, quantitative indicator of land. This is the term of its lease, in relation to which the new functions of expenditure, profitability and land use budget behave in general as well as in the case of an indefinite land purchase and sale market, that is, they obey the general law of diminishing production efficiency under the premise of ceteris paribus. The marketron of the land rental market looks similar to that

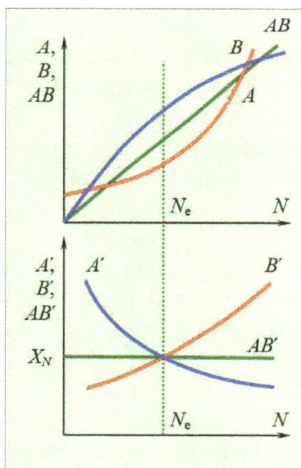

Fig. II.10

shown in Fig. II.10, but its abscissa shows the streaming indicator of the lease term (t_N), for example, the number of years, and the ordinates show the indicators of general and marginal income (A, A), expenses (B, B) and contract budgets (AB, AB) for the entire rental period. Balancing the rental market for land leads to the formation of the corresponding indicators: an equilibrium lease term ($t_{N(e)}$) and its equilibrium price – annual rent (C_e), which is the sum of the costs of restoring productivity (amortization) and a certain accumulation of leased land.

Since the land lease market as a whole is derived from the land purchase-sale market and is directly related to it, when analyzing the multifactorial

---

[1] In order not to clutter the figures and text with complex designations, here and further in the monograph, when describing specific marketrons, the indexing of parameters A, B, AB and the corresponding functions, meaning that they belong to a particular market, is omitted.

lease payment C, its second factor is always the amount of land, with an increase in which all functions of the land lease market are shifted in a certain way to states of double equilibrium.

Consider the market for capital goods, which we also referred to the structure-forming mechanisms of the economy.

An important distinctive feature of this market is that a traded product is a resource produced and reproduced in society. And it would seem that the man-made nature of these goods facilitates the determination of their value, but the issues of units of measurement of the amount of capital goods and their market valuation have not been completely clarified. Moreover, these issues in the middle of the last century caused the beginning of the fierce 'dispute of two Cambridges' mentioned above, which does not subside until now, since it affects the fundamental principles of economics.

In his book *Economic Philosophy* (1962), Robinson, the initiator and the most active participant in the 'dispute' on the part of the British 'Cambridge', wrote the following about the problem: "Models continue to appear in which the volume of 'capital'[1] appears and not a word is said about what is meant by the volume ... From the question of what is the volume of capital, mathematics obscure: K – capital, dK – investment. What is K? Yes, capital! K has some economic meaning, so let's go ahead and not pay attention to the intrusiveness of pedants who pester with the question of what is K" [150, p. 70]. As you can see from this passage, Robinson, when raising the issue of measuring capital goods, does not just casually call them capital. In an even earlier work, The *Production Function and The Theory of Capital* (1953), we find the roots of its fallacy. Considering that the monetary value of capital goods depends on the profits they supposedly bring, Robinson is perplexed: "We are used to talking about the rate of profit received by a businessman on capital as if profit and capital ... were the sums of money ... But these two never exist at the same time. As long as capital exists as a sum of money, profit is not yet created. When profit is created, capital has ceased to be money and has become a factory" [151, p. 84]. As a result, Robinson not only failed to find a measure for K, but also began to deny the correctness of the marginal distribution of the value created in production to factor income, which caused a protracted 'dispute'. Later, Robinson, without resolving the issue, nevertheless used the English word 'steel' (iron), written in the reverse order of letters, to denote non-financial means of production of durable use. It turned out "leets-capital". But why did it have to be done when the terms 'capital goods' or 'technical capital' already exist.

The problem lies not in the name of the assets, but in the nature of their

---

[1] Robinson, like many other economists and authors, calls capital goods capital, which is not accurate.

valuation. Capital goods and profits are money, moreover, 'simultaneous' money, but the sum of money of capital goods measures their stock, and the sum of profits measures the flow of net income.

A deep misunderstanding in the study of capital goods has arisen from the misguided evolution of neoclassical profit theory. Marshall began to ascribe it to the fourth, 'organizational factor' of production – at the micro level to the organizational abilities of an entrepreneur who is responsible for economic decisions: what to produce, in what quantity, in what technological way, etc. Since time passes between making a decision on the production and sale of a product and the entrepreneur bears the risk associated with fluctuations in the market situation, Knight (*Risk, Uncertainty and Profit* 1921) declared profit a "payment for risk". And then, mixing profit with interest on capital, on the basis of the earlier concept of Böhm-Bawerk (*Capital and Interest*, 1884) "rewards for the preference of future goods for the present," Fischer (*Theory of interest*, 1930), considering the universality of intertemporal preferences of people, he absolutized capital and interest, considering the varieties of the last profit, rent and wages. "The stock of wealth that exists at a given moment in time, – wrote Fischer, – is called a capital. The flow of services over a period of time is called a percentage" [140, p. 101]. After the declaration of land, and then labor force, as capital, the difference between financial and physical capital was leveled, the latter in market models began to be estimated as a percentage. In neoclassical theory, unfortunately, many models have appeared, with the help of which complex economic phenomena began to be described from a simplified position of the universality of interest. Models did not solve problems, but only gave them a certain scientific quality and led the theory in the wrong direction.

It should be emphasized that Robinson in the 'dispute about capital' spoke about different things: about the contradiction in measuring capital by interest and the alleged impossibility of measuring the amount of capital goods. These problems relate to different markets, the first – to the credit market, which we will consider a little later, and the second – to the stock market, which we will analyze further.

The modern American neo-Ricardian Alfred Eichner (1937-1988), echoing Robinson, declared: "It is impossible to aggregate capital investments in kind" [132, p. 347]. But the number of specific capital goods is easily determined. As for the set of heterogeneous capital goods, natural-material indicators for them are also applicable, for example, the number of 'jobs', it is possible to measure them in monetary units. The indicator of the number of jobs is convenient at the macro level, since it simultaneously denotes the number of employed labor resources, it differs from the indicator of capital-to-labor ratio, which is private from dividing the value of the entire production apparatus by the total number employees employed in it – and is calculated taking into account the shift coefficient of the functioning of the economy.

The measurement of capital goods in monetary units should not cause difficulties, since such is the growing sum of current nominal prices for the production of capital goods of a particular type or even a set of their different types. This perfectly homogeneous monetary indicator can represent two identical quantitative coordinates of the marketron of capital goods.

In the process of exploiting a capital good, its value changes significantly under the influence of physical and moral deterioration, which is fixed by the stock market. Its corresponding characteristics determine the current unit price of a capital asset. Therefore, an important issue of the functioning of markets and the reproduction of capital goods is the accurate accounting of their value when moving from a stock (resource, fund) to a stream (part of the value of a stock) and vice versa.

Physical wear and tear, for example, of a machine tool in the form of natural and operational wear and tear and obsolescence with a reduction in the cost of its production, as well as the appearance on the market of better quality machines, affect the current value of the operated copy. The accepted names for the value of capital goods corresponding to accounting (+) or not accounting (−) of their forms of wear are presented in the table in Fig. II.11. The best in market conditions is the

		Physical wear of capital goods	
		−	+
Obsolescence	I	Full initial cost	Residual initial cost
	+	Full replacement cost	**Residual replacement cost**

Fig. II.11

'residual replacement' value. Without it, either a 'remainder' of value undistributed among the factors of production appears in the product, which is usually declared to be the product of some special, 'specific' assets, or an 'underestimation' of the output that distorts the economic potential of producers. In addition, an accurate assessment of capital goods is necessary when calculating their profitability and when privatizing state property and its market turnover.

With proper consideration of the value of capital assets, an efficient market automatically adjusts its price. If their number is measured, for example, in rubles at the full initial value, then the market price of each ruble of capital goods will be expressed already in the current residual-replacement value. The complete graphical model of the market, marketron, of any capital good looks similar to the model of the land market and is shown in Fig. II.12. Only on its abscissas is the stock of a specific capital asset (K) deposited according to the full initial, for example, ruble estimate, and on the ordinates − the value of production consumption (B, B'), the purchase and sale budget (AB, AB') and

92

the profitability of using (A, A') capital goods. The point of intersection of the curves A' and B', which are functions of supply and demand for this market, corresponds on the axes to the equilibrium values of the current price of one ruble (X_K) and the number of rubles (K_e) of the capital good. These equilibrium parameters of the market provide maximum profit to producers and consumers of capital goods. Due to physical and moral deterioration and recovery that occur during the service life of a capital good, as a result, X_K does not coincide with each of its fixed nominal rubles.

The fixed-term, rental, capital goods market can be described by a standard marketer, which does not fundamentally differ from the model of the natural resource rental market considered above. In the differential part of such a model, the equilibrium number of years of using the capital good (t_K), deposited on the streaming quantitative abscissa, will also correspond on the ordinate to the stream indicator of the equilibrium rent equal to the 'gross profit' (M_g), otherwise – 'cash flow' [15, p. 333, 88] as the sum of net profit M and depreciation of capital goods B_K^1. As in the case of land lease, M_g depends on the amount of capital goods K and at K_e the market will be in a double equilibrium – in the markets for their purchase and sale and lease.

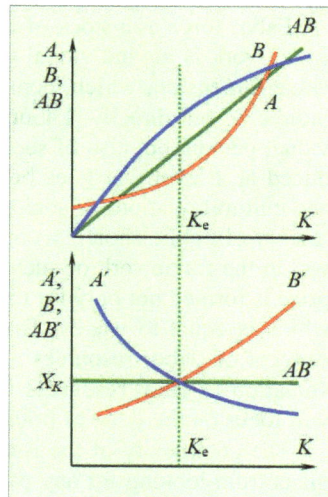

Fig. II.12

An essential feature of the rental market for any capital good is its direct connection with the labor market. Let's consider the latter in more detail.

Marshall stated categorically that "the human factor of production is not bought or sold, like machines and other material factors of production. The worker sells his labor, but he himself remains the owner of himself" [71, p. 355]. But, without challenging this property of the employee, which has always been recognized by the classics of political economy, it is nevertheless necessary to agree with Marx that labor power, like other factors of production, is a tradable commodity, but only a commodity of the rental market, on which the amount of labor power is measured by the time of its lease, the time of work.

It is also important that the impossibility of indefinite purchase and sale of labor does not mean that this stock of active abilities does not have its own

---

[1] The rent of capital goods, combined with the rent of labor, as will be shown below, is the main form of their functioning in the production sphere of the market economy, and the rent M – an integral part of the value of products.

full price. In this regard, Marshall wrote that "we can define 'personal wealth' in such a way that it includes all those powers, abilities and skills that directly serve the production efficiency of a person ... based on the fact that they are usually amenable to some kind of indirect measurement" [Ibid, p. 108]. This 'personal wealth' was practically the first concept of 'human capital'[1]. The concepts of human capital existing in modern economics interpret it purely qualitatively. The very word 'capital' only complicates the understanding of the essence of human labor resources, and above we have shown how the 'capitalization' of all factors of production leads in theory only to the erroneous absolutization of 'interest'. A clear separation of the moment indicators of stocks and period indicators of value streams makes it possible to dispense with the term 'human capital' and restrict ourselves to the corresponding already established concepts of 'labor force' and 'labor', investing in them more advanced content.

Labor force as a stock of a person's physical, mental and professional ability to work is his individual resource, a factor of production that has its own value dimension, which, contrary to Marshall's ideas, can be carried out not indirectly, but directly. Labor power is the highest value not only of an individual person, but also of society as a whole, it is a public good that is reproduced at a level that goes beyond the economy into the spheres of political and cultural relations of society. But these relations are also interpreted by the 'theory of public choice' as market relations, as supply-demand relations. It is within the framework of such a complex market and 'social contract' that the price is formed not only for the supply of 'labor', but also for its consumption, which is equal to wages. Taking into account the social significance of the concept of 'labor resources', we will consider the theory of direct monetary valuation of labor resources in section 11 of the monograph, and further we will focus on the issue of pricing in the national labor market.

The complexity of the issue led to the refusal of many theoretical economists from looking for any patterns in the functioning of the labor market. So Hicks declared that it is not supply and demand that act on him, but a huge number of heterogeneous factors. We have to agree with the last statement, but, nevertheless, there are laws in this area.

This market becomes more understandable if all of its many factors are di-

---

[1] Marshall referred to the English mercantilist Charles Davenant (1656-1714) and quoted him as saying: "People as such constitute, undoubtedly, the most valuable treasure of the country." It is believed that the priority in the use and development of the concept of 'human capital' belongs to the Americans Theodore Schultz (1902-1998) (*Building Capital Through Education*, 1960) and Becker (*Human Capital: A Theoretical and Empirical Analysis*, 1964). But after Marshall, the question of the absolute assessment of the labor force was developed by the Americans Friedman (*Theory of Consumption Function*, 1957) and Jacob Minser (1922-2006) (*Investments in Human Capital and Personal Distribution of Income*, 1958).

vided into perfectly and imperfectly competitive and logically built from the point of view of consistent neoclassicism[1] and formulate the following theoretical propositions.

1. The commodity here is the human labor force in its active manifestation – labor-flow, which acts only as an expenditure of the stock of labor-power. With Marshall's provision that the worker "sells his labor" [Ibid, p. 535] we do not agree, and agree with Marx's thesis on the sale and purchase of labor. The amount of labor is measured by the time of work during the day, that is, the duration of the working day ($t_{\text{тр}}$). The amount of labor is the main factor in its price (X_{la}, $X_{\text{la}} = f(t_{\text{la}})$), and not vice versa.

2. An employee is the bearer and owner of the labor force, and the employer is the owner of immovable capital goods and jobs. Therefore, the labor market, unlike other markets, is also a job market (vacancies). The act of employment is a transaction between an employee and an employer on mutual lease, provision for temporary use of their factors of production.

3. The functions of labor supply and demand for it are derivatives, respectively, of the functions of the expenditure of reproduction of labor and the profitability of its use. All functions are shifted under the influence of numerous other pricing factors in the given market.

4. Wages are rent, the price of human labor X_{la} – the monetary remuneration necessary for the reproduction of his labor force, that is, for the replenishment and certain accumulation of labor, household funds and social infrastructure that he uses.

Labor markets have a number of imperfections: 1) a lot of dependence of a little labor on labor in the household and leisure, due to which the function of expenditure turns into a vertical, often having a branch – a curve that bends in the opposite direction; 2) the existence of non-wage labor characteristics (general conditions, the possibility of professional or personnel growth, etc.); 3) the existence of non-labor elements of wages (internal (payment for downtime, vocational training) and external (payments for social insurance and security, as well as unemployment); 4) attracting and retaining employees by firms using non-salary funds (investments in education and training, provision of housing or other benefits); 5) incomplete elasticity of wages for labor, its

---

[1] Classical political economy interpreted wages as a kind of fund that remains after deducting the entrepreneur's profit from the net income and is constantly at the level of a person's living wage. The 'iron law of wages', according to 'Ricardianism', operates in such a way that an increase in the wage bill as a result of improving production causes, according to Malthus, an increase in population and labor resources, and this returns wages to the minimum level. Marxist science, which remained on the positions of the classical labor theory of value, actually agreed with this 'law', explaining it, however, by the 'exploitation of labor by capital'.

immobility to the lower side ('ratchet effect'[1]) due to the state's policy of social protection of the population; 6) the uniqueness of some jobs; 7) dividing markets into markets for prestigious and non-prestigious jobs; 8) the presence in firms of 'internal labor markets'; 9) the existence of stable groups of jobs, interconnected technologically, organizationally or traditionally and requiring the coordination of wages (the influence of labor markets on each other); 10) frequent collusion of participants of one or each of the market parties and pressure on counterparties.

Marshall's views on modeling the labor market were very controversial, he especially insisted that "marginal productivity ... for analyzing the problem of the general level of wages" was not suitable, and, at the same time, believed that the latter was "subject to the action of the law of supply and demand" [100, p. 307]. But the law of demand for labor is also a function of the marginal productivity of labor. Therefore, neoclassical economics as a whole easily coped with the demand function; it was recognized as standard, monotonically decreasing. Difficulties arose with the labor supply function. But, proceeding from the obvious division of the day into working and non-working hours, the theory, as well as for the capital goods market, has developed an abstract and highly controversial model of 'leisure – earnings', in which the sought quantitative and monetary indicators are also derived indirectly. Direct pricing in the rental labor market can be shown using the appropriate marketron (Fig. II.13).

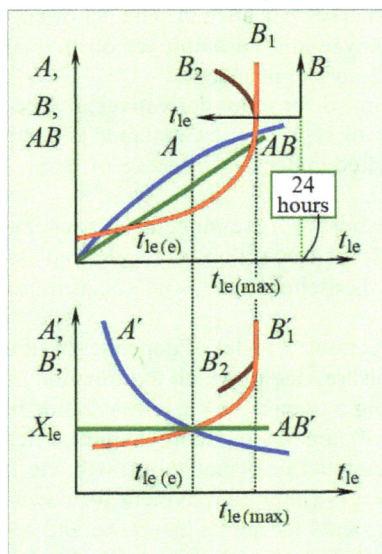

Fig. II.13

Under the standard premise ceteris paribus and the law of diminishing consumption efficiency, function B on the graph is concave, characterizing the increasing expenditure of reproduction of a particular labor force in households, and the marginal form of this function B' – a concave labor supply curve. Functions B and B' 'when reaching the maximum wage employment $t_{la(max)}$, which exists due to a certain necessary employment in households, become superelastic and line up vertically. With such an increase in the cost of reproduction of their labor force, some workers, as noted, prefer to reduce

---

[1] Ratchet – a technical device that prevents the wheel from turning back. In a modern market economy, there are also mechanisms that allow only an increase in wages.

their main wage employment, which is characterized by the sections B_2 and B_2 of functions bending in the opposite direction. In these areas, the inversion of the factor is observed, the independent variable is not the time of labor, but the consumption of its reproduction B. It is the further growth of B that determines the reduction in the time of hired employment. On the integral graph of the marketron, this is shown by an additional, rotated 90° counterclockwise, coordinate system, in which additional non-working time, 'leisure' time, (t_{le}) is a function of the cost of reproduction of expensive labor ($t_{le} = f(B)$).

The profitability function A of the use of labor by firms, measured by the time of its lease, the time of labor t_{la}, under the same condition that all other factors of pricing remain unchanged, is convex, and its marginal form (A') is a decreasing function of demand for labor.

The equilibrium time of renting labor ($t_{la(e)}$) corresponds to its equilibrium price X_{la} – the hourly rate of payment for its rent – and the maximum rental profit, which is divided by the contractual function AB into the consumer surplus (profit) of employees and the profit of employers. It becomes clear, and this is very important for understanding the phenomenon of unemployment, that maximum employment in labor markets is not achieved due to the lack of profit in this situation for both workers and employers.

Above, we have modeled pricing mechanisms in the structural markets of the economy, which can function effectively only with the help of a developed infrastructure, which includes a large number of intermediary, auxiliary and operating (service) markets[1]. All infrastructure markets have a certain specificity, but in general they obey the universal laws of pricing – the law of diminishing production efficiency and the law of supply and demand – and can be described by a standard marketer.

The capital market, or loans, is one of the most important infrastructural national markets, an understanding of the mechanism of operation of which is necessary for the development of macroeconomics. Therefore, let us turn to a brief theoretical description of it.

When someone saves a portion of their income, they give up the opportunity for current purchases. At the same time, another consumer can spend money in excess of his income, making loans. The financial futures market is a set of institutions that implement the movement of money savings to borrowers and back with interest.

Money as a commodity provided for temporary use through intermediaries is exchanged not only for a financial instrument, that is, a document evidenc-

---

[1] The assignment of infrastructure enterprises and organizations to the commercial or state sectors of the economy is not of fundamental importance, since the benefits created by the state, from the point of view of the 'theory of public choice', are also subject to the laws of pricing discussed above. We turn to a more detailed presentation of this issue in section 15 of the monograph.

ing a debt (deposit insurance, promissory note, bond, certificate of deposit, etc.), but also further for another good, which is loan security, collateral, since urgent transactions, like perpetual transactions, involve, first of all, the exchange of money for goods.

Microeconomic entities that mediate between savers and borrowers include commercial banks[1]. If firms and households localize production and consumer goods, then banks localize the funds of business entities. Since there are two groups of creditors (borrowers) in the forward money markets – depositors and banks and two groups of debtors (debtors) – banks and borrowers, and banks are simultaneously creditors and debtors, they, as commercial organizations, are engaged in reselling loans, which, by in essence, it means lease and sublease of funds. Therefore, the main interrelated parameters of the money market are the equilibrium values of the credit time ($t_{cr(e)}$) and its price (X_{cr}). Since commercial banks make passive and active monetary transactions, we call their loans passive loans, and loans from them – active loans.

The existing theory of credit contains a number of inaccurate and erroneous provisions. First, neoclassicism considers the amount of capital (Z_{cr}) as a traded commodity, and the price of its unit – the bank interest rate G_b), which is permissible, but not accurate from the point of view of the full lending model. The credit market in the monetary sphere is primary and the flow of time of the loan must also correspond to the flow indicator of its price.

Secondly, the sum Z_{cr} is considered as a function of G_b ($Z_{cr} = f(G_b)$), but the model of any market, including the credit one, should be based on the marginal principle: the quantity of goods determines its price. Therefore, the argument in this dependence should be the size of the loan (recall that this provision, however, does not mean that the inverse functions cannot be considered).

Thirdly, economics deduces the function of supply of credit from the model of the so-called intertemporal equilibrium of values, based on the typical preference of the current value for the future. But this model is complex, subjective, and most importantly, it is built on the basis of the function $Z_{cr} = f(G_b)$ as the only possible one. Such an approach is needed, but its 'price and income effects' are derivatives in theory, since they assume that the final sought price indicators are already known, and the interest rate is introduced into the comparison of values of different times, while this should use the discount coefficient. "To postpone the receipt of pleasure, so that in this way his saving speech for the future, – wrote Marshall, – is measured by the percentage of accumulated wealth, which just provides a sufficient incentive to save for the future" [71, p. 75]. And this is a fairly typical mistake of theoreti-

---

[1] In addition to commercial banks, credit firms include investment, financial and insurance companies, as well as pension funds and credit unions.

cal economists. Percentage measures credit, while deferral requires discounting the value. The first – profitability, the second – the growth rate of the quantity of goods, the growth of its value[1]. In addition, the analysis of two-factor models can only be considered as a development of the basic one-factor models.

In Fig. II.14 introduces the marketron of credit money. Its functions A, B, AB, A', B' and AB' are, respectively, integral and differential dependences of the cumulative values of income, expenses, the amount of loans and their price on the loan term t_{cr} tcr, measured, for example, in months. The function of banks' expense on passive loans B, like any expense function, at the starting point cuts off the segment B_{au} on the ordinate, which in this case is equal to the sum of these loans Z_{cr}. Function B with the growth of the loan term $t_{кр}$ progresses not only because of the ceteris paribus prerequisite, but also because of payments in this case to bank depositors of increasing interest income.

The profitability function A, on the contrary, characterizes the regression of the effect of active loans, and the contractual function AB expresses the linear dependence of the amount of contracts for the sale and purchase of loans on t_{cr}. The point of intersection of the functions of demand for active loans A' and their supply B' in our example corresponds to the equilibrium average number of months of lending ($t_{cr(e)}$), the maximum profits of banks and investors, and on the ordinate of the graph – to the equilibrium price of loans, then is the monthly credit income of banks (X_{cr}, $X_{cr} = dA/dt_{cr} = dB/dt_{cr} = dAB/dt_{cr}$), which includes the amount of loans per year and interest accrued on them, that is, the cash

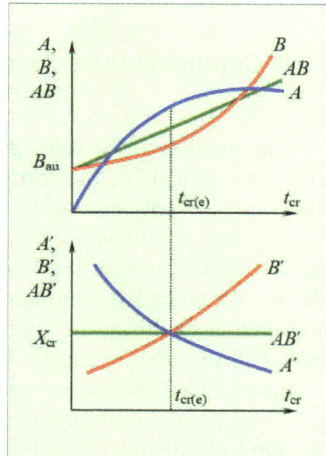

Fig. II.14

flow of banks. Keynes wrote similarly about the price of credit: "Suppose the immediate wheat price is £ 100. Art. for 100 quarters," then "the price of a 'long-term' contract for the supply of wheat in a year is 107 pounds. article ..." [53, p. 216]. The equilibrium price of a loan is a flow indicator and, as such, corresponds to a flow indicator of the loan-lease term of money. The ratio of these parts of income is called the bank interest rate (G_b).

As a commodity in the financial and credit market, not only cash or non-cash money can be used, but also liquid, various securities convertible into

---

[1] The question of the relationship between interest and discounting is detailed in section 16 of the monograph.

money. The annual income, for example, at the partial redemption of a regular discount long-term bond, is also considered its price.

At the end of the section, we note that from the point of view of the interaction of the mainstream and 'neo-Ricardianism', which assert the presence of a reproductive approach in their theories, it should be noted that modern marginal neoclassicism has an additional argument for such a statement, because by us, the revision of its models of factors and products of production allows us to develop a new generalized concept of "factors of reproduction".

From the point of view of the interaction of the mainstream and 'neo-Ricardianism', which assert the presence of a reproductive approach in their theories, it should be noted that modern marginal neoclassicism has an additional argument for such a statement, because our revision of its models of factors and products of production is based on allows you to develop a new generalized concept of 'factors of reproduction'.

8. Canonical three-factor product price and factor Marshall's 'organization of production'

This section of the monograph is devoted to a more accurate study of specific mechanisms of the formation of prices of goods than it was limited by the premise ceteris paribus above.

Marshall used this logic of moving from simple to complex, understanding the limitations of one-factor models, in his *Principles of Economics* he considered the so-called 'conjugate products', the phenomena of complementarity and mutual exclusion of goods. However, this small part of Marshall's work gave rise to major scientific problems in the mainstream, which will also be discussed in a constructive way below.

Since the price of any particular good in real reality depends on the quantity not only of this good, but also of all other goods reproduced outside this local market, then when creating a complete pricing model and, consequently, canceling the ceteris paribus premise, we automatically switch to the level of the national market and, strictly speaking, even of the entire world economy, which are not the level of microeconomics. But for a sufficiently complete understanding of the regularities of the action of pricing mechanisms, it is sufficient to consider the interrelationships of two or three good factors, in which the premise ceteris paribus continues to operate, and the researcher remains within the framework of microeconomics.

It is important to keep in mind that the number of pricing factors introduced into the analysis is always rather arbitrary. Among the many benefits of real consumer baskets of households and firms, one can find goods whose mutual relative prices are constant. Then such goods can be considered as one commodity – this is the so-called "compound commodity" proposed in the theory by Hicks (*Value and Capital*, 1939) and studied in detail by Sraffa (*Production of Goods by Means of Goods*, 1960) in his model 'standard system'.

On the other hand, according to the Australian economist Kelvin Lancaster (1924-1999) (*A New Approach to the Theory of the Consumer*, 1966), the choice of a particular product by the buyer is often determined by a number of its characteristics. For example, when buying a home, a whole gamut of its qualities is taken into account – comfort, cleanliness of the air in the area, remoteness from the place of work, the presence of shops in the area, etc., which can be considered as separate benefits. That is, the question arises about the one-dimensionality and multidimensionality of the usefulness of goods. Therefore, the number of factors in the price of a particular good, it would seem, can be both reduced and increased. But such and similar approaches in the economic literature, taking into account income, habits, fashion, culture, etc. as separate factors of production and consumption. they appear to us to be erroneous for a number of reasons. First, we have shown above that the amount of income is a dependent variable in the pricing model itself, and the indicated and other qualitative characteristics of goods are either its 'shift' factors, or only modify its functions of expense and profitability. Secondly, any distinguished, including the 'shift' factor must be divisible and homogeneous, and its marginal product must be computable.

The idea of a generalized theoretical utility function for several goods originated with Edgeworth (*Mathematical Psychology*, 1881), developed by Fisher (*Mathematical Research*, 1892) and other economists. For the two-factor case, we use the volumetric function $f(A, Q_1, Q_2)$, in which the 'utility' U is replaced by the profitability A of consuming two goods in quantities Q_1 and Q_2 (Fig. II.15). Since there are no restrictions on Q_1 and Q_2 in it, but with respect to the rest of the goods $Q_3,...Q_n$ the ceteris paribus assumption is valid, the restriction will be on the side of A, the value of which continuously increases with a decreasing rate (convex line A_1). The maxima of the function will be observed only in its vertical sections at fixed values of Q_1 or Q_2. Any horizontal section of the figure gives an open isoquant-hyperbola (in the figure it is also represented on the plane of coordinates '$Q_1 - Q_2$' in the form of a dotted line A_1), reflecting a narrower spectrum of preferences of rational economic entities in choice of mutually exclusive benefits.

But, taking into account the general position on the rarity of all goods without exception, the function $f(A, Q_1, Q_2)$ should acquire a bell-shaped form with the formation of an extremum (convex line A_2). The function can be defined as a model of the "law of utilities (traditionally – the '2nd law') of Gossen": "A person who can freely choose between many pleasures ... must ... provide all of them for himself partially, namely, in such a ratio that (the ultimate – *the author*) ... the magnitude of each individual pleasure ... would remain the same" [28, p.125]. This law in our interpretation means the existence of the maximum profitability ($A_{2(max)}$) of using the goods Q_1 and Q_2, as well as their equilibrium quantities $Q_{1(e)}$ and $Q_{2(e)}$. The equilibrium point (9) fixes the equality of marginal yields A'_1 and A'_2 between themselves and both of them to zero, and this indicates that the free goods under consideration are not goods.

Each level of profitability of consumption of goods located below A_{max} corresponds to a wider set of equilibrium quantitative proportions of goods – an isoquant in the form of a concentric closed line (see the oval of the volu-

Fig. II.15

metric figure and its projection A_2 in Fig. II.15). But, since the profitability does not increase in the areas of complementarity and convex mutual exclusion of the benefits of isoquant-ovals, then only the one that falls on the darkened sector remains the area of effective choice. Therefore, the real economic choice as a whole becomes even narrower.

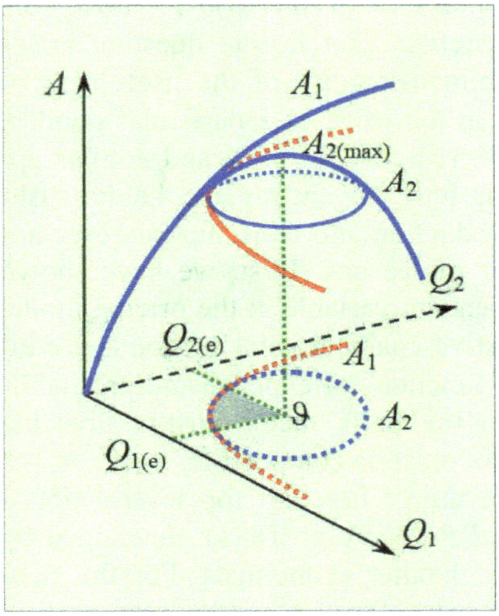

'Gossen's law of utilities' has a general character, in relation to it, all the other six Gossen's laws are his special cases. So the 'Gossen's law of utilities', for example, the good Q_1, is illustrated by the vertical section of the volumetric function A_2 under the premise ceteris paribus – a constant value of the quantity Q_2, and according to the 'law of value of Gossen' the value of the good Q_1 is measured by the area under the curve A_2 in this section, or the volume under the curves A'_1 and A'_2 within the specified sector of effective choice.

Since Gossen showed that when consuming goods created in society, utility maximization is not absolute, but relative, and is always correlated with the expense of producing these goods, then there is no restriction in the choice of business entities. only from the side of profitability, but also from the side of firms-producers of goods. Therefore, in modeling two-factor pricing, function A should be considered in conjunction with the concave function of consumption of goods B ($B = f(Q_1, Q_2)$). The relationship between these functions is shown in the integral part of the marketron of benefits, shown in Fig. II.16. Due to the nature of the functions A and B, they intersect in two places and further restrict the preferences of market counterparties to a cigar-shaped volumetric area, which A_{max} is no longer included. According to the 'law of Gossen's surplus', the choice becomes unambiguous, since the model should reflect the maximization of the profit of the transaction for the sale and pur-

102

chase of goods, that is, the difference $A - B$, and the corresponding point of joint equilibrium 9 falls on $Q_{1(e)}$, $Q_{2(e)}$ and the point of tangency of the projections of the concave isoquant of the maximum yield A and the convex isospenda of the minimum flow rate B. In this case, the curves themselves, as horizontal sections of the volumetric figure of the model, are at different levels.

In the marginal part of the marketron of produced goods, the functions of their supply prices (B'_1, B'_2) and the demand for them (A'_1, A'_2) are depicted as partial derivatives with respect to Q_1 and Q_2 (for example, $\partial A/\partial Q_1$), as well as equilibrium nonzero prices X_1 and X_2.

Prices X_1 and X_2, multiplied by the corresponding equilibrium quantities of goods $Q_{1(e)}$ and $Q_{2(e)}$, give the amounts of purchases and sales AB_1 and AB_2, fixed in the integral part of the marketron by the linear contract function AB (Fig. II.17). Sections of the plane AB are not necessarily horizontal, since the prices of goods are usually not the same, in our case X_1 and AB_1 are less than X_2 and AB_2. The equilibrium budget of the contract function – the straight line AB_e – divides the darkened field of profit of the section of the figure into the profit of producers and the profit of consumers of goods, and its projection takes the form of an isocost. This straight line is also denoted by us by the symbol AB_e, is tangent to isoquant A and isospenda B at the point of equilibrium 9. The maximum profit that comes to the equilibrium isocost AB_e has

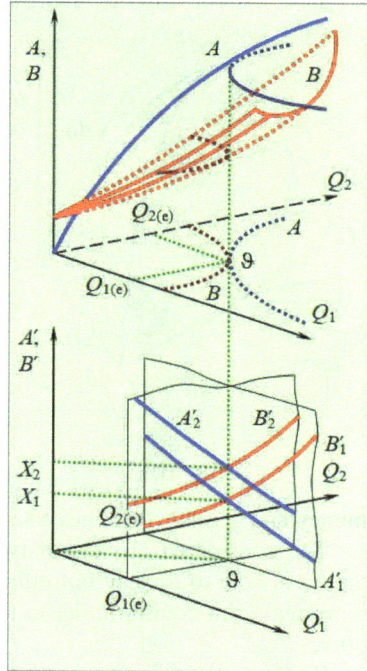

Fig. II.16

a double dimension: along and across rivers of the volumetric figure. Still, the rest of the isocosts characterize less profitable amounts of contracts, and the isocosts located closer to the origin of coordinates, for example, the one shown in the AB_{ra} figure, express generally a forced equilibrium with maximum, but reduced parameters parameters of the number of benefits and profitability due to budgetary imitations (rationing). The forced equilibrium of adjacent markets corresponds to the 'Gossen rationing law' discussed above.

Modeling the options in the ratio of the equilibrium quantities of goods Q_1 and Q_1, it should be borne in mind that the diagonal linear 'market development function' shown in Fig. II.18, there correspond smooth functions of profitability A, expenditure B and budget AB, lying in the same vertical plane, according to which the point of general unambiguous equilibrium of the two industries is determined. If their development acquires a nonlinear complex character, which is explained by the 'substitution effect' (see in Fig. II.18 a wavy line along the diagonal), then this distorts the ratio of functions and causes non-uniform value of balance. Marshall supplied such a two-factor analysis of markets with the concepts of "combined demand", "combined supply", "competitive demand" and "competitive supply" [71, p. 383-394]. But,

Fig. II.17

in this case, we are talking about the action of the third, fourth, etc. factors, which means the corresponding limitation of the premise ceteris paribus. That is, the persistence of 'shock' factors excludes the considered options for a more complex behavior of the system of markets. The options for the development of markets with changing proportions and 'washing out' of goods in fact reflect changes not in prices, tastes and fashion, but in the quantities of other real goods[1]. For example, a steady rise in the price of goods, or inflation, which is usually illustrated by the 'substitution and income effect', is associated with the marginal interaction of money and goods, which has a separate price modeling.

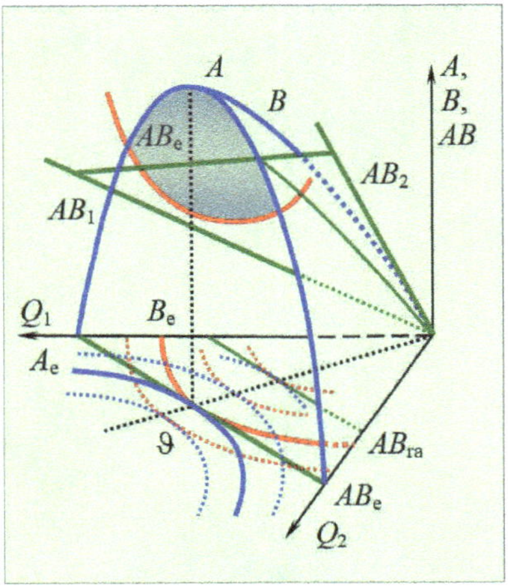

The considered models of two-factor pricing show that the mainstream theory is able to display not only a fairly abstract local equilibrium, but also more real joint equilibria, up to a multi-factor equilibrium of the entire economy.

If we go from factors-consumer goods to specific goods-frames that are consumed in production, then not only theoretical, but also practical interest is a canonical three-factor model describing the formation of equilibrium quantitative proportions and prices of natural (N), capital (K) and labor (L) factors. The classical three-factor theory of Say's value was significantly advanced by marginalists, it acquired a more meaningful, clear and broad analytical expression. The priority in extending the marginal toolkit to such a factorial analysis of production should be given to Clark, who, however, in his book *The Distribution of Wealth* (1899) did not cite volumetric figures. We'll try to do this to

---

[1] The list of 'shock' factors, first proposed by Edgeworth (*Mathematical Psychology*, 1884), included: 1) tastes; 2) cash income; 3) the prices of goods closely related to the goods in question; 4) prices of unrelated goods; 5) expected future prices.

map a three-factor market.

Due to the impossibility of depicting a completely production, budgetary and consumer functions, in Fig. II.19 shows a figure of mutually positioned three projections of their cross-sections. On it, the sectoral production of goods is characterized by its consumability by a convex iso-slant B, the amount of purchase and sale – by the triangular plane of the isocost AB and the profitability of consumption of the industry's products – by the concave isoquant A. B, A and AB touch at a point 9, which on the coordinates of the figure measures the equilibrium quantities of natural (N_e), capital (K_e) and human (L_e) factors of production.

A notable feature of this model is its reproductive isolation, in which the volume of production (Q) is not indicated by a separate coordinate, but is fixed by the location of the isoquant. The figure demonstrates that the com-modity as a value stream is created, fully distributed[1] and spent on the reproduction of the equilibrium amount of expended factors of production. The model simulta-neously reflects a single and continuous process of production and consumption of goods and serves as a graphical basis for clarifying the theory of distribution of the equilibrium price of a unit of production (X_Q) to factor income.

The issue of dividing the created value into factor income has always been central to the mainstream theory, but it was solved from different positions. The aforemen-

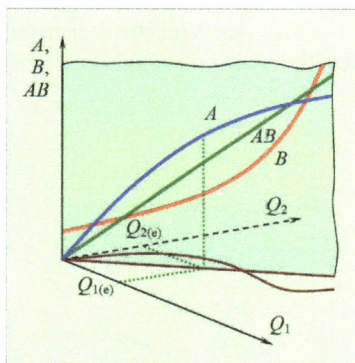

Fig. II.18

tioned attempts by the classics of political economy and neoricardians to sub-stantiate the distribution of 'value' by class are also significant and we will return to their analysis later. But then let us turn to the neoclassical theory of distribution.

Because Clark was the first to use limiting analysis to describe production, he also has priority in the marginal theory of factor distribution of the value of goods, some new elements of which were outlined by him in early articles and their collection of Philosophy wealth (1886). In the next book, *Distribution of Wealth*, he wrote: "Each agent is given a certain share in the product and each has an appropriate reward, – this is the natural law of distribution" [56 , p. 35],

---

[1] The Russian word 'distribution' corresponds to two English ones: allocation – the concentration of goods in certain areas of application, and distribution – the distribution of income between goods. But you can find Russian words that are more suitable for denoting these processes: "combining costs" – "sharing income". In this context, 'distribution' corresponds to the second meaning of the word.

"Each factor of production receives the amount of wealth that this factor creates" [Ibid, p. 46]. It is important to note that Clarke's formula is dual, it characterizes both the 'share' of expenses and income of production factors of a product in its value.

Wickstead, being familiar with Clarke's articles, in his Essay on the Coordination of the Laws of Distribution (1894), but published earlier than Clarke's Distribution of Wealth, developed the expenditure theory of pricing, for the first time in fact the price of a product X was determined in the form the sums of the marginal factor costs: $B_N + B_L + B_K = X$, $\partial B / \partial N + \partial B / \partial L + \partial B / \partial K = X$. Thus, Wickstead was the pioneer of the microproduction function, since, as the studies of the American economist A. Chang have shown (*Basic Methods of Mathematical Economics*, 1972), the integral form of the given the equation has the form $B = N^{\alpha_N} \cdot L^{\alpha_L} \cdot K^{\alpha_K}$, similar to the form of the Cobb-Douglas macro-production function.

Since the Wickstead distribution formula, in his opinion, is valid only under the assumption of zero profit, then, apparently, their depreciation should

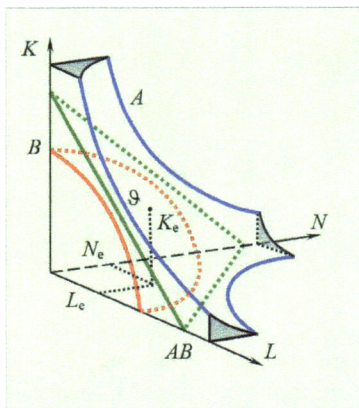

Fig. II.19

be considered as the limiting expenditure of capital goods. In addition, Wickstead believed that the function of supplying a product is the reverse of the function of demand, and therefore, in the analysis of markets, one can supposedly get rid of the first altogether. However, this sentiment contradicts the above constructions of the author, it contains a fundamental error. The absolutization of demand, which is inextricably linked with the profitability of a good, should exclude the use of expenditure functions in the model, as Clarke did. But it was precisely from the point of view of expenditure that Wickstead approached the question of value formation. Wickstead's mistake was that with all the symmetry of the marginal supply and demand curves and their determinism by a single law of decreasing efficiency of reproduction factors, they are not reciprocal and both are necessary in modeling the price-like Vania.

In their works, Clarke and Wickstead did not widely apply mathematics in their theoretical constructions and were limited to their graphic illustrations. As it later became clear thanks to the English statistician Alfred Flax (1869-

1942), who made a deep analysis of Wickstead's *Sketch* in a review of it[1], Wickstead's discoveries are connected with the evidence proven back in the XVIII century. Swiss mathematician Leonard Euler (1707-1783) theorem, which in relation to the problem of depletion of created value says: the price of a product is completely decomposed into the marginal costs of factors. Flux also showed that the theorem is valid only for conditions of perfect competition and the absence of scale effects: "Payments to production factors ..., – wrote Blaug, – will exactly exhaust the product if, and only if, the production the function is linearly homogeneous" [14, p. 418]. However, it should be added that the complete depletion of the price of a commodity requires the absence of not only internal effects of scale, but also external effects, the so-called externalities, as well as, and this is the main thing, the prerequisites for ceteris paribus.

To illustrate such a four-factor reproductive function ($f(N, L, K, Q)$), recall that hired workers and employers enter the market in a relationship of mutual lease of labor L and jobs K. Therefore, these factors of production can be combined into one indicator of the lease time of this complex ($K(L)$) and postpone it along one abscissa. Then, on the second factorial abscissa, the amount of land used (N) will be measured, and the ordinate of the model is freed to display the mone-

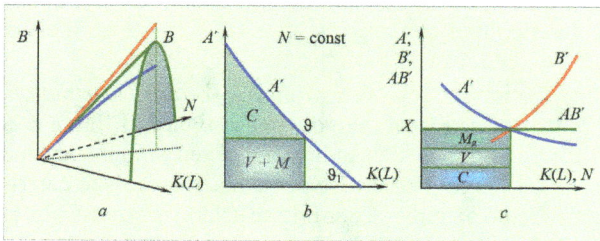

Fig. II.20

tary indicator of output Q (Fig. II.20, *a*, volumetric figure). This issue is presented not in physical, but in monetary measurement of expenditure (decreasing function $Q(B)$), profitability (increasing function $Q(A)$) of production and contract (linear function $Q(AB)$).

Under the ceteris paribus premise and negative economies of scale and externalities, that is, the Wickstead pricing option (convex $Q(B)$), incomplete factor payments should be expected due to the lack of total revenue from the sale of the product, and its price will be understated. The undistributed balance of this proceeds appears with positive effects of scale and externalities (concave $Q(A)$). According to this option, other economists developed the theory of factor income.

This variant of the division of proceeds, corresponding to the actually ob-

---

[1] The Work of Flax *A Review of the Books "Value, Capital in a New Theory of the National Economy" by Knut Wicksell and "An Essay on the Coordination of the Laws of Distribution" by Wickstead"* were published in 1894.

served nonlinearly decreasing function of the differential profitability of the goods, also does not allow finding the equilibrium factor proportions of the value of the product, since, like the Wickstead variant, contradicts the strict Euler theorem.

Edgeworth and Pareto criticized Wickstead's model, pointing out that there is generally no constant marginal cost of production. In the book *Common Sense in Political Economy* (1910) and Wickstead himself refused to absolutize his approach to pricing, although the American economist George Stigler (1911-1991) (*Theory of Production and Distribution*, 1941) believed that he had only doubts about mathematical interpretation of your model. In parallel with Wickstead's pricing model, the theory of not pricing, but of 'price distribution', based on the same classic three-element structure of Say's value, which is already being considered, was becoming more relevant in the mainstream. in terms of profitability.

This theory was presented by Clarke. He analyzed the results of already profitable production, which he considered not only effective, but also fair, that is, it was considered as positive-normative, not requiring the redistribution of factor income. The Clarke pricing formula looks like the sum of the marginal returns of the classic three factors: $X = A_N + A_L + A_K$, $X = \partial A / \partial N + \partial A / \partial L + \partial A / \partial K$.

Clarke's graphical distribution model, taken from his *Wealth Distribution*, is shown in Fig. II.20, *b*. It is a section of the volumetric figure of figure *a*, a section parallel to the abscissa $K(L)$, which indicates a fixed amount of land used in production (N = const). Only in the case of such a prerequisite ceteris paribus in relation to any factor of three according to Clark is it possible to determine their share in the income received by A.

In his marginal constructions, Clarke recognized and took into account the operation of two Gossen laws — the 'law of utility' known to us in detail (according to the names adopted in the mainstream, this is 'the first Gossen's law'), which shows the diminishing function of the marginal utility of consumed goods, and his 'law of value'[1], According to which the entire area under the curve A' at any of its points (for example, at the point 9 shown in the figure) is the value of A. Clarke made these Gossen laws concretized, in them 'utility' was replaced by 'productivity-profitability', the functions of expenditure, including the product supply curve, as well as market equilibrium were not taken into account and were not depicted by him.

---

[1] Elsewhere in the treatise *Development of the Laws of Social Exchange and the Resulting Rules of Human Activity* (1854) Gossen quite clearly formulates the conditions for the exchange of goods: "Each of the objects after exchanging them between (the subjects – *the author*) A and B ... should be distributed in this way so that the last atom ... would create equal value for both" [28, p. 129]. This theoretical position, the seventh in our count, can be called "the law of Gossen's exchange".

The area of the rectangle formed by the point 9, according to Clark's concept, should express the income of the employee and the owner of capital goods - the sum of wages (V) and profit (M), respectively, and the area above this rectangle — rent, but in the form of surplus (C). Clark's model by design was such that in it the payment to a variable factor was always supplemented by the sum of payments of two other fixed factors in the form of an indivisible surplus. This circumstance makes it incomprehensible the mechanism of the distribution of double factor income.

There are other features of Clark's model that do not allow it to be considered satisfactory. It is known that the owners of production factors strive to obtain not just surpluses, but maximum surpluses. This criterion of competitive activity should shift the dividing horizontal between factor income down to the abscissa (in the figure it — point 9_1), where the surplus of a fixed factor is maximum, and variable factors have no income at all. It is clear that such a situation is absurd, in reality, the function of offering products is excluded, it balances the market and the distribution of income. Since the supply function is not considered in the Clarke model, the result of the division of income in it is also distorted.

It should also be noted that since in the Clarke model, not an equilibrium, but an arbitrarily limited amount of a factor is taken, there can be no question of an equilibrium distribution of income in it. In his graph, the fixed land receives only the surplus of rent, while any factor of production represented in the created value must receive not only the surplus, but also the main part of the income, in this case all the rent.

Marshall adhered to the variant of dividing the output estimated by the yield (in Fig. II.20, a — the convex function $Q(A)$), according to which the unallocated remainder of the price of the goods appears. He attributed this balance to the factor of 'organization of production'. This concept of Marshall, like several other elements of his theory, caused misunderstandings, controversy and errors.

So, Seligman (*The Main Directions in Modern Economics: Economic Thought after 1870*, 1962), referring to land, labor and 'capital', wrote: "Marshall adds an organizational factor to the famous trinity, resulting in income corresponding factors received from him the form of rent, wages, interest and profit" [100, p. 307]. That is, Marshall allegedly attributed the profit entirely to the organizational factor. Elsewhere, the author writes somewhat differently: "According to Marshall, profit breaks down into management wages, interest, interest on capital, and risk fees. To explain the last component and include it in his theory of distribution, Marshall invented a new factor of production — organization, behind which is the institutional superstructure of society" [Ibid, p. 309]. Thus, Seligman has a chain of contradictions: interest is the income of capital and, at the same time, is included in profit, which only partly relates to the organization, and even that turns out to be not internal, but external institutional factor. But, since with the cost-based approach to value, profit is excluded, then, according to Marshall, the value of the product contains only rent, wages of employees and the cost of organizing production.

In the *Principles of Economics*, Marshall mixed profit with his 'organizational' factor of production, which meant not only literally 'organization' as a system of coordination and subordination relations in society, industries and firms, but also division and cooperation of labor, machine technology, territorial concentration and large-scale production, as well as enterprise management and organizational skills of people. At the microeconomic level, Marshall personified the organizational factor in an entrepreneur who is responsible for economic decisions: what to produce, in what quantity, by what method, etc. If you adhere to scientific rigor and exclude interest from profit, then, according to Marshall, it will be entirely attributed to the 'organization', which becomes not the fourth, but the third factor of production.

Marshall often used biological concepts in his economic theory to emphasize that economics is an 'organism'. Therefore, he had the idea of the fourth factor of production – its organization. But, having designated this factor, he does not even give it a definition. He simply lists the short-term and long-term, as well as the intra-industry and externally borrowed effects of this factor: "Organization promotes knowledge; it has many forms, that is, the form of a separate enterprise, different enterprises of the same industry, different branches from each other, and, finally, the form of a 'state' that provides security for all and assistance to many" [71, p. 181]. Analysis of the organization of production Marshall, unfortunately, does not try to bring up to a specific model level of pricing, which is characteristic of him as a whole, I think, and because this is impossible. There are other counterarguments as well.

First, Marshall reduces his very broad concept of 'organization' to which he devotes five chapters in a row in the *Principles*, at the microeconomic level, to the qualities of an entrepreneur-organizer of production. Such a focus only on 'entrepreneurial abilities' is hardly correct, since organization as a general phenomenon affects all participants in production and business entities as a whole.

Secondly, Marshall, investigating the organization of production, departs from the principle of one-factor pricing, which leads him to erroneous conclusions, which we noted above when analyzing the nature of the function of supply of goods. Marshall conducts, in fact, a multifactorial description of the economy, in particular he writes that "an increase in the volume of labor and capital costs usually leads to an improvement in the organization of production, which increases the efficiency of the use of labor and capital" and activates the "law increasing returns" [Ibid, p. 328]. As can be seen from this passage, Marshall is referring to long-term progressive changes in production, which are not directly related to the current modeling of the formation and distribution of market prices, are 'shift' price factors. So half of the Marshall *Principles*, where the various types of supply functions are clarified and, in general, a preference for a decreasing supply function is given, as we showed above, becomes not only unnecessary, but also erroneous.

Thirdly, there is no 'organizational remnant' as such in reality, because under the current ceteris paribus premise, only a decreasing efficiency of the use of factors is observed, so that the functions of total expenditure and product supply are purely concave. Otherwise, "Hotelling's thesis would come into force that cost-based pricing in all sectors of the economy would require subsidies for any industry with a declining supply price"[14, p. 418, 419]. We add that this total need for subsidies would arise in the presence of gigantic profitability of the markets. Therefore, many theorists, for example, Wicksell and Edgeworth, rightly did not recognize the Marshallian 'organizational' factor.

Fourth, and this is the most important argument against factor accounting for the organization of production, which we cited above, any selected factor must be divisible and homogeneous. The same argument forces us to abandon 'risk' as an independent factor claiming a share in the price of a commodity in the form of all profit, which, according to Knight (*Risk, Uncertainty and Profit*, 1921), is a 'payment for risk'.

With that said, we remain supporters, although like Marshall, of the four-factor theory of pricing, but as the fourth factor of reproduction we consider not the organization of production, but its products.

At the same time, we must pay tribute to Marshall, since his view of the problem of price distribution, in fact, was the beginning of a modern, very effective and constructive development of 'institutionalism'. But, and the fashionable theory of 'transaction costs' that appeared in 'institutionalism', some economists[1] also unreasonably associate it with the organizational factor of production, they call these costs "costs in addition to prices arising from trade in goods and services" [105, p. 498]. In reality, however, such additional costs are practically included in the overhead costs of production and are taken into account in the income of the corresponding traditional factors. It is not advisable to separate transaction costs from the flow of value due to the lack of a divisible and homogeneous source in the form of a value-stock.

However, the above does not mean that the distribution of value does not depend on the functions B and A in the above figure, they are important for determining the equilibrium quantitative and price parameters of the market. Moreover, the nature of these curves is influenced not only by the scale of

---

[1] See, for example: [17, p. 35-38].

production[1], but also by the externality and emergence of economic activity, but also by the very premise of ceteris paribus in the form of the appearance of non-linear elements of 'overspending' *B* or 'underprofit' *A*.

Most likely, internal effects of scale and external effects (externalities) of activity are interrelated, since both directly relate to its cost and profitability, externalities and are defined as inseparability (inseparability) of consumption and production functions. Externalities undoubtedly affect the efficiency of subjects and, thus, to a certain extent manifest themselves in economies of scale. Thus, a negative external effect, as the expenditure of a good, not reflected in its price, can cause a negative economies of scale for the consumer and a positive economies of scale for the producer of the good. Positive externality can cause a chain of opposite effects of scale. In the area of consumption of public goods, these links determine the effects of the 'free rider' ('free rider', or 'hare') and the 'forced free rider'. The systemic, emergent, effect, in which the flow of total value exceeds the sum of the terms (for example, $3 + 2 > 5$, the terms seem to be multiplied, $3 \times 2 = 6$) is actually observed often. But this means that the terms should not be multiplied, but adjusted to the value of the corresponding reserves of reproduction factors. For the correctness and transparency of the theory of pricing and price allocation, it is important to neutralize internalities and externalities in it, that is, to transfer them from the category of exogenous factors to endogenous ones. This is possible in two ways: by introducing, in appropriate cases, the 'Pigou tax' proposed by Pigou (*Economics of Welfare*, 1920), in the amount of externalities, or by selling certificates on externalities. But it is better to do this without state mediation by making a clear delineation of property rights in the areas of joint competitive interests of economic entities.

This shift in theory concerns the emergence of commercial activity. It must be remembered that in economics there is a "law of conservation of value", according to which value can only pass from the form of a stock to the form of a stream and back. So the emergent effect can be interpreted as inaccurate accounting of the value of stocks and flows. An important means of matching stocks and flows can be 'continuous inventory', a reassessment of factors of production taking into account scientific and technological progress, proposed by the American economist John Kendrick (*Formation and Accounting of Full Capital*, 1976) [54], and the corresponding most accurate definition of the value of the output. An adjusted estimate of the factors of production allows one to free oneself in theory from complicated production

---

[1] It should be borne in mind that scale effects are observed in the activities of not only firms, but also households. So there are 'income equivalence ratios' of families of different sizes, which are used to determine the same standard of living of individuals and which reflect the nonlinearity between the expenses and incomes of families of different sizes.

functions, for example, the Dutch economist Jan Tinberchen (1903-1994) (*Mathematical Models of Economic Growth*, together with H. Bose, 1962), or Solow (*To the theory of economic growth*, 1956) and other research tools, in which special multipliers are introduced, taking into account the effects of scale or scientific and technological progress. We have already spoken about such a possibility, considering the relationship between the obsolescence of capital goods and their prices.

The main constructive conclusion that we make from the shown prehistory of the formation and refinement of the theory of factorial determination and distribution of the price of goods is that this theory has a direct connection not with the functions of expenditure or profitability, but with a linear contractual function, which, under conditions perfect competition, which we are only considering here, in the market model appears primarily due to the fact that all its participants are 'price recipients', while the equilibrium price is clearly divided into three factor incomes − rent, wages and gross profit (Fig. II.20, *c*):

$$X = C + V + M_\text{в}, \quad X = \partial(AB)/\partial Q = \partial(AB)/\partial N + \partial(AB)/\partial L + \partial(AB)/\partial K.$$

Let's move on to the question of the structure of three factor incomes. Earlier, in some places of our study, it was shown that the structure of rent, wages and gross profit is unified and dual, in them, in normal competitive conditions, there are parts that are equal, respectively, to the consumption of the value of land, labor and capital goods, and maximum profits. Where do the latter come from if pricing and price distribution is carried out according to the general law of preservation of value: value, if properly taken into account, can only pass from the form of a stock to the form of a stream and vice versa?

The analysis of the model of macroeconomic equilibrium of the neoricardian Sraffa, carried out by us in section 5 of the monograph, showed that in *Chapter X* of his book *Production of Goods by Means of Goods*, he considered the depreciation fund as a source of not only compensation, but also a certain accumulation of capital goods. Sraffa practically tried to solve the age-old question of the origin of the profitability of production. True, in the further description of his model, he not only pointed to the amortization origin of net profit-investments, but also, following Ricardo, is trying to prove the need to regulate its share in the national income based on the correlation of "class forces" in society.

But if we accept such a mechanism of self-expansion of stocks acting in the reproduction of not only capital goods, but also other factors of production − land and labor, then the profit of rent and the profit of wages in the form of workers' savings should form in a similar way. Then the above equation for the depletion of the price of the good produced should take the form: $X = R_N \cdot N + R_L \cdot L + R_K \cdot K$, where R_N, R_L, R_K are indicators of the return on production factors in the form of their depreciation rates, which are values, inverse from the calculated service life (exhaustion) of these factors (τ_K, τ_L, τ_N). However, in the model, capital productivity is a constant value, which means the equality of annual depreciation costs, which are not included in the cost of the product due to the fact that only labor costs are taken into account in it, but, at the same time, are a source of net profit, and Sraffa's annuities, including percentages must be non-linear. Such constructions are extremely contradictory and cannot be accepted.

The mainstream theory does not exclude the use of depreciation funds to expand the production apparatus of the economy, but, despite doubts and disputes, it has developed a rather controversial provision that any value flow that is a product of a stock-value and a period indicator should be supplied with interest, taking into account the need for expanded reproduction of this stock. Fisher (*The Theory of Interest*, 1930), considering the universality of intertemporal preferences of people, absolutized capital and interest, considering the diversity of the latter to be profit, rent and wages. "The stock of wealth existing at a given moment in time, – he wrote, – is called capital. The flow of services over a period of time is called a percentage" [140, p. 101]. But unlike Fischer, Clark clearly distinguished between 'capital' and 'capital goods' and the percentage of profits. He, characterizing land assets, wrote: "What ... is interest? ... These are five dollars, annually delivered by one hundred dollars ..., but what concrete means of production bring is not interest, and rent" [56, p. 135].

Therefore, the need to include in the value of the product interest, developed in the marginal theory, does not mean that it is the same in all factor elements of this value. As a relative value, interest at the level of bank interest in all intertemporal calculations can be the same, but with different values of the monetary value of 'natural', 'human' and 'technical' capital, it also corresponds to different values of the net profit of factor income as part of the value of goods.

However, these arguments can be considered correct only for the conditions of existence in the economy of absolutely perfect competition. Monopolism, to the theory of which we are passing, forces us to make adjustments to them.

9. Development of consistently marginal models imperfect competition

Sraffa in his early work, the article *Laws of Return in Competitive Conditions* (1926), noted that one should start the study of the economy with its monopolistic structures as specific phenomena. He began then criticism of the 'Marshall cross' precisely with the discrepancy between its monopolized market. But neither Sraffa nor other neoricardians have created the corresponding models. With their intersectoral, technological methodology, the development of such models is simply impossible.

Therefore, neoclassical models of imperfect competition, taking into account the forms of organization of the economy, retain their importance, although they need improvement. But first, let's turn to the prehistory of their creation. The state economic monopoly of the era of 'mercantilism' was already criticized by Smith *(Study on the Nature and Cause of the Wealth of Nations*, 1776), but the classical market, which successfully developed thanks to the laissez-faire principle, moved to a new stage of large-scale machine production and numerous phenomena of imperfect competition acquired a massive character. However, the monopolization of the economy was the main means of overcoming the systemic crisis, the average profitability of production, which reached a record low level, began to rise in the subsequent period and the market acquired a 'second breath'.

This natural process was also facilitated by other circumstances: acceleration of scientific and technological progress, making innovations a means of gaining a competitive advantage; the impossibility or inexpediency of competition in some industries and spheres of the economy, mainly in the transport of water and sewage, gas, heat, electricity, oil and oil products, cargo and passengers, information and mail, where so-called natural monopolies; private ownership of unique factors and products of activity (land, structures, human abilities and his creations); economic policy of the state, aimed at obtaining benefits and competitive advantages by one or another business entity.

Production monopoly has attracted the attention of economists throughout the development of the phenomenon, but its systematic theory emerged only at the end of the XIX century. Cournot *(Study of the Mathematical Principles of the Theory of Wealth*, 1838) was the first to model monopoly, considering this form of market organization as the starting point for the theory of perfect competition. He came to the conclusion that the equilibrium volume of output is established when the marginal cost of production and marginal revenue are equal. Marginalists Marshall *(Chapter XIV. The Theory of Monopolies of Book V of Principles of Economics)*, Edgeworth *(Pure Theory of Monopoly*, 1897), Clark *(Problems of Monopoly*, 1904), Robbinson *(The Economics of Imperfect Competition*, 1933), the Americans of Chemberlin *(Theory of Monopoly Competition*, 1933), Galbraith *(American Capitalism, the Concept of Balancing Power*, 1952), and Arnold Harberger (b. 1924)) *(Monopoly and Resource Allocation*, 1954) and other more modern authors.

The first neoclassicist Marshall analyzed in detail in *Principles of Economics* (1890 et seq.) Monopoly pricing using the example of the state gas company, accompanying the analysis with four graphs, one of which we reproduce in Fig. II.21.

Removing numerous dotted hyperboles from the figure and replacing the author's designations with those adopted in our work, we place it in the lower, differential, part of the marketron of the product, the only one at that time in the gas industry of the company (Fig. II.22). The model includes a standard diminishing gas demand function (A') and its supply function, which is also diminishing due to Marshall's ideas about the increasing efficiency of the industry (B'), but the slope of which is that it intersects A' first from below, and then from above. Marshall believed that the difference between $B' - A'$ was a "monopole income" (the zone of which is shaded in the figure) — the amount "by what dividends exceed what is properly possible attributed to the account of interest on the capital and the insurance fund " [71, p. 462] (the maximum of this difference falls on the equilibrium volume of gas sales by the "monopoly of Marshall", $Q_{m(M)}$).

However, Marshall's reasoning and constructions are objectionable.

First, we should not talk about 'monopoly income', which Marshall says is "layered" on other elements of profit — for this, the term 'excess profit' is more appropriate, but about the integral indicator 'monopoly profit', that is, about the profit of a monopoly in excess of the cost of production of goods (M_m).

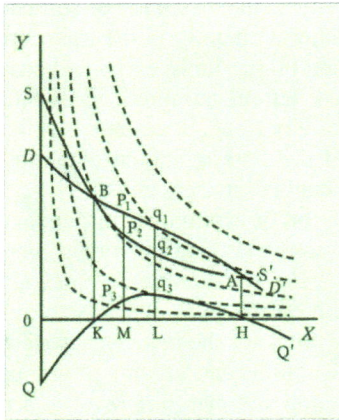

Fig. II.21

Secondly, we must remember that the supply and demand functions are always the first derivatives of the functions of profitability and consumption of goods, and if we add the integral part of the pricing model to the Marshall chart, it turns out that curve B has an unrealistic form. That is, at first it behaves typically, but as Q grows, it rises above A. Therefore, the area between intersecting A' and B' cannot be attributed to monopoly profit, as Marshall believed, its first half characterizes a 'non-working' diminishing profit, and the second is losses. The conclusion suggests itself: the expenditure functions under monopoly pricing have a standard concave form, since in this case the ceteris paribus premise and the law of diminishing efficiency of factors of production continue to operate.

Thirdly, even if the nature of the function B' is preserved, the equilibrium output of products according to Marshall ($Q_{e(M)}$) is much higher than the volume of output (Q_e) falling on the first intersection of B' and A', and this contradicts the position that monopoly always diminishes production[1].

---

[1] For all the fallacy of the Marshall monopoly model, its characteristic double crosshair of supply and demand functions may have been the prototype of the "firm breakeven" model developed later by Weiner (*Cost Curves and Supply Curves*, 1931).

Marshall made mistakes not only in the positive theory of monopoly, but also in its normative part. Declaring the main institution of the market not competition, but 'freedom of entrepreneurship', he, at the same time, legitimized the existence of monopoly, elements of which he saw in competition in the form of 'quasi-rent' of ordinary entrepreneurs.

Thus, in terms of monopoly pricing, Marshall turned out to be superior to his contemporaries in terms of instrumentation, but made mistakes, which in the following gave rise to a whole series of misunderstandings that have survived to this day in the description of monopolies. their pricing policy and anti-monopoly policy of the state.

In order to cleanse the monopoly research from unnecessary model burdens that have formed in the mainstream theory, and to build them into the consistently marginal theory of imperfect competition, let us give a list of the main conditions for perfect competition, for the first time comprehensively formulated by Stigler (*Perfect Competition, Historical Approach*, 1957), in our version, covering not only producers, but also consumers of goods, that is, both groups of counterparties of any markets, as well as several supplemented:

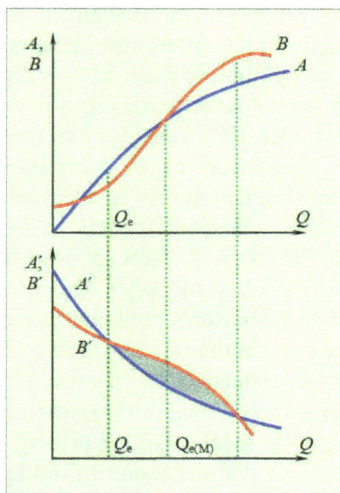

Fig. II.22

1) maximization by producers and consumers of profits from the sale of goods; 2) a large number of sellers and buyers of goods; 3) the sale and purchase by one market participant of quantities of goods that are negligible in comparison with the total volume of transactions in the industry; 4) homogeneity, identity of the goods produced; 5) the possession of complete and free information by market participants on the cost of production and profitability of consumption of goods, as well as market conditions; 6) the absence, both among sellers and buyers of collusion, of consistency in making decisions and actions; 7) freedom of entry into the industry and exit from it for producers and consumers of goods[1]; 8) free mobility, movement of products and factors of production.

Perfect competition is considered either a purely theoretical, abstract con-

---

[1] Usually, the economic literature speaks of the freedom to enter and exit the industry only for manufacturers of products. A typical characteristic is: "Sectoral equilibrium is a situation when firms do not have a tendency to enter the industry, leave it, or change their size" [23, p. 113]. Between them, from a theoretical point of view, it is important to take into account the availability of similar abilities among consumers of products.

struction, or is associated with the classical market economy or its industry, which, at least approximately, correspond to the specified conditions. For example, these can be considered the grain markets, or loans. The apparent absence of any of the above conditions means the existence of imperfect competition, which is closer to the real economy and a huge number of specific market structures. Imperfect competition multiplies the contractual basis of the industry, in which not only counteragents, but also competitors agree with each other, and the market structure acquires a powerful character, subjects, objects (space) and means of market power appear, which consists in influencing market prices, and, consequently, the volume of purchase and sale of products.

The first item in the 'Stigler's list' was added by us taking into account the new interpretation of profit as the goal of all economic entities, including households. Therefore, the analysis of imperfect competition on this point, in our opinion, is reduced only to the issue of redistribution of the total profit of market counterparties. But in the economic literature, this analysis looks much broader. Let's consider it in more detail.

Robinson, as we have shown above, was a universal researcher of economics. But her name is associated, first of all, with the creation of microeconomic marginal models in her book *Economics of Imperfect Competition* (1933), that is, the expanded model of Marshall's 'price scissors'. Chamberlin's book *Monopoly Competition* (1933) was published several months earlier than Robinson's book and is devoted to only one of the manifestations of monopoly, although its subtitle *Reorientation of the Theory of Value*, like the later collection of 16 articles by the author, *Directions to a More General Theory of Value* (1957), was very ambitious, but did not add knowledge of the general mechanism of pricing in conditions of imperfect competition. Many believe that the issues raised by economists coincide, but a careful reading of the works shows that Robinson considered the problems more broadly, carried out a comparative analysis of perfect and imperfect competition, investigated not only monopoly, but also monopsony, as well as monopoly demand for factors of production and social consequences of price diktat. Consider the general approach of Robinson in solving these issues, which is associated with pricing.

Robinson considered the monopoly of one manufacturing company and many consumers of industry products, the lack of substitute products and free entry into the industry (due to the absolute cost advantage of the firms operating there, the need for large start-up capital and the existence of difficult to overcome legal entities). or bureaucratic barriers), as well as a fairly complete information of producers about the economic conditions for the consumption of products. The latter circumstance is more important for a monopoly as a 'price fixer' than for perfect competition, in which all market counterparties are 'price receivers'. The monopolist, however, should know not only the consumption of its own production, but as a minimum the nature of the profitability function of consumers of the good and their differentiation by solvency.

Robinson used the marginal return function (A') to model monopoly, and the marginal expense function (B') for monopsony (Fig. II.23). These functions are located, respectively, below and above the functions of the middle functions of the same name (A_{mi}, B_{mi}), and the point of their intersection, according to Robinson, characterizes a special, imperfectly competitive equilibrium of the market with parameters that differ from the parameters of "perfect competition" (X, $Q_{mi(e)}$): twice the volume of the industry's output (Q_e) ($Q_{mi(e)} = 2Q_e$), reduced by the "price of monopoly Robinson" ($X_{m(R)}$) and the inflated "price of Robinson's monopsony" ($X_{m-s(R)}$). The interpretation in these constructions of the curves A'_{mi} and B'_{mi} as functions of sectoral demand and supply causes confusion. Robinson writes: "It is *convenient* to consider the demand curve as the curve of the average income of the seller" (highlighted by *the author*) [87, p. 59]. But 'convenience' in science cannot be considered an acceptable argument. It is known, and we have shown above that the functions of supply and demand of a perfectly competitive market are the functions of marginal profitability and marginal expense, A' and B', respectively. Since this state of affairs is associated with production and consumption technologies, it remains in any organizational structure of the market, including for an imperfectly competitive market. Business entities are guided by marginal rather than average indicators due to the maximum profitability of their activities only in the marginal 'range' of the market. Equilibrium of the averaged output is disadvantageous for both counterparties of the market, no matter what configuration

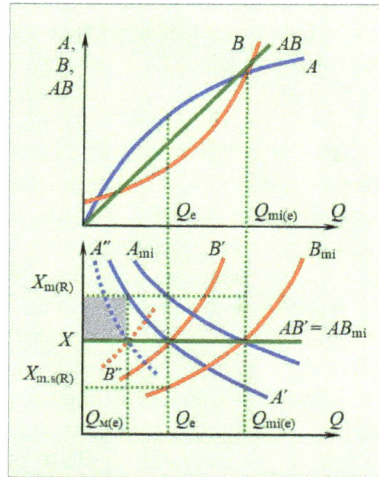

Fig. II.23

it may be. The volume of $Q_{mi(e)}$ in the integral part of the pricing marketron shown in Fig. II.23, the second point of intersection of functions A and B corresponds, at which the aggregate surplus (aggregate profit (M_{ag}) takes zero value. Therefore, the only correct and universal toolkit for finding the balance of any standard market certain combinations of marginal functions of production costs and profitability of consumption of goods should be considered.

Unfortunately, in the pricing study, neither Marshall, nor Robinson, and

Chamberlin used integral functions, the graphs of which clearly show the actual parameters of market equilibrium. Robinson, presenting the application of the marginal profitability function in his model as an innovation, in the *Preface* to her book indicated: "For the first time, I learned about the problem associated with the marginal yield curve at the lectures of Mr. J.G.R. Gifford, who prepared us in Cambridge for the exam for a doctoral degree" [Ibid, p. 34]. But this curve as a function of demand has been known since the time of the *Investigation of the Mathematical Principles of the Theory of Wealth* (1838) Cournot. In the Robinson model, the A' and B' curves are of an auxiliary character, they are a tool for determining the maximum size of the market counterparties' surplus assigned by the monopolist and monopsonist, respectively. The segments on the ordinate $X_{m(R)}$ and $X_{m-s(R)}$ cannot be considered prices, since they appear in the model as a result of the transformation of real 'triangular' surpluses into some rectangles equivalent in area. The actual price of the goods in both cases should be considered only the price of perfect competition X, within its framework, due to a certain relationship of the market power of counterparties, there is one or another structure of their aggregate surplus (M_{ag}), which is always entirely included in the price of X^1.

In his concept of imperfect competition, Robinson erroneously states that the model does not have the function of supplying a product under monopoly pricing and the function of demand for it under monopolytic pricing. In fact, the model retains not only the indicated functions, but also integral and differential contract functions. The latter only become nonlinear and coincide in the case of monopoly with the profitability functions ($AB = A$, $AB' = A'$), and in the case of monopsony, with the expense functions ($AB = B$, $AB' = B'$). For a monopolist, the profitability of consumers, as well as for a monopsonist, the expense of producers of goods, becomes a kind of limitation in pricing. If in perfect competition all market participants are price recipients, then imperfect competition makes them, as it were, 'recipients' of supply or demand functions.

As for the volumes of imperfectly competitive output, then the mechanism of their change must be approached from several positions: 1) a gradual increase in the sale and purchase of goods from zero to its equal competitive volume; 2) regular sale in the industry of a non-competitive volume of goods; 3) the transition to a new equilibrium quantity of goods of any of the parties to the market due to its transformation into a monopoly or monopsony. According to the first position, the monopolist, starting the release of the goods, each time sets the price at the level of the current maximum, but increasingly decreasing value of the demand function and at the point of its intersection with the supply function reaches perfectly competitive equilibrium market pa-

---

[1] We have shown this in section 6 of the monograph.

rameters (X, Q_e) and, in addition to the usual profit, 'captures' the complete surplus of the consumer. In the case of a monopony with an increasing volume of purchase of goods, she also gets a double surplus M_{ag}.

In the real economy, there are no monopolies or monopsony that would constantly operate in the market according to the described ideal scheme. There are special mechanisms of either more complex market structures, or the so-called 'price discrimination', but in these extreme conditions of concentration of market power, there is usually a regular sale of the entire volume of industry products. Proceeding from these realities, in the refined Robinson monopoly model, the equilibrium release of a product should fall on the crosshair of the second derivatives of its profitability and expense functions (A'', B''), since only under the conditions of a halved output $(Q_{m(e)})$ the maximum consumer surplus assigned by the monopolist is achieved (Fig. II.23, shaded rectangle). Equilibrium parameters and the 'monopsony marke' are determined in a similar way.

Based on Robinson's false ideas about the market of averaged parameters, Harberger (*Monopoly and Resource Allocation*, 1954) proved that the damage from monopoly is proportional to the reduction in industry output $(Q_{mi(e)} - Q_e, \Delta Q)$ and the increase in price $(X_{m(R)} - X, \Delta X)$. This is the so-called 'Harberger triangle', which expresses the 'net losses of welfare of society' $(A_{lo}$, shaded area 1 in the upper graph of Fig. II.24), calculated by the formula: $A_{lo} = 0.5(\Delta Q \cdot \Delta X)$. The author's calculations showed that Apot in the manufacturing industry in the United States amounted to only 0.1% of GNP [1, p.

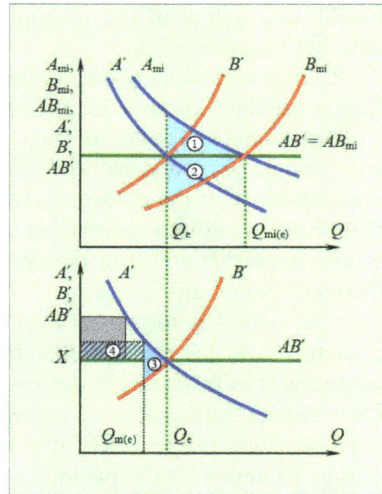

Fig. II.24

77]. The studies of other economists, who considered Harberger's calculations inaccurate, although they received somewhat higher numbers, nevertheless characterized the 'evil of mono-polyism' as very modest.

But Harberger's calculation method contains fundamental errors. First, the 'losses triangle' should occupy the entire vertical area between the supply and demand functions, that is, include triangles 1 and 2. Therefore: $A_{lo} \approx \Delta Q \cdot \Delta X$. Secondly, the real 'triangle of losses' is in the zone of marginal rather than average market parameters, that is, between the functions A' and B' in the range of $Q_{m(e)}$ and Q_e output (see the lower graph of Fig. II .24). Thirdly, the 'loss triangle', like the symmetrical triangle to the right of the point of competitive equilibrium, is a zone of losses not for society and not for both sides of the product market, but only for monopoly or monopony.

Fourthly, all the above calculations cannot be considered always consistent with the methodology for halving the uncompetitive release of Robinson, since, for example, a monopoly that has already appropriated the entire consumer surplus, or a newly formed the monopoly, in its expansion, is forced only to reduce the output of goods, but at the same time and proportionally increase the 'triangle of losses' (in Fig. II. 24 this is a shaded area 3). Therefore, the monopoly does not increase the surplus of consumers, but the positive difference between it and the growing losses of the aggregate surplus, which is maximized much earlier than 'Robinson's equilibrium'. This means that with this behavior of the monopoly, the real value of the appropriated surplus of consumers (in Fig. II.24 it is represented by the shaded rectangle 4) turns out to be significantly less than the 'marginal-maximum', while the equilibrium output of the monopoly $Q_{m(e)}$, as our calculations show, is not half, but a quarter of Q_e.

Robinson, analyzing the forms of monopolism, declares them unfair, the reason for the existence of unemployment, low welfare and exploitation of workers, under-utilization of the capacities of firms, weak scientific and technological progress and economic growth, in a word, the reason for all negative manifestations of the modern market. But, in our opinion, many of these conclusions turn out to be associated with factors that are far from the real possibilities of market power or disappear as a result of the above correction of the theory of monopolistic pricing.

"The only way to combat exploitation, – wrote Robinson, – is to establish ... control over the price level so that the monopolist would produce as much output as it is produced under conditions of competition" [87, p. 173, 174]. Control over monopolies, of course, in a social market economy is necessary, but Robinson's recipe turns out to be false, because in the market the supply is always balanced by the paying-capable demand, and if the monopolist manages to reduce the equilibrium volume of output, then this is supported by a corresponding reduction in equilibrium income. products consumers. Therefore, control should be directed to the profits of the monopolies, as well as the wages of buyers of the goods.

With regard to Robinson's assertion that the bargaining power of monopolies does not stimulate them to reduce expenditures and develop production, there is a long discussion on this issue in the economic literature. Of course, there is such a thing in the multifaceted market economy, including monopolies, but it is important to consider the dominant phenomena, confirmed by facts. They also show the opposite: monopolies were, on the whole, the locomotives of industrial development and the growth of welfare in the XX century. We agree with the opinion of Schumpeter, according to which monopoly as such is a powerful factor of innovation, since it gives double profits, greater opportunities for updating technologies and organizing production. It is known that it is corporate science, which invests enormous funds in R&D, that still creates the most important scientific discoveries and innovative products.

Robinson, in the book *Economics of Imperfect Competition*, analyzes the rarely encountered in practice bilateral market power, or the monopoly-monopsony structure, inaccurately referred to in the literature as bilateral monopoly, or bilateral monopoly. She gives the example of a city with one enterprise, the owners of which are negotiating with the branch trade union about the terms of employment of workers, and makes the model constructions shown by us with 'ineffective for society' deformations in the price and volume of output. But, an interesting from a theoretical point of view, a monopoly-monopsonic design is in fact identical to the model of a completely competitive market, because as a result of bargaining, a certain balance of the price power of counterparties is established on it and the total profit is distributed approximately in the same way as with perfect competition. In the model of such a market, there should be a restoration of the linear contract function and its derivative — the linear price function, which divide the total profit into the consumer's profit and the producer's profit. This quasi-perfect market situation is consistent with Galbraith's concept of "balancing power" (*American Capitalism. The Balancing Force Concept*, 1952), according to which the bargaining power of producers can and should be compensated for by the bargaining power of consumers.

The methods of imperfectly competitive pricing discussed above do not exhaust all the possibilities of appropriation by the pricing setters of the incomes of their numerous counterparties. For this, there is also the so-called price discrimination, which is either theoretical speculative constructions or specific economic phenomena observed only in certain specific markets.

Pigou (*Economics of Welfare*, 1920) was the first to turn to the study of discriminatory pricing, without sufficient justification singled out and fluently described its three 'levels'. Other theorists subsequently identified a different number of 'types' or 'degrees' of such discrimination: from two [105, p. 396] to four [1, p. 233]. Rather skeptical about the feasibility of price discrimination, Pigou wrote: "The first level is expressed in the assignment of different prices for all different units of the commodity, so that the price of each of these units is equal to the corresponding demand price, and the buyer does not have to There is some excess" [83, v. I, p. 348]. A modern textbook on economics defines this price discrimination in about the same way, that is, as "selling each unit of a good at its price of demand" [102, p. 277], and the Oxford *Dictionary of Economics* calls it "a situation when the only monopoly firm sells its products in several markets at different prices" [15, p. 202].

However, in this case, we should talk about one and the same market saturated with goods, and not about increasing output by a monopolist, which cannot be considered discriminatory pricing, since it involves purchases by all numerous consumers less and less rare at decreasing prices. The Latin word discriminatio means 'division', in this case the division of the entire mass of consumers into individual buyers, when each of them "must pay for the product the amount indicated by its place on the aggregate demand curve for a given market" [1, p. 230]. That is, price discrimination of the first type, which is often called 'perfect', should ensure the implementation of all units of the equilibrium production volume Q_e among the multitude of buyers differing in solvency. And this is extremely difficult to accomplish for a number of reasons.

First, the distribution of consumers in terms of income and desire to purchase goods at fixed prices cannot coincide with the diminishing function of sectoral demand, which delineates the boundary of solvency. It should also be borne in mind that with such a purchase of a product, individuals are unfairly deprived of their consumer surplus, and the monopolist is not able to force it to do so. All this points to the problematic nature of the systematic appropriation of the entire consumer surplus by the monopolist.

Secondly, 'perfect' price discrimination can be realized only when the monopolist is fully informed about the entire spectrum of the current profitability of market counterparties, which, even with developed modern marketing, requires high costs, and the exclusion of commodity arbitration – the resale of products by consumers for more high prices, which sharply narrows the scope of discrimination to markets for certain types of high-yield services and natural monopolies.

Third, the English auction procedure proposed as a mechanism for implementing price discrimination of the first type [Ibid, p. 229], starting with a minimum price, is hardly suitable for consumer goods.

Fourthly, the system of the two-part price of the monopolist's product considered in the economic literature, according to which each consumer pays with a lump sum first the right to purchase this product in the amount of the consumer surplus, and then a certain amount of it, must be considered ineffective in the modern economy and subject to a ban under antitrust laws.

Therefore, the essence and possibilities of individual price differentiation by a monopolist is expressed by the following characteristic made by the English economist John Sloman (b. 1947): "Price discrimination of the first degree exists when a firm takes from each consumer the maximum price that he agrees to pay for each item of the product. For example, the owners of kiosks in the bazaar try to do this when they conclude deals with their customers" [106, p. 230].

The next form of price discrimination Pigou was interpreted rather vaguely: "The second level assumes that the monopolist is able to set n different prices ... and ... sell the goods in batches ..." [83, v. I, p. 348-349]. In practice, we are talking about the sale of goods in large batches, that is, a variety of individualized price discrimination of the first form, more similar to simply a system of discounts in wholesale trade. Consignments of goods, as their sum approaches the equilibrium perfectly competitive quantity Q_e, must be larger and cheaper in order to cover the total consumer surplus of the product market with the corresponding total income, and this is even more difficult to carry out than perfect price discrimination. This form of discrimination means a deviation from the third point of the above list of Stigler's perfect competition conditions, according to which the sale and purchase by one market participant should be negligible in comparison with the total volume of transactions in the industry.

Pigou characterized the last, third form of increment of the superprofit of the price setter as follows: "The third level means that the monopolist is able to single out n different groups among its buyers, which can be more or less practically distinguished from each other, and the monopolist is able to assign its own monopoly price to buyers from each group" [Ibid, p. 348]. Pigou considered this form of appropriation of consumer surplus to be the most realistic. But selling goods to different buyers at different prices also requires even more market research costs than in the case of 'perfect' and 'wholesale' price discrimination, since knowledge is required not only of the profitability and solvency of many consumer groups, but also the demand functions of the latter. In addition, this form of price differentiation practically means the existence of several product markets and goes beyond the study of imperfectly competitive sectoral pricing.

If, in the list of the main conditions for perfect competition of Stigler, we consider the second item, which requires a large number of sellers and buyers of goods, and introduce only three gradations of the number of market participants - many (multi-), a little (oligo-) and one (mono-), then the analysis gives already nine market configurations, the dual names of which are shown in Fig. II.25. Of these, only multipole-multi-union, marked with a '*' sign, refers to completely perfect competition, all others are more realistic, they to a certain extent and on one side of the market reflect price power. These are symmetric oligopoly-oligopsony and monopoly-monopsony, four somewhat asymmetric configurations and two polar opposite power structures with "price-setting". Imperfect competition multiplies the contractual basis of the industry, in which not only counterparties, but also market competitors negotiate with each other, and the market structure acquires a powerful character, subjects, objects (space) and means of market power appear, which consists in influencing market prices, and, consequently, the volumes of purchase and sale of products. Our task is not to examine in detail all and even the main designated structures with imperfect competition, but only to clarify the pricing mechanisms operating in them and their impact on macroeconomic indicators.

Therefore, we do not consider the problems of points 6, 7 and 8 of the above 'Stigler's list', considering them the subject of a special discipline 'Theory of industrial markets' or theories of individual sectors of the economy.

Modern economic theory also considers several new forms of price discrimination. This is an analysis of sales by a monopoly of mutually complementary goods, durable goods in which the so-called 'Coase's time paradox'[1] manifests itself, goods with replaceable, separately sold parts and devices, etc. All of these various specific forms of trade do not affect the general issues of pricing and should be studied in a special 'Theory of industry markets'.

The next question requiring specification concerns the non-observance of point 3 of the 'Stigler's list', which requires a negligible amount of sale and purchase of goods by an individual market participant in the total volume of operations in the industry, that is, a quantitative assessment of the level of imperfection of competition. In the corresponding part of economics, a number of all available indicators are usually presented without ranking, but with a description of their pros and cons. In our opinion, the indicators should be divided into two groups: the one in which the characteristics of the level of concentration and centralization of capital are given − these are, so to speak, strategic indicators, indicators of the progress of manufacturing firms to monopoly, and the one in which the level of price power of already formed monopolies.

For the first group of indicators, we only mention the 'Hirschman index' (φ_X), proposed by the American economist Albert Hirschman (1915-2012) (*Exit, Voice and Fidelity: Responses to the Decline of Firms, Organizations and States*, 1970) and defined as the sum of the squares of the shares (g) of individual firms (i) operating in any market: $\varphi_{Hi} = \Sigma g_i^2$. The index, which takes a value from 0 in case of perfect competition to 1 in case of monopoly, quite accurately responds to the redistribution of the market between producers and is used in the development of antimonopoly policy of the state.

The second group of indicators is more numerous. The possibilities of measuring the level of price power of monopolies have been investigated by many specialists. One of the first was the American economist Abba Lerner (1903-1982) (*The Concept of Monopoly and the Measurement of Monopoly Power*, 1934), who graphically interpreted and expanded Marshall's price theory to include the concepts of imperfect competition Robinson and "monopolistic competition" Chamberlin, and a fairly simple index is proposed. Lerner

---

[1] The 'Coase's time paradox' consists in a decrease in the current demand for cheap durable goods due to the connection between consumer expectations of price discrimination applied by the seller with the service life of such goods (see: [1, p. 246-248]).

laconically writes about his indicator: "If X = price and B' = marginal cost, then the index of the degree of monopoly power (φ_{Le}) has the form $(X - B)/X$" [65, p. 536-566] (our notation – *the author*). However, the φ_{Le} index only measures the efficiency of the monopoly's pricing policy, while the theory of imperfect competition needs a more universal indicator covering monopony, as well as other intermediate market structures.

Does not reach such a generalized measurement and the 'Bane coefficient' (φ_{Ba}), proposed by the American economist Joseph Bane (1912-1991) (*Industry Organization*, 1959). The φ_{Ba} index is calculated as the ratio of the difference between accounting profit and 'normal' profit to the capital assets of the industry. The idea behind this coefficient' is that, given the constancy of normal' profit, any excess and growth of the entire indicator is associated with market power. But, since in reality profit can be increased not only by price setting, but also by the usual competitive method, the applicability of $\varphi_{Б}$ as a tool for measuring market power itself becomes controversial.

Developed to optimize the portfolio of financial assets by Tobin (*National Economic Policy*, 1966), the so-called 'q-coefficient' has been used for some time to measure the level of monopoly. The indicator is the ratio of the market value of shares and bonds of firms on the stock exchange to the recovery value of the corresponding assets at current prices. Although it was found that the q-coefficient reflects well the uniqueness of the technology or products of firms or industries, these phenomena are also characteristic of perfect competition, when manufacturers temporarily create a competitive innovative

		Number of producers (-poly)		
		Many (Multy-)	A little (Oligo-)	One (Mono-)
Number of consumers (-psone)	Multy-	Multypoly – multypsony*	Oligopoly – multypsony	Monopoly – multypsony
	Oligo-	Multypoly – oligopsony	Oligopoly – oligopsony	Monopoly – oligopsony
	Mono-	Multypoly – monopsony	Oligopoly – monopsony	Monopoly – monopsony

Fig. II.25

advantage. In addition, the growth of the q-coefficient can reflect not only the strengthening of monopolistic competition, but also other market circumstances. All this also does not allow us to consider the q-coefficient as an adequate measure of deviations from perfect competitive pricing.

Since we have shown that, in fact, under any market power, only the redistribution of the profits of factor income occurs, then a simple generalized indicator of competition (φ) in the form of the ratio of the difference between the profit of the producer (producers) (M_{pr}) and the profit of consumers (consumer) (M_{co}) to their sum in conditions of perfect competition (M_{ag}): $\varphi = = (M_{pr} - M_{co})/ M_{ag}$. The index φ varies from 1 in the case of a monopoly to -1 in the case of a monopsony with total price discriminatory takeovers of the profits of the market counterparties. Other values of φ reflect other real structures of the industry with a variety not only in proportion to the number of participants on the parties to market transactions, but also according to other conditions of perfect competition above, which corresponds to a zero value of the indicator φ.

Continuing the study of imperfectly competitive pricing, we turn to the situation with a small number of manufacturers as a deviation from the requirements of paragraph 2 of the 'Stigler's list', that is, to those contained in the middle column of Fig. II.25 oligopolistic market structures in which few firms are not independent and can interact in a wide variety of ways.

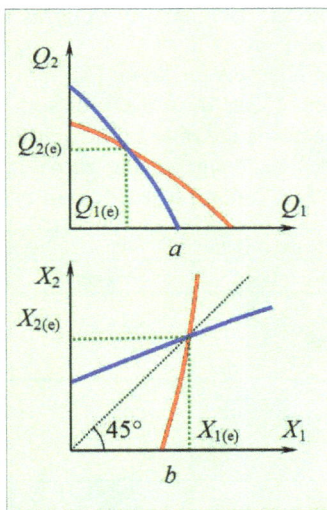

Fig. II.26

The first theoretical model of oligopoly, producing homogeneous products, was the dopoly model developed by Cournot in *Chapter VII* of his *Investigations of the Mathematical Principles of the Theory of Wealth* (1838), in which he considered fur the establishment of equilibrium in the volumes of output of two equal firms in the industry. The model is graphically presented in Fig. II.26, *a*.

In the coordinates of the interdependent volumes of Q_1 and Q_2 outputs, the corresponding 'reaction functions' are depicted – curves limiting the output of competitors in the event of any change in the output of one of them. The point of intersection of the response functions falls on the equilibrium output volumes of firms ($Q_{1(p)}$, $Q_{2(p)}$), which in total turn out to be less than the output of a perfectly competitive industry. Studies have shown that Cournot's 'dopoly model' can be expanded to a broader oligopoly, as well as to a variety of manufacturers (n). In this case, the price of the traded goods will decrease, and its quantity will increase to the level of perfect competition. In any case, the output of the industry (Q) will be equal to: $Q = k \cdot n$, where k – the share of an individual firm in the industry output, $k = 1/(n + 1)$.

German economist Heinrich von Steckelberg (1905-1946) (*Market Dominated Form*, 1934) modified Cournot's pre-pole model, in which one of the producers becomes the leader in terms of the volume of output and this al-

128

lowed him to extract increased profits. This model describes an even more monopolized structure of the industry. French economist and mathematician Joseph Bertrand (1822-1900) (*Mathematical Theory of Social Wealth*, 1883), criticizing Cournot's model for the fact that it varies the volume of output, and not the price of a product, proposed an equilibrium model with a price interaction ('price war') in the duopoly (Fig. II.26, *b*), which already contains two 'price reaction functions', which also limit the behavior of oligopoly participants and orientate them on the use of more and more convergent and as a result of equilibrium equal ($X_{1(e)} = X_{2(e)}$) commodity prices.

Cournot and Bertrand's dopoly models absolutize, respectively, the quantitative and price rivalry of firms, which in reality use both. Therefore, we propose a synthesis model of accessibility (Fig. II.27), the graph of which shows the 'reaction functions' of competitors in three coordinates: the output

volumes of firms Q_1 and Q_2 and the equilibrium price of the product (X_e).

Let's move on to the analysis of competition that violates point 3 of the Stigler's list and is associated with the heterogeneity of products produced in the industry, although historically this so-called 'monopoly competition' or 'mono-competition' was studied in detail by Chamberlin first. He drew attention to the fact that buyers of the industry distinguish the heterogeneity of its products and give preferences, show commitment to the product with the trademark of a particular manufacturer, which thereby practically

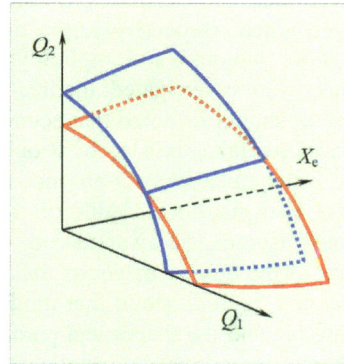

Fig. II.27

creates its own industry market, protected from substitute goods and becomes a monopolist. This market phenomenon was mentioned in the book *Economics of Imperfect Competition* by Robinson, but she categorically stated that if competing manufacturers begin to create their own industries, then the traditional theory of competition should be discarded. Chamberlin himself was more restrained and tried to describe the phenomenon of product differentiation from the standpoint of the existing marginal theory. It also seems to us that mono-competition can only confirm the correctness of the neoclassical theory of value and does not require a revision of any of its principles.

Of great importance in modern economics and its theory is the violation of point 5 of the list of conditions for perfect competition, which requires full, symmetrical and free information of market participants about the quality of goods. We are talking about natural or artificial incomplete and asymmetric awareness of market counterparties about their conjuncture, purchasing capacity, as well as the existence of situations with 'unfavorable, negative, screening' and 'moral hazard' in some markets for goods of 'uncertain quality'.

We would like to note that the phenomenon of concentration in the market of substandard goods has been known for a long time. Back at the beginning of the XVI century Polish thinker Nicolaus Copernicus (1473-1543) (*On the Evaluation of Coins*, 1519) drew attention to the displacement of full-value coins from precious metals by inferior ones, and later this phenomenon entered political economy as 'Gresham's law', formulated by the English financier Thomas Gresham (1519-1579). The law is really based on the ignorance of sellers of goods about the quality of money of buyers who acquire a competitive advantage. In modern times, the originally American economists George Akerlof (b. 1940) (*Market of Lemons: Quality Uncertainty and the Market Mechanism*, 1970) and Michael Spence (b. 1943) (*Market Signaling: Information Transfer in Hiring and Related Processes Screening*, 1974) investigated, respectively, the markets for cars, including secretly used cars, called 'lemons', and implicitly heterogeneous labor markets. Then other markets were investigated: medical services, insurance and even 'marriage'.

It should be noted that economics, which studies asymmetric informational markets, takes into account only the side of sellers of goods, while in reality the incompleteness or absence of information about the solvency of their buyers also matters. In addition, a characteristic feature of such markets is not only asymmetric awareness of market counterparties, but also the heterogeneity of the quality of goods that violate item 4 of the 'Stigler's list'. Further, it should be understood that modeling in the 'information economy' means going beyond the theoretical paradigm of the 'scarcity of the good' of marginalism, since market information should be considered as an inalienable and nonexhaustible good: when it is provided to someone, it does not decrease in others. The guarantor of possible losses is the state system of licensing economic activities, insurance of relevant risks, standardization, certification and examination of goods, as well as their private honest advertising and the reputation of firms. The old principle 'let the buyer beware' (Latin caveat emptor) is gradually being replaced by the principle 'let the seller beware' (caveat venditor). In addition, economic information in the age of the information society can be approached as an important market product and described by an appropriate industry model that allows one to determine the equilibrium values of prices and quantities of various necessary information.

Thus, the phenomena of competition in the modern representative market are a complex of structures, including: 1) classical competition between a large number of small and medium-sized enterprises; 2) competition between monopolized firms and outsiders; 3) competition between large firms that are part of the oligopoly; 4) competition of enterprises that are part of a monopolistic structure, but strive for independence. Therefore, the mainstream theory

130

is faced with the task of developing a unified theory of competition and pricing. Morgenstern (*Game Theory and Economic Behavior*, 1944) and promoted by American John Nash (1928-2015) (*Non-Cooperative Games*, 1951).

In general, given that our subject is the 'dispute of two Cambridges', and recalling the opinion of the leading representative of the British Cambridge Sraffa on the priority of studying the monopolies of economics, it is necessary to state the existence in the modern mainstream of a sufficiently developed theory of imperfect competition, which, based on from the scientific principle of 'moving from simple to complex', nevertheless, it should follow the theory of perfect competition.

10. Equilibrium of production, exchange, distribution, consumption and accumulation of goods

The economy is very multifaceted, but only six fundamental stable structures can be distinguished in it, shown by us in Fig. 1 in the form of cube faces: reproductive, factorial (resource), subjective, property (ownership structure), territorial and sectoral.

In Fig. II.28 presents the complete reproductive structure of the economy (1), in addition to the traditional elements – production, consumption, exchange and distribution of goods – we include in the reproduction the process of their accumulation, which is important from the point of view of the characteristics of modern macroeconomic theory, the peculiarity of which is is to focus on research and investment optimization.

In the factorial structure of the economy (2), we include, in addition to the canonical natural, capital and labor factors of production, its product and money, which, thanks to neoclassicism and 'Keynesianism', should take a worthy place in this structure. The modern neoclassical theory considers consumed products as a factor of obtaining 'utility', and 'Monetarism' shows the non-neutrality of money, the amount of which affects not only prices, but also the quantitative proportions of the economy and therefore is also an independent factor of reproduction – factor of the exchange of goods.

Subject (3), property (4) and territorial (6) structures are indicated in the figure in a rather traditional way. The economy should have a standard set of economic entities, it has production units in the form of households, firms, the state, public organizations, as well as foreign firms operating on the territory of the country ('nonresidents'). The property structure corresponds to a combination of the goods of different property, which usually coexist in any modern economy. Since social production is always located spatially, it has a territorial structure, which is quite specific in each country, the figure shows its elements that exist in the Russian Federation: local, municipal, regional, interregional economy, as well as the economy of special territorial rhetoric (coastal waters, recreational areas and zapoveniki, national parks and special economic regions).

Significant changes are required by the traditional sectoral (branch) structure of the economy (5), which provides for three elements: primary, associated with direct use of natural resources, secondary, processing raw materials, and tertiary, providing services. The overdue changes are due to both practical and theoretical reasons.

The vastly expanded modern service sector, often referred to as "infrastructure" in documents and literature, needs functional separation. First, an increase in the share of costs in public production for services for all business entities requires their new classification to avoid repeated counting and duplication. Secondly, our study of households, showing the complete archaic and ineffectiveness of the concept of 'usefulness of a good' and the need to replace it with a more specific concept that reflects the result of the functioning of households, a concept that is not important only for the theory of pricing and formation in individual markets, but also for determining the value of the aggregate product. Thirdly, the production of many services by the state necessitates the development of an appropriate standard nomenclature and the calculation of direct prices of public services, regardless of whether they are paid or free of charge, in the composition of the prices of all products produced in the economy. The attribution of infrastructural enterprises and organizations to the commercial or state sectors of the economy is not of fundamental importance, since the benefits created by the state, from the point of view of the 'theory of public choice', also obey the universal laws of pricing.

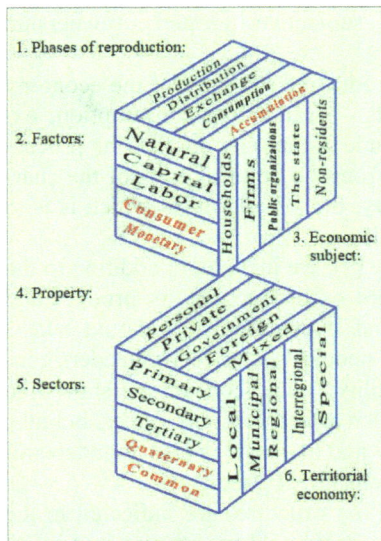

Therefore, in the tertiary sectors of the sectoral structure of the economy, we include economic units that provide services to production: 1) firms that provide producers with land (land plots), labor (labor exchanges and employment firms), capital goods-real estate (stock exchanges trading perpetual securities - shares), means and items of production (wholesalers, trading houses and commodity exchanges); 2) repair and engineering organizations; 3) institutions for retraining and advanced training of personnel of firms.

In the 'quaternary' sectors of the economy, we include households and enterprises with a wide social infrastructure that contribute to the reproduction

Fig. II.28

of labor resources ('collective worker'): 1) retail trade enterprises (shops, fairs and auctions); 2) public catering enterprises (kitchen factories, buffets, cafes, canteens, restaurants); 3) health care institutions (maternity hospitals, pioneer camps, physical culture institutions, fitness clubs, dispensaries, boarding houses, home and recreation centers, sanatoriums, hospitals); 4) institutions of upbringing, education and religion (nurseries, kindergartens, schools, boarding schools, colleges, technical schools, universities, libraries, Internet companies, places of worship); 5) consumer services enterprises (home service firms, dry-cleaners, laundries, hairdressers, ateliers, repair firms, ritual firms); 6) housing and communal organizations (housing cooperatives, homeowners' associations and housing repair enterprises); 7) leisure and entertainment establishments (television and radio companies, theaters, cinemas, museums, clubs, societies, stadiums, tourist and recreational firms and organizations, hippodromes and other gambling establishments).

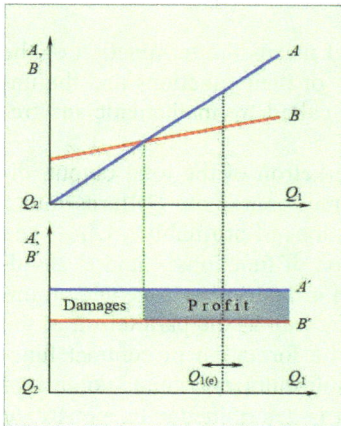

Fig. II.29

Finally, in the national market there is also a sphere of general economic services (in the sectoral (sectoral) structure 5 in Fig. II. 28 – this is the heading 'General'), including: 1) enterprises of heat, electricity, gas, water supply and sewerage; 2) transport enterprises (railway, automobile, water, air, pipeline), postal, electrical, television and radio communications); 3) savings market firms (financial organizations that trade in urgent primary securities and their derivatives (derivatives), universal, innovative, investment, venture and clearing banks, as well as pawnshops); 4) auxiliary firms (consulting, information, advertising, legal, arbitration and insurance); 5) intermediary firms (barter, dealer, real estate, distribution, agency, brokerage, rental and leasing).

Since the equilibrium of the economy is a situation in which the entire set of acting forces is in a state of mutual balance, then macroeconomic theory in a broad sense should consider the equilibria between the elements of all six structures indicated above. Therefore, there are theories of reproductive, interfactorial, intersubjective, intersectoral, territorial equilibrium, as well as the equilibrium of forms of ownership. which we list in the sequence corresponding to their importance for maroeconomics. This monograph mainly examines the existing ones and proposes new concepts of reproductive and interfactor general economic equilibrium (GEE). The criterion for such a selection is the very nature of macroeconomics – it is the reproductive and factor approaches, as well as the possibilities of aggregating indicators, imple-

133

mented in this part of the economics.

Further, we will consider the reproductive balance of the economy.

The theory of this form of equilibrium, using only aggregate indicators, is usually part of macroeconomics[1]. But there is also a technique in microeconomics that allows you to carry out a multivariate analysis of the equilibrium of the national market. It consists in opposing one good (Q_1) to all others in the form of an aggregate indicator (Q_2). The trick will also simplify our modeling with the help of a set of functions and operations usual for the study of local equilibrium.

But the emerging new quality of the model means the termination of the ceteris paribus prerequisite, the 'straightening' of their functions and the uncertainty of the sought equilibrium, which is called by mathematicians 'redefinition of the system of equations'.

In Fig. II.29 depicts the corresponding marketron of the total output, divided into Q_1 and Q_2, (on the graphs, the output coordinate Q_2 turns into a point) with linear integral and differential functions of profitability (A, A) and consumption (B, B) production. The intersection of functions A and B, dividing the entire output field of the model into an ordinary loss zone and an unboundedly increasing profit zone to the right, as well as the parallelism of the demand functions A' and supply B', exclude the formation of contract functions AB and AB' equilibrium price. The equilibrium maximum volume of output ($Q_{1(e)}$) in this case, if it is established, it is determined exogenously, or by the limitations of market counter-agents – the resource capabilities of producers and the paying capacity of consumers of the goods, – or an arbitrary norm world. The total profit for a given interposition of the model's functions also cannot be reasonably divided by the profits of the market counterparties.

Such an extreme embarrassing situation in marginal neoclassics is similar to the approach adopted in the theory of the GEE by the neo-Ricardian Sraffa, which directs us towards solving this methodological problem, which is relevant for both directions of modern economics.

The problem will be removed if we apply the ceteris paribus premise to the foreign market of the economy under consideration, which will mean not its isolation, 'closedness', but only the invariability of the quantitative characteristics of foreign economic activity, but also the preservation of the usual tools of nonlinear functions in the study of the GEE.

To preserve the tools isospend, isocost and isoquant in the analysis of reproductive macroeconomic equilibrium, the literature usually opposes two of any kind, which makes this analysis rather abstract. But it is possible to oppose a separate good to the rest of the mass of goods in the form of an aggregate indicator. However, we will concretize the analysis of the economy as

---

[1] The methodology for aggregating the most important indicators of the economy is discussed by us in section 11 of the monograph.

much as possible, considering it as a two-sector one, according to the abscissas Q_1 and Q_2 we will postpone the sums of total outputs, respectively, of means of production and consumer goods in real terms, and according to the ordinate – the sums of production costs, sales and profitability of consumption these benefits in nominal terms.

To quantitatively characterize the definition of perfectly competitive Pareto equilibria, we will use, as the author himself did, the 'Edgeworth-Bowley diagram' ('box', 'packing-case') – a research tool, developed by Edgeworth[1] and his compatriot Arthur Bowley (1869-1957) (*Mathematical Foundations of Economics*, 1924) (hereinafter – 'Edgeworth diagram'). Not only competitive, but also contractual (contractual) relations of business entities are assumed.

In Fig. II.30 presents the Edgeworth diagrams of equilibrium of production of goods. This is a rectangle formed by two identical coordinates directed one against the other and corresponding to the volume of production of means of production (Q_1) and consumer goods (Q_2). The abscissas show the size of the labor force (L) and the amount of capi-

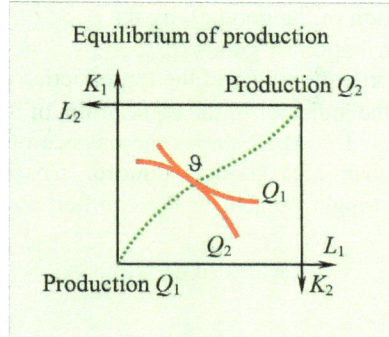

Equilibrium of production

Fig. II.30

tal goods, including land (K), available in the economy. The dotted diagonal curve on the diagram, consisting of all points of the combination of outputs Q_1 and Q_2, we call the function of production competition[2]. The study of the diagram shows that equilibrium at the points of contact (Ɵ) of production functions (isoquants) requires equality of the coefficients of the limiting technological substitution of capital goods by the labor force of producers of two groups of goods (β_{pr}): $\beta_{pr} = -dK/dL$. β_{pr} we call the indicator of equilibrium of production. A touch of the isoquants of the diagram indicates the Pareto efficiency of the equilibrium of production, since an increase in employment in it can only occur due to a reduction in the use of capital goods.

Next, we turn to the equilibrium of the second phase of reproduction – distribution. His Pareto analysis is important because it covers the distribution of

---

[1] However, Edgeworth's priority in the study of economics using this model is disputed (see: [14, p. 564]).
[2] This curve was erroneously called by Edgeworth a "contract function", but its name stuck in the economic literature (see, for example: [116, p. 210]), although, for example, the American economist Kenneth Boulding (1910-1993) spoke about it as a "conflict curve" (see: [7, p. 44]). The element of the Edgeworth diagram, which is really a 'contract function', will be discussed below.

both factors and production results. To do this, we represent the competition curve in the coordinates of the quantities of goods produced '$Q_1 - Q_2$' (Fig. II.31) in the form of isospenda B, since it, first of all, reflects the constant monetary expenditures of all combinations of volumes of passage production of these goods. Function B is convex with negative slope due to the law of diminishing production efficiency under the premise of ceteris paribus. At the equilibrium point of the distribution process (9), falling on the maximum possible total output, an increase in the output of means of production, according to the Pareto-optimal criterion, is possible only by reducing the production of consumer goods. We call the corresponding coefficient of marginal substitution of the good Q_2 by the good Q_1 the indicator of the equilibrium of the distribution of goods (β_{dis}, $\beta_{dis} = -dQ_{2(B)}/dQ_{1(B)}$), which, under the conditions of proportionality of the reproduction process in the economy, should be equal to the indicator of the equilibrium of their production: $\beta_{dis} = \beta_{pr}$.

Fig. II.32 shows the balance of the third phase of reproduction – the exchange of goods produced. This is done with the help of isocost AB – a straight tangent at the equilibrium point 9 of isospenda B. Isocost, being a projection of the horizontal section of the actual contractual (budgetary) function of the same name AB, characterizes the counterparty market relations of producers and consumers of products. Unlike nonlinear functions A and B, each equilibrium function AB is directly proportional to the amount of goods sold, and its slope is determined by the ratio of the prices of these goods (X_1, X_2). Therefore, the process of market exchange between counterparties of the national market is Pareto-optimal if an increase in sales of some good (dQ_1) is possible only by reducing purchases of another good ($-dQ_2$). The corresponding coefficient of the marginal exchange price substitution of goods (β_{ex}, $\beta_{ex} = -dQ_{2(AB)}/dQ_{1(AB)}$) we call the Pareto-equilibrium indicator of exchange, which, under conditions of proportionality of social reproduction, should be equal to the equilibrium indicators production and distribution: $\beta_{ex} = \beta_{dis} = \beta_{pr}$.

In the economic literature, the study of the fourth phase of reproduction – the consumption of goods – has long been carried out on the basis of the concept of 'utility' (U). The corresponding Edgeworth diagram (Fig. II.33, a) is a rectangle formed by two coordinate systems located opposite each other in such a way that the aggregate volumes of means of production (Q_1) and objects consumption (Q_2) are constant. All possible proportions in the consump-

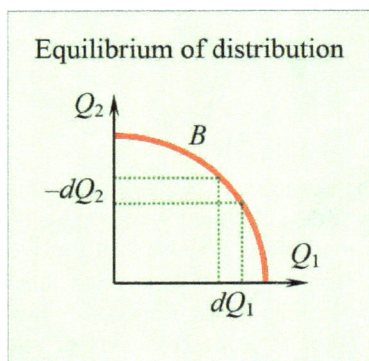

Equilibrium of distribution

Fig. II.31

tion of these goods fit into the function of consumer competition (dotted line in the figure).

The analysis of this diagram shows that here the Pareto efficiency is established when the isoquants of utility of the coefficients of the marginal substitutability of the good Q_2 with the good Q_1 are equal at the points of contact 9 for all their consumers. According to the existing methodology for the study of multifactorial equilibrium, the function of consumer competition is transformed into the so-called 'function of consumption capabilities' (U), similar to the isospende B, which is formed during production modeling, and is already depicted in the coordinates '$U_1 - U_2$', which began, in fact, to replace the utility of real mass consumers of products or households with the utility of abstract individuals (Fig. II.33, b). The function U is also convex, reflecting the action of the ceteris paribus premise, that is, the diminishing efficiency of the process of consumption of substitutable goods.

Based on the foregoing, the consumption process should be interpreted as Pareto-equilibrium if it can increase the utility of any individual (dU_1) only by reducing the utility of another individual ($-dU_2$). The quantitative expression of the Pareto equilibrium of the consumption process is the negative coefficient of the marginal substitutability of the utilities of the consumed goods (β_{co} $\beta_{co} = -dU_{2(U)}/dU_{1(U)}$).

The Pareto consumption efficiency model has been used in the theory of welfare. Since the function U characterizes a certain upper limit, limiting the growth of utility, it began to be interpreted as a general expression of the maximum Pareto welfare. However, since a specific set of actions of business entities can lead not only to an increase, but also to a redistribution of welfare, not all of these actions have begun to be assessed as preferable. Pareto proposed a criterion for the growth of welfare, which is considered quite simple and excludes the redistribution of welfare. According to this criterion, the growth of welfare, say, from the point of the initial level of utility U_0 lying inside the region bounded by the function U (and this growth is called 'Pareto improvements'), should occur only in a rectangular sector of the graph in radial directions, indicated by dotted arrows (Fig. II.33, b). All other changes in the economy, including the movement according to the very function of consumer opportunities, cannot be assessed by the Pareto criterion, except as unwanted.

It is important to emphasize that Pareto believed that all movements along

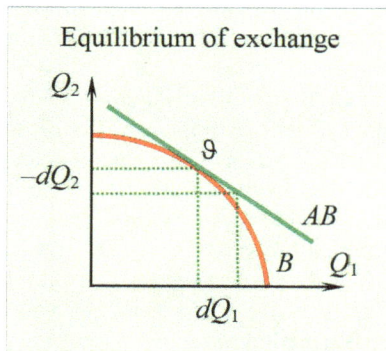

Equilibrium of exchange

Fig. II.32

137

the U line should be excluded due to the fact that they characterize a pure, allegedly 'unfair' redistribution of welfare. However, the specific state of "society can be Pareto optimal, – notes the Indian-English economist Amartya Sen (b. 1933) (*Collective Choice and Public Welfare*, 1970; *On Ethics and Economics*, 1987), – but at the same time some may be in extreme poverty, while others – to swim in luxury, since the poverty of some cannot be mitigated without reducing the level of luxury of the rich" [103, p. 53].

It is believed that in the matter of human well-being, the positive part of economic theory collides with its normative part[1]. It is accepted that well-being has a dichotomy, includes 'economic well-being', which is the result of competitive consumption of goods, and 'social welfare' defined by equity. Therefore, in practice, one supposedly always has to choose between efficiency and fairness. But supporters of the existence of the welfare dichotomy have methodological problems associated with the need for concrete expression of such ethical concepts as 'good', 'fair', 'desirable', 'undesirable', etc. And here the problem of welfare uncertainty reappears, as the English economist Ian Little (1918-2012) (*Critique of Welfare Economics*, 1950) has shown.

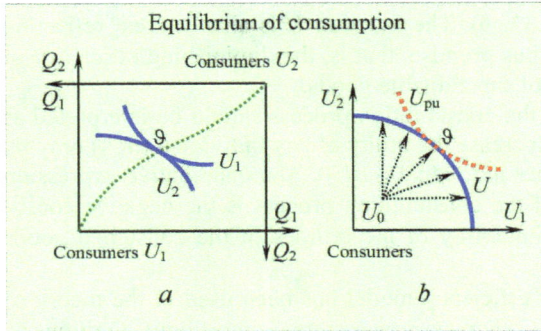

Fig. II.34

Contrary to the Paretian model of welfare and the concept of its dichotomy, Pigou (*Economics of Welfare*, 1920) believed that the redistribution of wealth in favor of low-income social groups can increase aggregate welfare, since in an 'unfair' society the relative standard of living of the poor grows $(\omega_p = (dU/U)_p)$ more significant than the decrease in the standard of living of the rich $(\omega_{ri} = (-dU/U)_{ri}, \omega_p > |\omega_{ri}|$, the vertical lines at the second coefficient of elasticity denote that that they are considered without regard to the sign, that is, as modules). But even with this approach, an effective measure of the redistribution of the welfare of members of society also remains uncertain and very subjective.

In the future, the theory of welfare tried to overcome its own limitations in two ways: 1) using the 'Kaldor-Hicks compensation criterion' proposed by

---

[1] This problem exists not only in macroeconomics, but also in microeconomics. For example, there is a positive 'behavioral theory of the firm' and a normative 'management theory of the firm'.

Kaldor[1] (*The Theorem of Welfare in Economics and Interpersonal Compari-sons of Utility*, 1939), Hicks (*Foundations of Welfare Economics*, 1939) and developed by the American economist Tibor Skitovski (1910-2002) (*Welfare and Competition*, 1951); 2) the introduction into the Pareto model of the 'function of public welfare (public utility)' (U_{pu}), which provides for a certain rule (*f*) for the inclusion of individual utility (U_i) in this public utility ($U_{pu} = f(U_i))^2$.

Kaldor and Hicks, also not recognizing this dichotomy of welfare, deep-ened Pareto's purely economic approach and proposed a monetary criterion for compensating for injustice arising from the redistribution of utility. They substantiated the conduct of first virtual, and subsequently real compromise calculations between economic entities (determining payments-compensation) for their new, redistributed welfare. However, many economists disagree with this approach due to the alleged incompatibility of the emerging forms of wel-fare. Thus, the American economist William Bowmoll (1922-2017) (*Eco-nomic Theory and Operational Analysis*, 1961) and Sen (*Collective Choice and Public Welfare*, 1970) believe that such a criterion cannot solve the prob-lem, because it translates it on a monetary basis unacceptable for social wel-fare. In our opinion, social welfare, like economic welfare, has a competitive basis and monetary dimension.

In general, the calculations of compensation proposed by Kaldor and Hicks also do not lead to finding a positivist balance-well-being due to their subjectivity.

Despite the fact that the very convexity property of the 'consumption func-tion' U (see Fig. II.33) allows us to determine its equilibrium point ('hap-piness point') corresponding to the maximum sum of total utility, the Ameri-can economist Abram Bergson (1914 2003) (*Reformulation of some Aspects of Welfare Economics*, 1938), in fact, unwittingly artificially complicating the task, proposed a 'public welfare function' in the form of an indifference func-tion (isoquants) (this is the dashed curve in Fig. II.33), superimposed on the 'function of consumer possibilities'. The 'Bergson function' in combination with the economic function of demanding capabilities U supposedly allows you to optimize the latter (the optimum is at the point of tangency of 9 func-tions).

Following the 'Bergson function' in the theory of welfare, a whole series of functions was proposed, built according to different criteria of social justice

---

[1] According to the Russian economist Rustem Nureyev (b. 1950) [78, p. 368] Barone was the first to make similar proposals for achieving social justice in his article *The Ministry of Industry in a Collectivist State* (1908). However, the article deals only with the use of 'shadow prices' in the planned economy.

[2] In modern economic theory, the concept of the inclusion of public utility in the individual utility of goods has appeared (see: [30]).

(Fig. II.34, the dotted bisector characterizes the fair, equal, utility of consumers of goods):

1) the maximax 'Nietzsche function' ($U_N = \max(\max U_i)$), adequate to the ideas of the German philosopher Friedrich Nietzsche (1844-1900) about the need to further maximize the welfare of the rich, the elite of society;

2) 'Bentham's function' ($U_B = \Sigma(U_i)$), which allows the redistribution of welfare and is consistent with the views of the English sociologist Jeremiah Bentham (1748-1832) (*Introduction to the Principles of Morality and Legislation*, 1780) on the need to sum up the utility of individuals, providing "the greatest happiness to the greatest number of people" [8, p. 321] (therefore, the point of an unjust society U_0 according to Bentham may correspond to the maximum total welfare);

3) 'Nash function' ($U_{Na} = \Pi(U_i)$) – a version of the 'Bergson isoquant' developed by Nash (*Cooperative Games of Two Persons*, 1953) from the standpoint of game theory, which provides for a product (in the function of this operation is indicated by the sign 'Π') of the 'weighted' utilities of individuals;

4) the maximin 'Rawls' function' ($U_{Ro} = \max(\min U_i)$), which maximizes the growth of the well-being of the poor within the limits, developed on the basis of ideas about justice of the American philosopher John Rawls (1921-2002) (*Theory of Justice*, 1971).

Analyzing the issues of the existing theory of welfare, it is impossible not to dwell on the so-called welfare theorems, formulated by Lerner *(Economics of Control. Principles of the Economics of Welfare*, 1944), Lange (*On the Economic Theory of Socialism*, 1936, 1937; *Foundations of Economics Welfare*, 1942), and strictly reformulated by the American economist Kenneth Arrow (1921-2017) (*Public Choice and Individual Values*, 1951).

Since there are three such theorems, of which the first and second have retained their names in the economic literature, and the third has an initial key value, we will call it the "zero" welfare theorem.

The zero welfare theorem, considered by Arrow as a "theorem of possibility", but rightly renamed by Sen as a "theorem of impossibility"[1], states that the function of social preference cannot be derived from data on the totality of individual preferences (welfare, public utility). Having developed a strict logical algorithm for solving the problem of constructing a function, Arrow formulated the "public welfare dilemma", which consists in the fact that with the assumption of the existence of sovereignty and rationality of consumers, it is impossible to determine the social a priority that would correspond to individual priorities, and this or that welfare that actually exists in society is built on the sovereignty of a 'dictator' – a person or institution that influences the

---

[1] Some authors call this theorem "Arrow's paradox" (see, for example: [2, p. 201]).

choice of individuals. Society itself is not in a position, as Arrow believes, to form a collective opinion about what it should strive for.

Such a pessimistic view of the problem completely undermines the possibilities for the development of the theory of welfare and the reproductive GEE in general.

The conclusion about the impossibility of developing a function or indicator of public welfare, made by Arrow on the basis of the marginalist principle of 'methodological individualism', led to the development of mathematical and statistical aggregate indicators that comprehensively characterize the welfare of society. For example, as an alternative to the indicator of the average per capita product, the 'human development index' (*Human Development Report (1991-2000)*, 1990)[1] was developed, taking into account material well-being, the quality of the labor force (level of education) and human longevity.

However, even the most perfect statistical indicators should have a general theoretical basis, which is currently absent in the theory of welfare.

Many researchers note the weakness of modern welfare theory. "In general, the conclusions reached by the economic theory of welfare are predominantly negative: economists have failed to formulate indisputable rules for deciding which results are desirable and which are not" [85, p. 632]. The authoritative authors of the economic dictionary *New Palgrave*

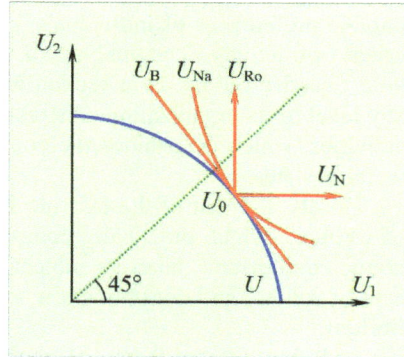

Fig. II.34

also note the lack of validity of the welfare policy: "What can be said about the economic theory of welfare today? The first and second theorems indicate that the market mechanism has great merit: competitive equilibrium and Pareto optimality are rigidly connected. But measuring the size of the economic 'pie' or making judgments about its division leads to paradoxes and insurmountable difficulties, generalized by the third ('zero' – *the author*) theorem. And this is a tragedy. We feel like we know, like Adam Smith, which policies are improving the well-being of nations. But due to theoretical difficulties we cannot prove this" [118, p. 885].

However, let's not indulge in pessimism and look at the problems of welfare theory from the perspective of the new knowledge we presented in the monograph above. More specifically, three weaknesses can be justified in the existing theory of public welfare and GEE.

---

[1] See, for example: [94, p. 107].

Firstly, this is the above-examined non-elaboration of the category 'utility of a good', which lies at the basis of the category of 'public utility'. The operations of summation, multiplication, division, 'compensation', 'weighing', etc. proposed by different authors. usefulness does not make sense if we do not know the specific expression of the indicated category. In fact, Bergson and his followers piled up on the already known isoquants of utility other, also inoperative, isoquants, which cannot solve the problem of the theory of welfare.

Secondly, it is erroneous to base the theory of welfare on the principle of 'methodological individualism' – a simplified notion of the 'atomicity' of society, a notion that leads to Arrow's late-peak 'impossibility theorem'. Let us pay attention, in this regard, to the fact that in the models of Pareto efficiency we should talk not about individuals, but about firms and households, the functioning of which is built, although on the sovereign and often incomparable preferences of individuals. , but according to universal, 'end-to-end' criteria of activity. The analysis of the criteria for the functioning of households, carried out by us in section 6 of the monograph, shows that society at any level of its organization adheres to a single criterion of the profitability of activities, which determines the competitive and natural formation of public welfare. states.

Thirdly, the exit of the existing Pareto modeling to a kind of 'philosophy of welfare', which practically completes the existing theory of 'general economic equilibrium', takes its subject aside, into the 'jungle' of the useful concept of welfare and does not allow solving the problems of reproductive equilibrium.

And, fourthly, the theory of 'general economic equilibrium' does not consider all five reproductive processes, limiting itself to the analysis of production and consumption or only exchange in an arbitrary sequence, which also does not give the desired scientific result – the parameters of the only equilibrium of the economy.

The first welfare theorem was for the first time not strictly, intuitively formulated by Smith: "Each individual person ... takes into account his own benefit, ... he certainly helps to ensure that the annual income of society was as large as possible" [109, p. 441-443]. The first and second welfare theorems in Arrow's strict version are reciprocal and state only obvious connections. If his first theorem asserts that a perfectly competitive economy is Pareto efficient[1], then the second theorem proves that a Pareto efficient economy is per-

---

[1] The first theorem, which equates the competitive equilibrium of the economy with its maximum efficiency, Arrow himself formulates as follows: "If competitive equilibrium exists at all, and if all goods ... have market prices, then the equilibrium is necessarily optimal in ... the exact sense (according to Pareto) ..." [134, p. 294].

142

fectly competitive[1]. It can also be argued that Arrow's null 'impossibility theorem' does not reflect reality. Thus, the long history of the development of welfare theory as an integral part of the GEE theory returned to the original Pareto methodology. And this is symptomatic, since the improvement of the already become classical model of Pareto efficiency allows you to move the object from the 'dead center'. To do this, in the Edgeworth diagram describing the consumption of goods, we introduce instead of utility U the indicator of profitability-welfare of society A and make some other adjustments in it.

In Fig. II.35, a, depicts a model of the reproductive equilibrium of the economy with a three-coordinate interaction of the producers and consumers of goods available in it. The figure shows only the coordinates themselves, which form a full-fledged, three-dimensional Edgeworth diagram. Its content in the form of a set of functions has been omitted for simplicity. But rice. II.35, b, is a section of this diagram, in which the interconnected functions of total expenditures B and income A completely coincide and merge into one dotted line, on which there is a common one for economics is the equilibrium point of a particu-

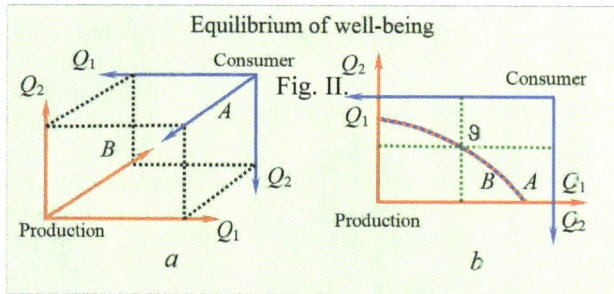

Fig. II.35

lar countable welfare. In the light of the proposed "eocardinalism", the above definition of the equilibrium of consumption acquires operationality and can be reformulated as follows: the process of consumption is Pareto-equilibrium if the gain of any good can be increased (dQ_1) only by reducing the consumption of other or other goods $(-dQ_2)$. The coefficient of the marginal demand substitution of goods (β_{co}, $\beta_{co} = -dQ_{2(A)}/dQ_{1(A)}$) we call the indicator of the Pareto equilibrium of consumption. Since the proportions of the equilibrium of consumption, as well as the proportions of the equilibria of distribution, exchange are determined by the equilibrium point of production, the following general equilibrium of these phases of reproduction will be fair: $\beta_{co} = \beta_{ex} = \beta_{dis} = \beta_{pr}$.

Comparison of the new and traditional concepts of well-being, which can be conditionally called "A-concept" and "U-concept", respectively, shows that

---

[1] Arrow himself formulates the second welfare theorem as follows: "... if there is no increasing return in production, and if other secondary conditions are met, then each optimal state – a competitive equilibrium corresponding to some initial distribution of purchasing power" [134, p. 295].

the above 'unfair' reto-improvements, as well as 'Pareto-deterioration', leading to a redistribution or decrease in utility, in the 'A-concept' are quite admissible and fair, since they only testify to changes in the efficiency of business entities, firms and households. That is, welfare is also competitive. If the household functions ineffectively, then the equilibrium theory has no right to introduce a Paretian ban on the redistribution of welfare, which should be decided not in the theory of competitive GEE, but in the theory of state regulation of the social market economy. In fact, the Pareto criterion of efficiency, establishes the framework for the growth of well-being, is an instrument of normative economic theory. The issues of modeling competitive GEE are related to the positive theory.

Let us turn to the last, fifth phase of the reproduction of the economy – the accumulation of goods. What is its Pareto equilibrium and how does it compare with the above equilibria? Note that these questions in paretian and subsequent economic theory are not covered at all.

To answer the questions, first of all, we point out that in a mutual equilibrium state the functions A, B and AB on the plane $Q_1 - Q_2$ touch each other at the same vertically point (ϑ), but in the volumetric figure $f(Q_1, Q_2, A, B, AB)$ are located at different levels (Fig. II.36), since in magnitude the total income exceeds the amount of the contract, and that is more than the total costs. The difference between A_e and B_e on the darkened horizontal sections of the figure represents the aggregated profit of the M_{ag} economy, which is maximized under market conditions, turns into pure investment and characterizes the scale of the process of accumulation of benefits, any displacements of the vertical plane of equilibrium from the point ϑ will mean a decrease in

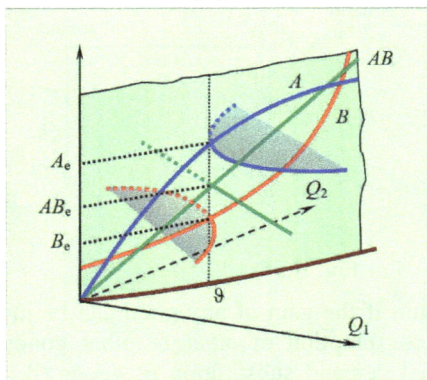

Fig. II.36

M_{ag} and will be considered ineffective. Therefore, the process of accumulation is Pareto-equilibrium, if in a growing economy it is possible to increase the output of means of production (dQ_1) only through a proportional increase in the number of consumer goods (dQ_2).

The points of contact of the series isospend, isocost and isoquant, B, A, AB, depicted in the usual form in the coordinates '$Q_1 - Q_2$' (Fig. II.37), concretize the balance of expanded reproduction, as well as the direction of economic development. The curve with an arrow (D) connecting the points ϑ_1 and ϑ_2, which we presented above as a function the development of a sepa-

144

rate market, now as a function of the equilibrium economic growth preferable for society, can be called a "preference" (from the Latin word praeferre – to establish a preferention, prefer). "The line of preference ..., – wrote about the curve Edgeworth, – is perpendicular to the line of indifference" (unimportant – *the author*) [139, p. 22]. The ratio dQ_2 to dQ_1 on preference D as the coefficient of the marginal complementarity of these goods is called the Pareto-equilibrium index of accumulation (γ_{ac}): $\gamma_{ac} = dQ_{2(D)}/dQ_{1(D)}$.

Thus, the process of extended reproduction of a perfectly competitive economy is Pareto-equilibrium if its indicator (θ) is equal to the indicator of the marginal complementarity of goods in the accumulation phase and to the indicators of the marginal substitutability of goods in the phases of their consumption, exchange, distribution and production, which can be expressed by the following marginal equation: $\theta = \gamma_{ac} = \beta_{co} = \beta_{ex} = \beta_{dis} = \beta_{pr}$ (all indicators here are given in the form of modules).

At the end of the analysis of the multifactorial reproductive GEE, it should be emphasized that the Edgeworth diagram as a theoretical tool allows one to determine the proportions of an idealized, maximally effective and perfectly competitive self-balancing economies. The real economies, for a number of reasons, first of all, the presence of market defects[1], does not reach the maximum efficiency, which means that in reality the isospendas and isoquants of the diagrams do not concern are each other at one point, and intersect with an overlap, forming a certain area – the so-called core of the model[2], which contains a certain compact set of equilibria and indicates the presence in the economy unemployed workers and jobs. And here the very type of the GEE model considered by us is manifested – although it is reproductive, it does not explain the reasons for the formation of

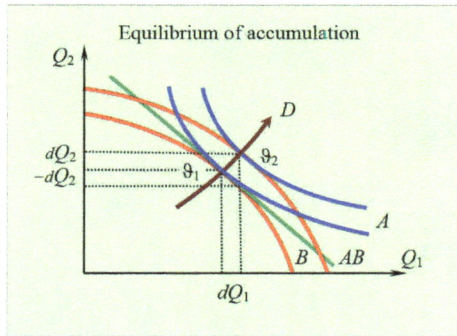

Fig. II.37

an excess of reproduction factors. macroeconomics requires not only models that show general objective reasons for the formation of equilibrium, but also those that substantiated recipes for neutralizing market defects.

One more conclusion can be drawn – a conclusion from a comparative

---

[1] The system of defects in the market mechanism for the functioning of the economy will be discussed in section 15 of the monograph.

[2] In the language of game theory, this means the presence of coalitional (cooperative) decision-making by a part of economic entities, and the model of the economy itself is called a game with a nonzero sum of participants' gains.

analysis of the mainstream and 'neo-Ricardianism': the rate of profit of the Sraffa model of 'production price' improved by us above can be filled with the results of the just conducted marginal research multi-factorial GEE, which made it possible to determine the equilibrium value of the total accumulation.

Since this section concludes the second chapter of the monograph, we express the hope that the corrections contained in it and certain advances in solving the problems of mainstream microeconomic theory allow us to approach the exhaustion of the 'dispute of two Cambridges'.

CHAPTER III
SYSTEM UPDATE MACROECONOMIX TO COMPLETE THE 'DISPUTE OF TWO CAM-BRIDGES'

11. Aggregate indicators of economics and neoclassical her equilibrium model

The issues of aggregate indicators are of fundamental importance for the analysis of the economy, its structure, growth and regulation, neoclassical and Keynesian GEE schemes, as well as the 'dispute of two Cambridges'.

The issues of aggregate indicators are of fundamental importance for the analysis of the economy, its structure, growth and regulation, neoclassical and Keynesian GEE schemes, as well as the 'dispute of two Cambridges'.

The concept of 'production potential' is defined as the achieved actual annual total output at current prices, averaged over a number of years, that is, as the capacity of the economy.

To select a specific aggregate indicator of the flow of physical aggregate output, let us first consider the so-called gross social product (Q_g), that is, the value of the entire mass of material goods produced in the economy for a year. Q_g is formed by aggregating sectoral or territorial gross products: $Q_g = \Sigma(Q_g)_i$, or $Q_g = \Sigma(Q_g)_j$, where i – the number of the industry, and j – the number of the territorial unit of the economy.

The concept of gross social product has been known since the time of classical political economy, but as a scientific tool it has drawbacks (Fig. III.1). Q_g contains a multiple value account for the sale and purchase of goods along an inter-sectoral technological chain and is characterized by extreme inconsistency, dependence on the organizational structure of production. Only the intensification of the processes of concentration or deconcentration of production, merger or, on the contrary, separation of enterprises, cause respectively a sharp decrease or increase in the so-called total intermediate (Q_{in}) and gross products, while the dynamics of the total end product (Q_{en}), as can be seen from the figure, remains fairly uniform. These circumstances make the Q_g indicator unsuitable for displaying the true results of the functioning of the economy.

Smith (*Investigation of the Nature and Causes of the Wealth of Nations*, 1776) was the first theorist of national wealth, but reduced it only to annual aggregate output. Knowing the main drawback of the country's 'gross income', he considered it necessary to exclude all intermediate product from Q_B. Being one of the pillars of the labor theory of value, Smith interpreted material expenditures as expenditures of the materialized and accumulated past of living labor. He also did not consider the primary, unprocessed natural resources used in production as a price-forming factor.

In fact, in the *Wealth of Nations*, Smith used the 'national income' (Y) of the country as an indicator of the total output, since it is he, according to the labor theory of value, that embodies the costs of living labor. Y is calculated by subtracting all material costs from Q_g. The indicator does not reflect the measure of the use of all its factors in production, but is used in macroeconomic analysis, although it cannot be considered the best for characterizing production potential.

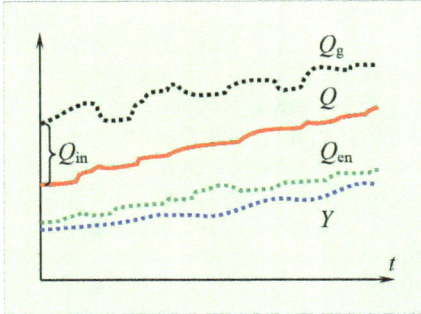

Fig. III.1

The neoclassical three-factor theory of value has not developed in its entire long history of an adequate aggregate indicator of total output. The methodology of national accounts of the American economist Simon Kuznets (1901-1985), created by him at the US National Bureau of Economic Research, gave practice and theory an indicator of the total final product Q_{en}, which distinguishes from Y by including depreciation costs of capital goods for production purposes. This indicator is used by modern international market statistics in the form of gross domestic product (GDP) and gross national product (GNP), which are varieties of Q_{en}. GDP is calculated by the territorial sign, and GNP – by the sign of registration of producers as national economic entities, residents. However, in our opinion, both Q_{en} and its two varieties are also not suitable for characterizing the aggregate output of production and the production potential of the modern economy, since they do not include net costs natural resources[1].

As we have shown[2], the full product contains the costs (depreciation) of all three factors of production, therefore it is the best for characterizing the production potential of the country and at this level can be called simply 'aggregate product' (or simply 'aggregate output') (Q, $Q = C + V + M$, where C, V and M denote land rent, wage and cash flows in real terms)[3]. It is

---

[1] See: [111].

[2] See work in more detail on this issue: [38, c. 265-277].

[3] Usually, in the economic literature, when presenting the issue of aggregate indicators of output, it is immediately indicated on its composition in the form of disposable income, government spending and net exports. We single out these elements from the aggregate product only when considering the production of public goods and foreign trade in sections 15 and 14 of the monograph, respectively.

calculated by subtracting from Q_g not all current material costs, but only their multiple intermediate accounts. The aggregate product also has varieties: 'aggregate domestic product' and 'aggregate national product'.

Since macroeconomic theory examines the national market, it needs not only an indicator of the country's production potential, but also aggregate price indicators that correlate aggregate nominal value streams of adjacent time periods. Economists have developed several price aggregates (deflators): 1) the index proposed by the German statistician Etienne Laspeyres (1834-1913) (X_L) and calculated for the current time period (t) according to the nomenclature of production of the past time period ($t - 1$): $X_L = \Sigma(X_t \cdot Q_{t-1})_i / \Sigma(X_{t-1} \cdot Q_{t-1})_i$ (X_L underestimates price dynamics); 2) the index proposed by the German statistician Hermann Paasche (1851-1925) (X_{Pa}) and calculated as a whole according to the existing nomenclature of production: $X_{Pa} = \Sigma(X_t \cdot Q_t)_i / \Sigma(X_{t-1} \cdot Q_t)_i$ (X_{Π} overestimates price dynamics); 3) Fisher's index (*Compilation of indexes*, 1922) (X_F), calculated as the geometric mean of the indices X_L and X_{Pa}: $X_{\Phi} = \sqrt{X_L \cdot X_{Pa}}$.

The Fisher index, in our opinion, can be modified and represented in the form: $X_F = X_L^k \cdot X_{Pa}^{1-k}$, where k – the coefficient that distributes the 'weights' of the factors. Depending on the nature of the long-term trend of price dynamics, the coefficient k should be given values that allow to compensate for the systematic errors of the Laspeyres and Paasche indices.

All three indices are periodic, and therefore, when presenting the macroeconomic theory, we will use marginal, momentary, price indices.

Price indices allow you to determine the size of stocks and flows of values in real or nominal terms. Dividing, for example, the aggregate product in nominal monetary terms Q_n into X_L allows us to determine the 'real total product' (Q), which we will use as an aggregate indicator-substitute (substitute for) physical aggregate output. Indices inverse to X_L, X_{Pa}, X_F and other similar indices, characterizing the real, market, price of the national monetary unit, can be called inflationary.

Strictly speaking, all factors of production within the framework of the general marginal methodology should be designated as stock values, subject to the amortization mechanisms of their expenditure, reimbursement and accumulation. Value only transforms from one form to another and remains in size. Such a reproduction, amortization, approach to all types of reserves, in theory, is unified and the most effective.

The transformation of a stock into a value stream is the initial phase of depreciation, while its reverse phase – capitalization of value – completes the process of stock reproduction. We analyzed the first phase of depreciation in section 5 of the monograph, but here, at the level of the economy as a whole, we will consider how, based on the data on the total factor expenditures and incomes (depreciation), it is possible to determine the resource and economic potentials of the country. If we have chosen a three-factor aggregate as the total output-value stream, then the resource aggregate-value stock must also be a three-factor one.

Let us give a specific example of a full monetary assessment of the country's resource potential, that is, the stock of its national economic factor resources, which can be considered a complete indicator of its 'national wealth'.

If we consider the modern economy, then, for example, let us take the data for the USSR for 1990, that is, a year characterized by the reliability of statistical data. The total end product of the USSR was in nominal prices 1,2 tril in current prices rubles, and its factorial structure was as follows: $Q_{n(1990)} = 1.2$ tril. rub $= 0,4_{-\Delta N} + 0,5_{-\Delta L} + 0,3_{-\Delta K}$, where the indices $-\Delta N$, $-\Delta L$ and $-\Delta K$ denote costly full flows, including profits of natural, labor and capital resources, respectively. Expressing the equation as the sum of expenses (depreciation) of production factors, we can write: $Q_{n(1990)} = B_N + B_L + B_K$. Multiplying these depreciation by the corresponding average life (service, or exhaustion) of production factors (τ), we get their absolute monetary values[1].

The most obvious is the calculation for capital goods, for the so-called production apparatus of the economy. If its average service life (τ_K) in 1990 was 30 years, then multiplying the total 'inflow of 0,3 tril. rubles of cash' as the sum of compensation for depreciation (0,1) and accumulation (0,2) of the production apparatus (B_K), we get: $K_{1990} = B_K \cdot \tau_K = 0,3 \cdot 30 = 9$ tril. rub.

For a monetary estimate of the labor force (total labor force) of a country, data on the service life of an average economic worker is required – the length of his working life (τ_L), which we will define by the demographic pyramid of the population for 1990, that is, by the momentary ratio of different age groups. groups of the population, divided into female and male components. In fig. III.2, *a*, a typical age pyramid of the population (*T*) is presented in the form of a histogram, along the vertical of which is the age of a person (ψ), and horizontally to the left and to the right of zero – the shares of female and male settlements falling on the corresponding small age intervals ($\Delta T_w/\Delta\psi$, $\Delta T_{ma}/\Delta\psi$).

We will not further divide the population into female and male and instead of a histogram we will take a smooth function of the age distribution of the population. The corresponding coordinate system '$\psi - dT/d\psi$' rotated by 90° is shown in Fig. III.2, *b*. The integral (area) of the function $dT/d\psi =$

---

[1] Calculations of resource and economic potentials in this section are simplified by not taking into account discounting of streaming indicators. The question of the economic essence of the discounting standards used to bring values to one point in time is considered by us in section 16 of the monograph.

$= f(\psi)$ is the total population. The vertical lines on the graph indicate formal, legal (dashed lines) and actual, economic, lower (16, 20 years) and upper (57.5; 60 years), the boundaries of the working life of the average statistical individual. type of the USSR in 1990. Zones I and IV of the schedule correspond to unemployed persons of young and old ages, zone III – to persons physically or mentally incapable of work and evading it, as well as the unemployed, and zone II – busy labor resources (shaded part of the graph).

The ratio of the area of zone II to the entire area under the curve of the demographic pyramid is the employment rate of the population (k_{emp}): $k_{emp} = L/T$. It characterizes the labor potential of the population. Even Smith believed that the growth of the wealth of nations depends on the productivity of labor (division of labor) and "the ratio between the number of people engaged in useful labor and the number of people not engaged in it" [109, p. 66]. Therefore, from an economic point of view, the coefficient of the labor potential of the population is best calculated as the ratio of its employed and unoccupied parts ($k_{l.p}$): $k_{l.p} = L/(T - L)$. The reciprocal of the coefficient ($1/k_{l.p} = (T - L)/L$) expresses the demographic burden on labor resources, which is important for calculating wages and pension contributions in the country. In this form, the coefficient $k_{l.p}$ is approximately equal to one for almost all countries, regardless of the level of their socio-economic development. This means that, on average, one working person maintains one dependent, or rather, six working individuals contain three young people, two pensioners and one unemployed person.

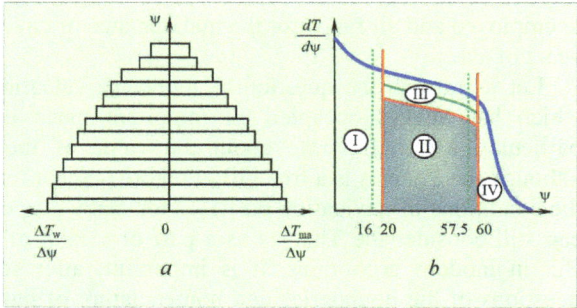

Fig. III.2

There is another important demographic and economic characteristic of the total labor force – the indicator of the rate of its reproduction (ω_{rep}), which is equal to: $\omega_{rep} = (\Delta L + \Delta L_{rel})/L$, where ΔL – the demographic growth of labor resources, and ΔL_{rel} – the number of technologically released workers who need new employment. The indicator reflects not only natural (quantitative, extensive), but also economic (qualitative, intensive) factors of expanded reproduction of the 'aggregate worker'. The intensive component ω_{rep} will be positive also in the case when ΔL_{rel} you exceed the natural decline

151

in labor resources ($-\Delta L$). An analysis of the age structure of the population makes it possible to determine not only the demographic potential of economic development, but also an important parameter for calculating national wealth – the average period of a person's labor activity (τ_L).

The formal, legal, lower limit of a person's work activity in the USSR was 16 years, while the actual, economic border, taking into account the study of some young people in secondary and higher educational institutions, shifted to 20 years. Since the retirement age for women was set at 55 years, and for men – 60 years, then, assuming rounded equal shares of women and men in the population, the average legal retirement age of a person was 57,5 years. Taking into account the availability of working pensioners, the economic upper limit of the country's labor resources was at the level of 60 years. Thus, τ_L was equal to 40 years.

Based on these data and that part of $Q_{H(1990)}$ that was spent on the maintenance of labor resources, that is, the nominal flow of expenses for the reproduction of the total labor force (B_L), we determine its moment value in monetary terms: $L_{1990} = B_L \cdot \tau_L = 0,5 \cdot 40 = 20$ tril. rub. Moreover, it should be noted that 500 billion rubles. were spent on expanded reproduction not only of labor resources, but also of the entire population of the country, since the accrued total wage fund included pension funds, payments to temporarily unemployed and all funds for the maintenance of children and youth under 20 years of age.

Let us turn to the question of monetary valuation of natural resources, which has always occupied an important place in economic theory. In particular, Marshall wrote about the value of the River Thames: "And although the Thames is a free gift of nature (except for the costs of improving the conditions of navigation on it) ..., for many purposes of our research, we can still consider the Thames as a part of wealth of England" [71, p. 109]. But in modern economics, it is important, after solving the fundamental questions of the boundaries and nomenclature of natural wealth, to develop specific calculation schemes for its assessment. With the absolute immensity and inexhaustibility of natural resources, they are always localized and limited in the economy, therefore, they have not a 'service life', but a conditional 'expiration date', the average value of which (τ_N) depends on the structure The flow of these benefits in 1990 was about 100 years. It is the costs of 'adapting' natural resources for use, multiplied by their service life, that will make up their value-stock.

Accordingly, the nominal monetary value of the stock of the entire mass of this natural wealth is calculated in the same way as it was carried out above in relation to capital and labor resources: $N_{1990} = B_N \cdot \tau_N = 0,4 \cdot 100 = 40$ tril. rub.

The monetary expression of the country's resource potential as a whole

(W_{1990}) is also equal to the sum of monetary estimates of all three factors of production: $W_{1990} = N + L + K = 40 + 20 + 9 = 69$ tril. rub.

When the question of assessing the 'economic potential' of an object of any level – firms, industries, regions, national or world economies – is raised, the answer is usually twofold: data are given either on the production capacity of the object, or on the availability of economic resources – natural, capital, labor and others. These data individually can distort the idea of economic potential. To achieve unambiguity, objectivity and comparability of economic potentials, we propose to express them in the form of a ratio of production and resource potentials (efficiency of the economy, a general indicator of production efficiency, R). For the same 1990, the R indicator was equal to: $R_{1990} = Q_{n(1990)}/W_{1990} = 1,2/69 = 0,017$ (1,7%). In the USSR, it was 2.5 times lower than in highly developed countries. R is the ratio of the value stream to the value stock, therefore the essence of the indicator is quite simple – it is the depreciation rate of the national wealth (v) as the reciprocal of its average service life (τ), equal in our example to 58.8 years. Of course, this period is mobile and 'sliding', it is a constantly existing 'horizon' of the country's development. Since all elements of the aggregate product – rent (B_N), wages (B_L) and gross profit (B_K) include surplus parts, 'dividends', the ratio of their sum as a 'national dividend' to the national wealth is an indicator of the rate of growth of the latter.

When calculating the potential of the country's total labor force, we used normative and empirical data on the service life of workers. The existing general historical tendencies of an increase in the educational level of the labor force and an

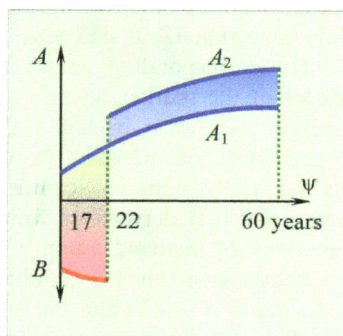

Fig. III.3

increase in both the average age of a person's entry into the working period and this period itself can be modeled.

The justification for the shift in the actual lower age limit of the labor force associated with higher education can be illustrated using the Minser model (*Investments in Human Capital and the Distribution of Personal Income*, 1958), which compares educational costs and incomes over the entire adult life of a representative individual (Fig. III.3). The model has a coordinate of a person's age, starting with a 17-year decision to find a job or continuing for five years of university studies and ending with a 60-year completion of employment, as well as coordinates of the corresponding educational expenses (B), measured down, and income from work without higher education (A_1) and with that (A_2), measured up the graph of the model.

It is assumed that B, A_1 and A_2 increase over time, A_2 is greater than A_1, and earnings for the period 17-22 years are considered lost profits when studying at a university and are included as indirect costs (B_{ind}) along with direct costs (B_{str}) in total costs education: $B = B_{str} + B_{ind}$. The concept of the efficiency of investments in higher education of Minser is to calculate its profitability (G_{ed}) as the ratio of profit (($A_2 - A_1$)$_{43}$ − (B)$_{43}$) discounted for the entire 43-year period and costs ((B)$_{43}$) of additional education (these indicators are equal to the areas under the curves B, A_1 and A_2). Investments in this education and the corresponding shifts in the lower limit of labor resources will be advisable in the case of an approximate equality of G_{ed} to the bank's percentage G_b.

Minser's model was created quite a long time ago and it, of course, could be developed by supplementing the calculations on the shift of the lower economic boundary of labor resources with the calculations of the shifts of their upper boundary. But it would be much more interesting from a theoretical and practical point of view to determine the equilibrium values of the entire period of labor activity of the joint employee in years and, so to speak, the price of a year of his labor, since this would allow to optimize not only educational, but also pension sphere of the economy.

The corresponding 'marketron', that is, a complete integral-differential model of the market, in this case, the labor market by the service life of workers, is shown in Fig. III.4. In its integral part, there are functional dependences of income (A), expenses (B) and the amount of the labor contract (AB) on the service life of the joint employee (τ_L), and in its marginal part – the first derivatives from A, B and AB (A', B' and AB'), which are functions of demand, supply and price (X) of the service life τ_L. The marketron shows the profitability of both the labor of the aggregate employee (M_{la}, $M_{la} = A - AB$) and the aggregate educational costs for it (M_{ed}, $M_{ed} = AB - B$). Equilibrium X_e and $\tau_{L(e)}$ account for the maximum overall profitability of the functioning of the aggregate employee.

Thus, similar models can be developed to optimize the life of the land and the production apparatus of the country.

We examined the extremely aggregated value indicators of the economy. But neoclassical and many Keynesian models of macroeconomy are built on other indicators, often more convenient and visual, but simplified. This is the 'number of people employed', instead of the 'labor lease time' for the market of the same name, this is 'interest' as a price for capital markets, savings and investments instead of 'the amount of debt repaid with interest' and others are not quite correct. Correct indicators. Since they have already entered the well-known models of economics, we keep them in the author's form in further critical analysis. But when considering certain issues of the theory of equilibria, requiring homogeneity in functional dependencies, we will also

154

operate with precise aggregate indicators.

In macroeconomics, there is still no full justification for the various monetary aggregates used in practice. To describe the money market, in our opinion, an incorrect system of coordinates is used, in particular, the same 'percentage' is considered the price coordinate. The complete modeling of money as a factor of exchange will be the subject of section 10 of the monograph, and here further we will turn briefly to the functions and history of the theory of money, as well as to the issue of monetary aggregates.

Since money is practically transactional, non-cash (account), cash and full-value, advance and credit, we define it as a special public good[1], which is, first of all, an instrument of exchange, as well as measurement (accounts), preservation, prepayment, and increase the value of goods, respectively. In the general historical aspect of the development of the market in the transi-tion from subsistence farming to barter and a commodity-money economy (Fig. III.5), one must always bear in mind that the appearance of money greatly simpli-fies the exchange of goods. If, for exam-ple, 100 goods are exchanged in the mar-ket without money (barter), then each of them is valued by the remaining 99 goods, and the total number of such prices, as suggested by combinatorics, will be equal to $100 \cdot 99/2$, that is, 4950, instead of the usual cash 100 prices. Therefore, the main function of money is to rationalize the mechanism for the ex-change of goods.

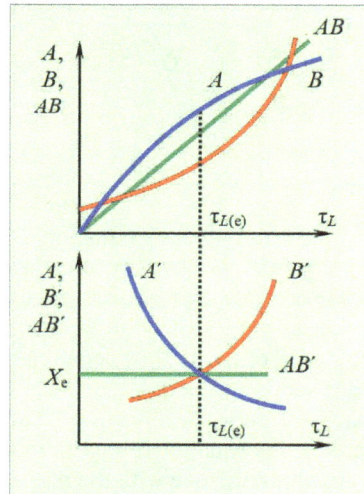

Fig. III.4

The theory of money in general followed the development of the technology of commodity exchange. Historically, the first nominalist theory of money as conventional symbols that have no intrinsic value arose during the transition in antiquity in the exchange from bullion money to coin money, which was subject to massive damage. Such fiduciarism, that is, the idea that money does not have its own value and that it functions only thanks to trust in the state, in market conditions was replaced by another extreme theory – metal theory, which identified money and precious metals. In modern conditions, a compromise quantitative theory of money has been successfully

---

[1] Note that the Austrian economist Friedrich von Hayek (1899-1992) (*Denationali-zation of Money – the Cleaning Argument*, 1976) substantiated the concept of money as a private good that can be issued by all economic entities.

established in economics, the value of which has begun to be linked to its quantity. This theory is methodologically fully consistent with marginalism, but has not yet developed a generalized model for the functioning of money-reserve.

Fundamental difficulties on this issue in the quantitative theory of money arose in connection with a comparison of the interpretations of the 'Say's law of markets' and Walras' GEE. For the economy as a whole, it is always possible to write down the equality of supply and demand: $\Sigma(X_i \cdot Q_i)_d \equiv \Sigma(X_i \cdot Q_i)_s$, where i are the numbers of types of manufactured goods. This means that there are no significant differences between the monetary and barter economies, since here and there all manufactured products are bought up over time, and there can be no chronic surplus or shortage of goods, that other goods are immediately bought with the money received from the sale of goods, and money as a whole does not affect the quantity of goods, it is neutral to them and is, in Say's expression, a "veil" of goods.

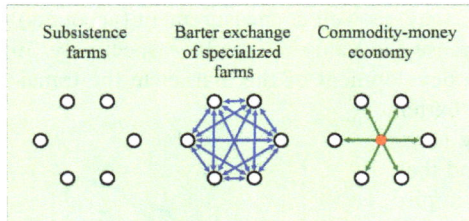

Fig. III.5

Walras's monetary equation differed from the above identity by separating money from commodity circulation by assuming that one of the goods is designated as having a unit price of nominal money-turnover (Z), opposed to the mass values of all other goods: $1 \cdot Z = \Sigma(X_i \cdot Q_i)$. In aggregated form, the right side of the Walras equation is equal to the product of the already known price index of goods X_Q and the total product in real terms Q. The equation takes the form: $1 \cdot Z = X_Q \cdot Q$. Thus, according to Walras, the left and right sides of the equation represent flows of goods and are constructed in the same way, in accordance with the thesis about the marketability of money.

American economist Don Patinkin (1922-1995) (*Money, Percentage and Prices: Integration of Monetary and Value Theories*, 1956) consistently proposed the marginal concept of "real cash remainders"[1], according to which Z is on the left side of the Wal race are momentary cash balances (in the hands of the population, in the cash offices of firms, on the accounts of banks, other credit and other institutions), representing property, 'money wealth', stock, the unit price of which (X_Z), as and the price of any other product changes depending on its total quantity. According to Patinkin, the

---

[1] The concept of 'real money remainders' should be distinguished from Patinkin's concept of the 'effect of real money remainders'. The latter has an independent meaning and refers to the issue of the so-called 'wealth effect' of the theory of GEE, which is considered in section 14 of the monograph.

monetary equation looks like this: $X_Z \cdot Z = X_Q \cdot Q$. The author describes the mechanism of the change in the price of money as follows: "Exogenous growth of the nominal amount of money ... creates inflationary pressure ..., the rise in prices then reduces the real amount of money and thus reduces the inflationary pressure that disturbs the equilibrium" [82, p. 179].

However, analysis of the monetary equation in Patinkin's version shows that it is contradictory. So, if we assume that the amount of money in the economy, for example, doubles, then by virtue of the classical postulate of neutrality of money, which changes only the absolute prices of goods and preserves their relative prices and quantities, the price index of goods also doubles, and the monetary equation is violated and turns into inequality: $0,5 \cdot 2Z < 2X_Q \cdot Q$; $Z < 2X_Q \cdot Q$. It shows that any change in the amount of money has only a price effect that disturbs the equilibrium of the economy.

It is this contradiction of the modified Walrasian monetary equation, in our opinion, that caused the subsequent large and long confusion in the theory of money. Some economists, Klauer (*Keynesian Counterrevolution: a Theoretical Assessment*, 1965), Leyonhufwood (*Revision of the Microeconomic Foundations of the Theory of Money*, 1967) and others, began to talk about the absence of a money market in the economy and about the erroneousness of the Walras equation itself, which does not correspond to reality.

To restore the balance in the Walras equation, as well as to build a full-fledged general model of money, we will make some clarifications, taking into account the division of values into stocks and flows.

First, it must be recognized that the price of a unit of money X_Z is not an autonomous variable, but the inverse of the X_Q commodity price index ($X_Z = 1/X_Q$, $X_Z \cdot X_Q = 1$), which must be included either in the right , or in the left part of the monetary equation, and the relationship X_Q with the variables 'nominal money turnover' (Z) or 'real money turnover' (Z_{re}) should be written as follows: $Z = X_Q \cdot Q$, $Z/X_Q = Z_{re} = Q$. Secondly, it is also important to emphasize that the nominal amount of money, in contrast to the nominal value of other goods, expresses the physical volume of this money. Then the monetary equation will take the canonical form: $Z = Q_n$. Thirdly, the indicator Z of the left side of the monetary equation is heterogeneous, it is a complex set of money-aggregates, which occupies the main place in the structure of means of payment.

We will use the following simplified but functionally strict aggregate structure of financial payment instruments: Z_1, Z_2, Z_3 and Z_4. Their content and relationship are shown in Fig. III.6. The ratio between the nominal amounts of these assets and their liquidity, that is, the ability to quickly exchange without losses for other values, are presented in Fig. III.7.

The indicator of monetary availability Z_1 is included in the well-known equation of the quantitative theory of money by Fisher (*The Purchasing Power of Money. Its Definition and Relation to Credit, Interest and Crises*, 1911)[1]. It is deduced from the canonical monetary equation, which, taking into account the reduced system of indices of monetary aggregates, can be written in the following form: $Z_3 = X_Q \cdot Q$. Representing the money supply Z_3 as the product of the amount of cash Z_1 by the average number of revolutions made by all cash flows during the year (the rate of circulation of money, r), we obtain the Fisher equation: $Z_1 \cdot r = X_Q \cdot Q$, or: $Z_1 = (X_Q \cdot Q)/r$.

It is possible to obtain a more accurate equation of the emission of money needed by the economy if we go from real to nominal commodity turnover and its elements: $Z_1 = X_Q (Q_n/X_Q)/r$, $Z_1 = (Q_n - Q_{cr} + Q_{ad} - Q_{c.s})/r$, where Q_{cr} – the balance of credit sales of goods (commodity credit, the term of which has not yet expired minus the loan to be repaid); Q_{ad} – the balance of advance sales, calculated in the same way; $Q_{c.s}$ – the amount of cashless sales (barter, fat settlements, clearing, mutual accounting of bills, etc.).

Financial means of payment (Z_4)			
Money supply (Z_3)			Securities (quasi-money, monetary surrogates): stocks, bonds, traveler's checks, (letters of credit), promissory notes, etc.
Cash money (Z_1)		Non-cash money	
Bank-notes	Coins	Central bank accounts	Commercial bank accounts
Central bank money, the 'monetary basa' of the contry (Z_2)		Commercial bank money	

Fig. III.6

The so-called 'Cambridge monetary equation' is also known, first proposed by Marshall (*Money, Credit and Commerce*, 1923) and important for modeling the GEE, it is derived from the canonical equation: $Z_1 = 1/r(X_Q \cdot Q)$; $Z_1 = p \cdot X_Q \cdot Q$, where p is the coefficient of monetization of total income, equal to the reciprocal of r.

We will further use the 'Cambridge monetary equation' in the analysis of the neoclassical GEE scheme. But let us first formulate the main provisions of this equilibrium, developed by Walras (*Elements of Pure Political Economy, or The Theory of Social Wealth*, 1974-1877) in the form of five specific postulates:

1) the existence of the GEE, that is, such a state of the economy, in which due to perfect competition and movable prices of goods, full and free information of business entities about the market conditions, the equality of the sum of demands (ΣQ_c) to the sum of offers is established (ΣQ_n) benefits: $\Sigma Q_d = \Sigma Q_s$;

---

[1] Schumpeter called this equation "the Newcomb-Fisher equation" [129, p. 1442], since Fisher, when constructing his monetary equation, referred to the American economist Simon Newcomb (1835-1909) (*Principles of Political Economy*, 1886) as his discoverer. For the sake of fairness, it should be noted that before Newcomb, a monetary equation of this type was first encountered in Marx (*Capital: a Criticism of Political Economy. Vol. 1. The Process of Capital Production*, 1867).

2) the stability of the GEE under short-term and long-term market fluctuations of an internal or external nature, that is, the equality of the sum of excess demand $(\Sigma-\Delta Q_d)$ to the sum of excess supply $(\Sigma-\Delta Q_s)$ and the advancement of both of them to zero: $\Sigma-\Delta Q_d = \Sigma-\Delta Q_s \to 0$;

3) the homogeneity of the GEE, which means the equality of all incomes to all expenses in the economy, that is, the equality of the sum of factor income $(\Sigma A_i$, where i – the number of the factor of production) to the sum of factor costs (ΣB_i): $\Sigma A_i = \Sigma B_i$;

4) the uniqueness of the GEE, meaning that if $n - 1$ markets of the economy are in equilibrium, then the remaining market and the entire economy are in equilibrium: $(n-1)_e \to (n)_e$;

5) the monetary value of the GEE, that is, the equality of the real money turnover (Z) to the real commodity turnover of the economy in nominal terms (Q): $Z_{re} = Q$.

It should be noted that Walras adhered to the classical 'law of Say's markets', which in the author's formulation (*Treatise on Political Economy*, 1803) states that "sales for products are created by production itself" [114, p. 43] and means that demand is derived from supply: Demand = f(Supply). Therefore, in all the postulates formulated above, the indicators of demand, income and money are located in the left parts of the equations. The process of advancing the economy to equilibrium in the Walrasian model – the so-called process of successive approximation of tâtononnement, 'groping' – turns out to be indefinite in duration and is carried out due to the mechanism of actions of the virtual agent – 'auctionist' eliminating the surplus of supply and demand in the markets.

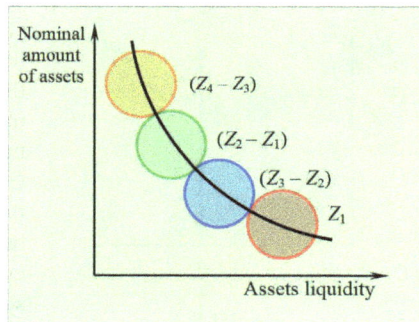

Fig. III.7

The first Walras postulate is the basis for modeling the GEE, it was intensively developed by other neoclassicists of the XX century. If Walras proved the existence of GEE only by simply counting the number of equations and unknown variables of his model, then the Americans Arrow and Gerard Debreu (1921-2004) (*Existence of Equilibrium in a Competitive Economy*, 1954), and also Debreu (*Theory of Value: an Axiomatic Analysis Economic Equilibrium*, 1959) developed a canonical model of the Walrasian type and proved the existence of an informal equilibrium in it, with positive roots of equations – prices of goods.

The second postulate about the stability of equilibrium was the most controversial in the post-Walrasian era of the development of economic theory. Although Samuelson (*Stability of Equilibrium: Linear and Nonlinear Systems*, 1942) and created an abstract theory of the stability of the GEE, the economic practice of the interwar period indicated the instability of the market economy and the possibility of 'dumping' it into a crisis. Therefore, 'Keynesianism' denied the postulate of equilibrium stability, but in some other later concepts the mainstream, despite everything, defended this postulate.

The third postulate of Walras is confirmed by the marginal microeconomic theory of the formation and distribution of product value, it will be used by us to construct aggregate macroindicators, and his fourth postulate simplifies the search for GEE due to the optional inclusion of descriptions of all markets in the model (from the attention of the theory, usually the money market was leaving, which turned out to be the most difficult for researchers).

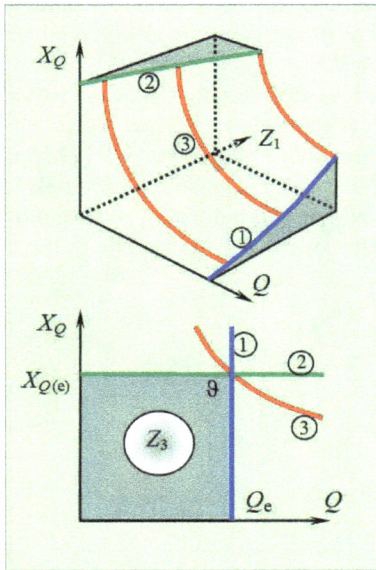

Fig. III.8

The fifth postulate of Walras in the above form, as will be shown below when analyzing Keynes's theory, allows you to get rid of erroneous ideas about the neutrality of money, to develop a theory of monetary aggregates, to introduce them into generalizations. a new model of money and an interfactor GEE scheme. We attribute this postulate to Walras due to the fact that he was the first to investigate commodity-money proportions in the section *Theory of Circulation and Money* of his *Elements*.

The term 'neoclassical scheme' of GEE should be understood with a reservation, since the first neoclassicists, being market researchers, saw only cyclical fluctuations ('business cycles' in the macro system and did not create complete GEE schemes. Therefore, we are talking, in fact, about a modern macroeconomic structure, built on the general theoretical principles of neoclassicism and only some statements of marginalists about the economy as a whole.

The neoclassical GEE scheme, as well as all similar constructions, have an analytical expression in the form of systems of equations. We set the task not so much of a rigorous consideration as of the development of the

160

methodology of the theory of the equilibrium of the economy, and therefore we give mathematical equations only when necessary, focusing on the graphical side of the problem for clarity.

In the economic literature, the neoclassical GEE scheme is built in real price parameters and with the assumption that there is no monetary component in it. We consider this a fundamental mistake, since neoclassicism retained the classical ideas about monetary neutrality ('veils', 'illusions'). Therefore, into the scheme we introduce nominal current prices and the 'Cambridge monetary equation' $Z_1 = p \cdot X_Q \cdot Q$, which is not just an element, but the core of the scheme, since it contains the indicator of total output (product) and necessary for the theory of GEE, the corresponding aggregate functions of supply and demand.

In Fig. III.8 depicts a volumetric model of the 'Cambridge monetary equation'. Its three sections represent the so-called 'Cambridge effects'. In the economic literature, the 'Cambridge effect' means only an increase in the price index of goods in proportion to the monetary mass at $Q = $ const: $X_Q = k_1 \cdot Z_1$, where k_1 – the coefficient of proportionality, $k_1 = 1/(p \cdot Q)$ (lines 1 in the figure). The actual confirmation of this effect can be found in the economic literature [73. p. 614].

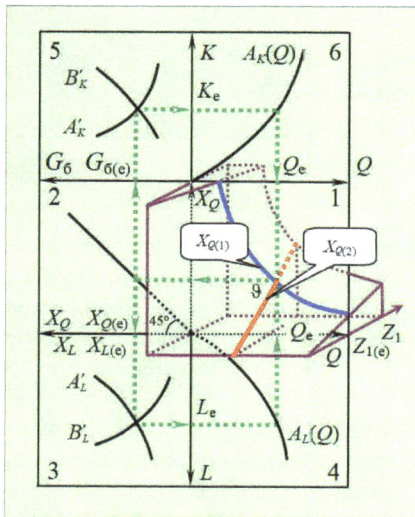

Fig. III.9

But in general there are three effects associated with the analysis of the equation $Z_1 = p \cdot X_Q \cdot Q$. So, in addition to the well-known and presented above effect, which we designate as number 1, there are effects of the 2nd and 3rd. The 'Cambridge effect-2' is opposed to the first one and consists in increasing Z_1 in proportion to Q at $X_Q = $ const: $Z_1 = k_2 \cdot Q$, where k_2 – the proportionality coefficient, $k_2 = p \cdot X_Q$ (lines 2). This effect is also confirmed by the facts of the functioning of the economy [Ibid, p. 613].

The 'Cambridge effect-3' means a reciprocal inversely proportional growth of X_Q and Q with a constant nominal cash flow: $X_Q = k_3/Q$, where k_3 – the proportionality coefficient, $k_3 = Z_1/p = Z_3$ (line 3).

Taking into account the neoclassicists' view of the constant striving of the market for equilibrium, it can be argued that each point of the function X_Q corresponds to the nominal money supply Z_3, equal to $Z_1 \cdot r$ (shaded rectangle under the equilibrium point 9). A more complex curve can correspond to the real economy, for example, reflecting a certain combination of all three 'Cambridge effects', but in any case, the intersection of the curves at one point will mean equilibrium in the model, at the lower the graph of the figure are the values of $X_{Q(e)}$ and Q_e.

In Fig. III.9 we have presented the neoclassical interfactor GEE scheme in a new graphical form. It consists of eight quadrants with sixteen coordinates, six of which are aligned, and either simply coincide, or are 'homogeneous', linearly connected – they can 'slide' over each other, providing docking of indicators. Three price ($X_{Q(e)}$, $X_{L(e)}$, $G_{b(e)}$) and four quantitative (Q_e, L_e, K_e, $Z_{1(e)}$) equilibrium parameters of the circuit connect the quadrants into two closed circuits: the 'labor' circuit, counterclockwise moving, and the 'capital'

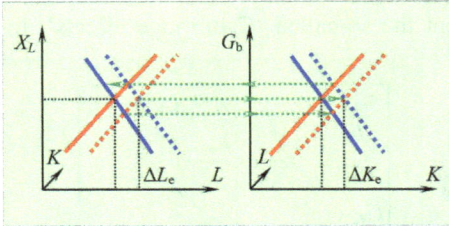

Fig. III.10

contour moving clockwise[1]. The contours originate from quadrant 1 and are closed in it – this is a graph of the main market of the economy, the market of manufactured products in the coordinates 'price index, X_Q – total output, Q' containing the functions of the aggregate demand ($X_{Q(1)}$) and aggregate supply ($X_{Q(2)}$). These functions belong to the figure of the 'Cambridge monetary equation', conjugate to the plane of quadrants 1-6. The hyperbola $X_{Q(1)}$ reflects the result of the 'Cambridge effect-3'. The function $X_{Q(2)}$ is a volume straight line, and in the plane of quadrant 1 there is a superelastic vertical, which characterizes the 'Cambridge effect-1'. The point of intersection of these functions is 9 and determines all the equilibrium parameters of the given GEE scheme.

In the figure, quadrants 3 and 4 make up the marketron of 'labor' with the functions of supply of 'labor' B'_L, demand for it A'_L and the integral function $A_L(Q)$, and quadrants 5 and 6 make up the marketron of 'capital' with analogous functions B'_K, A'_K and $A_K(Q)$. Here we keep the conclusion and interpretation of these functions in the neoclassical style. So the supply function of 'labor' is derived from the well-known model 'leisure – earnings', the supply function of 'capital' – from the model of intertemporal equilibrium of the value of Fisher's goods, and the demand functions for 'labor' and 'capital' – from the usual aggregated production functions $Q =$

---

[1] The classical names of the factors of production 'labor' and 'capital', which are still preserved in economic theory, are cited by us in quotation marks since they are not correct, in section 7 of the monograph we showed that the traded goods are 'labor power' and 'capital goods'.

$= f(L)$ and $Q = f(K)$, with the help of which the equilibrium values of employment (L_e), 'capital'(K_e) are determined, according to exposure of the aggregate supply function $X_{Q(2)}$ and, therefore, the equilibrium volume of the aggregate output (Q_p).

Quadrant 2, called the price quadrant, contains a directly proportional price converter – a beam emanating from the origin at an angle of $45°$, with the help of which the X_Q price signal is bifurcated and through offset X_L price scales and $G_b{}^1$ enters the 'labor' and 'capital' marketers.

The presented scheme reproduces the interfactor GEE, which is unique and stable, that is, it reflects the classic price mechanism of self-balancing of the factor and output markets. The 'labor' and 'capital' markets of the scheme are conjugate, since the quantities L and K are factors of mutual shock shifts in the supply and demand functions (Fig. III.10). Due to this, for example, with an exogenous increase in the supply of 'labor' for demographic reasons, meaning an increase in demand for 'capital', a shift in the corresponding function and an increase in prices occur, which, in turn, is the cause of shifts functions of demand for 'labor' and supply of 'capital'. As a result of these cyclical processes in the markets, there is a shift in the equilibrium indicators of employment of production factors $(\Delta L_e, \Delta K_2)$, exchange $(\Delta Z_{1(e)})$ and consumption (ΔQ_e), as well as restoration of the initial price levels $(X_L, G_b$ and $X_Q)$.

The scheme also corresponds to the classical idea of the neutrality of money: for example, with an increase in the economy of money by ΔZ_1 with ceteris pari-bus, only the price variables of the markets are proportionally adjusted $(\Delta X_{L(e)}, \Delta G_{b(e)}$ and $\Delta X_{Q(e)})$ while maintaining the technological quantitative proportions between the factors and the results of production.

In general, the described scheme of the interfactor GEE is rather simplified, but quite acceptable for describing the economy of the era of perfect competition with market price regulators that work automatically under the laissez-faire principle.

In the economic literature, any market models of the ancestors of neoclassicism are usually qualified as long-term ones. But in fact, these models are abstract, and when their inconsistency with reality is found, it is asserted that the models are correct, since they reflect a natural long-term tendency towards harmony and basic lance of the productive forces of the market without the participation of the state. In this regard, can the considered GEE scheme be considered long-term? See-dimo, no. It would be more correct to characterize it as a simple and basic one for our further analysis of the mainstream theory. But in contrast to it, the Sraffa GEE model

---

[1] The validity of measuring capital goods and investment by the interest rate is discussed in detail in sections 13 and 16 of the monograph.

considered above looks even more simplified, since in it this equilibrium is established instantly.

Since our graphical marketron framework of the neoclassical GEE scheme is universal, we will save it for further analysis and construction of other macromodels.

12. 1st approximation to Keynes's concept of equilibrium: 45-grain Samuelson model

Keynes's major theoretical work, *A Treatise on Money* (1930), was innovative but not well done. Keynes is a mathematician by education, a supporter of the concept of an equilibrium of economics and a marginalist; in a relatively small following work, the *General Theory of Employment, Interest and Money* (1936), he intended, judging by his correspondence with colleagues, to clearly show the essence of his new ideas. but the book also did not turn out to be sufficiently systematized and did not differ in an intelligible style. It is also known that it was written in a hurry, since the author wanted to publish it as soon as possible and convey to theorists, politicians and practitioners his recipes for the exit of the world market from the Great Depression.

Consistency as the most important requirement for any scientific research in Keynes is perhaps indicated only in the title of the book, its content does not have a common whole, its sections exist on their own and are weakly connected logically. Undoubtedly, such a whole should have been a specific new GEE scheme, replacing the neoclassical GEE scheme discussed above.

Keynes, as you know, criticized predecessor economists on many issues – market equilibrium, the ratio of the importance of supply or demand, wages, prices, etc., which, by virtue of what began in the late 1920s. systemic market crisis could no longer be covered traditionally. Keynes' criticism of the 'classics' was generally constructive, he developed a new system of aggregated coordinates and indicators for the study of 'employment, interest and money', as well as an active state policy in the relevant spheres of the economy. But the multifaceted 'Keynesianism' that arose and developed on the basis of different interpretations of the *General Theory* turned out to be not very similar to Keynes's theory. Let's try to reconstruct his vision of the GEE, which was presented only in fragments.

Before turning directly to the analysis of the main element of the latest macroeconomics – the so-called 'Keynes cross' and its interpretation by Samuelson – we need to clarify two important methodological points.

In the *General Theory*, in contrast to the Seev's concept of the primacy of 'market supply', 'aggregate demand' was updated, which, in Keynes's opinion, determines the scale of employment and production in the economy.

Therefore, we can talk about the 'law of Keynes markets' with the priority of aggregated demand. In the context of the outbreak of the crisis of the market economy, Keynes was interested in the phenomenon, as he expressed it, of "price rigidity"[1] (including wages) and "forced unemployment." The latter he considered for the market more typical than full employment, immoral, but completely eliminated by the state. Justifying the rejection of the classical principle of laissez-faire, he imputed to the state, as the largest consumer and investor in the country, the solution to the problem of increasing aggregate demand and employment through budget-deficit growth of investment costs and monetary reduction in the cost of entrepreneurial credit. Therefore, we can talk about the emergence of the principle of non-laissez-faire Keynes.

Further, for Keynes, it was not the change of long-term analysis to short-term analysis, as is commonly believed, that was important, but a more accurate concept of aggregated display of the real economy than the classics. But Keynes's new task was, of course, dictated by the protracted crisis market conditions of those times, the need for urgent action, as well as his ideas about the uncertainty of the future.

The British economist and Keynesian researcher Robert Skidelsky (b. 1939) generally correctly writes that the traditional view of economics did not explain its negatives and gave people vague expectations [104, p. 112]. But the reasons for this 'uncertainty', in our opinion, lay deeper. The need for long-term reasoning of economic entities began to be conditioned by the saturation of durable property in the process of industrialization of the economy. Keynes himself wrote about this: "It is because of the existence of equipment with a long service life in the field of economics that the future is connected with the present" [53, p. 156]. Long-term expectations of people due to the weakness of their knowledge of the details of the economic mechanism turned out to be uncertain (Keynes had this idea when he wrote his *A Treatise on Probability* (1930)). In turn, the monopolization of markets, which turned a significant amount of labor, land and capital goods into surplus factors of production, became socially unacceptable and actualized a deeper knowledge of economics and scientifically grounded information reform. institutions of society, established since the time of the classical market. Thus, if the neoclassical macroeconomics was reduced to a superficial description of fluctuations in business activity, Keynes's macroeconomics began not only to study in detail the underlying causes of the same fluctuations, but also to put forward recipes for their leveling, smoothing.

---

[1] Instead of the often used by Keynes, in Keynesianism and economic theory as a whole, the epithets 'rigid' and 'flexible' to the word 'prices' we will use, in our opinion, more general and corresponding to the meaning of price behavior, the epithets 'mobile', 'weakly mobileand' and 'motionless'.

The question arises about the time required for a new detailed modeling of the GEE. Robinson noted that short-term is "a period during which changes in capital equipment stocks can be neglected" [87, p. 179]. Other economists-Keynesians associate the effectiveness of macroanalysis with the invariability of the prices of capital goods or the prices of all factors of production while maintaining the mobility of product prices. But Keynes himself wrote: "... I ... attach fundamental importance to the concept of the period of production. By definition, which I prefer ..., the product has a production period of n, if n units of time are needed, from the moment of warning of an impending change in demand, in order to achieve the maximum elasticity of employment" [53, p. 268]. We, starting the analysis of Keynesian models, in which not only employment is considered, but also inertial, so-called 'multiplicative' processes of the propagation of investment waves across sectors of the economy, we believe that it is impossible to exclude the action of any factor of production from the analysis.

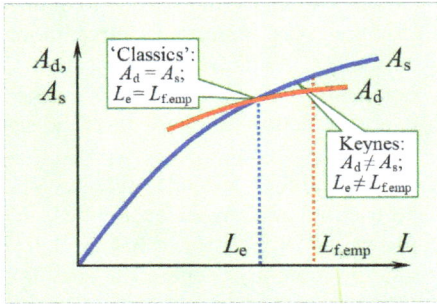

Fig. III.11

In addition, it is known that many interpreters of Keynes's work consider the 'short-term' of his analysis of economics to be the reason for the regidity, or lagging of reactions, of wages and prices in general. But in all dynamic systems there are time lags, and the comparative statics method neutralizes them.

Therefore, in the study of all Keynesian macromodels under the period of comparative-static study of the economy, we mean the time sufficient to establish equilibrium prices and quantities of all resource and produced goods, that is, the time the economy reaches a 'stationary' state, or a state of static equilibrium. news. At this time, there is an internal (between the moment of establishing the need for action and the moment of making decisions by business entities) and external (before the implementation of decisions) administrative lag, as well as a technological lag of establishing the GEE itself.

The inconsistent and contradictory form of Keynes's presentation of the *General Theory* noted above caused confusion in his definitions already in *Book One, Introduction*, when he considered two types of aggregated function of nominal income with the abscissa 'employment, L' (Fig. III.11). Keynes wrote that "the total income received with a given volume of employment, it is advisable to call the proceeds from this employment. On the other hand, the aggregate price of the supply of products for a given volume of employment is the expected revenue ..." [Ibid, p. 58, 59]. That is, he introduced different concepts – "received revenue" and "expected revenue", which actually denote the same value, the function of which, literally in the next paragraph, was already opposed by another function: "Let's designate the aggregate offer price of products (that is, 'received revenue' – *the author*) when L is employed by a person through A_s; the relationship between A_s and L, which can be written in the form $A_s = f(L)$, will be called the aggregate supply function. The revenue expected by entrepreneurs when L people are employed will be denoted by A_d, the relationship between A_c and L, which can be written in the form $A_d = f(L)$, will be called the aggregate demand function" [Ibid, p. 59] (the designation of indicators in the quote is our – *the author*). At the same time, Keynes made a special note that the indicators 'aggregate supply price' and 'aggregate demand price' should not be confused with unit prices, which should be similar to the first, but refer to the Marshall local equilibrium model.

Since $A_s(L)$ and $A_d(L)$ are, in fact, one-factor production functions, then, proceeding from the action of the premise ceteris paribus, they are depicted by us as convex. A_d has a smaller slope and therefore the curves intersect at the point corresponding to the equilibrium employment (L_e). It must be assumed that the 'Say's law of the market' with the priority of market supply corresponds to the function A_s, merging with the demand function A_c, at all points of which the full employment of the labor force ($L_{f.emp}$) must also be achieved. According to Keynes, with such equilibria, there can be 'involuntary unemployment', the elimination of which requires a shift to a higher level of the 'demand price' function A_d. The version went down in the history of macroeconomics as Keynes's concept of chronic "insufficient demand".

He also put forward the concept of "effective demand", according to which the maximum profit is achieved in the crosshairs of the curves A_s and A_d. In the same *Introduction*, Keynes formulates the concept as follows: "It is at this point that the profit expected by entrepreneurs will be greatest. The value of A_d at that point of the curve of the aggregate demand function, where it intersects with the function of aggregate supply, we will call the effective demand" [Ibid, p. 60] (the designation of our value – *the author*). This concept is correct in that profit maximization falls on the intersection of supply and demand curves, as for the statement that these are the functions A_s and A_d, then our subsequent analysis of Keynes's ideas about the equilibrium of the economy will require significant adjustments.

It should be noted that in the constructions of Keynes, which we call the "Keynes-1 cross", one can find many other fundamental errors and absurdities. So in his words repeatedly repeating that "demand is a total income (or revenue)"[1] is a mistake, since demand, like supply, is always an indicator of the physical quantity of the considered good or resource, in this case – the number of employees, deferred on the abscissa, and not the cash flow. It is important to keep in mind that, according to marginalism and contrary to Keynes, it is not cash flow indicators that determine employment, but, on the contrary, employment is a determinant of income in the economy.

To give his macromodel a more Marshallian look and adapted for its further analysis in the *General Theory*, Keynes in *Book Third, Propensity to Consume* the abscissa 'employment, *L*' of the model was replaced by the indicator of real national income (national product, *Y*). In this regard, he wrote: "The function of the aggregate demand connects the given level of employment with the 'profit'... It is more convenient, however, to investigate a slightly different function, namely the function that connects consumption ... with income ... corresponding to the level of employment *L*" [Ibid, p. 112] (Fig. III.12). We call this Keynes model "Keynes-2 cross".

It may seem that the replacement of indicators speaks of the inconsistency of the author. But in fact, Keynes's first coordinate system was necessary to criticize the existing neoclassical interpretation of the issue of employment, and the model with a new abscissa allowed Keynes to significantly expand his theory. There were reasons for choosing the indicator of the real national product as the aggregate output.

First, in the 30s. there was still no statistical standard of GDP (GNP), therefore, choosing an indicator to display total output in the chapter *Determining Income, Savings and Investment*, Keynes faced the problems of calculating, as he put it, "the cost of using equipment" (its amor tization) as part of the aggregate product and even devoted a separate *Appendix* to the chapter to this issue. As a result, he considered it possible, as did many economists of that time, not to take into account depreciation and settled on unit *Y*. Secondly, to show new macroeconomic functions – consumption and accumulation (savings and investment) – Keynes was comfortable with *Y*, since it consists of consumption and accumulation funds. Thirdly, *Y* allowed Keynes to organically introduce new key marginal indicators into the model of the economy – "marginal propensity to consume" and "investment multiplier", which should be homogeneous. nym for the comparison of monetary values.

And to be precise, it should be noted that the functions A_s and A_d Keynes proposed to measure in special "units of wages" in order to preserve the correctness of their relationship with the natural indicators of employment and output. But for this, subsequent 'Keynesianism', without complicating the theory, preferred to simply use the units of output, as well as supply and

---

[1] See, for example: [53, p. 82].

demand in real terms. We will return to the question of what indicators and functions are the most adequate to Keynes's theory.

Let's continue the analysis of Keynes's theoretical constructions. In *Book Three* of his *General Theory*, a decreasing convex "consumption function (H)" appears as a constant part and therefore is located parallel to the 'aggregate demand pric' A_d (see the dotted line in Fig. III.12). Curve H, as well as A_d, intersects Keynes A_s 'aggregate supply function' and expresses the dependence formulated by the author as follows: "The basic psychological law, in the existence of which we can be sure ..., with The point is that people tend, as a rule, to increase their consumption with an increase in income, but not to the same extent as income grows" [Ibid, p. 117]. Confidence in the existence of the law was based on the empirical facts of consumption established by the German statistician Ernst Engel (1821-1896) (*Modern Housing Shortage*, 1873). Accordingly,

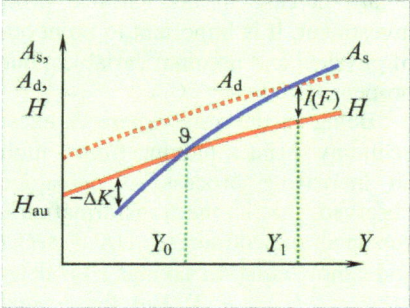

Fig. III.12

Keynes introduces two measures of the consumption function: 1) the 'marginal propensity to consume' income (H'), that is, the increase in total consumption dH attributable to the increase in output dY ($H' = dH/dY$), this Keynes's decreasing indicator characterizes the slope of the consumption functions and the 'aggregate demand price'; 2) "autonomous consumption" (H_{au}), that is, the minimum level of household consumption that does not depend on the output and remains at zero output of the national product. Thus, H consists of Havt and the so-called "induced consumption" (H_{ind}), that is, consumption depending on the "marginal propensity to consume" and output: $H = H_{au} + H_{ind} = H_{au} + H' \cdot Y$.

The parallelism of the functions A_s and H is also explained by Keynes s assumption of "autonomy", but already in the sense of independence from the output of the accumulation fund (investment), the size of which is determined by factors that are supposedly exogenous for this model: demographic growth of labor resources, their employment, the development of scientific and technological progress and other circumstances that, as the American Keynesian Alvin Hansen (1887-1975) said, "expand" and "deepen" the functioning capital goods. In the 'Keynes-2 cross', under such a strong assumption, the point of intersection of the functions A_s and H (ϑ) corresponds to a 'balanced' (without investment) output (Y_0) and a constant volume of capital goods.

In the zone, at first growing, and then stabilizing (after point Y_1 in Fig.

III.12) positive difference between A_s and H, savings (F) and investments (I) are carried out, capitalization of the corresponding part of the national income occurs, that is, an increase in wealth countries including land, financial assets and other reserves. In the case of an economy with investments, one can write down the differential equation: $dY = \rho \cdot dI$, where ρ – the so-called Keynes' 'investment multiplier': $\rho = 1/(1 - H)$, $\rho > 1$. The value of ρ is a marginal measure of the multiplier effect of the spread of investments in technological inter-sectoral relations of the economy, resulting in an increase in the national product exceeding the increase in initial investment. It is important to point out that ρ in the model expresses the ratio of physical and nominal variables, but the inverse of ρ, – Keynes's "marginal propensity to invest" (I').

Being in the zone where H exceeds A_s is possible, but only when the economy shrinks, moving from a high level of output to a low one, at which an increasing process of de-capitalization of the economy should be observed, that is, the transformation of the stock of wealth into a stream of consumer expenditures ($-\Delta K = \Delta H$). The volume of investments (in general and simply equal to savings F) is determined as follows: $I = -H_{au} + (1 - H')Y$, or: $I = -H_{au} + I' \cdot Y$. But these equations also show that, along with the propensity to save, business entities in the event of a significant drop in production should show, so to speak, the necessary 'propensity to wastefulness'[1].

A joint analysis of the curves A_s, A_d and H, shows that Keynes's constructions in terms of 'expected income' and 'actual income' turns out to be erroneous. The so-called 'unplanned' reductions or increases in inventories in the economy at the locations of the 'deflationary gap' ($A_d > A_s$) and 'inflationary gap' ($A_d < A_s$) models, further in the *General Theory*, Keynes did not use and seem to be invented by the author only to demonstrate their discrepancy. This can be explained without the complex arguments and assumptions of Keynes shown above, by the very Engel's law of consumption. But even being within the framework of Keynes's concept, we are forced to designate his function A_s as A_d, since his very concept contradicts the Marshallian canon that had already been formed before him: A_s is the production yield curve corresponding from its first occurrence. water, that is, with a demand function. Correcting this error requires a number of alterations not only in the theory of Keynes himself, but also in modern macroeconomics, since this error persists in it to this day. 'Keynes-2 cross', in its original form, became the macromodels of many theorists,

---

[1] In addition to 'balanced capital goods', one can consider the stock of the entire national wealth of the country. A vivid example of 'wastefulness' is the situation with the depleted territorial and natural resources, the production apparatus of firms and the property of households in the disintegrated USSR.

which led to an incredible clutter of 'Keynesianism' and the rest of mainstream economic theory with often conflicting concepts, as well as distorted conclusions and recommendations on state economic policy. The question arises, how could this happen? The fact is that in the current macroeconomics[1], the AD-AS^2 model is first considered separately, that is, the 'Weintraub's cross' proposed by Weintraub (*General Theory of the Price Level*, 1959), built on the basis of neoclassical principles and representing only the differential part of the marketron of the collective release. Its integral part is analyzed in the following sections, also separately in the form of 'Keynes-2 cross'. But, if these models are combined into one, then their semantic discrepancy becomes absolutely obvious.

Thus, both curves of the 'Keynes-2 cross' are functions of production profitability, and the point of their intersection does not correspond to the true equilibrium of the economy, which should be determined by the intersection of the marginal functions of demand for products and their supply. Therefore, in order to get rid of unnecessary elements of Keynes's macroeconomic theory, we again combine the curves A_s, A_d into one integral function of profitability (A), which we further consider together with the consumption curve H in the Keynes model, and in general the case with the function of expenditure of total output (B). The meaning and relationship of Keynes's functions A and H is of key importance in the theory of self-balancing and state regulation of the economy.

Keynes did not intend to republish the *General Theory* and wrote about the prospects for its formulation in the article *General Theory of Employment* (1937) as follows: "For me, the relatively simple fundamental ideas underlying my theory are more important than specific forms in which I have embodied them, and I have no desire to give them final form at the present stage of discussion. If simple basic ideas become familiar and acceptable, then time, experience and cooperation of several minds will allow finding the best way to express them" [53, p. 358]. The 'minds' of neoclassicists first of all tried to adapt all the new content of the book to their already existing systematized and formalized models. This is how 'Keynesianism' and 'post-Keynesianism' arose with different hybrid macroeconomic concepts.

Common to all the main versions of Keynes's teachings are their claims to be adequate to the original and universality, but also the actual eclecticism, the remaining confusion in names and interpretations. Let us turn to one such version – Samuelson's 45-degree model, which we regard as an important

---

[1] See, for example: [96].

[2] The sequence '$AD{\to}AS$' in the name of the model corresponds to Keynes's idea of the priority of demand. However, the sequence of reality 'production $\to$ consumption' and the construction of models 'supply $\to$ demand' suggests a more accurate name: AS-AD.

first approximation to Keynes's GEE concept.

The 45-degree model appeared in the *Collection of Articles in Honor of Hansen's 60th Birthday* (1948), and then in the third and all subsequent editions of the textbook *Economics: An Introduction to Analysis* (1955) by Samuelson. Some authors believe that "the model was and remains the central part of the Keynesian approach to economics"[1], although in fact, given that the model contains elements that Keynes himself was not the author, it can only be qualified as an attempt to display the economic representations of the "Master"[2].

In the economic literature, there are different assessments and interpretations of Samuelson's model. The model is often ignored or its significance is belittled, for example, in the monograph of the Belgian economist Michel De Frey the *History of Macroeconomics from Keynes to Lucas and Beyond* (2016), there is no worthy assessment of Samuelson's construction, which historically entered the macroeconomic canon earlier than other Keynesian developments. Many authors consider the model to be simplified[3], but the criterion of simplicity should not express the principle of gradation of Keynesian models. It would be most correct to call it a model with fixed prices, which allows demonstrating the idea and the mechanism of quantitative balancing of Keynes's economy.

The 45-degree model, or simply 'Samuelson's cross', can be modified, in it, first of all, it is necessary to correct one mistake of Samuelson himself, some of the errors of Keynes and Keynesians discussed above, and also to present the model in full integral-differential form, that is, in the form of a markron.

In the 45-degree model (Fig. III.13, upper graph) Samuelson, to display the aggregate output as an independent variable on the abscissa, instead of the national income, the standard deflated GDP, that is, the end product (Q_{en}), was deflated. On the ordinate of the model, repeatedly demonstrated by Samuelson[4] himself and often by other authors to this day, one can find, in addition to the indicator of aggregate income (A), the indicator of consumer spending (H). But the measurement of aggregate output by the value of the end product Q_{en}, which includes in real terms, in addition to the accumulation fund and consumption, depreciation, makes it necessary to correlate it with the total costs of production (B), and not just 'consumer costs'. Removing the indicated incorrectness, we can say that in the model there is an equality of the total end output Q_{en} to the total income A, the corresponding function of

---

[1] See, for example: [67, p. 85].
[2] This is how Skidelsky called Keynes figuratively [104].
[3] See, for example: [49, p. 46].
[4] See, for example, the model in one of the latest editions of Samuelson's textbook [96, p. 152].

which is located at an angle of 45°. The function of expenditure B has a smaller angle of inclination, which expresses the 'basic psychological law' of Keynes considered above, and extends to the beginning of the abscissa, measuring the autonomous expenditures B_{au} on the ordinate.

In the economic literature, the indicator of total expenditures is usually structured in a special way, in it, in addition to investment expenditures, government expenditures are highlighted, as well as the foreign trade balance to demonstrate and analyze the effect of the corresponding multipliers. This complicates the 45-degree model and is not so important for understanding its essence. Therefore, we will turn to the issue of mapping the work of the state and foreign trade sectors of the economy in the theory of Keynes and Keynesians in section 14 of the monograph.

Both functions of the 'Samuelson's cross' are fundamentally different from the functions of the 'Keynes-2 cross' in their linearity[1]. The 'linearization' of functions in this case does not so much simplify, as it is commonly believed, Keynes's constructions, as it makes it possible to show his theoretical propositions about the uncertainty of the future of the industrial economy and the need for a non-price, quantitative mutual adjustment of its markets in conditions of the immobility

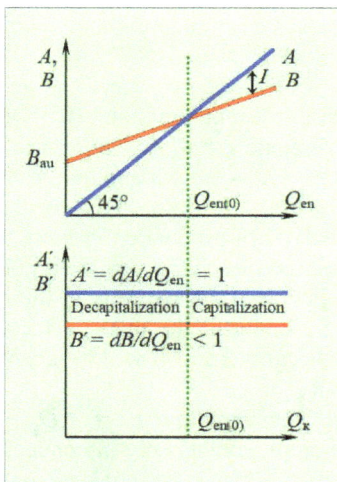

Fig. III.13

(rigidity) of wages. To do this, we represent the model in the form of a marketron, in the differential part of which there are the first derivatives of A and B with respect to Q_{en} – the functions of demand for Q_{en} and its supply (A' and B'), the horizontal nature of which shows the uncertainty of the price balance and prospects of the economy. The function A' expresses the marginal price index (X_Q, $X_Q = dA/dQ_{en}$), unchanged in value in this model, which differs from the periodical indices of Laspeyres, Paasche and Fisher in greater sensitivity to changes in the economy. Function B', which can be considered the 'Keynesian section' of the supply function AD, is located below A' and simultaneously expresses the indicator of the 'propensity to spend' the total income, which is also a constant in this model. The point of intersection of functions A and B does not show the equilibrium of the

---

[1] In economic cybernetics, a special mathematical operation of linearization of functions is used, which greatly simplifies their analysis (see, for example: [58, p. 59]).

economy, as Keynes believed, but simply divides the area between A' and B' into zones of capitalized profit and loss coverage by decapitalization of the economy.

The presented 'cross' of the marketron does not show the equilibrium of the economy, and even more so the main idea of Keynes – the equilibrium with 'forced unemployment' but, being a product model, it is convenient for developing Samuelson's interfactor GEE scheme, built on the basis of our standard scheme presented above in the study of the neoclassic GEE scheme. To do this, we reconstruct the models of economic reproduction factors – employment, interest and money, described by Keynes and formalized by other Keynesians.

In Keynes, in the *Book of the Fifth General Theory*, there appears a "employment function" ($L = f(Y)$), which, although "only differs from the aggregate supply function (more precisely, the aggregate production function $A_s = f(L) – the author$) that in fact it is its inverse function" [53, p. 262]. The new curve is introduced by the author into the theory specifically for the analysis of production growth, when "we consider changes in employment in response to changes in the amount of investment" [Ibid, p. 263]. We use this function in this capacity in the new GEE scheme to illustrate the quantitative adjustment of the markets for the reproduction factors of the economy, but the argument in it will be the value of the aggregated end product Q_{en}: $L = = f(Q_{\kappa})$.

The function $L = f(Q_{en})$ can reflect the equilibrium with 'forced unemployment' only in connection with the model of the labor market itself, which Keynes did not develop, repeatedly spoke about the existence of an indirect connection between unemployment and the immobility of wages. Macmillan's authoritative *Dictionary of Modern Economics* characterizes Samuelson's concept of 'neoclassical synthesis' as follows, under which he created the 45-degree model: Neoclassical synthesis is the statement "that the existence of an equilibrium in underemployment is a consequence of the Keynesian assumption (but no Keynesian assumption! – *the author*) about the inflexibility of wages in monetary terms" [105, p. 352]. Modigliani, Hicks and Samuelson interpreted Keynes's *General Theory* on the basis of the assumption that wages were immovable. So Samuelson wrote that "if Keynes had simply said in his early chapters that he considered it realistic to assume that in modern capitalist society wages are regular and difficult to lower, then most of his insights would remain valid"[1]. The meaning of the 'neoclassical synthesis' lies in the inclusion of a neoclassical, but somewhat modified model of the labor market, into the GEE scheme with the 'Samuelson's cross'.

---

[1] Cit. according to: [104, p. 133].

174

Such a model in the form of a marketron, already known to us in detail in section 7 of the monograph, is shown in Fig. III.14. Its integral part depicts the aggregate nominal-monetary production function A_L by the factor of labor force L. In the differential part of the marketron, the derivative of the A_L function – the function of the limiting labor productivity A'_L – at the same time a function of the demand for labor. The labor supply function B'_L in 'Keynesianism', as well as in neoclassicism, is derived from the well-known microeconomic model 'leisure – earnings'.

It is believed to have added the labor market model to Hansen's Keynesian equilibrium theory (*Business Cycles and National Income*, 1951). This is so, but only concerns the graphical side of the theory, the analytical part of it we find already in Modigliani (*Preference for Liquidity and the Theory of Interest and Money*, 1944). However, both were generally of a standard neoclassical look. To display the notion of 'frozen' wages, we will use Stigler's more advanced labor market model (*Economics of the Minimum Legislative Wage*, 1946). Stigler's modification is that, taking into account trade union activity, the long-term employment contracts, which we mentioned in section 7 of the monograph of the social 'ratchet effect', the action of other institutional factors, as well as the conditions of a depressive economy, both functions, A'_L and B'_L are cut off by a horizontal line of a fixed and increased so-called 'legislative price' ($X_{L(1)}$), which blocks the entire price mechanism for balancing the economy.

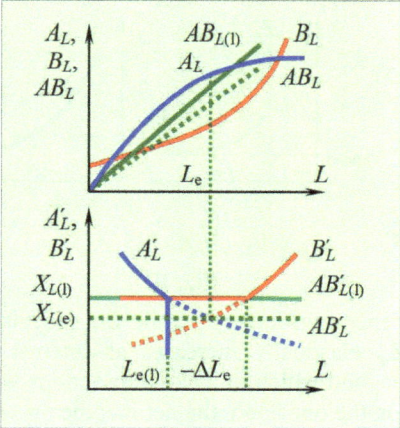

Fig. III.14

It should also be added that the labor market is a futures market in which mutual lease agreements are concluded between workers and employers, which provide for taking into account the growth of firms' profitability when setting wage rates. Therefore, the 'frozenness' of the market can be explained by the 'stickiness' of the prices of labor and capital. In addition, the stability of wages is also determined by a fairly stable price of labor, that is, the price of 'human capital'.

Due to the above reasons, the standard functions of labor demand and its supply themselves become broken lines and intersect at low equilibrium employment (L_e), denoting all, so to speak, 'legislative' unemployment ($-\Delta L_e$), which is qualitatively and quantitatively not corresponds to Keynes's

175

'forced unemploymen' equal to $L_{f.emp} - L_e$.

Perhaps the money market was described in the most detail by Keynes in the *General Theory* and developed graphically by Samuelson in economics, a feature of which is its direct connection with the investment market. In Fig. III.15 such a combined model is presented.

At one time, the classic of political economy Say asserted that "even in the case when money is being saved, ... their purpose, in the end, is still to buy something with it, for ... they cannot have any other use" [114, p. 43], but Keynes drew attention precisely to his contemporary 'other use' of money. He considered the multifunctionality of money and, in addition to the usual transactional ("commercial" [53, p. 195]) and insurance demand, introduced the so-called "speculative" demand for money associated with the purchase and sale of valuable boo-

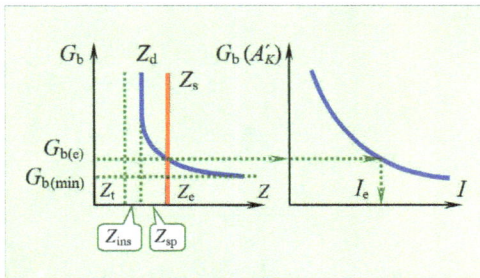

Fig. III.15

magician. The corresponding amounts of money Z_t, Z_{ins} and Z_{sp} in the figure are plotted along the coordinate of the amount of money, which is a function of the bank interest (G_b): $Z = f(G_b)$.

According to Keynes, the first two forms of demand for money Z_t and Z_{ins} do not depend on interest, while the speculative preference of money for securities Z_{sp} elastically increases as interest decreases to a certain limit $(G_{b(min)})$, beyond which to make transactions with the price new papers is unprofitable. On the one hand, the net income on securities is made up of their appreciation and interest. If the fall in the price of securities exceeds the interest on them, then losses are formed and the players, in this case, tend to preserve their savings only in a liquid, monetary form. On the other hand, the market rate of securities is inversely proportional to the interest rate, and if there is a significant rise in interest, then this is identical to a sharp drop in securities prices, which again forces business entities to own only money, since they do not monetary risky assets, unlike money, can depreciate to zero. This logic of human behavior was outlined by Keynes in his *A Treatise on Money* (1933).

Thus, in the coordinates '$Z - G_b$' the money demand function (Z_d) goes from vertical to horizontal. Since the amount of money in the economy is set exogenously by the central bank of the country, the superelastic vertical money supply function (Z_s) at the point of intersection with the money demand function Z_d determines the equilibrium parameters of the amount of money (Z_e) and interest rate $(G_{b(e)})$.

For Keynes, such a money market is closely related to investments that

176

'absorb' savings and should be profitable, should be estimated by bank interest at the level of the expected "marginal capital efficiency".

In economic theory, in connection with this innovation of Keynes, there is a controversy over the question of what he meant: capital goods or investments? Lerner (*Ekonomiks Kontrol*, 1944) even suggested replacing Keynes's term with the concept of "marginal investment efficiency". But, in our opinion, the misunderstanding can be eliminated if we consider the marketron of capital goods (Fig. III.16), which presents the functions of the general ($A_K = f(K)$) and limiting ($A'_K = f(K)$) efficiency (productivity) of capital goods in the form of their monetary profitability[1]. Within the

framework of a fragment of the model, bounded in the figure by vertical dashed lines and representing investments dI on the K axis, the curve A'_K and is a decreasing function of investment demand – 'the maximum capital efficiency': dA/dK. We have already demonstrated a similar approach to the issue when constructing a neoclassical GEE scheme and will apply it in the further analysis of macroeconomics. So for now, one should not abandon Keynes' terminology in this matter.

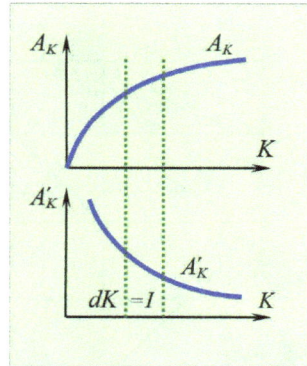

Fig. III.16

Keynes's A'_K curve is balanced not by the investment supply function, as in neoclassicism, but by the equilibrium interest rate $G_{b(e)}$, which is formed not in the credit market, but in the money market (see Fig. III.15). This statement, borrowed by Keynes from the English economist Dennis Robertson (1890-1963)[2], was justified by the fact that savings and investments are not necessarily equal, since they are made by different economic entities – households and firms, who can act with different motives and goals[3]. Equilibrium interest is the criterion for the selection and implementation of investment decisions that have an expected marginal profitability A'_K higher than $G_{b(e)}$, a tool for determining the equilibrium total investment volume (I_e). Keynes wrote in this regard that "the value of investments tends to the point on the investment

---

[1] The designations 'A_K' and 'A'_K' in this and the previous graphs were adopted by us in the capital goods marketron (see section 7 of the monograph).
[2] Keynes writes about this as follows; "The idea of this diagram was suggested to me by R.F. Harrod. See also D.H. Robertson's somewhat similar scheme in *Economic Journan* (1934). Desember. [p. 652])" [53, p. 182].
[3] Keynes believed that investment is a function of the interest rate ($I = f(G_b)$), and savings are a function of national income ($F = f(Y)$). However, in reality, both in savings and investment activities, there is no such clear subjective division, savers also claim interest, and investments from firms' profits are realized without interest.

demand graph where the marginal efficiency of the aggregate capital is equal to the market rate of interest" [53, p. 148].

Keynes, referring negatively to the classic 'Say's law of the market' with the priority status of the supply of goods, considered the joint functioning of money and savings markets without taking into account the supply of savings, which undoubtedly, like the rate of interest, affect the equal volume of investments. In addition, it should be noted that the analysis of the marketron of fixed capital and savings shows that the 'marginal efficiency of capital' (the "natural" rate of interest [Ibid, p. 232]) and bank interest are not identical. This circumstance was only mentioned by Keynes of the *General Theory*, but was actively used later by Hicks when creating the *IS-LM* model.

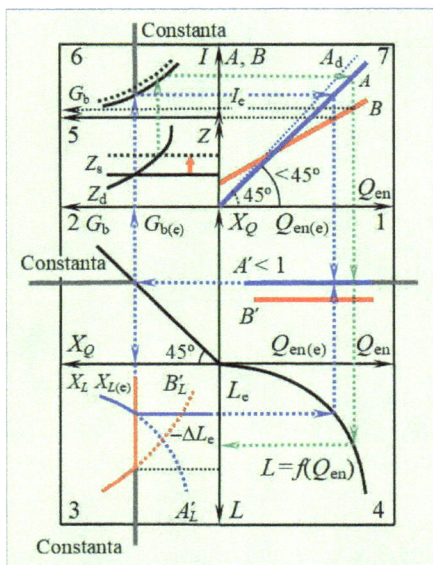

Fig. III.17

In Fig. III.17 depicts the Keynesian interfactor scheme of the GEE with a quantitative adjustment of its elements – the marketrons of the end output Q_{en} and the labor force L, as well as the model of the money-investment market '$Z – I$'. Collecting everything in a closed complex, we make one more modification of Samuelson's Keynesian constructions. We present the monetary indicators of the 45-degree markron in nominal prices, which allows its use in describing not only the deflationary economy during the Great Depression, but also the subsequent Great Inflationary Boom. Accordingly, the profitability function A is located in Fig. III.17 at an angle slightly less than 45°, and its derivative-price index A' is at a deflationary level equal to less than one.

Since in a crisis economy the usual price equalization does not work, in the model the indicators X_Q, X_L and G_b of price coordinates are 'frozen' with the help of end-to-end fixed horizontal and vertical lines 'Constanta', I form There are two contours of market signals. The equilibrium horizontal is formed in the output quadrant 1, bifurcates in the price quadrant 2 into verticals, which, passing through the labor marketron of quadrants 3 and 4, as well as the money-investment model of quadrants 5 and 6 and the 'Samuelson's cross' of the quadrant 7, returns to the initial point of

178

equilibrium (in Fig. III.17 – a closed dotted line with arrows).

To demonstrate the quantitative agreement of the markets of the economy, our GEE scheme provides for a special Keynesian 'employment function', $L = f(Q_{en})$, which is an integral part of the labor marketron.

Placing the function $L = f(Q_{en})$ in the scheme allows us to understand the mechanism of a balanced rise in a crisis economy with additional emission of money, in proportion to which only it can be realized, for example, exogenous increase in output and employment [Ibid, p. 274, 275].

The first part of the money impulse propagation mechanism – the so-called 'Keynes effect'[1] – (see the open dashed line passing clockwise through quadrants 5, 6, 7 and 1) the author describes as follows: "Money influences the value of effective demand primarily by influencing the rate of interest ... The quantitative effect could be derived from three elements: a) a liquidity preference graph showing how much it should to drop the rate of interest so that an additional amount of money can be absorbed by those who want to keep cash; b) a graph of maximum efficiency, showing how much a given drop in the rate of interest will increase investment, and c) an investment multiplier, showing how much effective demand will increase with a given increase in investment" [Ibid, p. 276].

The second part of the mechanism of quantitative balancing of Keynes's economy (see a fragment of the open dashed line under consideration, passing through quadrants 1 and 4) consists in transforming the increase in output into an increase in employment by reducing 'institutional' unemployment.

This mechanism clearly demonstrates Keynes's principle of non-neutrality of money. A direct monetary method of regulating bank interest and the growth of a crisis economy, described, surprisingly, by Keynes himself, devalues his proposals for an indirect rather complicated credit and fiscal deficit stimulation of economic growth.

Keynes in the *General Theory* showed that the equilibrium under laissez-faire does not ensure full employment, considered the reason for 'forced unemployment' not to immobility of wages, but to insufficient aggregated demand due to a spontaneous flow of funds into the financial sector and achieved a forced return of these funds in the production sector in the form of public investment in jobs. Therefore, the policy of large expenditures of the state was applied during the 2nd World War and until the 70s, when Keynes's theory "lost its dominant position" [43, p. XIII]. But the theory turned out to be not only unpopular, but contained, as the above analysis showed,

---

[1] In macroeconomics, the 'Keynes effect' is associated with the function of aggregate demand, but in reality should refer to the function of aggregate supply. Since in our GEE scheme these functions are inelastic, the monetary impulse directly determines the equilibrium volume of final product output.

fundamental errors. First of all, this is the substitution of 'insufficient demand' for insufficient supply, which, in our opinion, explains the spontaneous emergence of the theory of 'supply economics' (the theory of 'seplisders'). The real policy of stimulating aggregate demand instead of Keynes's aggregate supply, imputed to the state, turned into inflation, and subsequently, stagflation.

The set of models presented above shows well such Keynes's achievements as the concept of 'propensity to consume', 'multiplier effect', 'uncertainty' of the future of the economy and the need for state regulation of it. But, at the same time, the GEE scheme shows that the economy's exit from the 'equilibrium trap in a depression' can be implemented in a monetary-emission way, that is, in a simpler way than the one proposed by Keynes himself. This circumstance served, in our opinion, the reason for the emergence of 'Monetarism', whose representatives generally considered Keynesian measures of state regulation of the economy ineffective and periodically justified the policy of expanding business activity precisely by a moderate increase in the amount of money in the economy. 'Monetarism' quickly replaced 'Keynesianism' from macroeconomics.

Samuelson, on the basis of the 'neoclassical synthesis' developed by him, considered his '45-degree model' applicable to describe any state of the market economy. We have shown that the model cannot claim the universality that Keynes was striving for in the *General Theory*, since with its linear functions it is able to describe only a deflationary crisis economy with a built-in regulator of its quantitative proportions. In addition, and this, please, most importantly, the considered scheme does not reproduce the total equilibrium with Keynes's 'forced unemployment', which, according to the postulates of Walras' GEE, should not only exist, but be the only one. and sustainable. 'Institutional' unemployment, as time has shown, disappears with the transition to free pricing in the labor market.

We noted above. that the concept of 'neoclassical synthesis' as interpreted by Samuelson himself meant that after a quantitative settlement of full employment, the economy could move to traditional automatic functioning. But in Samuelson's GEE scheme with legislative wages, an increase in investment and output in a monetary manner runs up against regularity and interest rates, and the economy falls into an ineffective deflationary liquidity trap.

Modern neo-Ricardians talk about the 'organic' proximity of the theories of Keynes and Sraffa. For example, Kurz writes, "that the analyzes of two of the most significant critics of orthodox economics in the XX century, Keynes and Sraffa ... complement each other ... The question is ... to bring together the theoretical alternatives to orthodox science developed by ... Keynes and Sraffa, that is, the theory of effective demand and the theory of normal prices and distribution" [63, p. 21]. We support this goal, but so far we see in the theories of meters only a few formal similarities: 1) the origin of Sraffa's theory as 'left Keynesianism'; 2) upholding by both the principle of non laissez-faire and the need for state regulation of market defects; 3) their search for the effective distribution of the same aggregate indicator – national income.

Since the teachings of Keynes and Sraffa refer to different areas of economics that are arguing in reality and in our theoretical analysis – mainstream and 'neo-Ricardianism' – it is too early to talk about their 'organic' relationship.

13. 2nd approximation to Keynes's equilibrium concept: Hicks *IS-LM* synthesis model

Interpretation of the content of the *General Theory*, proposed by Hicks (*Mr. Keynes and the 'Classics': An Attempt at Interpretation*, 1936) in the form of the *IS-LM* model chronologically, as you know, appeared earlier than Samuelson's interpretation, but was used in macroeconomics only in conditions post-crisis market with movable prices and inflation instead of deflation, its model was more in line with the 60s. development of the Western economy, when, thanks to the implementation of the policy of 'neoclassical synthesis' by Samuelson, the market mechanism has already started working again. But for all the vulnerability of his 'cross' to criticism from monetarists, 'seplisders' and representatives of other areas of economics, 'Keynesianism' demanded and presented Hicks's model as supposedly more adequate to the 'spirit' of Keynes's theory. Hicks' article is only 15 pages long, divided into four unnamed sections, and contains three figures mainly illustrating the *IS-LM*[1] 'cross'.

It is important to note that Hicks's article was based on his 1936 scientific report and was published after Keynes's article *General Theory of Employment* (1937), devoted to some of the responses to the book *The General Theory of Employment, Interest and Money*, and containing important additional explanations of the theory. capital, which makes it possible to more accurately understand its original point of view on the mechanism for forming the interest rate and its role in balancing the economy.

In the economic literature, there are conflicting and extreme assessments of the Hicks model. Thus, one Oxford dictionary says that the "intellectual

---

[1] We keep the Latin letters *S, L* and *M* as designations of the elements of the 'Hicks cross' only when studying it, since in the monograph the letters are also used for other symbolism (see the *Preface*).

peak" of economics – the *IS-LM* model – "serves to teach and is not a realistic model of any existing economics" [15, p. 407]. However, some authors note the value of just its applied nature: "The *IS-LM* model is an excellent tool for analyzing the results of the policies of the conjunctural rise ..." [18, p. 124]. In textbooks on economic theory, the model is either not applied at all [68, 73, 96], or is used as the basis for the presentation of macroeconomics [25, 67, 95].

Let us clarify that the Hicks model is more correlated with the 'Keynes-2 cross' shown above, in which the volume of the real national product was used by the author as a measure of the total output, which created problems with his stated short-term theory. Hicks also used the indicator of the national product Y, but he incorrectly wrote that Keynes "ignored the entire side of the matter concerning depreciation, as well as the temporal aspect of the processes under consideration" [125, p. 356]. We have already considered these issues in the previous section of the monograph and noted Keynes's attention to "the costs of using capital equipment" [53, p. 92]. Hicks did not try to solve the issue of amortization and noted: "I will ... proceed from the fact that amortization can be neglected, that is, the release of investment goods coincides with new investments" [125, p. 344]. Only later, Samuelson, though not quite neatly, simply replaced Y with GDP. The problem of short-term, associated not only with amortization, but also with the investment process, was not solved by Hicks as well as by Keynes and Samuelson. He wrote: "So, I will proceed from the assumption that we are dealing with a short-term period, within which the amount of available physical equipment of all kinds can be considered unchanged" [Ibid, p. 344]. But this premise does not fit with Hicks' demonstrations of shock shifts in the *IS* function and other investment manipulations that inevitably change the volume of fixed capital. Note also that Hicks also introduced into his model simplifying, but fundamentally important, prerequisites for the equality of investment to savings, and the supply of money to demand for them. However, much in the *IS-LM* model should be evaluated positively. For example, if Samuelson had money, and therefore investments, were exogenous factors of the economy, then Hicks made them endogenous.

We will consider the *IS-LM* model in its essential aspect briefly and critically, without going into minor details and deeply into mathematical details.

Essential for the model, in our opinion, is the question of the prices applied in it. If in the Marshall model of local equilibrium prices and quantities were mobile, while in Keynes only quantities remained mobile, then in the more complex Hicks model the neoclassical standard can be restored on the scale of the entire macroeconomic system. According to many authors, the *IS-LM* model differs from the 45-degree model in that it 'takes into account the price factor' is the presentation of all indicators in real prices[1]. But in Hicks's article itself there are no corresponding statements, on the contrary, he wrote about nominal indicators [125, p. 344]. Therefore, in his model, on the abscissa, we will postpone the output indicator in real terms, and for monetary ordinates, we will use nominal and movable prices, which corresponds to the modeling canon and is convenient for constructing an OER scheme with a 'Hicks cross'. In addition, the use of nominal prices will free us from the need to demonstrate the numerous price shock shifts that have filled the macroeconomic literature of the model functions.

The insignificant details of the modern *IS-LM* model include its foreign economic mechanism. Without imploring its widespread use as a tool for analyzing trade and monetary policy of the state in open economy models, as well as the role of the model in applied research, we do not touch on these topics in this section.

In its original form, the theoretical construction presented by Hicks in 1937 was designated '*IS-LL*'. Later Modigliani (*Preference for liquidity and the Theory of Interest and Money*, 1944) slightly modified the model and renamed its equilibrium curve of money to *LM*. Hansen (*Monetary Theory and Fiscal Policy*, 1949) and other economists took part in the further development of the model. Although the model has entered the modern macroeconomic canon, in our opinion, it still has certain defects, made not so much by Hicks as by its interpreters. The functions *IS* and *LM* by Hicks were not deduced graphically and were justified only logically, and in the educational literature, into which the 'Hicks cross' migrated, the presentation of its analytical basis cannot be considered completely correct.

Let's start with the fact that the sequences '$I \rightarrow S$' and '$L \rightarrow M$' in the author's name of the model correspond to Keynes's idea of the priority of demand, while the sequence is actually 'production $\rightarrow$ consumption' and the construction of models 'supply $\rightarrow$ demand' is it is believed to use the reverse sequences: '$S \rightarrow I$' and '$M \rightarrow L$'. Moreover, the derivation of the model curves by Hicks was also carried out in full accordance with the mechanism for balancing these economic markets established by Keynes and demonstrated by us in the GEE scheme with the 'Samuelson's cross': the initial variable that sets the impetus for economic growth is the money supply by the emission center of the country. Therefore, the *LM* curve must be displayed first, and then the IS^2 curve. But in the literature, the analysis of curves is still carried out in the reverse order.

Further, we argue that the name of the model 'IS-LM', which stands for '*Investment–Saving – Liquidity–Money*', does not correspond to the letter and

---

[1] See, for example: [48, p. 509].
[2] Taking into account these two clarifications, corresponding to reality and the rules accepted in neoclassical literature, the name of the model should have been *ML-SI*.

meaning laid down in it by Hicks himself. In his article, the symbol *I* did not denote investment when he wrote that "we can draw the *IS* curve, which reflects the ratio between income *I* and interest *i*, ensuring equality of savings and investment" [Ibid, p. 350], and the national income, *Y*. Therefore, the exact interpretation of the model should be as follows: '*Income – Saving– Liquidity*'. It is clear that the renaming of the curves occurred either due to a misunderstanding, or in order to emphasize the equality of investment with

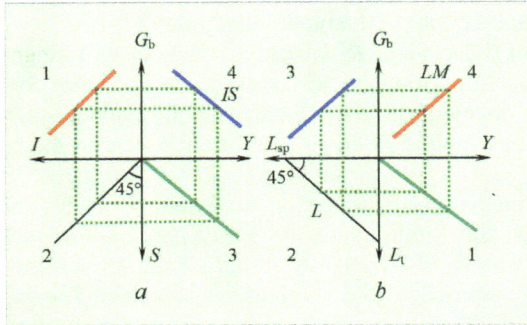

savings and the demand for money from their supply, respectively. But the name "*YS*" was given by Hicks not for this, but to indicate that "savings *S* depend on ... income" [Ibid, p. 345] *Y*. The name '*LL*' simply corresponds to the accepted designation of any curve segments on the graphs. In order not to

Fig. III.18

confuse the reader, in the further consideration of the model, we keep its name and its general structure, established in the literature. The original author's names of the curves – '*YS*' and '*LL*' – force a critical approach to their subsequent renaming and the accepted sequences of curves derivation, and also radically changes the existing idea of Hicks's concept, embedded in his model.

In fig. III.18 presents typical modern graphs for the derivation of the functions *IS* (*a*) and *LM* (*b*), which we present in the form of two four-quadrant diagrams (all functions in them are presented so far in a simplified linear form that does not violate model building logic). In diagrams, by changing the value of the initial variable and advancing these changes to adjacent coordinates, the points and the nature of the sought functions are determined (see dotted closed contours imitating equilibria). However, this method of comparative statics in this case is applied incorrectly. Diagram *a* of the figure includes the functions: a) investments $I(G_b^1)$ (quadrant 1); b)

---

[1] Immediately, we note that both models are incorrect – *IS* and *LM*. Model *IS* – from the point of view of the measure of the cost of savings used in it, because their exact price *IS* should not be considered the interest rate, but the amount returned per unit of the loan term, as we showed in section 7 of the monograph. The percentage can be considered, although convenient in macroeconomics, but a "converted" indicator of the cost of savings and investments. The incorrectness of the *LM* model is the measurement of the price of money as a percentage, while it is more correct to evaluate money by its purchasing power (for more details, see section 14 of the monograph).

184

equality of investments to savings $I(S)$ (2); c) the share of savings in the national product $S(Y)$ (3); d) IS (4). A decrease in the value of G_b, provided by the growth mechanism of Keynes's economy, leading to changes along the closed chain $G_b{\rightarrow}I{\rightarrow}S{\rightarrow}Y{\rightarrow}G_b$, allegedly generates the points of the IS function.

In fact, in this mechanism, an increase in investment should not form the same IS function, but shift it to a new, higher position (Fig. III.18, a). In addition, the adopted mechanism does not allow depicting the volumetric IS model, that is, the functions $f(G_b, I, Y)$. These circumstances make it necessary to reconstruct the corresponding part of the 'Hicks cross'.

There are defects in the typical construction and function of the LM. But before proceeding to clarify these defects, the essence and correction of the LM model, we recall that the letters L and M of its names are already used in the monograph for other symbolism. But in order to avoid confusion, further only in this section we keep the original name of the model and introduce the following new designations: L_t – demand for transaction money, L_{ins} – demand for insurance money, L_{sp} – demand for speculative

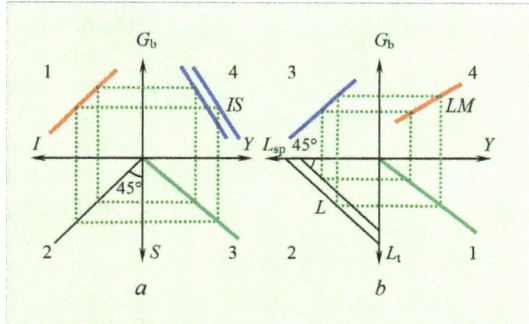

Fig. III.19

money. The corresponding diagram in Fig. III.18, b includes the functions: a) shares in the national product of transactional money demand L_t (it also includes insurance demand L_{ins}) $L_t(Y)$ (quadrant 1); b) the total demand for money (the sum of L_t and the speculative demand L_{sp}) $L(G_b)$ (2), located at an angle of 45°; c) the function $L_{sp}(G_b)$ (3) itself; d) bank interest $G_b(X_Y)$ (4). The decrease in the value of L_t, provided for by the growth mechanism of Keynes 'economies and leading to changes along the closed chain $L_t{\rightarrow}L_{sp}{\rightarrow}G_b{\rightarrow}Y{\rightarrow}L_t$, supposedly should, according to Hicks' representations, generate the points of the LM function.

But if in this mechanism the value of the total demand for money is assumed to be unchanged and only a redistribution between L_t and L_{sp} occurs in it, then G_b cannot decrease and the output Y cannot be increased, as shown in the diagram. The growth of the economy occurs only with an additional supply of money by the emission center of the country, which should be shown by the offset in quadrant 2 of the straight line L from the origin (Fig. III.19, b). The adopted diagram also does not allow drawing the volumetric model *LM*, that is, the function $f(G_b, L(M), Y)$. These circumstances indicate defects in construction and this second part of the 'Hicks cross' that need to be eliminated.

We are forced to carry out the reconstruction of the *IS* and *LM* models in the order adopted by the author himself [Ibid, p. 348, 349] – first constructing *LM*, and then *IS*, that is, the order corresponding to the priority given by Keynes to the model of the 'money-investment' market, simultaneously correcting the inadequacies of the latter. Whereas in other places in the monograph a different sequence of descriptions of numerous models has been and will be applied simply for stylistic reasons, in the case of a complex Hicks design, accuracy is important.

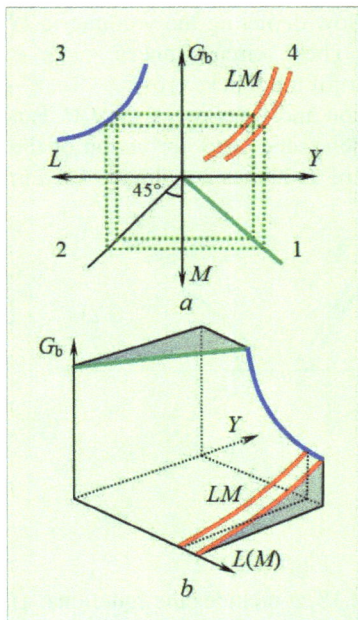

Fig. III.20

Consider Fig. III.20, *a*. His four-quadrant diagram presents a new approach to the derivation and characterization of the essence of the Hicks *LM* function. Since we noted that the starting point of the Keynesian money market model is the money supply *M*, this indicator is indicated on the ordinate of quadrant 1 of the diagram, the argument of which is the national product *Y*. Here, a ray emanating from the origin of coordinates at a certain angle indicates by the directly proportional share of *M* in *Y*: $M = k \cdot Y$, where k – the proportionality coefficient. Since the supply of money determines the demand for it, then quadrant 2 of the diagram with the ordinate *L*, showing its equality *M*.

Keynes's money market concept assumes a dual demand for Keynes's money: L_t, determined by the 'Cambridge monetary equation' $L_t = p \cdot X_Y \cdot Y$ (total output *Q* is replaced by *Y*) and L_{sp}, determined by the "liquidity preference" equation $L_{sp} = k/G_b$, where k – the proportionality coefficient. Therefore, the total money demand *L* will be equal to: $L = L_t + L_{sp}$, $L = p \cdot X_Y \cdot Y + k/G_b$. To illustrate and detail the first component of the equation, that is, the process of transactional spending of money in the literature, they resort to the works of Baumol (*Transactional Demand for Personality: An Inventory Theoretical Approach*, 1952) and Tobin (*Percentage-elastic Transactional Demand for Cash*, 1956), in which the so-called 'sawtooth function' is built on the basis of the 'theory of reserves'. But we see in these

186

constructions an important theoretical proposition: the conversion by economic entities of their bank deposits into cash, entailing the corresponding interest losses, cause an inversely proportional dependence of L_t on G_b. Thus, it follows from the Baumol-Tobin model that the function of the total total money demand also has such a dependence: $L = f(1/G_b)$, located in quadrant 3. The money market equilibration circuit ends on a nonlinearly increasing function LM in quadrant 4 of the diagram with coordinates '$G_b - Y$'.

By combining the coordinates M and L into one $L(M)$, we get a three-coordinate function $f(G_b, L(M), Y)$, the volumetric image of which is shown in Fig. III.20, b. LM functions simply express the dependence of the bank interest on the volume of the national product: $G_b = f(Y)$. Two such functions, shown in the figure, have two different values of $L(M)$ on its volumetric figure. Equilibrium of the money market is characterized not only by the points of the function LM of the section perpendicular to the coordinate $L(M)$, but also by any points on the surface of the function $f(G_b, L(M), Y)$.

At the heart of the graphical-analytical constructions of the IS curve of Hicks, who is considered the ancestor of 'neoclassical synthesis', is not Keynes's model of the money market, but the neoclassical model of the accumulation market. In this regard, he noted that "a significant part of Keynes's reasoning ... is not a general theory ... A general theory is something significantly more orthodox" [Ibid, p. 349]. Keynes also has a chapter in the *General Theory*, *The Classical Theory of Interest*, in which he agreed with the concept of the then existing accumulation market model, recognized its coordinates, the functions of demand, supply and the mechanism of their balancing. He wrote: "This is something on which we were all brought up and that until the very last time we accepted almost without reservations" [53, p. 179]. In the chapter, Keynes even included the graph of this model, which we mentioned above. Not accepting the neoclassical theory of the model, Keynes in his book unreasonably categorically stated that "this is an absurd theory" [Ibid, p. 182], since it allegedly "ignores the influence of changes in the level of income" [Ibid], and its model "curves ... tell us nothing about the rate of interest" [Ibid, p. 183].

In the aforementioned article, *General Theory of Employment*, Keynes returned to characterizing the well-known model. "The orthodox theory, – wrote Keynes, – considers the marginal efficiency of capital as a determining factor" [52, p. 366], that this theory is supposedly based on the full use of resources, including labor. But, since there is unemployment, Keynes concludes in the article: "Thus, instead of the statement that the marginal efficiency of capital determines the interest rate, or rather ... that it is the other way around. the interest rate determines the marginal efficiency of capital" [Ibid, p. 366, 367].

But, it is impossible to agree with these estimates and the statement: the model takes into account the level of income on the third coordinate, and the corresponding shifts of known functions and their equilibrium points always show the value of the interest rate. Keynes, a mathematician by education, could not help but understand a fairly simple graph and we dare to assume that all his long critical discussions in the chapter *The Classical Theory of Interest*[1] are explained simply by his desire to associate the volume of investments not with the 'classical offer' of savings, but with the bank interest, which determines the 'propensity to invest'.

Hicks, being in the position of 'orthodox' neoclassicism, deliberately showed (Fig. III.21) that the equilibrium of the economy is established in the savings market and is determined by the crosshair of the functions of investment demand for savings (A'_{inv}) and their supply (B'_{sa})[2], and the equilibrium the interest rate of this market, which he called the "investment rate of interest" [125, p. 353] ($G_{inv(e)}$) may not coincide with the money market rate (G_b). Thus, Hicks not only retained the double, monetary and investment,

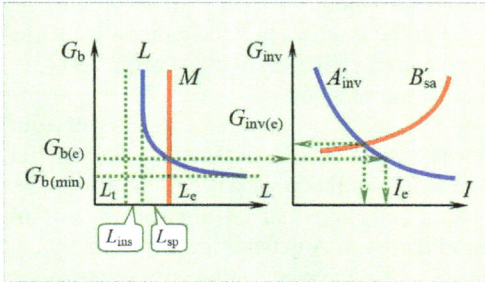

Fig. III.21

determination of interest rates, but also built his model of the economy on their automatic equalization.

Therefore, to fully understand the derivation of the *LM* curve, we will use the supply savings function (*S*) explicitly. Only in this case can the *IS* model be formed in the form in which it was presented by Hicks. In Fig. III.22, a shows a four-dimensional diagram intended for a new output of the *IS* functions located in quadrant 1. Quadrant 2 of the diagram contains a linear function of the share of investments *I* in the national product *Y* *I(Y)*, quadrant 3 is a ray at an angle of 45°, denoted the equality of *I* and *S*, and quadrant 4 – instead of the investment function, the savings function *S(G_b)*. Since under the assumption that *I* and *S* are equal, instead of the auxiliary quadrant 3, we can form one coordinate *I(S)*, then from the three coordinates of the diagram we compose a function *f(G_b, I(S),Y)*, the volumetric figure of which is is

---

[1] See: [53, p. 182-184].

[2] The designation here of the functions by the symbols 'A'_{inv}' and 'B'_{sa}', as in the investment function of Keynes (section 12 of the monograph), is due to the fact that the graph containing them is a differential part of the marketron of capital goods, in the integral part of which there are functions of profitability of use *A* and the cost of production *B* of capital goods (see section 7 of the monograph).

shown in Fig. II.22, *b*. It clearly shows three dependences on the corresponding planes, and all points of its concave surface can correspond to the equilibrium of the savings market.

In the economic literature, it is often indicated that the *IS* function is special. In one of the textbooks it is written that "*IS* reflects not the functional relationship between the interest rate and income, but a multitude of equilibrium situations in the commodity market, which are obtained as a result of the projection of the saving function and the investment function" [46, p. 208]. But, we are not talking about the 'commodity' market, but about the savings market, the *IS* curves in the model are the most common, they are just a function $G_b(Y)$.

In Fig. III.23 we show the complete model of the 'Hicks cross' as the union of two volumetric figures along the coordinates $I(S)$ and $L(M)$. The combination of the corresponding sections of the figures gives the graph of the *IS* and *LM* functions. The model allows not only to visualize the interrelationships of the four indicators, but also to carry out all kinds of model transformations used in macroeconomic theory and politics. The model shows that the equilibrium of the economy according to Hicks is such an interaction of its accumulation markets and money, which leads to the exit of the equilibrium investment interest $G_{и(p)}$ to the level of the equilibrium monetary interest $G_{b(e)}$ which, in its turn determines the equilibrium volume of the national product Y_p.

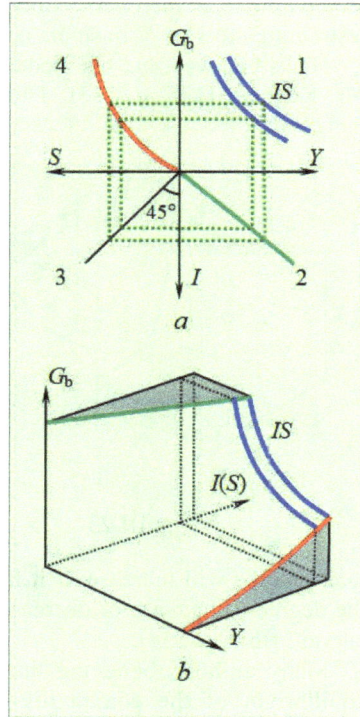

Fig. III.22

It is usually argued that the *IS-LM* model demonstrates the balance of the 'real and monetary' sectors of the economy, but based on the above, it can be said more precisely that the essence of the model is the functional relationships of three markets, since in it the *IS* curve is an elemental the accumulation market model, the *LM* curve – an element of the money market model, and the combination of the curves forms the product market graph.

From the point of view of production as the final point of the entire process of balancing the national market, the combination of the *IS* and *LM* functions represents a complete double assessment of national income, that is, an assessment of both the supply of income and the demand for it. The 'Hicks cross' contains a well-known meaning: *IS* expresses the deterrent, and the *LM* function – the stimulating effect of the interest rate on production. With the growth of G_b (rise in the cost of credit), production is curtailed and vice versa, but since the interest rate also characterizes the average profitability of the economy, its growth activates entrepreneurship and production. The establishment of the equilibrium percentage $G_{b(e)}$ and the total output Y_e at the intersection of *IS* and *LM* – a balance of stimulating and restraining motives of business activity.

Hicks believed that his model "somewhat develops ... the construction of Mr. Keynes" [125, p. 355]. Therefore, he not only proved a rather simple thing that "income and interest are determined by the intersection of the curves *IS* and *LL*, at which the investment rate of interest is equal to the money rate", but also tried to clearly show all the complexity of the mechanism of the national market, as well as 'Keynesian market': "Any change in the urge to invest or the propensity to consume will shift *IS*; any change in liquidity preference or monetary policy will shift *LL*. If, as a result of such a change, the investment rate rises above the monetary rate, income will increase; if it falls below the money rate, income will fall; the degree of increase or decrease in income depends on the elasticity of the curves" [Ibid, p. 354].

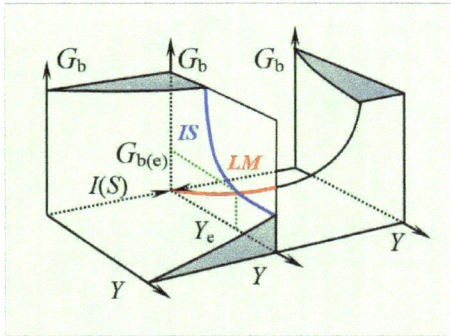

Fig. III.23

Many authors, believing that the 'Hicks cross' fully characterizes the equilibrium of the commodity and money markets, do not consider its interaction with the models of factor markets [21, 29, 46]. From our point of view, such an analysis is absolutely necessary to complete the picture. Hicks, almost forty years after the publication of his article, was surprised that his cursory analysis of Keynes's book "will be considered ... completed" [142, p. 6]. It requires not only the reconstruction of his *IS-LM* model, but also the construction of a new GEE scheme on its basis. Hicks, after his brief analysis of Keynes's *General Theory* and a description of the *IS-LM* model, in some subsequent publications, spoke about some elements of the mechanism for establishing the GEE. Even in his famous article there are a lot of corresponding statements, in one place, for example, we find: "With a given graph of the marginal efficiency of capital, the rate of interest determines the cost of investments, and that, in its queue ... determines the income. The level of employment ... is then determined through ... income" [125, p. 349]. However, Hicks did not provide any complete schemes for balancing the economy. After the publication of Hicks's article, repeated attempts were made to advance the theory in this direction by other economists, in particular, as we noted above, Hansen in 1951 (*Business Cycles and National Income*) added the *IS-LM* model to the 'cross' labor market (albeit more suitable for Samuelson's GEE scheme) and the usual production function, which discord Keynes's 'employment functions'. In the macroeconomic literature, there are more complex constructions[1], which also do not quite correspond to the ideas of Keynes and Hicks.

In our opinion, it is more correct to combine the 'Hicks cross' with the well-known model of aggregate output *AD-AS* ('Vinetraub's cross'), Keynes's employment function and Phillips function. The corresponding complete closed circuit of the Hicks GEE is shown in our standard six-quadrant arrangement in Fig. III.24. The scheme demonstrates the quantitative adjustment of markets while preserving their price interaction;

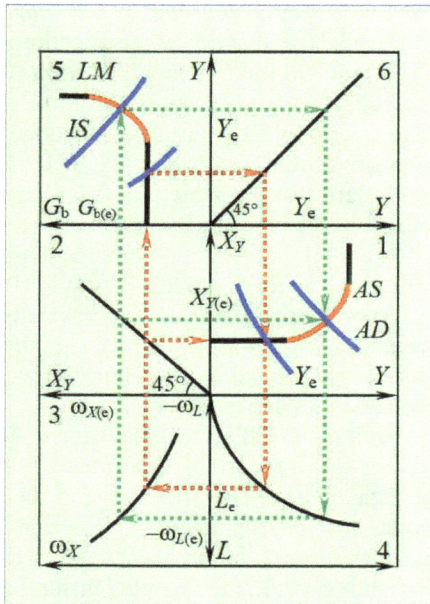

Fig. III.24

therefore, Keynes's 'employment function' $L = f(Y)$ is more appropriate in it than its inverse ordinary one-factor production function $Y = f(L)$. The existence of not only unemployment in the economy, but also inflation, the Phillips function reflects better than the labor market model. The GEE scheme is based on Keigan's concept of "adaptive expectations" (*Monetary Dynamics of Hyperinflation*, 1956) and therefore assumes the possibility of a choice in the 'inflation-unemployment' alternative.

Let's take a quick look at the origin and modern form of the Phillips function. At the time of the adoption of the 'Hicks cross' in 'Keynesianism', the article *The Relationship between Unemployment and the Rate of Change*

---

[1] See, for example: [25, p. 219-257].

in Nominal Wages in Great Britain in the Period from 1861 to 1957 appeared in economic theory. (1958)[1] New Zealand economist William Phillips (1919-1975). The original statistical 'Phillips curve' is the dependence of the rate of wage growth (ω_V) on the share of unemployed ($-\Delta L$) in the total number of labor resources L ($-\omega_L, -\omega_L = -\Delta L/L$) ($\omega_V = k/-\omega_L$, where k – a constant) (Fig. III.25). After the publication of the article, the statistical curve was confirmed by many other researchers. The English economist Richard Lipsey (b. 1928) (*The Relationship between Unemployment and the Rate of Change in Monetary Wages in the United Kingdom, 1862-1975: Further Analysis*, 1960) made a theoretical justification for the empirical curve, and Samu Elson and Solow (*Analytic Aspects of Anti-inflationary Policy*, 1960) generalized it by replacing ω_X with the rate of growth of the price index (ω_X). In this form and already as a function, the 'Phillips curve' turned out to be adequate to the market practice of those times, which faced unemployment and inflation at the same time (stagflation), and was considered an effective tool of the state's economic policy.

The Phillips function immediately sparked a theoretical and practical debate that continues to this day. We will turn to these disputes in more detail in section 15 of the monograph, specially devoted to the defects of the market economy, and in this section we are interested in the possibilities of using the function in modeling the interfactor GEE in the framework of Hicks' neoclassical synthesis.

Unlike the GEE scheme with a 45-degree model, which implements Keynes's system only as a theory of a crisis market with uncertain expectations, the GEE scheme with the *IS-LM* chart practically contains two models of the economy – Hicks and Keynes. As in all previous similar schemes of ours, in the new structure there are two balancing circuits – 'labor' and 'capital', but the relationship between them again acquires a peculiar character, due to the peculiarities of the interpretation of the work of the money market and savings Hicks.

Moreover, we find a certain contradiction in Hicks. On the one hand, he noted: "Most of our curves, in fact, cannot be determined unless something is said about the distribution of income and its magnitude, because they express a kind of relationship between the price system and the system of interest rates. .." [125, p. 355, 356]. But all the curves and the specified ratio can be determined and Hicks, on the other hand, definitely hinted at how this can be done: "Income and interest rate are determined at ... the point of intersection of the *LL* and *IS* curves. They are determined jointly – just as in the modern

---

[1] The relationship between wages and unemployment was considered by Phillips in *Stabilization Policy in a Closed Economy* (1954). There is evidence that before Phillips, similar issues were considered by Fischer and Tinberkhan.

192

theory of supply and demand, price and output are jointly determined" [Ibid].
That is, to address the issues raised, it is sufficient to supplement the savings
market model with the above-mentioned standard model of the aggregate
output of Weintraub.

Therefore, we combine the 'Hicks cross' in the coordinates '$G_b - Y$' with
the above-mentioned aggregated 'cross $AS\text{-}AD$'[1] in the coordinates '$X_Y - Y$'.
'crosses' are similar analytically and graphically, if in the first of them the
national product is assessed by the interest rate, then in the second – by the
price index. Accordingly, the initial interest rate in the scheme $G_{b(e)}$ of the
'capital' contour (quadrant 5) is transformed using a 45-degree transmission
(transfer auxiliary function) (6), Keynes's 'employment function' (4), Phillips
function (3) and a 45-degree ray of the price quadrant (2) into a chain of other
equilibrium parameters – Y_e, L_e, $-\omega_{L(e)}$, $\omega_{X(e)}$, X_Y и Y_e, which denotes a closed
'labor' contour of the GEE scheme, acting clockwise.

The positive side of this construction with two 'crosses' is that it contains
a substantiation of the synthesis universal function of the aggregate supply of
products AS, which shows with its vertical section the 'classical' state of the
economy with full employment, and with
its horizontal section – its 'Keynesian' state
with unemployment. Both sections of the
AS function in this GEE scheme are
derived from the same sections of the
Hicks LM function. The aggregate demand
function for products AD, like the function
AS, has vertical and horizontal sections
(Fig. III.26), and in its intersections with
the function AS, in addition to the usual
equilibrium point (9), there are four more
special equilibrium zones, called 'traps'[2] in

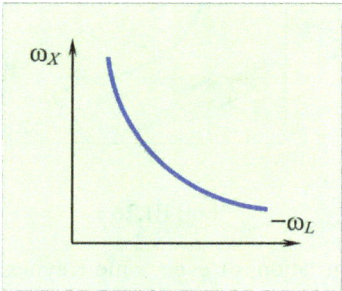

Fig. III.25

which the growth of the economy stops. We already know the 'liquidity trap'
– the cross-section on the horizontal section of the AS function (9_1), where
the additional emission of money does not lead to an increase in investment.
The crosshair area on the vertical section of the AD function (9_2), in which
the cumulative release is also blocked, is called an 'investment trap'.
However, in addition to these two well-known traps in the graph in Fig. III.26
there are two more extreme intersections of functions (9_3 and 9_4), which,

---

[1] In the name of this model, we nevertheless swap the abbreviations AD and AS
according to the 'production – consumption' sequence.
[2] Many authors mistakenly attribute the term 'trap' to Keynes (for example, in one
textbook it is noted that the preference for liquidity "Keynes called a liquidity trap" [106,
p. 496]). However, Keynes wrote only about a "truly absolute" preference for liquidity).
The term first appeared in *Outlines of Monetary Theory* (1956) by Robertson.

although they cannot be considered traps, are special zones, since the phenomenon of full employment of the labor force is observed in them.

Hicks wrote in his article that "*General Theory of Employment* – the economic theory of depression" [125, p. 352], "special theory" [Ibid, p. 349], in relation to which his own theory became 'general'. Therefore, he assigned Keynes's theory in his model of economics to the place of a viscous trap, in which the equilibration is depicted in Fig. III.24 in the form of a second circuit. In it, the synthesis, horizontal-vertical function of the aggregate supply shows the tendencies of the crisis economy: less cheap production, employment and more unemployment.

But the complex scheme of the GEE presupposes, along with self-regulation, state regulation of the economy, as advocated by Keynes (Fig. III.27). Such regulation means in the scheme of movement of volumetric functions *IS* and *LM* relative to each other along the coordinates '$I(S) - L(M)$' and the block of functions *IS-LM* relative to the plane with the rest of the elements of the scheme. If our analysis of the GEE scheme with the 45-degree Samuelson model has shown the effectiveness of simple monetary-emission regulation of the economy, then the considered Hicks model directs practice to the use of a mixed monetary-fiscal regulator. It realizes the possibility of reaching a compromise between unemployment and inflation, or even some Keynesian reduction of unemployment at the cost of rising inflation and emission coverage of the state budget deficit. The use of the Phillips function in one or another choice actually forced all macroeconomists to forget about solving the problem of achieving full employment.

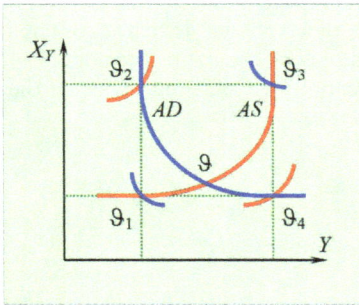

Fig. III.26

The combination of the neoclassical and Keynesian extremes into one common function of the aggregate supply of the national product Y as an initial variable in the ordinates of the interest rate G_b or the price index X_Y expresses the essence of Hicks's 'neoclassical synthesis'. The synthesis in Samuelson's interpretation assumed that the economy would enter a laissez-faire mode of operation only after it was 'treated' by the state, and Keynes linked such a transition to 'neoclassical orthodoxy' with achievements in labor force employment, in the final chapter of the *General Theory* he wrote that "if our system of centralized control leads to the establishment of the total volume of production, as close to full employment as possible, then from that moment on the classical theory will regain strength" [53, p. 337].

194

The same synthesis in the interpretation of Hicks turned out to be more organic, since it showed the transition to the given parameters of the economy within the framework of the same model.

Hicks investigated, as he put it, "the meager construction of Mr. Keynes" [125, p. 355] and called his own interpretation of it "very primitive and crude" [Ibid], with which one can only partially agree. Its design turned out to be more accurate than Keynes's model, closer to reality and contained generalizations that improve macroeconomics. Hicks also wrote: "... I will try to build my typical classical theory in a form similar to that in which Keynes presented his theory" [Ibid, p. 344]. In our opinion, he constructed not a classical, but a new theory, and not in the form of Keynes's theory, but in a form that included the latter as its particular case.

In contrast to the concept of spontaneous and socially acceptable macro-equilibrium of the neoclassicists, the Keynesian models of Hicks and Samael-son are united in the concept of recognizing money, taxes, subsidies, transfers and other public goods as necessary and effective instruments of state regulation of the market economy, in accordance with the principle of Keynes's non-leassiz-faire. In both models, the source of economic growth was the savings market, which was in line with the neoclassical doctrine and contributed to the successful development of Western countries in the postwar years. But, if Samuelson's model was based on linear functional dependencies of variables and, therefore, it focused on the monetary growth mechanism

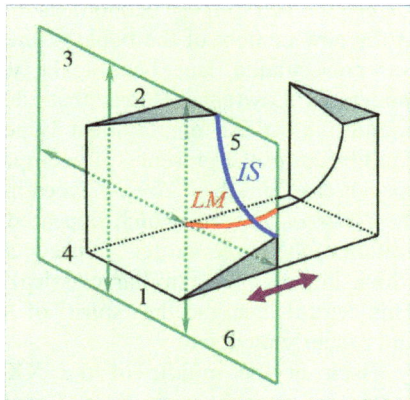

Fig. III.27

through quantitative coordination of markets, then the Hicks model already contained non-linear functions that allow one to display and regulate the natural market price mechanism for balancing the economy.

The GEE scheme, built on the foundations of the Hicks *IS-LM* model, reproduces the equilibrium with unemployment, but interprets unemployment as a removable phenomenon. Further in the monograph, we will show that forced unemployment is a common and unavoidable attribute of a market economy; we will prove that Keynes was close to this conclusion.

Hicks at the very end of his article noted: "In such a generalized form, Mr. Keynes's theory begins to resemble Wicksell's theory ..." [Ibid, p. 355], which back in 1898 in the book *Interest and Prices* separated the money market interest rates from the 'natural rates' determined by the marginal productivity of fixed capital. Keynes considered the 'Wicksell effect' in the *General Theory* in some detail, but did not use it in his macroeconomic system. Hicks, without going into the essence of the 'effect', used the difference in the indicated percentages as the basis for the *IS-LM* model. By design, the monetary, or rather the credit interest G_b, and the so-called 'investment interest' G_{inv} are different ($G_b = dK/K$; $G_{inv} = dY/dK$), that is, they are fundamentally different indicators[1], and this is the our opinion may require a revision of Hicks's economic modeling.

14. Third approximation to Keynes's equilibrium concept: full *AS-AD* model according to Marshall

Samuelson's 45-degree model and Hicks' *IS-LM* model can explain some of the phenomena of the pre-war and post-war market economies, respectively, but they do not fully reflect Keynes's theory. His *General Theory* seemed to these economists insufficiently general and therefore much of the new content of the book by the authors of the 'neoclassical synthesis' was emasculated. But, once again, we emphasize in the words of English monetarist Lawrence Harris that "Keynes saw his task in showing that equilibrium at full employment is not a general case. The general case is equilibrium in the presence of unemployment, and full employment is only a special case" [122, p. 269]. Keynes himself on this subject in the *Preface* to the *General Theory*, which appeared in Russia only in 2009, in the sixth edition of the book, wrote: "Consequently, we come to a more general theory, which includes the familiar classical theory as a special case" [53, p. 40]. This central idea and the 'spirit' of Keynes's system needs to be preserved and properly modeled.

Back in the middle of the XX century, when 'Keynesianism' was considered both theoretically and practically flawless, but there were studies criticizing 'Keynesianism' and calling for a return to the authentic teachings of Keynes. These are the publications of Patinkin (*Money, Interest and Prices. Integration of Monetary and Value Theories*, 1956), Klauer (*Keynesian Counter-revolution: Theoretical Assessment*, 1965) and Leyonhufwood (*On Keynesianism and Keynesian Economic Theory: a Study of the Monetary Economy*, 1968), relating to the so-called "nonequilibrium Keynesianism" [93, p. 197]. In our opinion, they mistakenly believed that in the modern economy there are strong frictions and delays in the mechanism of its balancing. Many economists who reproached Keynes in the absence of

---

[1] We will use the interaction of these indicators not in the theory of static equilibrium of the economy, but in modeling economic growth (see section 16 of the monograph).

a microeconomic basis for his teachings represented either a 'new classical macroeconomics', that is, an old school in a stricter form, or a 'new Keynesianism' engaged in founding (justifying) Keynes's teachings with complicated microeconomic models. But both essentially also acted in the direction of 'dissolving' Keynesian 'heresy' in orthodoxy even more than Samuelson and Hicks did. We see a regularity in this stable scientific trend: the more accurately and more systemically economists reflect in their models the innovations of Keynes's theory, the more it resembles neoclassicism Certain steps will be taken in the same direction in this section of the monograph after a brief comparison of early and recent 'Keynesianism'.

The ability to derive from the *IS-LM* model the key unified function of the aggregate supply *AS-AD*, as it turns out, was already in 1937 and even a year earlier, when the *General Theory* itself was published, with a careful analysis of its text, but contained in the book against Conversations and confusion in the definitions made by Keynes led to the development of economics along the wrong path.

Let's start with the contradictions. Thus, Keynes's famous "paradox of frugality" – an unexpected absolute reduction in savings when people show a tendency to save and incomplete investment of money – is not, as it is believed, obvious. The mechanism of the inverse multiplier effect can show in the 'Keynes-2 model' (see Fig. III.12) such a decrease in the output of the national product Y, in which savings cannot exist at all. But, in our opinion, the right field of large output values, in which the equilibrium volume of investments reaches gigantic proportions, looks really paradoxical in the model. There is doubt about the possibility of such proportions in the economy, which should also be attributed to the contradictions of the Keynesian model itself. Apparently, he was not just joking when he said that in the "long term, we are all dead"[1], but had in mind his hypothesis "about eternal stagnation" associated with this unrealistic trend in the ratio of consumption and investment. He wrote that, "when it comes to significant changes, then one must take into account ... the progressive change in the marginal propensity to consume ... as employment increases. In other words, as real income increases, society wants to consume a constantly decreasing part of it" [53, p. 137]. Therefore, Keynes's marginal propensity to consume is decreasing, and the integral function of consumption H itself is convex, that is, as Y grows, it becomes more and more flat. But this kind of addiction is contrary to common sense. In addition, in the *General Theory* we read: "The aggregate supply function ... can be represented as follows: $A = f(L)$, where A is income, the expectation of which will stimulate the achievement of the employment level L. Therefore, if ... employment L provides the

---

[1] Cit. according to: [104, p. 108].

production of Y ..., then it follows from here that the expression $A' = A/Y$ is an ordinary sentence curve" [Ibid, p. 73] (our notation – *the author*). But, firstly, based on really It was not about the supply function, but about the demand function, and, secondly, both of them always have a marginal form: $A' = dA/dY$, $H' = dH/dY$. The same confusion and the contradiction, that is, the impossibility of the 'paradox of frugality' and the 'paradox of super accumulation', remained with the linear 'consumption function' of Samuelson in its marginal zones, even when in his 45-degree model in I used GDP as an output indicator.

We know that Samuelson, following Keynes, postulated a one-factor form of the function of total expenditures B, which depended only on the volume of end output: $B = f(Q_{en})$. Samuelson's references to Kuznets's research (*National Product since 1869*, 1949), allegedly confirming the stability of the B/Q_{κ} value at the level of 0.867-0.879[1], cannot justify the linearity of B. The data obtained by Kuznets relate to the development of the economy as a whole, while the 'Samuelson's cross' models the dependence of consumption only on output under the ceteris paribus research premise. And since the B curve theorists continued to call the 'aggregate demand' function, and the income curve – the 'aggregate supply' function, the macroeconomics developed from the point of view of Keynes's ideas along the wrong path, it began to consider the most controversial elements of consumption theory.

The first economist to severely criticize Keynesian consumption functions and to show the multifactorial nature of consumption was the American James Dusenberry (1918-2009) (*Income, Savings, and Theory of Consumer Behavior*, 1949). Then a lot of publications appeared that developed the theory of consumption from the standpoint of the concept of 'expectation' used in the economic sense by Keynes[2] in the *General Theory* (apparently, after opposing Myrdal (*Monetary Equilibrium*, 1931) to "supposed", 'ex ante', savings and "realized", 'ex post', investments). Expectations of business entities – there are their opinions on the future values of economic variables, formed in conditions of uncertainty. But, as you know, subjective comparisons of incomes in time were investigated by Fisher (*Theory of Percentage*, 1930). It was on the basis of the neoclassical model of 'intertemporal equilibrium' and 'expectations' of Keynes, created by Fisher, that various modifications of the simplest consumption function of Keynes and Samuelson were carried out. Since Keynes wrote about short-term and

---

[1] See, for example: [75, p. 292].
[2] In five editions of the *General Theory* in the USSR and Russia, the English word 'expectations' was mistakenly translated as 'assumptions' and only in the sixth edition it was correctly translated as 'expectation'. For this reason, in Russian-language economic literature, the first use of the term 'expectations' is attributed to Mut (*Rational Expectations and the Theory of Price Movement*, 1961), who actually considered the more developed concept of "rational expectations".

long-term expectations [53, p. 157], then the concept of "permanent income", formulated by Friedman in 1950 and described by him in the book *Theory of consumer function* (1957), was based on the summation of adaptively averaged short-term expected incomes and a certain part of discounted long-term incomes. expected income. As a result, the 'Friedman's consumption function' differed from Keynesian ones in that the volume of consumption in it depended not only on current, but also on permanent income. At the same time, Friedman showed the variability of the 'propensity to consume', and, consequently, the 'Keynes multiplier'.

Another idea that consumption can depend not only on income, but also simply on accumulated property was first expressed by Tobin (*Relative Income, Absolute Income and Savings*, 1951), and was embodied in the form of a conceptual model of the "life cycle" Modigliani (*Utility Analysis and the Consumption Function: Interpreting Overlapping Generations*, with R. Brumberg, 1954). The Modigliani model and its numerous modifications took into account the dependence of current consumption on the wealth acquired during the working period of people's lives.

In general, the theoretical approach from the position of long-term expectations and empirical tests of the models of 'permanent income' and 'life cycle' have significantly clarified the process of consumption itself. However, the revealed details of consumption did not advance the theory of the equilibrium of the economy; the multifactor nature of consumption in general was known to Keynes and Keynesians, as well as to all economists.

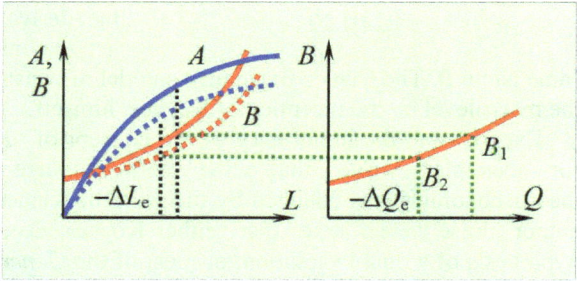

Fig. III.28

But we are talking about the so-called 'shift' factors of consumption, which should remain unchanged in the study of its main factor – output, since this is the requirement of the premise ceteris paribus.

In 1965, a different kind of shift took place in the theory of consumption, the concept of Klauer's "double solution" (*Keynesian Counter-revolution: Theoretical Assessment*, 1965) appeared, which was subsequently developed using Patinkin's labor market model (*Forced Unemployment and Keynesian supply Function*, 1949) Barro (*Money, Employment and Inflation*, with H. Grossman, 1976). The neoclassical-type model developed by the concept claimed to derive Keynes's aggregate consumption function based on new assumptions about the microeconomic behavior of households in conditions of unemployment. Due to the analytical and graphical complexities contained in the Klauer-Barro model of 'double solution' [25, p. 465-499], we will use to explain the essence of the authors' approach by the integral part of the marketron of employment and consumption of goods by a representative household (Fig. III.28).

The term 'dual solution' refers to a change in the costs of all consumers due to a change in their income due to a decrease in overall employment. Accordingly, the left graph of the figure shows the dependences of the profitability of production (A) and consumption consumption (B) on employment L, the equilibrium value of which falls on the maximum profit of the sale and purchase of 'labor' $(A - B)$. In the case of a decrease in the equilibrium profitability of households, they decrease the equilibrium

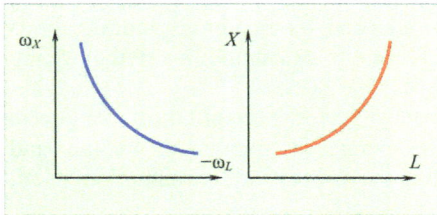

Fig. III.29

expenditure (dotted curves in Fig. III.28), and its equilibrium employment $(-\Delta L_e)$ also decreases, and these changes on the right graph with coordinates '$B - Q$' correspond to the points B_1 and B_2, the integral consumption function B, taking the derivative of cator, you can get the marginal function of the same name B'. The Clauer-Barro micromodel of consumption is transferred to the macrolevel by the reception of Keynes[1] himself.

Experts note the importance of the concept of 'double decision', Blaug, for example, wrote that "the entire course of development of macroeconomics was changed by the work of Klauer" [13, p. 119], and the author himself even states that "either Keynes, deep down, adhered to the hypothesis of a double solution, or most of the *General Theory* is theoretical nonsense" [57, p. 405]. However, one should not exaggerate the importance of the concept, which, firstly, is obvious, and, secondly, it changes the object of research, in fact, it is not aimed at deriving the function of aggregate supply, but the study of market behavior of households.

Many theorists were enthusiastic about the emergence of the Phillips function in macroeconomics. So, in the *New Paulgrave* dictionary, Itwell writes: "The Phillips curve filled the empty fourth quadrant of graphs familiar to everyone from textbooks, bringing the number of unknowns in line with

---

[1] Keynes in many places in the *General Theory* spoke about the absence of a fundamental difference between the analysis of the behavior of an individual economic entity and the economy as a whole. He also often cited formulas for converting micromodels into macromodels [53, p. 262].

the number of equations and thereby closing the model" [136, p. 456]. But, we believe that the Phillips function should not just be placed in the GEE scheme, but it can be a direct element of the aggregate supply function of the economic model described in the *General theory* by Keynes. Blanchard (*Macroeconomics*, 1997) generally asserts that the Phillips curve is the aggregate supply function [11, p. 185]. And with this thesis, with certain reservations, you can agree. Let us clarify that Phillips himself did not make these identifications, and Blanchard's thesis will be valid only when transforming the coordinates '$\omega_X - (-\omega_L)$' of the Phillips function into coordinates '$X - L$' (Fig. III.29), in which Second, the question of the relationship 'unemployment – inflation' becomes close to its interpretation by Keynes.

In this regard, let us once again turn to Keynes's 'aggregate demand – aggregate supply price' model. *Chapter XXI. The theory of prices* of his book, he first briefly described a very important theoretical position as follows: "As long as there is underemployment of factors of production, the degree of their use will change in the same proportion as the amount of money; if they are fully employed, then prices will change in the same proportion as the amount of money" [53, p. 274, 275]. We will give a graphic illustration of this statement in the form of an angular broken figure in the coordinates '$X - L$', placing in it the

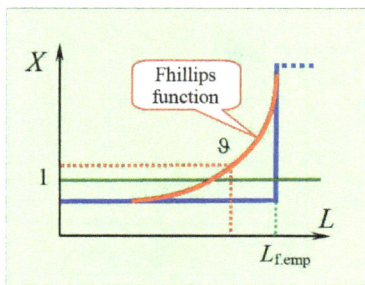

Fig. III.30

transformed Phillips function (Fig. III.30). The model has a point '1' on the X coordinate, corresponding to a 'normal' economy, and a lower horizontal segment of deflationary values of the variable L, which after the point of full employment ($L_{f.emp}$) turns into an inflationary vertical. This figure, or "Keynes's angle", expresses the effect of emission of money described by Keynes: the growth of employment in the economy first, and then prices. The Phillips function we reworked, or the "Phillips angle", is a skewed 'Keynes angle', therefore, for example, at its point 9 there is unemployment and inflation at the same time.

Comparison of the curves shows that according to the aforementioned statement of Keynes, the simultaneous existence of unemployment and inflation, that is, stagflation, is excluded, whereas according to Phillips and in reality it exists. How can this contradiction be explained? Keynes, in the same chapter mentioned, writes further: "Generally speaking, an increase in *effective demand* [of money] will be spent partly on increasing the use of resources and partly on raising the price level" [Ibid, p. 275] (italics ours –

the author). And he gives five reasons for this phenomenon of stagflation, which can be briefly reduced to the ceteris paribus principle. If Keynes examines in detail the use of all factors of production, then in the model with one factor of employment L this will mean 'other things being equal'. Note also that Keynes's all operating factors are represented by money, which corresponds to his concepts of 'liquidity preference' and 'non-neutrality of money'.

Thus, both functions shown above are correct and compatible, only the 'Keynes angle' is a crude, simplified one, and the 'Phillips angle' is a realistic relationship between employment and the price index. Both figures represent only fragments of the aggregate supply function B' – the 'Keynes

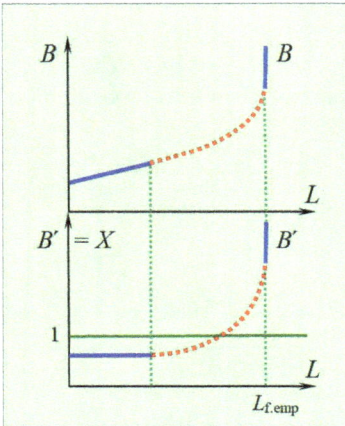

Fig. III.31

angle' is the initial and final, and the 'Phillips angle' is its middle part (Fig. III.31). Since B' is a marginal function, it is possible to restore its integral form B. Both functions are represented in the employment marketron. The nature of the curves does not fundamentally change when the argument 'employment' L is replaced by 'cumulative output' Q, which, however, as already noted, will require calling it the 'function of total expenditures'.

Our constructions relate to the function of the aggregate supply of products, but in the quotes and in the *General Theory* as a whole, paradoxically, Keynes speaks of the function of 'effective demand'. That is, we are again faced with Keynes's fundamental mistakes in the naming and meanings of their functions, which entailed in macroeconomics a whole series of studies of the consumption process instead of the production process. It is necessary to understand that the function B' is simply a homogeneous monetary expenditure of production, including rent, depreciation and wages. Therefore, any clarifications and revisions of the essence of consumption made by Dusenbury, Friedman, Modigliani, Klauer and other theorists themselves had scientific value, but did not solve the issue of developing an aggregate supply function adequate to Keynes's theory.

And, nevertheless, a fairly complete picture of the marginal and integral functions of *AS* can be obtained not only with the help of the *IS-LM* Hicks model, but also with a careful reading of the original source – the *General Theory* of Keynes.

Keynes did not use the term "general equilibrium" of Walras, as he

202

believed that "the theory of Walras and his other supporters is complete nonsense!" [43, p. 8] and wanted to develop Marshall's local equilibrium model to describe the economy as a whole. However, Marshall lacked the concept of unemployment, which occupied a key place in Keynes's theory. Patinkin wrote that in *General Theory* Keynes "analyzes general equilibrium. The voice of Marshall sounds in it ..." [148, p. 35], but his attempt to develop a model of aggregated supply and demand functions and link it with the concept of 'forced unemployment' was not entirely successful. Is it possible to reconstruct 'Keynes cross' on non-classical principles? Many economists answer the question in the negative. For example, De Frei (*History of Macroeconomics from Keynes to Lucas and Beyond*, 2016) writes: "With a high degree of probability, it can be assumed that consensus on this issue will never be reached" [43, p. 6]. But this opinion can be rather explained by the fact that the author prefers the newest models of 'dynamic stochastic general equilibrium' (*DSGE*-models) and only casually mentions the 'crosses' of Samuelson and *AS-AD*. But for all the importance of the dynamic approach of the 'new classics', the problems of static macroeconomics still remain unresolved. In our opinion, the mentioned 'consensus' is possible. Keynes, relying on the 'Marshall cross' methodology, actually replaced it with an integral aggregated model, which he presented in a confused form. Therefore, the task of macroeconomics is to bring both models into mutual correspondence – to add the corrected Keynesian integral model to the *AS-AD* marginal model, that is, to create a macromarketron of total output. which it would be fair to call the complete equilibrium model of the Marshall economy.

Let's imagine the economy as a firm and describe it with the help of the output marcetron, taking into account the data of the above analysis of the theory of Keynes and Keynesians (Fig. III.32).

In the integral part of the marketron, the function of nominal consumption B from the level of autonomous expenditures B_{au} grows as additional factors of production are drawn into the economy, first linearly, then nonlinearly due to the use, on the one hand, of low-quality and ineffective, costly reserve, on the other hand, high-quality, expensive, factors of production, including the unemployed, and then goes to the vertical corresponding to the maximum values of output and full employment ($Q_{f.emp}$). The nominal income function A rises convexly above the bisector of real income A_{re}. The growing and then decreasing difference $A - A_{re}$ in the entire range of the total output Q represents an 'inflation tax' on economic entities. The nature of both functions is determined by the action of the law of diminishing resource efficiency, that is, the premise ceteris paribus.

In the differential part of the marketron, which directly models the product market, the functions of the marginal price indices of aggregate demand (X_A, $X_A = A' = dA/dQ$) and the aggregate supply (X_B, $X_B = B' = dB/dQ$) are presented , which in this model expresses the dynamics of the "marginal propensity to spend" [82, p. 353] Keynes. For a complete explanation of the behavior of the B' curve, it is important to note that the functions A and B are in constant interaction, which distinguishes this macromarketron from the micromarketron, in which similar functions are independent. This feature characterizes the emergence of the macroeconomic system, that is, the presence in it of a property that is absent in its elements. Therefore, the "poverty effect" of small volumes Q, where $B > A$, divides, and the "wealth effect", of large volumes Q, where $B < A$, brings together the functions A and B. Accordingly, the aggregate demand function monotonically decreases with an increase in output , with the transition of the A' value across the important price-new border between inflation and deflation ($A' = X_Q = 1$), business entities observe the replacement of Keynes's "preference for liquidity" with a preference for goods and securities, "the effect of real cash balances" – an increase in the costs of business entities in the conditions of decreasing inflation in the economy, discovered by Pigou (*Classical Stationary State*, 1942), and studied in more detail by Patinkin (*Money, Percentage and Prices: Integration of Monetary and Value Theories*, 1956).

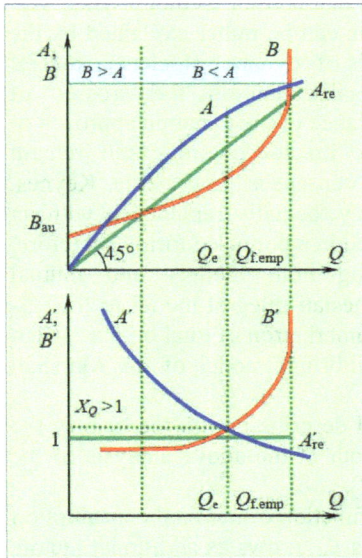

Fig. III.32

Keynes tried to overcome the neoclassicism, but adhered to the traditional criterion of economic activity and equilibrium, noted that "effective demand is ... such a value of the aggregate demand function ... that an entrepreneur can maximize the size of the expected profit" [53, p. 82]. But he was mistaken when he wrote that at the point of intersection of his supply and demand functions "the profit expected by entrepreneurs will be the greatest" [Ibid, p. 60]. First, according to Case, it turns out that there can be many such points, while in reality, the 'effective' equilibrium of output should be the only one, and secondly, the maximum profit is obtained not at the point of intersection of functions, but at the point of greatest difference between them. In the new 'cross' of output presented by us, the difference between A and B corresponds to the total profit of the economy, consisting of the main part, measured by the difference between the bisector A_{pe} and B, and the inflationary part. The maximum total profit falls on the crosshair of the functions A' and B', which measures the equilibrium values of the output volume (Q_e) and the price index (X_Q), which in Fig. III.32 is inflationary, slightly above one (at the bottom of the figure – the dashed line).

If Samuelson considered the cause of forced unemployment to be immobility of wages, and Hicks considered a 'liquidity trap', that is, certain special conditions of the economy, then its real permanent reason is the orientation of business entities to maximum profit. Keynes's proposal to stimulate effective demand and employment is not realistic because output exceeding the natural maximum profitable equilibrium is accounted for by lower total profit, which increasingly narrows the possibility of creating additional jobs. The problematic nature of employment can be exacerbated by a decrease in the share of the extensive component in investment that creates jobs, due to intensive investments that release workers. A market economy with maximum output is also unlikely, since in this case it becomes generally non-profitable.

It should be emphasized that Keynes, on the one hand, discovered 'effective demand' as a demand that brings maximum profit and 'forced unemployment' ("The lack of effective demand alone can lead and often leads to a cessation of employment growth even before how the level of full employment will be achieved" [Ibid, p. 63]), which allows us to consider his book a really general theory, but, on the other hand, he could not convincingly prove this, which caused a lot of different interpretations his statements. For example, many economists consider 'forced unemployment' to be an abnormal phenomenon [43, p. 6, 7]. But it is not so. Keynes considered it, on the contrary, a normal market phenomenon, but not acceptable from a humanitarian point of view and completely removable with the help of the state.

We give a new interpretation to the concept of 'unemployment'. If its Malthusian interpretation proceeded from 'natural' overpopulation, the Marxist one – from the growth of the 'organic structure of capital', the neoclassical one – from an excessively high level of wages, and its Keynesian version was based on insufficient aggregate demand, then in fact unemployment is an inevitable sacrifice of efficiency and therefore it is legitimate to talk about 'effective unemployment', that is, about such a level of underemployment, which ensures maximum profitability in the economy.

The presence of forcedly unemployed people in society should not surprise us, just like the 'unemployed' land, or capital goods. In general, a market economy operating for maximum profit always has surplus factors of production. We can say once again that market theory is the science of rational economic management already in conditions of not limited, but an excess of resources. If the equilibrium attributable to the maximum profit and not the maximum output does not surprise us in the 'Marshall cross', then why does the same objective phenomenon at the macro level cause so much controversy?

The complete model of the aggregate output of the Marshallian type presented above allows solving many problems of macroeconomics at the same time, and most importantly, reproaches against Keynes's theory about the lack of microeconomic substantiation[1] in it are removed, since del as the third approximation to Keynes's concept of equilibrium is this justification. At the same time, Keynes's theory is becoming more and more neoclassical.

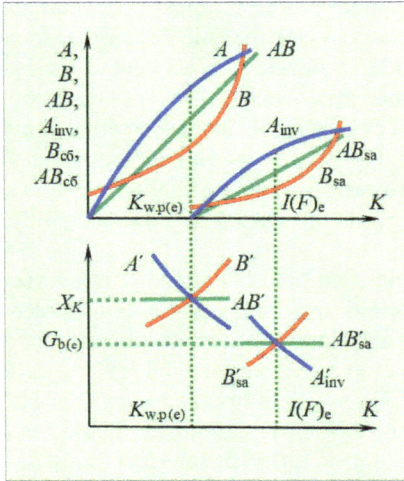

Fig. III.33

We consider the new marketron of the total output Q presented above as the main element of the unified GEE scheme, which should also contain models of production factors, and also, if we adhere to the completeness of research, exchange factors – money, as national and international.

A unified model of production factors is presented in the form of a marquetron of the total production apparatus K (Fig. III.33), the value of which is indicated on the abscissa by the number of work-places in the economy of $K_{w.p.}$. As we have already noted in section 7 of the monograph, such a measurement is convenient because it also characterizes the number of other factors of production employed in shifts – labor and land. On the ordinates of the marquetron, the values of integral and differential indicators of the discounted profitability of workplaces for the entire average life of their work (A, A), production costs (B, B) and the amount of the sales contract (AB, AB) the corresponding amount of capital goods. In the model, an equilibrium average cost of a job (X_K) and an equilibrium number of work-places $(K_{w.p(e)})$ are formed, which corresponds to equilibrium employment in the economy and is the most profitable for business.

The graph in Fig. III.33 is expanded by the model of savings, that is, investment-savings $I(F)$, as an increase in capital goods in the nominal-

---

[1] For example, the authors of one of the advanced textbooks write: "The fact is that Keynesian macroeconomic theory suffered from a fundamental flaw – the absence of solid microfoundations" [75, p. 282].

206

monetary terms. The model should be seen as a generalization of the non-classical and Keynesian theories of capital. In the integral part of the marketron $I(F)$, there are the functions of the return on investment A_{inv}, the expenditure of the B_{sa} and the realization of the savings AB_{sa}. The savings function B_{sa} divides the total profit from the sale and purchase of savings into the profit of commercial banks and the profit (interest income) of their depositors. The differential part of the marketron contains: 1) the increasing function of the offer price of savings B'_{sa}, since with an increase in the size of bank deposits, the interest rate paid to savers (depositors) increases; 2) a decreasing function of the price of demand for investments A'_{inv}, which characterizes a decrease in the payment for a loan as its amount (value) increases; 3) a linear function of the equilibrium investment price AB'_{inv} in the form of an equilibrium interest rate $G_{b(e)}$, at which the equilibrium investment volume $I(S)_e$ is realized.

Next, consider the monetary system, which, according to Keynes, plays an important role in the establishment of the GEE. In the previous sections of the monograph, we have already clarified the issue of monetary aggregates, showed their connections with product aggregates in the form of Fisher's equation for the amount of money and the 'Cambridge monetary equation', and got acquainted with the Keynesian theory of money. Here we will try to outline the complete model of money as a factor in the exchange of goods.

The fiduciary money market is one of the fundamental, system-forming elements of the modern economy, but, perhaps, the most complex and, despite the abundance of relevant publications, an insufficiently studied object of macroeconomics. Back in 1875, Jevons spoke about the difficulties of understanding monetary phenomena: "Money for economic theory is the same as squaring a circle in geometry" [146, p. 1]. Skidelsky writes: "If Marx is a poet of goods, then Keynes is a poet of money" [153, p. 543]. As we have already noted, Keynes did deal with money a lot, both in theory and in practice. But, nevertheless, he considered the theory of money unfinished, called his intellectual efforts in this direction the first step towards a "generalized **Q**uantitative **T**heory of **M**oney" [51, p. 445] and said that "we necessary a complete **T**heory of **M**onetary **E**conomics" [Ibid, p. 451][1]. But such theories of money and economics never emerged. Keynes's model of money presented above cannot be considered impeccable, a consistently marginal approach to the interpretation of money and the logical completeness of describing their market is also absent in monetarism. On the one hand, it is said about the market for such money as the whole set of relations between business entities that offer money and demand for it. On

---

[1] It is surprising that the latest edition of Keynes's works in Russia [53, p. 267, 273] does not contain the highlighted designation of the theories of money and monetary economy, cited in quotations.

the other hand, naming the sides and attributes of the money market, theories do not bring this concept to completion. In all the models of money available in the economics, the bank interest is considered as the price of money, and not the purchasing power of the money-reserve itself, while the indicator of their quantity, as a rule, is not specified.

Taking a systematic approach to modeling the national money market, first of all, it is important to note that of the monetary aggregates introduced by us, the amount of cash Z_1 is a reserve, and the money of the Central Bank of the country (monetary base) Z_2 and the money supply Z_3 are flows. Therefore, the only measure of the physical quantity of money and the independent variable of their market model should be the aggregate Z_1, while the rest of the monetary aggregates-flows are dependent variables. Cash issued by the Central Bank of the country for the purchase of gold, foreign currency and securities, the provision of loans to the government and commercial banks, as well as exchange for the obligatory reserves of commercial banks (at the request of their depositors), lives at the base of the entire 'monetary pyramid' of the state. Integral and differential functions expressing the relationship between the three main monetary aggregates will be considered in the form of a monetary marquetron, the graphs of which are shown in Fig. III.34. In addition to Z_1, Z_2 and Z_3, on the ordinates of the model in nominal terms, the total costs of production and circulation of money in the economy B are plotted. By virtue of the ceteris paribus assumption, the functions Z_1, Z_2 and Z_3 are convex, and the function B is concave.

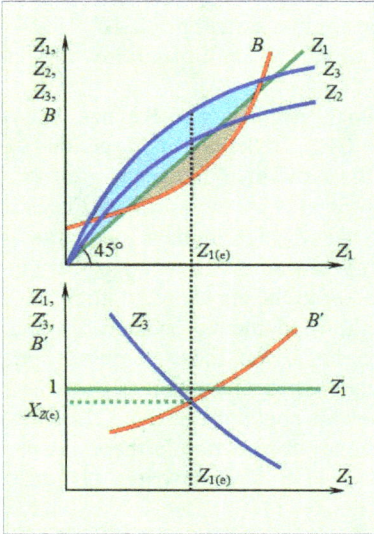

Fig. III.34

The contractual function Z_1 – a ray emanating from the origin at an angle of 45° – characterizes the regulatory and institutional framework for the implementation of money as a factor in the exchange of values in the economy, the relationship of fiduciarity between the state-producer of money and their consumers – business entities. The Z_2 function is located above the bisector, since the monetary base is equal to the sum of the cash flow and the required reserves of commercial banks recorded in the correspondent accounts of the Central Bank. Since the money supply ('broad money') Z_3 is the sum of the money turnover created by business entities, including commercial banks, the function Z_3 characterizes the entrepreneurial profitability of using cash, it expresses the law of falling efficiency in the form of diminishing money turnover as Z_1 grows.

The Z_3 indicator is calculated as follows: $Z_3 = r \cdot Z_1$, or in more detail: $Z_3 = [(1 + k_{mo})/(k_{res} + k_{mo})] \cdot Z_1$, where: k_{mo} – the deposit monetization standard ($0 < k_{mo} < 1$, for $k_{mo} = 1$, there is no banking system in it at all and all transactions are made only by means of cash); k_{res} – deposit reserve ratio ($0 < k_{res} < 1$, with $k_{res} = 1$ there are no commercial loans in the monetary system). The decisions of bank customers on the rate of monetization of deposits also affect the volume of active operations of banks, the more k_{mo}, the narrower the lending activities of banks. The decisions of the Central Bank on the deposit reserve rate determine the volume of active credit operations of commercial banks, the less k_{res}, the more active transactions and the greater the risk in the work of banks. In general, the operations of commercial banks do not affect cash (it is controlled by the Central Bank of the country) and their volumes depend on the money needs of business entities. The ratio Z_3/Z_1 is called an indicator of the turnover of cash or the speed of circulation of money r. The reciprocal of r, the fraction Z_1/Z_3, called the indicator of the level of monetization of total income in nominal terms (Q_n), is included in the 'Cambridge monetary equation' $Z_1 = p \cdot X_Q \cdot Q$.

The function B' of the differential part of the model will progressively increase. It, as a marginal dependence ($B' = dB/dZ_1$) is a multiplier of money emission and a money supply function, and the decreasing function of the marginal profitability of money Z_3 ($Z_3 = dZ_3/dZ_1$) – a demand function for money. The function Z_1 is a 'unit' horizontal corresponding to the non-inflationary equilibrium of the monetary system, it can coincide with the point of intersection of the money supply and demand functions, and then the marginal values of income Z_3, expenditure B' and cash Z_1 become equal to each other: $dZ_3/dZ_1 = dB/dZ_1 = dZ_1/dZ_1 = 1$. Fig. III.34 shows a more typical inflationary state of the economy. The intersection point of the corresponding marginal curves on the ordinate measures the equilibrium market price or the purchasing power of money ($X_{Z(e)}$), which in the case shown is below the nominal price. The same point on the abscissa Z_1 corresponds to the equilibrium cash ($Z_{1(e)}$), which ensures the maximum turnover of money and optimal reserves of banks, which guarantee the safety of their clients' deposits.

We can speak about the money market in the full sense of the word only if it includes mutually interested counterparties, and the traded good has a price and brings benefits to the parties[1]. As we have shown, money is a

---

[1] Such a broad interpretation of the money market, including producers and consumers of money, was justified in our monograph: [35, p. 368-380].

public good that has a price, it has a producer-issuer represented by the state, economic entities consume money, temporarily withdraw money from circulation, and give it away. But is the circulation of money profitable? The above modeling of the money market shows that money also has this attribute of the market; it brings profit.

From a financial point of view, all money is credit, provided by the state and other economic entities for temporary paid use. Therefore, in the money market, there are parties that claim and receive profit. The total surplus of the money market, which we call the 'national dividend', represents the financial result of all economic entities, including the state, is equal to the difference $Z_3 - B$, and is divided by the income of three factors of production – the sum of rent, wages and cash flow $(Z_3 - Z_1)$ (see Fig. III.34 the corresponding shaded area) and the profit of the state from the issue of money – seigniorage $(Z_1 - B)$ (see the corresponding shaded area). When the monetary system is in equilibrium, the 'national dividend' becomes maximum.

There is no unambiguousness about the seignorage of the state in macroeconomics. In the *Economic Encyclopedia*, seigniorage means "the exclusive right of the state to print banknotes, a way to cover the state budget deficit through the emission of money by the central bank" [133, p. 723]. In our opinion, this is an erroneous understanding of seigniorage. If we turn to the original meaning of the term, then initially it denoted a payment for the tolling (from the English word 'tall' – tax, duty, collection) minting money from the precious metal of private customers by the state mint, the face value of which covered the corresponding costs and delivered profit to the ruler. We also use this interpretation of the term. Seigniorage in the modern meaning of the word is "the profit received by the authorities from the issue of money" [15, p. 656][1].

It can be concluded that money, being a special public good, has all the attributes of an ordinary market product, the amount of money is measured by its nominal mass, and the price of money is not a percentage, but its purchasing power $(X_Z = 1/X_Q)$. The market approach to the analysis of money allows, firstly, it is reasonably considered in accordance with Keynes's theory to be non-neutral, secondly, the monetary system, which is traditionally a sphere of discretionary state regulation, can be included in the complex of self-balancing markets, and, thirdly, use a submitted model of money to new describe the interfactor GEE.

---

[1] In a narrower sense, the term is used in relation to a country whose currency is used by foreign states for trading purposes or as a reserve (for example, for the stability of the financial system and the economy as a whole, the Central Bank of Russia not only reserves part of the deposits of commercial banks, but also places a part their foreign exchange reserves in foreign banks). In this case, seigniorage means the income of the country from the corresponding issue of its currency.

Let's move on to the analysis of another monetary model – the marketron of the international currency market, which is officially the US dollar. A separate consideration of this model, which describes the functioning of the foreign trade sector of the economy, makes the theory of GEE more complete and specific.

The economy that interacts with the rest of the world has been studied since the days of classical political economy, and mercantilists were the first to point out the importance of foreign trade. Its mechanism, profitability and balance were studied by Smith and Ricardo, and later by many neoclassicists. However, the modern theory of open economics is still far from perfect.

Market transactions are always associated with payments, and foreign trade of countries is recorded in the form of accounting aggregate indicators in the so-called balance of payments. The term 'balance of payments' was first used by the English mercantilist James Stewart (1712-1780) (*Study of the Principles of Political Economy*, 1767), but only in 1923 did the League of Nations publish balance of payments of some countries. In 1943, the American economist D. Larry compiled the US balances of payments for 1919-1939. They served as the basis for the development of the Balance of Payments Scheme by the International Monetary Fund (*Balance of Payments Manual, 5th edition*, 1993). However, the accounting principles of constructing the balance of payments make it always balanced and do not show the general state of the external market in terms of its profitability and expense. Therefore, we

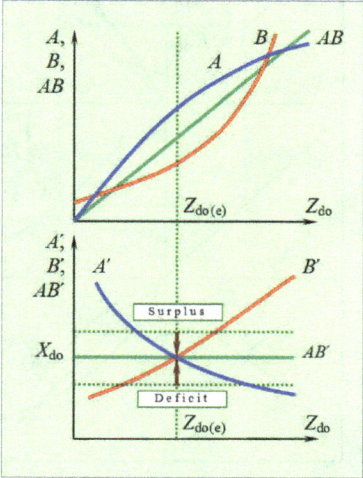

Fig. III.35

will represent all external flows of money in dollar terms in a representative country, including, for simplicity, all possible transfers in the corresponding factor income, in the form of volumes of sales to non-residents of the following economic benefits: 1) land and its rental services; 2) services for renting labor; 3) immovable capital goods and their rental services, as well as capital, shares and fixed-term securities; 4) finished products; 5) foreign currency intended not for foreign trade.

The amount of nominal dollars earned and spent on these transactions (Z_{do}) will be plotted along the abscissa of the currency market marketron. On the ordinates of the model, we will place the absolute and marginal values of indicators of expenses, incomes and prices (rates) in the national currency (B,

A, AB, B', A', AB' and X_{do}, respectively, in Fig. III.35). Since the foreign trade sector is only a part of the national economy, its analysis is carried out with the ceteris paribus premise, which automatically activates the law of diminishing efficiency of factors and determines the nonlinearity of the functions A, B, A' and B'.

Economic entities of the country, selling these goods to non-residents at world prices with a profit $(AB - B)$, buy everything they need with the proceeds of dollars and sell it inside the country also with a profit $(A - AB)$. With the equilibrium of foreign trade, the dollar rate in the national currency,

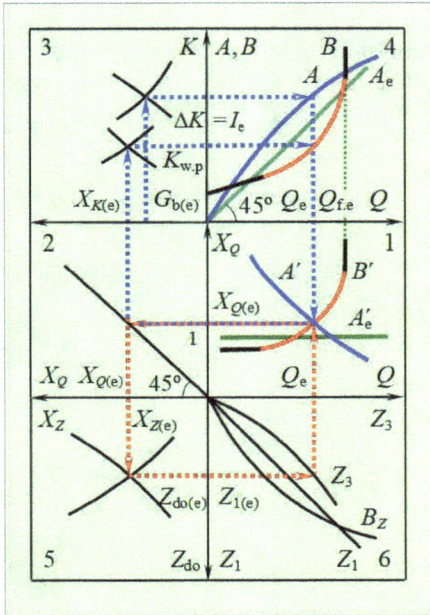

Fig. III.36

the equilibrium amount of dollars and the maximum total profit of such transactions are established. In the event of an imbalance in foreign trade with an unregulated internal market of currencies and their 'floating' exchange rate, a surplus or deficit of the country's payment balance is formed, measured by the volume of the reserve currency according to the same abscissa. When the government regulates exchange rates, balancing the country's foreign exchange market requires an official increase or decrease in the price (revaluation or devaluation) of the national currency. The corresponding arrows in the figure indicate the self-balancing of the foreign exchange market.

Let's combine the considered models of product markets, factors of production and exchange into a new scheme of interfactor GEE (Fig. III.36).

The scheme, as in the previously considered case of non-classical equilibrium of the economy, consists of six quadrants, the content of which, taking into account our theoretical innovations, has been slightly changed: there is a full marketron of the total output Q (quadrants 1 and 4), the price quadrant 2, the differential parts of the marketrons of factors of production (3) and dollars (5), as well as the integral part of the marketrons of the national currency (6).

In the GEE scheme, there are two full-fledged balancing contours –

commodity and money, indicated by dotted closed lines with arrows. The equilibrium typical somewhat inflationary price index of the product market $(X_{Q(p)})$ in quadrant 2 is transformed with the help of a directly proportional price converter into equilibrium prices of other factors – capital goods $(X_{K(e)})$ accumulations $(G_{b(e)})$ and valute $(X_{Z(e)}, X_{\pi(e)})$, and at the end of the cycles determines the equilibrium total output Q_e, which falls on a certain employment with 'forced unemployment'.

In the scheme, money, in contrast to the money of Keynesian models, acts as an independent non-neutral factor in the functioning and development of the economy, which is fully consistent with Keynes's interpretation of the issue. Coordinates Z_1 and Z_{do} of money markets are combined in such a way that the equilibrium amounts of national $(Z_{1(e)})$ and international $(Z_{do(pe)})$ currencies coincide. In addition, in this model, for the compatibility of the indicator of total output Q with monetary nominal indicators, the corresponding coordinates of quadrants 3 and 4 are horizontally shifted in proportion to the price index.

The demonstrated GEE scheme and its elements are of a unified nature, since they take into account both the basic marginal principles of neoclassics and the discoveries of Keynes, Keynesians, as well as theoreticians of other areas ofmacroeconomics. The diagram reproduces and explains the phenomenon of equilibrium with 'forced unemployment', describes such a normal, as well as extreme, undesirable states of the economy.

15. From the phenomenon of equilibrium with 'forced unemployment' to the system of market defects

When analyzing the multifactorial reproduction GEE in section 10 of the monograph, we noted that the modern real economy does not correspond to the Pareto-efficiency model (*The course of political economy. In 2 volumes*, 1896, 1897), built on the assumption of perfect competition and full use of resources. If we assume that the classical market largely corresponded to these conditions, then its subsequent evolution meant all kinds of Pareto impairments (Fig. III.37, gradually moving the GEE point in the model into the region $(\vartheta_0 \to \vartheta_1)$ outlined by the expense function (isospend) B, even though this area itself has been extensively and intensively expanded.This systemic inability of the economy to spontaneous, automatic, Pareto-improvements is the failure of the market mechanism of its functioning and development, which manifests itself in specific defects.

Thus, at the very preliminary consideration of the problem of Pareto-improvements, it can be stated that they are possible only with the help of special regulatory or even larger-scale, governing influences from the state, which comes from the distribution of Keynes' principle of non laissez-faire, seen above.

The reasons for market failure in the economic literature are interpreted in different ways. Many authors confuse the causes of the phenomenon with its consequences and point, for example, to "inequality in the distribution of income" [6. p. 388]. Due to the factual incomplete or invisible marginal rationality of economic entities, the American economist Harvey Leibenstein (1922-1993) (*Distributive Efficiency in Comparison with X-efficiency*, 1966) introduced the concept of "X-inefficiency", meaning the complex of numerous and supposedly difficult to identify deviations from the perfectly competitive and rational behavior of manufacturers , entailing an incomplete use of the resources of the economy. In fact, the specific reasons for such inefficiency are known. No matter how pun intended, the reason is also Keynes's 'effective demand', which is focused on maximum profit and minimum employment, leading to incomplete use of existing and new equipment and technology.

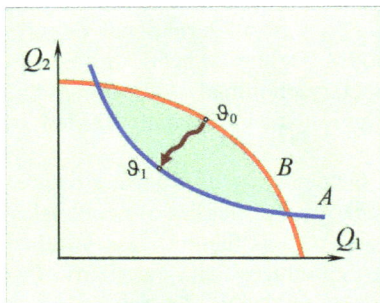

Fig. III.37

In an authoritative textbook on economic theory, four other reasons for market failure are indicated – existence: 1) monopolism; 2) incomplete and asymmetrical awareness of the counteragents of the markets about their conjuncture and the quality of goods; 3) externalities; 4) public goods [21, p. 301-303]. This list of market defects, of course, needs clarification, expansion and systematization, which we intend to do below, but for now we note that the information problems noted in the second item in the list are a kind of monopoly, and the externalities that follow monopoly should not be counted as market defects, since they can be eliminated, as we have shown above, by accurately taking into account the cost and profitability of the production of goods, as well as by regular revaluation of the factors of production available in the economy.

Let's take a closer look at the first phenomenon on the list – monopolism, since it can lead to colossal market pathologies known from its history, and a decrease in the efficiency of the economy and many current injustices and turmoil.

Monopoly, as a rule, is the result of the development of internal competition in the national market, but in models it can be considered an exogenous factor. This approach allows you to describe in a new way many states of the economy, differing in time and scale of action of this factor. From our point of view, the question of the role of monopolism in the emergence of the Great Depression of 1929-1939 is of historical, theoretical and practical interest. in the West. It is known that at the beginning of this period there was a slump, a 'collapse', in aggregate demand, prices, business activity and production. As for the reasons for the events that took place then, little is known about them even from numerous special studies[1], which, however, are not of a general theoretical nature. Friedman (*Monetary History of the United States in 1867-1960*, with A. Schwartz, 1963) argued that the cause of the depression was the mistakes of the American Federal Reserve System, in particular, the reduction in the money supply in the economy. But one can hardly agree with this explanation, since such mistakes could not have occurred over such a long period of time – the depression lasted ten years and was interrupted by the war. In our opinion, the reason is institutional in nature and lies in the revision of the status of large corporations and monopoly.

From the analysis of our marketron of aggregate output (Fig. III.38), it can be seen that the level of monopoly (φ) is closely related to modifications, changes in the function of profitability of production A. Antimonopoly legislation, which was forcedly introduced in the interwar period in the West, could have caused the depression in economy. The establishment of state control over prices means a decrease in the slope of the function A (A_1) and the

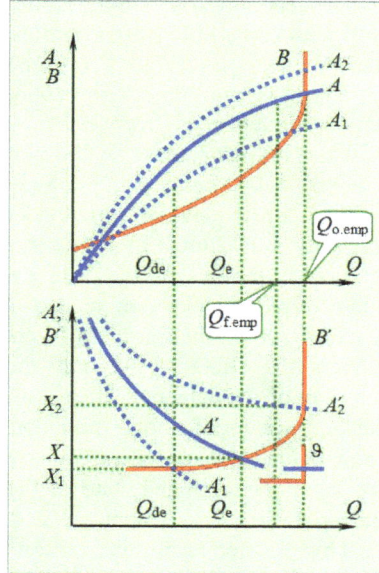

Fig. III.38

transition of the equilibrium of the demand (A'_1) and supply B' functions to significantly lower levels of prices (X_1) and depression release volume (Q_{de}), which corresponds to the equilibrium of the 'Samuelson's cross', or 'liquid traps' of Hicks, considered by us above and observed during the crisis of the world market. The gradual exit from the equilibrium of depression to the 'normal' equilibrium (X, Q_e) was obviously associated with the formation of monopsony, that is, with the organization of a system for protecting the rights of consumers, opposing the price dictates of producers. This market situation is consistent with Galbraith's concept of 'balancing power' (*American Capitalism. The Concept of Balancing Force*, 1952), according to which the bargaining power of producers can and should be offset by the bargaining

---

[1] See, for example, the following studies: [55, 41, 59, 90].

power of consumers, which is called a "wedge knocked out by a wedge". The interpretation of this 'edge' option in the economic model corresponds to the views of theorists of the so-called 'new classical macroeconomics' presented by us in section 1 of the monograph.

Another extreme state of the economy, opposite to the depression, corresponds to the 'cross' of the neoclassical GEE scheme with the parameter of equal output with over-employment ($Q_{o.-emp}$), which exceeds the output of full employment $Q_{f.emp}$[1]. This state is outwardly similar to the properties of a planned economy, a 'single factory economy', it is possible in the market only with some kind of extraordinary mobilization of resources. In any case, such an economy is to a certain extent 'state-owned', in which political monopoly is combined with economic monopoly, and it can be likened to a separate independent corporation, which is a complete price dictator. This is indicated by a decrease in the slope of the profitability functions A and A' upward (A_2, A'_2) and a high price level (X_2).

Such a price level did not exist in the planned, 'administrative-command' economy, but it must be borne in mind that considering any model without the ceteris paribus prerequisite means weakening the effect of the law of diminishing efficiency of factors and 'straightens' the corresponding return functions. If, on the third, 'shift' coordinate of the output model, we take into account the effect of not only the level of monopoly, but also the entire complex of other factors, then the functions B' and A' turn, respectively, into the 'Keynes angle' and 'Samuelson horizontal' we know, the intersection at a point 9 (see the 'cross' in Fig. III.38, right) rather accurately characterizes the super-monopolized state of the economy with understated stable prices and excessive employment.

This planned 'marginal' option in the economic model corresponds to the views of representatives of the so-called 'Left Keynesianism', or 'English Cambridge', but, first of all, the theoretical system of 'optimal functioning of the economy' (SOFE) and 'radical political economy' Orthodox Marxist persuasion, and the interpretation of this option was described by Keynes in *Book 5* of his *General Theory* as follows: "A flexible wage policy could be

---

[1] Keynes and the mainstream theorists consider possible output volumes that exceed the current resource potential of the economy, in particular, output beyond full employment. This implies, apparently, the involvement in production not of labor resources, but of the population (Some authors in this regard introduce the concept of "excess employment" (see, for example: [75, p. 204]), which, however, violates the rigor of macroeconomic constructions). If we measure employment in man-hours, then it is necessary to take into account the possibility of increasing the duration of work during the day, week and year. But even in this case and in the case of attracting foreign workers, the employment limit in the economy will exist. On the whole, such situations can be considered real only in a 'mobilization' economy, and in market conditions, purely hypothetical due to the fact that the price index of goods becomes incredibly high.

successfully pursued only in a society with strong authoritarian power, where sudden, significant, all-round changes in wages fees could be declared from above" [53, p. 251].

Since private property and competitiveness are the basis for self-regulation of markets, spontaneous order and efficiency of the economy, the guarantee of the preservation and development of these institutions is the most important function of civil society. The corresponding state policy provides for the creation of monopoly and antimonopoly norms, the combination of which should not lead the economy to extreme unfavorable conditions. Market monopoly can be prevented or controlled by state monopoly, but discretionary administration of competition in modern conditions should be supplanted by its high-quality institutionalization.

Let us turn to the analysis of the market defect caused by the increasing production in the modern economy of public goods. Many theoreticians impute the production of these benefits to the state. This was also done by the guru of the state economy, the American Richard Musgrave (1910-2007) (*Theory of Public Finance*, 1959). According to the Musgrayv triad, the state performs three functions: 1) stabilization, support of the existing economic mechanism; 2) redistributive, aimed at overcoming excessive or unfair market differentiation of incomes of the population, causing social tension; 3) allocation, associated with the production of public goods. But, if we take into account the fact that the state organizes the development, implementation and abolition of the rules of business, then the fourth, institutional function, the function of managing the institutions of society, should be added to the listed functions of the state. State-controlled 'institutional building' is effective if it is based on knowledge of the laws and trends of socio-economic development in a broad historical retro and perspective, that is, on a qualitative theory of economic growth and forecasting.

As for the above public goods, the implementation of which, in their properties, allegedly does not fit into market conditions and can only take place with state participation, then economic theory should carefully examine this, in our opinion, a confused issue. The concepts of "non-competitiveness" and "non-exclusion" of the consumption of a public good, introduced by Samuelmon, that is, its consumption by an individual, which does not protect other individuals from this, look too abstract. The world of consumption is very complex and changeable, sometimes traditionally public bugs are not different from the usual competitive and excluded goods sold privately. For example, freely available terrestrial radio and television signals, due to their coding technologies, can be sold and, on the contrary, market goods for one reason or another often become public goods. So all the functions performed by the state can be considered public goods, that is, goods that satisfy the needs of society as a whole, and the criterion for classifying goods as public is simply the public nature of their choice. It means that the set of necessary public goods, their prices and quantities are determined using the political procedures of democratic voting.

In 'institutionalism', there is a direction called 'public choice theory', which specifically examines the entire political and economic mechanism of rational tax behavior. The leading representative of this theory Buchanan wrote: "Politics is a complex system of exchange between individuals, in which the latter collectively strive to achieve their particular goals, since they cannot realize them through ordinary market exchange. There are no other interests here besides the individual. In the market, people exchange apples for oranges, and in politics, they agree to pay taxes in exchange for the goods necessary for everyone and everyone: from the local fire department to the court" [19, p. 23].

The theory of public choice can be summarized as follows: 1) the political sphere is viewed not as exogenous, but as endogenous in relation to the market sphere; 2) to describe human behavior in the political sphere, the same postulates are used as in neoclassical economic theory: following personal interest, completeness and variety of preferences, rational maximization of goals; 3) the process of identifying the preferences of individuals is described as a mechanism of market exchange and balancing.

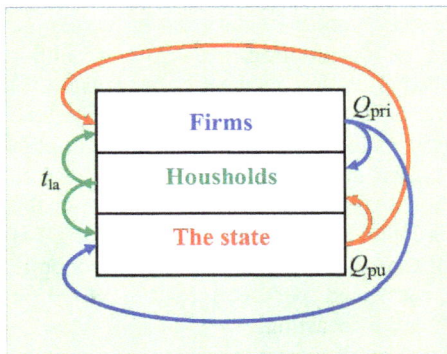

Fig. III.39

Thus, the state, as a body that ensures a certain mode of functioning of society, exists not because it contains public goods, but because of the political mechanism for their implementation. In a traditional society with a weak state, for example, such vital human benefits as health, education, employment, security, etc. were satisfied in a private way.

We divide the extended list of typical public goods into three groups of factors: 1) public goods consumed by both physical and legal entities – systems: public administration, mass information and communication (including automata), ecological safety (including the department for emergency situations and hydrometeorological centers), national defense, law enforcement agencies, state security, standards of measures and weights (including house of money); 2) general economic benefits: state systems of reserves, health care, upbringing, education and science; natural and

218

monetary transfers to individual economic entities (individuals, households, firms and territories) – some goods and services, scholarships, subsidies and subventions; the very macroeconomic equilibrium, proportional efficient and sustainable functioning of the economy, etc.; 3) social benefits that ensure the well-being of the non-working (temporarily and permanently) and poor for objective reasons of the population of the country, in the form of state benefits, pensions, benefits, subsidies and compensations.

The proposed typology of public goods requires a broader interpretation of public funding. In addition to the consolidated budget, consisting of federal, regional and local components, the source includes off-budget social funds (pension, social insurance, health insurance and employment). The use of just such an aggregate budget of the 'expanded government' is what we mean by 'state financing'.

The diagram of the relationship between the circulation of private and public goods in the economy is shown in Fig. III.39. The flow t_{la} characterizes the 'labor' offered by households and consumed by firms together with the public sector, the flow Q_{pri} corresponds to the production of private firms consumed by households and the state, and the flow Q_{pu} is the public goods produced the state and distributed among other business entities.

What should be the size of the state as a producer of public goods? Galbraith once correctly noted that an abundance society is characterized by "an excess of private wealth with a scarcity of public goods." This circumstance

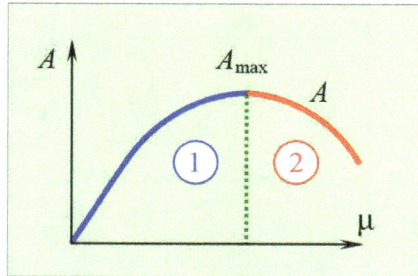

Fig. III.40

requires an increase in the state budget, which, at first glance, corresponds to the so-called 'Wagner's law' – the hypothesis that with the development of the economy there is an increase in the share of government spending in the total product. As the reasons for this phenomenon, Wagner considered the growth of expenditures on public administration, law, order and regulation of the economy, the growth in demand for cultural and charitable activities of the state in comparison with the growth of income, as well as the strengthening of state control as the economy was monopolized. The 'bias effect' also affects, that is, the tendency for government spending to increase during the war and other crises, which, however, do not return to their original level after the crisis. This phenomenon was investigated by the British Arthur Pickcock (1922-2014) and Jack Wiseman (1919-1991) (*Growth of Public Spending in Great Britain*, 1961). The authors argue that wars and crises help overcome taxpayers' resistance ('threshold effect') to tax increases and lead to increased centralization of various types of activities that remain under state control after the crisis.

But a more detailed study of the 'laissez-faire – non-laissez-faire' problem reveals that the scope of fiscal regulation has its limits. The representative of the modern 'supply theory' Laffer (*Economics of Tax Evasion,* together with D. Seymour, 1979) established a functional relationship between the tax rate (μ) and budget income (A), which was called the 'Laffer function' (Fig. III.40). According to Laffer, tax expansion is first accompanied by a proportional increase in budget revenues, then the increase in government revenue slows down and, having reached its maximum (A_{max}), it absolutely decreases due to a decrease in business activity, impossibility or evasion of taxes. The Laffer function shows the effective (left area 1 under the curve) and ineffective, excess (area 2) taxation. However, a comprehensive analysis of the function shows that the tax rate attributable to the maximum budgetary receipts A_{max} is not equilibrium. Let's try to prove this thesis and show the actual conditions for the balance of the state budget.

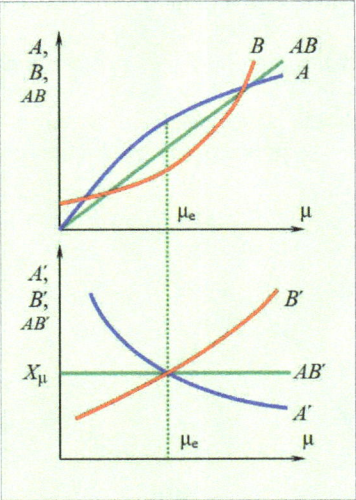

Fig. III.41

Since fiscal activity is reduced to the collection of funds, their current simple spending, investment and trans-fermentation (payments), the equilibrium of the state sector can be investigated using the appropriate marker (Fig. III.41) with the premise ceteris paribus, 'making' its functions non-linear. The quantitative coordinates of the public goods market model are represented by the tax rate μ as a percentage of the amount of taxes in real terms in the total output Q. The integral part of the marketron contains the functions of profitability A, flow rate B and public military contract AB budget, which characterizes the equilibrium of this market. Curve A in the model is the 'Laffer function'. The marginal part of the marketron contains the functions of the demand prices A', for public goods, their supply B' and the equilibrium price AB' of one percent of the tax rate (X_μ). X_μ corresponds to the equilibrium tax rate (μ_e), at which the maximum total profit of the public sector is divided into the profit of the direct producers of public goods and the profit of their consumers in the form of preferential and differentiated according to different criteria transfers paid from the budget by the economic subjects (households, firms, industries and territories). These parts of the total profit are, respectively, below and above the contractual function of the AB budget.

The proposed model of state activity as a whole is universal in nature and can be applied to describe the markets for individual public goods. In the economic literature, it is generally accepted that "the state is not guided by market principles of maximizing benefits and equivalent exchange" [135, p. 382]. However, it is not. We have shown that the state implements public goods with the help of the 'political market' on an equivalent and mutually beneficial basis. The inclusion of the Laffer function in the considered model, where its marginal form becomes a function of the demand for public goods, should be considered as one of the neoclassical interpretations of the basic provisions of the 'supply theory'.

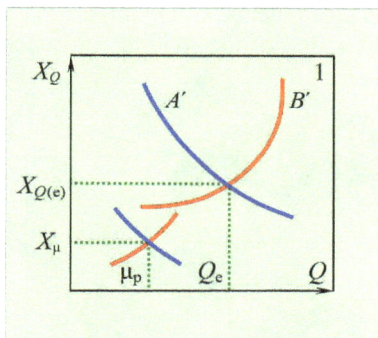

Fig. III.42

Thus, the thesis about the implementation of public goods outside the market mechanism should be considered erroneous, it does not take into account that the concepts of 'private choice' and 'market' cover a wider range of competitive and counterparty relations than is customary with their traditional interpretation.

In the case of a sufficiently fully institutionalized and effectively functioning political market of the country, the public sector marketron can be placed in the aggregate output quadrant 1 of our unified GEE scheme (see Fig. III.36 of section 13 of the monograph), shown in Fig. III.42. In the quadrant of the equilibrium share of public goods μp in the equilibrium output Q_e, taken as 100%, on the ordinate of the price index X_Q there corresponds the equilibrium price of one percent of the total tax rate X_μ.

The traditional discretionaryness of fiscal practice, taking into account the presented market model of the public sector, can be replaced by an automatically operating mechanism in the form of an 'embedded institutional market'. Within the framework of similar regulatory mechanisms, the implementation of many individual public goods, both material and monetary, can be formalized, which satisfy the corresponding urgent needs of people and ensure the well-being of society. Such 'embedded markets' make it possible to preserve the neutrality of the state regulation system as a whole to the competitiveness and motivation of economic entities, as well as to make this system more compact and inexpensive. For example, to maintain business profitability, it is more expedient to pay unemployment benefits (workfare) than to apply complex, costly and ineffective Keynesian employment regulation schemes.

And one more note about Keynesian fiscalism. It considers expenditures from the state budget to be a purely 'autonomous' variable, independent of the total output. But, since the actual value of public goods in real terms is part of the aggregate output of goods as a whole and can be determined in a separate market for public services built into the national market, then it should not be an external 'discretionary' variable. This does not mean a complete denial of the importance of fiscal regulation of the economy at the discretion of the state. It can successfully carry out modification and shock 'shifts' of many substantial dependences existing in the economy, promptly change its parameters, as a result of which the main market defects acquire socially acceptable my frames. But this requires substantial detailing of economic models.

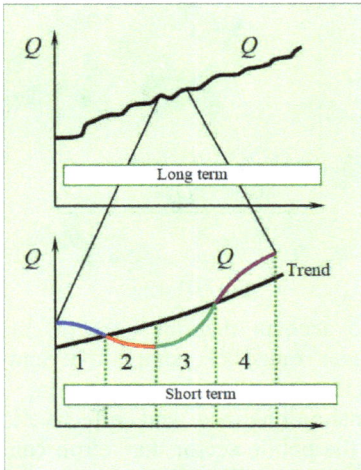

Fig. III.43

There is a defect in the economy that was not noted by the aforementioned authors, but is traditionally regulated by the state. It has a nature determined by the heterogeneity, and, therefore, by the imperfection of the fundamental institutions of the market. Such a defect is the well-known cyclical nature of economic development.

The real long-term trajectory of the indicator of total output Q, as shown in section 7 of the monograph, looks very complex (Fig. III.1 and III.43) and is the result of the interaction of many oscillatory processes that differ in origin, amplitude and frequency. Since these processes are at each moment of time in different phases, then there is an attenuation, neutralization or amplification of individual waves. However, any highlighted economic cycle observed in the medium term looks pretty standard and simple. It consists of the phases of recession (steady decline in production (1), stagnation (2), recovery (3) and recovery (4), which characterize deviations from the long-term average line of development of the economy (trend).

In economics, there are many models of cycles of technological, institutional, monetary, investment, sectoral, political, informational and psychological nature. The best known cycle model is the mathematical 'multiplier-accelerator model' developed by Samuelson (*Interaction between Multiplier Analysis and the Principle of Acceleration*, 1939) and Hicks

(*Contribution to the Theory of the Trading Cycle*, 1950). However, it, like all other cycle models[1], only reproduces fluctuations, but does not explain their immanent reasons, inherent in the market. In the entire conglomerate of ideas about the cycle, there must be a certain core that would characterize a regular microeconomic source, generator, and cyclicity. Such a core, in our opinion, is the idea of non-coincidence of criteria for the functioning of economic entities.

We considered the entire micro- and macroeconomic theory above on the basis of the idea of the existence of a single criterion for the maximum profit of economic entities. But the real economy is not so unified and combines different goals both among competitors and counteragents of the markets. For example, in the labor market, the unemployed are clearly not guided by the maximum profit. And, if the discrepancy between the criteria is or takes on a stable character, then this dissonance can serve as a deep reason for the cyclical functioning and development of the economy.

So, for example, the orientation of all or some of the firms in the economy is not on profit (M), but on the profitability of production (M/B) (Fig. III.44), which shifts the equilibrium to smaller volumes of output ($-\Delta Q$), as well as the desire to maximize the amount of sales or purchases distorts market signals, causes inconsistency in the expectations and decisions of business entities.

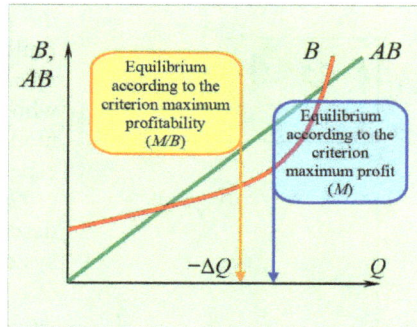

Fig. III.44

But even if the criteria for managing the producers and consumers of goods coincide, but the mismatch between their maxima (Fig. III.45, *a*) and the corresponding volumes of supply (Q_s) and demand (Q_d) (*b*), there will be a systematic sectoral indiscriminate stability in time (t) (*c*). All these primary market imbalances are the factor of macroeconomic cycle formation.

The state is able to minimize fluctuations in the economy, to smooth out the cycles by pursuing a policy of strengthening business activity (expansion)

---

[1] Other notable cycle models are the monetary cycle model by the English economist Ralph Hawtrey (1879-1975) (*Good and Bad Trade: A Study of the Causes of Trade Fluctuations*, 1913), a cycle-phase model by the American economist Godfried Haberler (1900-1995) (*Prosperity and Depression. A Theoretical Analysis of Cyclical Fluctuations*, 1937), the so-called "*IS*-model of the cycle" by Kaldor (*Model of the Trade Cycle*, 1940), the model of the cycle "predator-prey" by the Englishman R. Goodwin (*Cycle of Growth*, 1967) and the model of political cycle by American William Nordhaus (b. 1929) (*Political Business Cycle*, 1975).

in the phase of recession and its weakening (restriction) in the phase of economic recovery. As a result, its growth can become more even, but in the presence of criterion heterogeneity, multi-structured economy and especially during periods of change in the criteria of its functioning, for example, when moving from the profitability of land to the profitability of capital or from the latter to the "wages' of labor[1], institutional cyclicality will necessarily manifest itself.

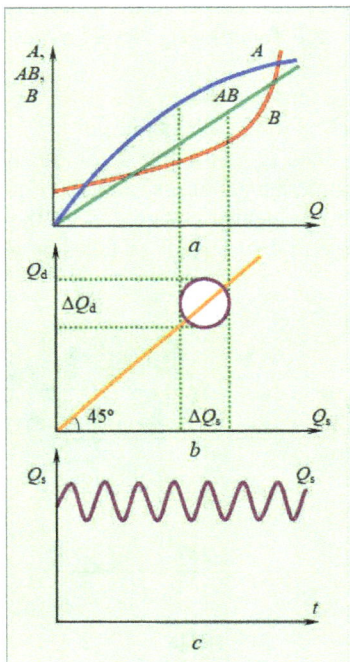

Fig. III.45

In the development of economic modeling, there is a tendency not only to mathematical concretization, but also to an increase in the number of all kinds of independent, dependent and regulated indicators. Fischer (*Mathematical Study in the Theory of Value and Prices*, 1892) and Phillips (*Mechanical Models in Economic Dynamics*, 1950) were also fond of this, who created mechanical[2] and hydraulic[3] models with many controllers, but especially American Lawrence Klein (1920-2013). He first turned the verbal description of Keynes' economics into a system of econometric equations (*Keynesian Revolution*, 1947), then worked on creating models of the American economy, the 'Klein-Goldberg model' (*Economic Fluctuations in the USA, 1921-41*, together with A. Goldberg, 1950), consisting of 20 equations and the 'Wharton Model' (*Econometric Model of the USA, 1929-52*, 1955), which already includes more than a thousand endogenous and exogenous parameters. Under the conditions of computer technology, Klein, under the UN LINC project, tried to unify and combine into a single system similar models of economies of other countries, created in other research centers.

Tinberchen (*Theory of Economic Policy*, 1952), being in the mainstream of the scientific gigantomania under consideration, but striving to unify the

---

[1] For more details on the patterns of change in the historical criteria of management, see the *Conclusion* of the monograph, as well as our work: [33].

[2] In Fisher's models "everything depended on everything" [74, p. 212] and his specified work contained a project of a mechanical machine to illustrate general equilibrium in economics (see: [12, p. 318]).

[3] Phillips' models were actually 'hydraulic' and he even constructed demo models with different colored fluids (see: [13, p. 312]).

regulators of the economy, identified three of their components: 1) short-term key goals (parameters) of social welfare; 2) a set of instruments, fiscal, monetary and other means of influencing the parameters of the economy; 3) the econometric model itself, linking goals and tools using a variety of multipliers, coefficients, elasticity indicators, etc., as well as the effectiveness of regulation (policy). The relationship between goals and instruments, according to Tinberchen, is such that there is a general rule "the number of regulatory instruments must be no less than the number of its goals", or, in other words, 'each goal must have its own instrument of implementation'. Note that the 'rule' did not limit the number of regulators in the economy in any way.

Canadian economist Robert Mundell (1932-2021) (*Dynamics of Adaptation of the World Foreign Exchange Market at Fixed and Floating Exchange Rates*, 1960), faced with the problems of implementation of 'management developments' in the currency sphere, pointed out that in fact the goals and instruments for regulating the economy often refer to different organs of the state, and proposed the so-called "effective market classification", according to which the goals, instruments and implementers of the policy should be organizationally connected. If we take into account the fact that in reality the subjects of economic regulation are not only state central and regional power structures, but also numerous non-state unions, organizations and associations, then to ensure the effectiveness of broad regulation of markets according to the proposed 'rules', as practice shows, it becomes It is very difficult to grow.

A peculiar reaction to the theoretical constructions of these neo-classical scholars, proposing the ordering of discretionary state regulation of the economy, was criticism from the representative of the 'new classical macroeconomics' Lucas (*Evolution of Economic Policy: Criticism*, 1976). From the standpoint of the concept of 'rational expectations', he believes that numerous normalized parameters of the economy already reflect the influence of politics and the rational responses of economic entities, which devalues government efforts to regulate, can lead to negative unpredictable results, and therefore proposes to abandon the very idea of state public regulation of the national market. However, the 'criticism of Lukas' looks rather controversial, and its conclusions do not reasonably close the possibility of achieving socially significant Pareto improvements in the real economy. This was shown by representatives of the 'new Keynesianism'.

The aforementioned grandiose work on the complication and mathematization of the theory of equilibrium and the regulators of the economy, done by macroeconomists, did not make it more effective; it showed large discrepancies with the actual data. The reason for this, in our opinion, is the same formal approach to all model variables, which is typical for development. It is not the quantity, but the quality of indicators that is important, the allocation of the most closely, systematically interconnected coordinates. An example of such a reasonable 'compressio' of models is the extremely simple model 'World-2' by the American researcher Jay Forrester (1918-2016) (*World Dynamics*, 1971), which describes the world economy, which is a much more complex system than a separate national economy ... The model, due to its high degree of endogeneity, aggregation of variables and the use of a new method of "system dynamics" of indicators in it, made it possible for the author to identify, and the world community to take control of the most dangerous trends in the development of the industrial community.

As for specific forms of Pareto inefficiency, or emergent, that is, observed only at the macro level, market defects, the settlement of which is possible only systemically, then, in our opinion, for the money market this is inflation, the labor market is unemployment, the market is a production – a stable recession, and to the external market – an increase in the balance of payments deficit, or, more simply, the export of capital, decapitalization of the economy (Fig. III.46). In these four negatives of specific markets, we are familiar with the strong relationship between the current levels of unemployment $-\omega_L$ and inflation ω_X in the form of a Phillips function (quadrant 1). But the increase in the unemployment rate is a consequence of the growth in the rate of decline in total output $(-\omega_Q)$, which characterizes the depth of the recession. The corresponding linear function (quadrant 2), introduced into the theory by the American economist Arthur Oaken (1928-1980) (*Potential GNP: Measurement and Meaning*, 1962), expresses the 'Okun's Law': the growth of unemployment entails followed by a recession. According to the average statistical data, a 3% drop in GDP leads to an increase in unemployment by 1% [88, p. 234].

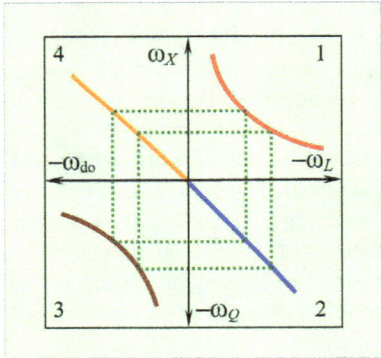

Fig. III.46

In turn, the recession is inversely proportional to the growth of capital export in dollar terms $(-\omega_{do}, -\omega_{do} = -\Delta Z_{do}/Z_{do(e)})$ (quadrant 3), and that is directly proportional to inflation (quadrant 4). Thus, all four market defects that characterize the measure of excess of money, labor, production and capital (currency) in the economy turn out to be functionally related to each other, and it is possible to write in general form the equation of dynamic equilibrium $f(\omega_X, -\omega_L, -\omega_Q, -\omega_{do}) = 0$, the solution of which gives the numerical values of the corresponding indicators, which are in mutual equilibrium proportions and on the graph constitute a closed loop. This system of defects is subject to constant monitoring and adjustment by the state.

When analyzing the Phillips function in the GEE scheme with the Hicks *IS-LM* model, we talked about the need to find a certain compromise between $-\omega_L$ and ω_X, but the development of the economy and monetarist economics shows that this choice becomes more complicated due to the hypothesis of the need to include in model of the third variable – expectations. The first to express this hypothesis was the American economist Edmund Phelps (b. 1933) (*Phillips Curve, Inflation Expectations and Optimal Long-term Employment*, 1967). He believes that inflationary expectations of business entities can shift the Phillips function over time (Fig. III.47), and on it there is a point of "natural unemployment rate" ($-\omega_{L(na)}$), which remains constant nym under any options for equilibrium and regulation of the economy. Keynesian Tobin (*Macroeconomic Effects of Public Works and Salary Subsidies*, together with M. Bailey, 1977), refusing to talk about this unavoidable unemployment, the corresponding point already on the inflation coordinate began to be called "not accelerating inflation rate of unemployment", NAIRU ($\omega_{X(NAIRU)}$).

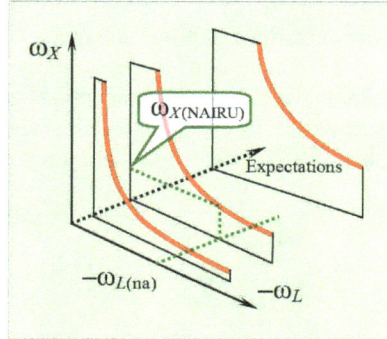

Fig. III.47

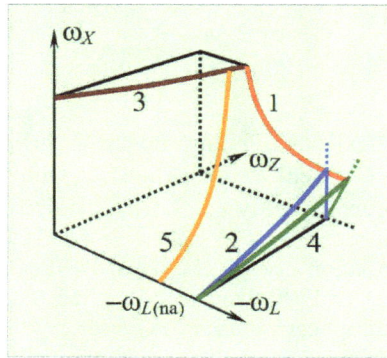

Fig. III.48

Friedman (*The Role of Monetary Policy*, 1968) also, on the basis of expectations, showed a certain mechanism of shifts in the Phillips function and argued that with a 'natural level of unemployment', the function turns into a vertical inflation growth (Fig. III.48, projection curve 2 with a dotted line). Some economists, for example, Blanchard, even believe that during a shock shift "the Phillips curve disappears" [11, p. 185]. The proof of the verticality of the 'Friedman function' was based on the necessary mobility of unemployment at a constant level of inflation, therefore, in the author's concept, there is a corresponding 'horizontal' of the transition in time from one Phillips curve to another, from 'current' to 'expected'. In a later book,

The Theoretical Framework of Monetary Analysis (1971), Friedman's vertical function turned into a line with a slope to the right (Fig. III.48, projection of curve 4 with a dotted line) and he began to talk not only about stagflation, which means the existence of unemployment and inflation, but also about 'slumpflation' – the simultaneous growth of unemployment and inflation, explaining this real phenomenon by 'unpredictability of prices', that is, not by expectations, but by 'unexpectedness'.

How can one systematically explain the seemingly incompatible phenomena discovered and investigated by Phelps and Phillips? It seems to us. that the only way is to consider the three-factor model, clearing it of all subjective 'rational' and 'not very rational', 'adaptive' and other 'monetary illusions', replacing them with an objective and specific coordinate with a dynamic indicator 'growth rate of monetary mass', or simply 'emission' (ω_Z). The volumetric figure of the function $f(-\omega_L, \omega_X, \omega_Z)$ of such

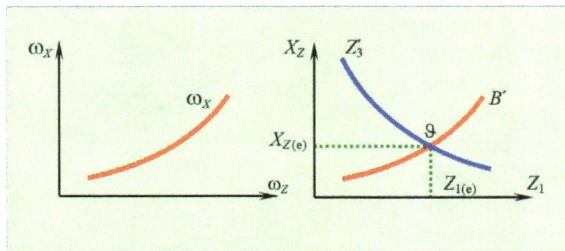

Fig. III.49

a 'extended Phillips model' is shown in Fig. III.48, and its balance equation is written in the following form: $-\omega_L \cdot \omega_X = k_{em} \cdot \omega_Z$, where k_{em} – the proportionality coefficient, 'emission constant' ($k_{em} = (-\omega_L \cdot \omega_X)/\omega_Z = $ const). Sections of the figure at fixed values of emission, unemployment and inflation give us the usual Phillips function (Fig. III.48, curve 1), 'vertical' (2) and 'horizontal' (3) Friedman. Moreover, all three functions do not 'disappear' and can exist for any values of the indicators. The inflationary 'vertical' in the model is not tied to the 'natural level of unemployment', which is always only reduced to a certain minimum due to 'frictions' and voluntariness in employment, and can be observed in any employment with 'forced unemployment', Providing maximum profit to employees and employers. The oblique 'Friedman curve' (4) is the result of the simultaneous growth of all three factors of the extended Phillips model and can have any other form depending on the ratio of the dynamics of indicators, for example, the form shown in Fig. III.48 curve 5, which characterizes both stagflation and slumpflation.

Summarizing what has been said, it can be argued that forcing money emission with fixed unemployment leads only to an increase in inflation, just as with 'frozen' prices, it only leads to an increase in unemployment, and a constant level of emission creates stagflation. The task of state regulation of

228

the economy is reduced to finding the optimal trajectory of its movement, displayed in the extended Phillips function.

Friedman used his both substantial, corresponding to the laws of the market, and some rather speculative marginalist constructions as evidence of the validity of his criticism of practical 'Keynesianism', wrote that budget deficit expansion cannot reduce unemployment and only leads to the growth of inflation. In theory, Friedman's monetarism as a whole looks more effective than Keynes's fiscalism. But speaking of the inconsistency of the policy pursued (*Research on the Quantitative Theory of Money*, 1956), Friedman suggested that the state use the mechanism of "fine tuning" the economy in the form of an exogenous discretionary "monetary rule", according to which the planned economic growth should be supported by proportional emission

money. But this 'rule' turned out to be too approximate, and the mechanism of 'fine tuning' was also ineffective due to the lack of a high level of institutional design in the social market economy of an adequate Friedman theory. This is evidenced by the testing of the so-called 'St. Louis model', created in the spirit of Friedman in the US Federal Reserve System by Leonell Anderson and Keith Carlson (*Monetarist Model of Economic*

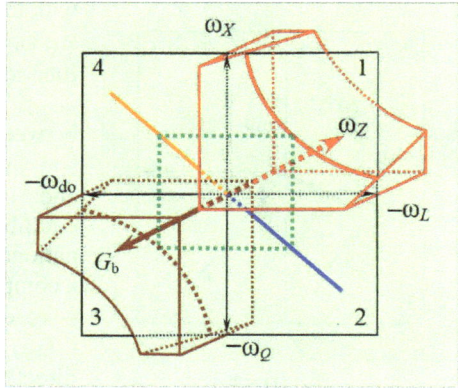

Fig. III.50

Stabilization, 1970). But even perfect institutions of a complex economy require a deep knowledge of the laws of its functioning and development.

The proposed model of the extended Phillips function with a completely uncontrolled coordinate of the money issue ω_Z can present the concept of regulation of the economy by Friedman in a new perspective. Let's take a closer look at $f(-\omega_L, \omega_X, \omega_Z)$. Behind each of its dynamic variables is another important macroeconomic indicator: behind unemployment – employment L, behind inflation – the price index X_Q, and behind emission – the cash aggregate Z_1. Therefore, in the section of the indicated volumetric figure with a constant level of unemployment, representing the graph of the Friedman 'vertical', $\omega_X = f(\omega_Z)$ (see concave curve 2 in Fig. III.48 and the left graph of Fig. III.49)[1], a graph of a function of money supply, $X_Z = f(Z_1)$, similar in form, derived by us in section 13 of the monograph, is seen. The function is

---

[1] The function $\omega_X = f(\omega_Z)$ has statistical confirmation (see, for example: [115, p. 333]).

an element of the generalized money market model, at the point 9 of which the equilibrium value of the total cash $Z_{1(e)}$ is automatically determined. Consequently, Friedman's monetary theory, embedded in the extended

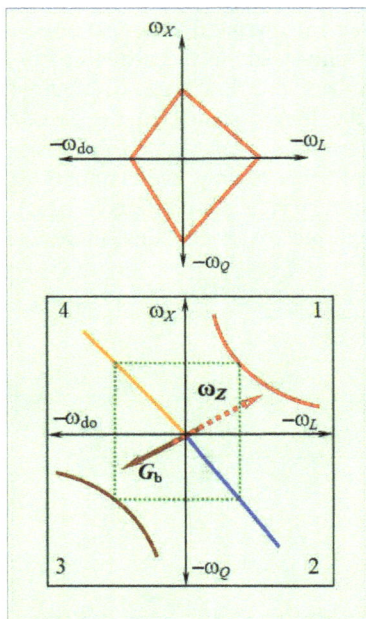

Fig. III.51

Phillips model, becomes endogenous, more specific and accurate in determining its parameters, the equilibrium value $Z_{1(e)}$ is easily determined by the growth rate of money issue ω_Z ($\omega_Z = dZ/Z_1$) according to Friedman's 'monetary rule'.

An in-depth analysis of the above model of four market defects (Fig. III.50) with the extended Phillips function $f(-\omega_L, \omega_X, \omega_Z)$ (quadrant 1) shows that the linear functions of the 'Okun's law' ($f(-\omega_L, -\omega_Q)$) and the law of proportionality between the levels of decapitalization and inflation ($f(-\omega_{do}, \omega_X)$) (quadrants 2 and 4) are transmissions in a closed equilibrium loop of these defects in the national market. But quadrant 3 also has a complex structure: both of its indicators – recession ($-\omega_X$) and decapitalization ($-\omega_{do}$) levels in the economy – are directly proportional to the average nominal bank interest rate G_b. The general connection between the indicators says: with an increase in the depth of recession in the economy, the rate of capital export from it decreases and vice versa, but both linearly depend on the interest rate. Therefore, we can write down the three-factor equation $f(-\omega_Q, -\omega_{do}, G_b) = 0$, the volumetric figure of which is also shown in quadrant 3 of Fig. III.50, and the solution to the equation takes the form: $-\omega_{do} \cdot (-\omega_Q) = k_{cr} \cdot G_b$, where k_{cr} – the proportionality coefficient, 'credit constant' ($k_{cr} = [-\omega_{do} \cdot (-\omega_Q)]/G_b = $ const). Despite the simplicity of the equation, it can be used in this form to regulate the economy only at a known optimal bank interest rate. But, since this rate concentratedly expresses, as shown in section 9 of the monograph, the dynamics of the scale of entrepreneurial activity, that is, it directly depends on the volumes of resources involved in the economy and total output , and in the model of the national market, this dependence is found out when optimizing the interaction of many socio-economic factors, then for effective regulation of the economy additional research is required to optimize the interest rate.

230

In the economic literature, the problem of joint control and regulation of inflation, unemployment, recession and payment deficit of a country is sometimes called the 'golden quadrangle' or 'rhombus' and is drawn in a simplified way, linking its parameters with straight lines (Fig. III.51, upper graph, on which indicates the coordinates and indices of our defect model). Emphasizing the difficulties of solving the problem, the quadrilateral is often called "magic"[1]. But, as soon as the functional relationships of the indicators and the specific content of the graph become clear to us, fundamental difficulties are eliminated, and the magic of the quadrangle dissipates.

Monetary indicators of the economy ω_Z and G_b are key in balancing the system of macromarket defects (Fig. III.51, bottom figure) and are functionally related to each other. The solution to the corresponding linear equation $f(\omega_Z, G_b) = 0$ has the form: $\omega_Z = k_{em.cr} \cdot G_b$, where $k_{em.cr}$ – the proportionality coefficient, "emission-credit constant" ($k_{em.cr} = \omega_Z/G_b = $ = const). Thus, regulation of the economy is reduced to regulation of the interest rate.

In this section, we have shown the need for a departure from the broad state-interventionist regulation of the economy, which means a certain displacement of Keynes's non-laissez-faire principle by the classical laissez-faire principle, significantly rehabilitated 'Monetarism'. But with the use of the new model of fiduciary money developed in section 14, government emission regulation seems redundant, and the emphasis in macroeconomic theory shifts from comparative statics to the study of economic growth and development in order to transform bank interest rate into an endogenous indicator of the GEE scheme. Macroeconomic dynamic meaning, the regularities of the formation of the optimal G_b level will be the subject of our further research.

Returning at the end of the section to the problems of the 'dispute of two Cambridges', the interaction and synthesis of two modern directions of macroeconomics, it should be noted that in 'neo-Ricardianism', the issues of market defects are not even touched upon. Therefore, the mainstream theory, which actively studies this part of economic reality, has a 'competitive advantage' over 'neo-Ricardianism', in which the theoretical constructions are 'standard system', 'basic and non-basic goods', capital goods and land as by-products of production, 'technology switching', 'dated quantities of labor', etc. should be recognized as defects of the intersectoral models of this direction, which are subject to elimination.

---

[1] See, for example: [101, p. 424], [80, p. 19] and [127, p. 96].

16. Optimization of the interest rate as integral regulator of the economy

Setting the task of studying the most important dependencies of bank interest, first of all, we need to clarify its formal structure. As Fisher showed (*The Theory of Interest, which Restrains the Expenditure of Income and Favors its Investment*, 1930), the nominal interest rate G_b, consists of the real interest rate ($G_{b(re)}$) and the inflation rate: $G_b = G_{b(re)} + \omega_X$. Strictly matematically, G_6 should be determined by a more complex formula: G_6 $G_{6(pe)} + + \omega_X + G_{b(re)} \cdot \omega_X$. In the economic literature, the percentage meter is often not specified, or used in real terms. But, since the modeling of interest provides for its linking with many other indicators, we emphasize that further we will consider the percentage and the few macro-indicators of the theory of economic growth associated with it in nominal terms.

Churchill once wittily said that 'looking too far ahead is shortsighted'. But it is impossible to keep a person, and even more so a scientist-researcher, from the desire to learn a broad perspective. The system theory of economic dynamics arose only after Keynes and Keynesians showed the complexity of the mechanism for balancing the national market; it was created in the conditions of the fastest development of the Western market economy in the post-war period, when 'Keynesianism', although it was the dominant scientific system, was already could not solve new problems of practice – the balance of the pace and quality of the expanded scale of production. Therefore, to relate the emerging growth theory to 'Keynesianism', as is often done in the economic literature[1], in our opinion, is not entirely correct; the development of growth issues in macroeconomic means, first of all, the rejection of the 'short-term' and static nature of Keynes's theory. The concepts of growth have indeed 'grown' on Keynesian soil, but in modern conditions, the dynamic approach claims to update the entire economic theory[2].

Formally, the dynamics of the economy differs from its statics, but according to the research method, they have a lot in common. This became especially evident after Samuelson's discovery (*Foundations of Economic Analysis*, 1947) of the coincidence of the instruments of comparative statics and dynamics, which became part of the theory called the "principle of correspondence". This is probably why static 'short-term' Keynesian models were easily transformed into models of long-term economic growth. The economists involved in these transformations began to disengage from

---

[1] See, for example: [75, p. 526].
[2] Currently, more and more works appear in which both macro- and microeconomic phenomena are considered from the standpoint of dynamics (see, for example: [108, 17]).

'Keynesianism'. But dynamic research in theory began even before the appearance of Keynes's *General Theory* with the help of constructions that differ from the comparatively static ones by clarifying the very mechanism of the transition from one equilibrium to another. His multipliers were first deduced by John Maurice Clark (*Business Acceleration and the Law of Demand*, 1917), and then by the English economist Richard Kahn (1905-1989) (*The Ratio of Domestic Investment to Unemployment*, 1931). If we use their approach, then the known Keynes multiplier can be derived dynamically.

Since the capital goods produced in the economy turn into investments I, which are exogenous and constant in magnitude, and the consumption of H – proportional to the output of the national product of the previous period (Y_0), then the current output Y_1 will be equal to: $Y_1 = I + H_1 = I + H' \cdot Y_0 = I + + H' \cdot I = I(1 + H')$. In turn, the size-measures of the issue in the following periods will be: $Y_2 = I + H' \cdot Y_1 = I(1 + H' + (H')^2)$, $Y_3 = I(1 + H' + (H')^2 + + (H')^3)$ etc. In general, in the t-th period, the output will be equal: $Y_t = I(1 + + H' + (H')^2 + ... + (H')^t)$. If we agree that the number of periods t grows indefinitely, then in the limit we can write the final equations $Y = (1/(1 - - H'))I$, $dY = \rho \cdot dI$, which coincide with the Keynesian formula, but according to the iterative procedure of derivation and graphical illustration (Fig. III.52) can be called "dynamic multiplier" equations.

The graph in Fig. III.52 is depicted as it is usually given in the literature[1], it contains a simplified, linear, kind of 'Keynes-1 cross' – Samuelson's 45-degree model with supposedly functions of 'total supply' A_s of product Y, 'aggregate demand' A_d on it and the point of intersection of functions ϑ, corresponding to the equilibrium volume of output Y_e, to which

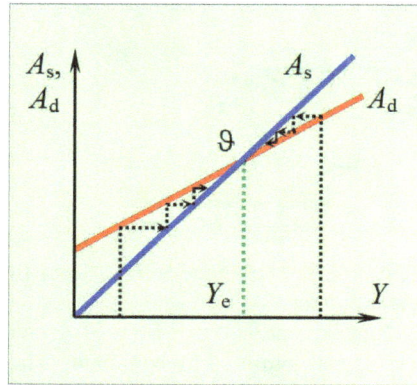

Fig. III.52

portions of investments invested in the zones of the so-called deflationary or inflationary gaps of the 'cross' lead. It is believed that this stepped model shows the action of the 'dynamic multiplier'. However, with a strict approach to Keynes's theory, shown in section 10 of the monograph (Fig. III.53), the multiplication processes should take place not stepwise, but smoothly with an increase in investment to the maximum corresponding to the equilibrium and

---

[1] See, for example: [113, p. 82].

stable volume of total output (Q_e). The opposite of this process, the movement from large output to equilibrium is quite logically possible, but for the entire economy it is unlikely. Thus, modeling economic growth seeks to show the mechanism and possibilities of increasing not just the total product, but its equilibrium volume.

The modern mathematized theory of economic growth dates back to the 30s. last century from the article by Neumann *Model of General Economic Equilibrium* (1937). The economy in the model was described using linearly homogeneous (with constant return) production functions. All goods in the model were raw materials for further production, that is, the sphere of consumption was considered by Neumann as a system of production of labor. It was assumed that land, labor and capital goods are available in the economy in an unlimited amount and do not limit the balanced stationary (with full consumption of the product for the period of time under consideration) growth of production sectors. The analysis of the model shows that the rate of expansion of production (ω_Q) in it coincides with the rate of the bank interest G_b. Therefore, the dynamic equilibrium of the economy is as follows: $\omega_Q = G_b$. This first growth model should be considered very successful, but too simplified, the real variability of capital return requires the inclusion in the right side of the equation of a term that takes into account the dynamics of this indicator.

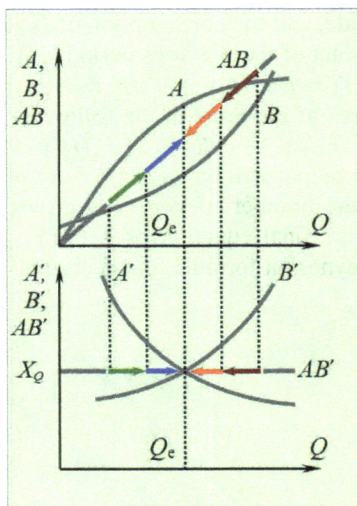

Fig. III.53

Subsequently, the theory of growth, in our opinion, departed from the correct path outlined by Neumann. The models of the English Keynesian Roy Harrod (1900-1978) (*Essay on the Dynamic Theory*, 1939) and the American economist Yevsey Domar (1914-1998) (*Capital Expansion, Growth Rate and Employment*, 1946)[1] appeared. Without going into the specifics and details of the two author's approaches, the corresponding generalized model can be represented as an expression of the "expected" rate of growth of the total product: $\omega_Q = \eta \cdot R'_K$, where η is the share of investments in the total product, or the so-called "capital ratio" (I/Q), and R'_K – the marginal capital return

---

[1] In this work, Domar refers to the growth model of his predecessor Feldman (*On the Theory of Growth Rates of the National Economy*, 1928).

indicator ($dQ/dK = dQ/l$), reflecting the dynamism of production, but accepted by the authors as an exogenous and constant value. In addition to Keynesian 'expected growth', Harrod introduced the concepts of "guaranteed growth", which implies full employment of available jobs, and "natural growth", which ensures full employment of the workforce. The coincidence of one with the other means a subtle dynamic balance, balancing 'on the edge of a knife', if the corresponding goals do not coincide in the economy, instability increases. The Harrod-Domar equation looks more like an identity than a full-fledged model, but, nevertheless, it was the basis for the subsequent development of the theory of economic growth.

The neoclassical model of economic growth developed by Solow (*Towards the Theory of Economic Growth*, 1956) and independently by Australian economist Trevor Swan (1918-1989) (*Economic Growth and Capital Accumulation*, 1956)[1], is more advanced, taking into account the dynamics of the labor force, depreciation and the growth of capital goods. It is built on the basis of the aggregated two-factor Cobb-Douglas production function (*Theory of Production*, 1928), obtained as a result of a statistical analysis of the manufacturing industry in the USA in 1899-1922: $Q_{en} = = 1.01K^{0.25} \cdot L^{1-0.25}$, where 1.01 – the parameter of the scale of production, Q_{en} – the volume of the aggregate end (gross domestic) product, 0.25 – the indicator of the elasticity of the product in terms of the volume of capital goods (α).

The model uses indicators that change significantly only in the long run in the form of the dependence of labor productivity (R_L) on the capital-labor ratio (E) (Fig. III.54). The R_L function is convex, since it reflects the law of diminishing efficiency of a factor, acting under the premise of ceteris paribus, and is derived from a production function of the form $Q = K^\alpha \cdot L^{1-\alpha}$ (we round the parameter 1.01 to 1, and the index 'к' for Q we omit for simplicity of further presentation) as follows: $R_L = Q/L = (K^\alpha \cdot L^{1-\alpha})/L = (K^\alpha/L^\alpha)(L/L) = = (K/L)^\alpha$, $R_L = E^\alpha$. Product Q consists of a consumption fund (H) and gross investment, consisting of depreciation of capital goods ($v \cdot K$, where v – the depreciation rate of capital goods, the ratio of the amortization flow A_K to the value of the stock K, $v = A_K/K$) and their gain (dK): $Q = H + v \cdot K + dK$. Then Q/L will be: $Q/L = H/L + v(K/L) + d(K/L)$. But, since $d(K/L) = (L \cdot dK - K \cdot dL)/L^2 = dK/L - (dK/L) - (K/L)(K/L \cdot dL/L) = I_L - \omega_L \cdot E$, where I_L – the investment per employee, or reduced investment, and ω_L – the rate of growth of the labor force, then in a compact form we obtain: $R_L = H_L + I_L - k \cdot E$, where H_L – the average consumption of the employee, k – the sum labor force

---

[1] There is evidence that the Norwegian economist Trygve Haavelmo (1911-1999) (*Study in the Theory of Economic Evolution*, 1954) developed a neoclassical one-sector model of economic growth before Solow and Swan (see: [76, p. 211]).

growth rate and depreciation rate, $k = \omega_L + v$.

The final neoclassical equation of economic growth, taking into account the production and distribution of the product, can be written in the following form: $R_L = E^\alpha = H_L + I_L - k \cdot E$. It is shown in the figure: the power-law function E^α, consisting of H_L and I_L, is at the top of the graph, and the linear function $-k \cdot E$ – at the bottom of the graph.

Since further analysis of this growth equation involves finding the marginal characteristics of the indicators included in it, the model is best viewed in the form of a marketron (Fig. III.55, in the integral part of which all three functions of the equation are depicted in such a way that the positive the function of the reduced national income H_L and I_L, the negative function $-k \cdot E$ is imposed. This allows you to clearly demonstrate the balancing of the model. In the marginal part of the marketron, a decreasing function of the marginal capital return appears ($R'_K = dQ/dK$) as the ratio of the differentials of productivity (dR_L) and capital-to-labor ratio (dE) of labor ($dR_L/dE = dQ/dK$). The intersection point of R'_K with the horizontal k ($k = (k \cdot E)'$) the value of the capital-labor ratio (E_p), which provides the maximum average consumption of the employee ($H_{L(max)}$, $H_{L(max)} = E_p^\alpha - k \cdot E_e$).

Phelps (*The Golden Rule of Accumulation: An Axiom for Students of Growth*, 1961) for the Solow model formulated the "golden rule of accumulation": investment should equal the factor income of capital goods at the point of maximum average consumption of the employee $H_{L(max)}$. Such a

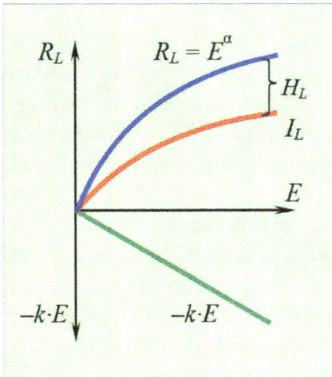

variant of the location of the reduced investment function I_L is depicted in Fig. III.55. It should be borne in mind that not every I_L function corresponds to the 'golden rule'. At all other points of intersection of I_L with the ray $k \cdot E$, investments will also be equal to depreciation, but the average employee consumption will be lower than the maximum.

Fig. III.54

Solow's model in the context of technological progress in the economy could not simply be based on new data on the elasticity indicator in the production function, and therefore, since the 80s. of the last century, attempts were made to develop the theory of growth in the direction of creating endogenous models containing internal impulses to increase the efficiency of production factors.

American economist Paul Romer (b. 1955) (*Increasing Returns and Long-term Growth*, 1986) began to consider, instead of two-factor, three-factor production functions – with labor, capital goods and 'knowledge'. The emergence of this line of research was undoubtedly influenced by Arrow's work *The Economic Consequences of Learning in Practice* (1962). Lucas (*On the Mechanism of Economic Development*, 1988) suggested taking into account the factor of 'human capital' as a result of learning in the process of production. And a little later, Rohmer, as well as his colleague Mankiw (*Contribution to the Practice of Economic Growth*, together with D. Weil, 1992) developed growth models, directly containing the factor 'human capital'.

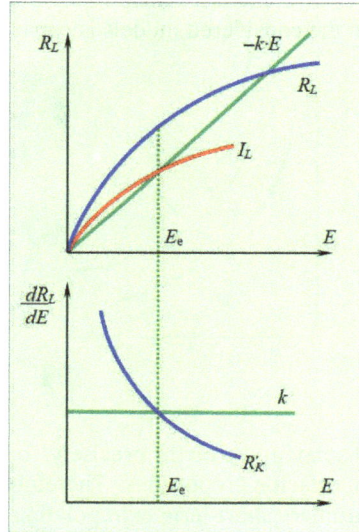

Fig. III.55

Evaluating the Solow model and its named modifications, one can point out their common shortcomings.

Attempts to formally include in the standard production function additional dubious factors – 'knowledge', 'human capital', etc., taking into account progressive changes in the economy, lead to mathematical heaps and fundamentally do not solve growth modeling problems. For example, in addition to the factor of 'labor' in the form of the number of employed labor resources in the models it turns out to be both a dubious factor and a factor of 'human capital', while he and 'labor' are one and the same factor 'labor force' in the form of a stock of value, that is, labor potential.

The second remark concerns the incorporation of technological progress into the growth model. In theory, there are many relevant developments. Let's consider the main ones. Tinberchen (*Mathematical Models of Economic Growth*, together with H. Bose, 1962) based on data on Germany, Great Britain, France and the United States, a special factor-factor (k) was introduced into the standard production function, which is defined as follows:

$k = (1 + \omega_R)^t \approx e^{\omega_R \cdot t}$, where: ω_R – the annual growth rate of production efficiency, e – the base of the natural logarithm, equal to 2.72, and t – the time of 'maturation' of innovations. Technological progress will be Harrod-neutral to capital productivity R_K (R_K = const), that is, materialized in the labor force, if k is attributed to the factor L ($Q = K^{\alpha}(k \cdot L)^{1-\alpha}$) (Fig. III.56, option 1), or neutral to labor productivity R_L (R_L = const) according to Solow, that is, materialized in capital goods, if k is referred to K ($Q = (k \cdot K)^{\alpha} \cdot L^{1-\alpha}$ (option 2) and neutral to the capital-to-labor ratio E (E = const) according to Hicks, if k will relate to both factors ($Q = k(K^{\alpha} \cdot L^{1-\alpha})$ (option 3).

From a methodological point of view, as we have shown above, it would

237

be more correct not to introduce additional factors-factors into production functions, but to develop a system of continuous revaluation of the factors of production themselves, including the factor of its scale, which makes it possible to avoid a gap between values. stocks and values-flows.

And one last remark. The search for an equilibrium capital-to-labor ratio in the considered models is carried out according to the criterion of maximum consumption, while the universal market criterion for the activities of business entities in the industrial economy is the maximum profit. It should be borne in mind that the modeling of economic growth with the target function of savings and investment exists, it was carried out by the Englishman Frank Ramsey (1903-1930) (*Mathematical Theory of Savings,* 1928).

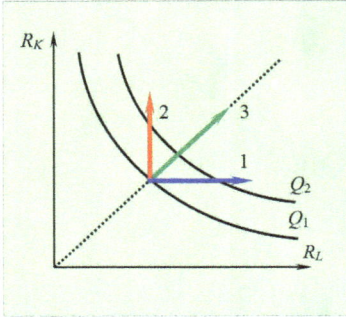

Fig. III.56

In our opinion, all models of economic growth, built on the basis of multifactorial production functions, are of little use for displaying growth precisely because of the difficulties in determining interfactor proportions. Therefore, it is rational to use such models only for ordinary short-term extrapolation.

One-factor growth models are much more useful, and among them one should single out a model built on the basis of the capital return $((R_K)$ indicator: $R_K = Q/K$ (Fig. III.57). In the model, the increase in the aggregate output for an extremely short period of time dt is equal to: $dQ = d(K \cdot R_K) = dK \cdot R_K + K \cdot dR_K + dK \cdot dR_K$. The first term in the sum represents an extensive increase in output (dQ_{ext}), the second term is an intensive increase in output (dQ_{int}), and the third term is an extensive-intensive increase in output $(dQ_{ext.-int})$. If we know exactly the trajectory of the economy's transition from point 1 to point 2, that is, if the dynamics of either the aggregate of capital goods or capital return is known for a period of time dt, then the equation can be simplified by distributing the third term between the first and the second (see wide arrows in Fig. III.57). Due to the relative smallness of the $dQ_{ext.-int}$ component, it can simply be ignored in simplified calculations. And then, in both cases, the dynamic equation of economic growth can be written as: $\omega_Q = \omega_K + \omega_{R(K)}$.

This model is preferable to a similar model built on the basis of the labor productivity indicator $(\omega_{R(L)})$ $(\omega_Q = \omega_L + \omega_{R(L)})$ for several reasons. First, the equation $\omega_Q = \omega_K + \omega_{R(K)}$ is more accurate than the Neumann growth model equation, since it contains an indicator of capital return, which, moreover, is adequate to the industrialized economy itself, characterized by intensive use

238

of accumulated potential of capital goods. Secondly, the capital return indicator, which is absolutely exogenous, changes in a long-term period cyclically, which simplifies its forecasting and use in a model of economic growth. Thirdly, the equation is homogeneous, there is no mixing of monetary indicators with natural ones. Fourth, the equation characterizes not just economic growth, but long-term economic development. And, fifthly, no less important, the equation $\omega_Q = \omega_K + \omega_{R(K)}$ reflects the relationship of all indicators of 'capital investment efficiency' used in the practice of evaluating and choosing investment projects, as well as optimisation of the bank interest as a final, integral regulator of the economy.

Economic development is inextricably linked with investment. Therefore, to regulate growth, it is important to provide a theoretical basis for decisions in the field of formation and use of capital resources. The theory of the efficiency of capital investments as a whole has become the most advanced and applied section of economic science. This is evidenced by the regular publication of relevant practical methods for evaluating and selecting investment projects[1]. To select investment options, three indicators are used: value discounting (π_{di}), relative (π_r) and absolute (π_a) investment efficiency.

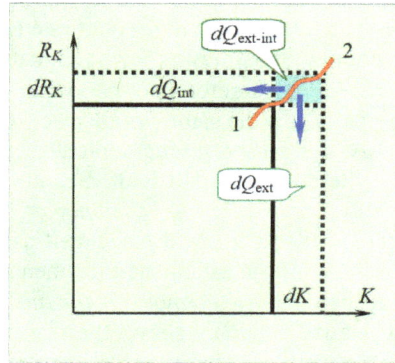

Fig. III.57

What is the economic content of these indicators and how are they related to each other? Despite the centuries-old practice and the theory of accumulation and investment, the question posed remains unclear to the end. In the economic literature, not only the concepts of 'capital' and 'capital goods' are still mixed, the place of interest in the theory of factor income is not clearly defined, but an exact description of the ratio of interest to indicators of capital efficiency is not given. investments, there is no sufficient scientific substantiation of the corresponding standards from the standpoint of the theory of economic growth and development.

It is known that different-period flows of value should be discounted, that is, brought to one point in time. Despite the subjective nature of intertemporal preferences, when reducing future values to current ones, current economic practice is focused on the average bank percentage G_b. For example, investments (I) made over a number of years ($I_1, I_2 \dots I_i$), to bring to the

---

[1] See, for example, quality development: [9].

beginning of the entire period t, are multiplied by the discount factor (k_{di}), calculated on the basis of G_b according to the rule of negative compound interest ($k_{di} = (1 - G_b)^t$) and are summed ($I = \Sigma(I_i \cdot k_{di})$). At the same time, investments are always associated with the corresponding effects in the form of an increase in production or profits. This means that both the costs and the effect for the entire investment cycle should be calculated cumulatively. If, suppose, it is 4 years, then the final effect for this period should be 'tied' to the volume of capital investment for 4 years as well.

Some authors[1], however, identify the effect of the time factor with an investment lag. But bringing values of different times to one point in time is not associated with an investment lag. If investment lags, or project cycles are precisely known, then the period for disregarding capital investments can be different and depends simply on the time frame for comparing costs or benefits. It is quite obvious that when discounting the value of goods, instead of the bank interest, a discount rate (π_{di}) should be used, which is equal to the economic dynamics as a whole, that is, the rate of increase in the aggregate issue (ω_Q). Therefore, we can write the identity: $\pi_{di} \equiv \omega_Q$. Moreover, π_{di}, as well as G_b, is the same for all specific calculations.

As for the economic content of the o indicator, it is often interpreted in the literature very difficult. So, the Soviet economist Dmitry Lvov (1930-2008) (*Measuring the Efficiency of Production*, together with A. Rubinstein, 1972) called the profit calculated using the indicator as costs that determine the "size of the established payments of the enterprise to the budget" [66, p. 18] (in a planned economy – *the author*). At the same time, it is said that "the normative economy shows the size of the national economic losses that arise not in the given, but in other enterprises that have not received the necessary capital investments due to their use in this production" [Ibid, p. 19], which completely confuses the solution to the question of the essence of the indicator of the relative efficiency of investments. But, judging by the statistical comparisons and their macroeconomic analysis [31, p. 26], we can conclude that the π_o indicator expresses the generalized profitability in the economy (M/K), that is, the growth rate of the total volume of capital goods (ω_K), and, consequently, the key rate bank interest G_b: $\pi_r = M/K = \Delta K/K = \omega_K = G_b$.

Based on this conclusion, the rationing of the π_r indicator would give certainty not only in the practice of solving the issues of selection and optimization of investments, but also in banking, since the percentage is an indicator of the business activity of economic entities. In our model constructions in the previous section of the monograph, we also showed that G_b – not just a financial instrument, but also a regulator of the system of four

---

[1] See, for example: [99].

defects and the general equilibrium of the market economy.

The indicator of the absolute efficiency of investment π_a in Keynesian macroeconomic theory is interpreted as the return on investment, dA/I, as the 'marginal efficiency of capital' (dA/dK), the equilibrium value of which is equated in the Keynesian investment selection model to the bank interest G_b (see section 12 of the monograph). Let's try to establish a real connection between all three indicators in the complete model of the capital goods market (Fig. III.58).

The integral part of the corresponding marketron contains the convex function of profitability A_K of capital goods K and the concave function of their production expenditure (B_K). The positive difference between the values of A_K and B_K is the total profit (M) invested in the growth and development of the production apparatus. In the differential part of the marketron, there are the marginal functions of the same name A'_K and B'_K, which are the curves of the supply of capital goods and the demand for them. It is important to point out that A'_K is also a function of limiting capital return: $A'_K \equiv R'_K$. The point of intersection of the functions corresponds to the equilibrium values of the aggregate of capital goods (K_p) and the rate of absolute efficiency of capital investments $\pi_{a(e)}$. This point also falls on the maximum aggregate profit (M_{max}), the capitalization of which gives an

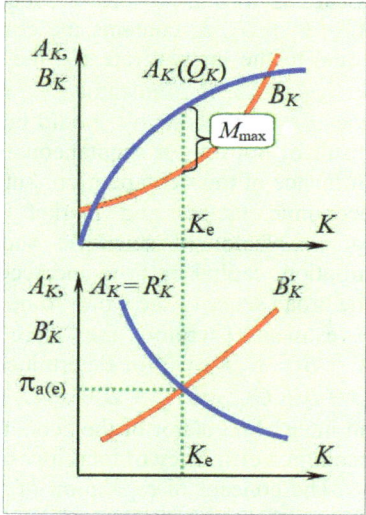

Fig. III.58

equilibrium increase in the production apparatus (ΔK_e), and the fraction $\Delta K_e/K_e$ is the equilibrium rate of the relative efficiency of investments $\pi_{r(e)}$, interest rate. Thus, the essence of the indicator $\pi_a - R'_K$, and the indicator $\pi_{a(e)} - R'_K$, which is at the level B'_K.

Therefore, according to Keynes's controversial money-investment model, considered in section 8 of the monograph, our conclusion is as follows: the price of money in the form of an equilibrium bank interest rate cannot be equal to the 'marginal efficiency of capital', since these are qualitatively different indicators, the first is equal to the relative, and the second – to the absolute efficiency of capital investments.

The marketron of capital goods shows clear interrelationships of all three indicators, π_{di}, π_a and π_r, which are included in the equation of our model of economic development: $\omega_Q = \omega_K + \omega_{R(K)}$, $\omega_Q = G_b + \omega_{R(K)}$, $\pi_{di} = \pi_r + \omega_{\pi(a)}$,

241

where $\omega_{\pi(a)}$ – the growth rate of the absolute efficiency of capital investments. The equation allows you to get rid of the calculation of the value of the discount rate $\pi_{\text{ди}}$ and determine it directly from the data on π_o and π_a. For example, in the 80s. in the USSR, the π_r and π_a standards were set at 12% and 40%, since the total product grew more slowly than the production apparatus, and capital productivity fell by about 2% annually: 10% = 12% – 2%. At the level of 10%, the π_{di} value was set for that period.

Note that the presented model of capital goods, as well as all the markrons of markets considered in the entire material of the monograph, are built on a single, end-to-end criterion – profit maximization. In our corrected neo-Ricardian formula of the 'production price' of the Marx-Sraffa GEE model $X_i = B_i + G_{mi} \cdot K_i$ contains the economy's average profitability. Since G_{mi} is equal to the interest rate G_b, the equation can be represented as: $X_i = B_i + + G_b \cdot K_i$. But, the indicator G_{mi}, and, therefore, equal to it G_b, and π_r, in a social market economy should be determined at the macro level and be the result of not only a spontaneous intersectoral overflow of capital under the influence of their competition, but also taking into account many other socio-economic factors and market defects, demographic and environmental factors, factor of scientific and technological progress, unemployment, inflation, capital outflow and recession, etc., that is, to be 'reproductive' in the broad sense of the word, to be the result of optimizing the volume of total investment. Therefore, the "price of reproduction" of an individual product, $X_i = B_i + G_b \cdot K_i$, will be determined by the "price of aggregate reproduction", $Q = B + G_{b(opt)} \cdot K$, $Q = B + \pi_{r(opt)} \cdot K$, where the key interest rate $G_{b(opt)}$ acts as an integral regulator of the economy, and $\pi_{r(opt)}$ – as a standard for the socio-economic efficiency of total investments.

The concept of regulation of the Keynesian economy considered above, which consists in fiscal and monetary support of the deficit and budgetary stimulation of business activity, pursuing the false goal of increasing employment only, is not suitable for optimizing the banking interest G_b and the standard π_r, since it generates new disproportion, in general, does not lead to a reduction in unemployment and entails other negative phenomena – an increase in inflation and public debt. There are not only factual, but also deeper, explanations for the inefficiency and limitation of the operation of Keynesian regulators of the economy. If, according to Keynes, an increase in government spending should multiply the total output by a multiplier mechanism, then in fact, even with a balanced budget, this recipe leads to the opposite result – the 'crowding out effect', a reduction in total private spending. Haavelmo (*The Multiplicative Effects of a Balanced Budget*, 1945) proved that a tax increase in government spending by a certain amount leads to an increase in output by the same amount, regardless of the redistribution of funds, "the multiplier will be equal to one" [98, p. 444]. "Theorem

242

Haavelmo" is explained by the fact that the 'state expenditure multiplier' (dQ/dB_{st}) is always greater than the 'tax multiplier' (dQ/dA_{st}). With a deficit fiscal expansion of the state, there is a decrease in the current real consumption, and, according to Ricardo-Barro's 'equivalence theorem' (*Is Government Bonds Pure Wealth?*, 1979), tax and credit financing is budget deficit give the same result in the economy.

Thus, the optimization of G_b more accurately and comprehensively characterizes the problem of normative regulation of the economy.

A fairly complete description of regulated economic growth is usually associated with the need to simultaneously solve a number of short-term and long-term problems. Some of these tasks are mutually complementary, some are mutually exclusive. Therefore, modeling the growth and development of the economy is multi-criteria and presupposes finding a certain compromise between individual formalized development tasks, its optimal proportions. In general, multi-criteria optimization of the long-term development of the economy without the use of empirical data turns out to be simply impossible due to the non-operationality of many goals.

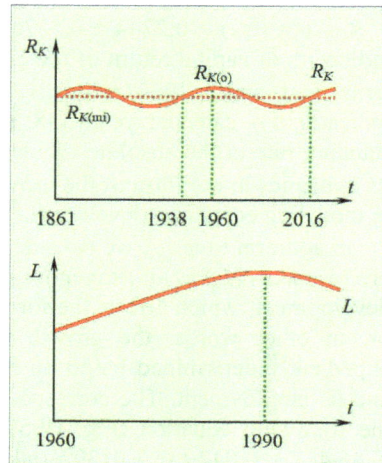

Fig. III.59

In our equation of economic development $\omega_Q = \omega_K + \omega_{R(K)}$, all of the above main factors are concentrated in only two indicators – extensive ω_K and intensive $\omega_{R(K)}$. But the optimization of even such a compact model, as we have shown above, is difficult to implement. The term $\omega_{R(K)}$ should be considered an explicitly not formalized factor, since it characterizes a complex phenomenon of scientific and technological progress. But this factor, as already noted, is quite accurately predicted due to the cyclical behavior of capital return.

For example, on the Russian-Soviet economy, statistics show that the R_K cycle can be clearly traced from the time of the economic reform of Russia in 1861 (Fig. III.59, upper graph), when the abolition of serfdom accelerated the industrialization of the country, due to which a large historical wave of capital return was observed. There is a reason to talk about the beginning of this process during the time of transformations in the Russian economy during the reign of king Peter I (1672-1725). By the beginning of the XX century the indicator monotonously decreased and took the lowest position during the period of revolutionary events in the country. The subsequent state government of the economy and the first 'five years' led to the completion of the process of industrialization of the economy and an increase in R_K again. But from the middle of the 60s to the middle of the 90s. The indicator began to gradually decrease again by about 2% per year, despite repeated attempts to prevent this negative phenomenon (hence the calculation of percentages, $10\% = 12\% - 2\%$, given above for the equation of efficiency standards the efficiency of capital investments, $\pi_{di} = \pi_r + \omega_{\pi(a)}$. The situation has improved since the second half of the 90s. after radical market transformations in the country, but the indicator will reach the average level for the period not earlier than 2030. The cycle of capital return, which takes an average of 80 years, can be calculated according to the empirical formula: $R_K = R_{K(mi)} + R_{K(0)} \cdot \cos(\sigma \cdot t) = 0{,}2744 + 0{,}537\cos(5{,}2941 \cdot t)$, where R_K, $R_{K(mi)}$ and $R_{K(0)}$ – indicators of capital return of the current year, average over 150 years (long-term trend) and in 1960, respectively; σ – the oscillation frequency of the R_K indicator; t – calendar years [38, p. 408]. The predicted values of R_K as a standard rate of the absolute efficiency of investments π_a and the indicator of its dynamics in the form of the growth rate of capital return $\omega_{R(K)}$ will be used in modeling economic development.

In addition to $\omega_{R(K)}$, we consider the indicator of the number of employed ore resources (L_t) as an exogenous empirical factor of the model of economic development, which affects the formation of the growth rate of capital goods, or, in other words, the growth rate of the average interest rate. L_t is expediently determined based on the long-term dynamics of the population and its employment. The corresponding data for Russia allow us to develop the following equation (Fig. III.59, lower graph): $L_t = L_0(a + b \cdot t + c^t) = 46{,}4(2 + 0{,}042 \cdot t + 1{,}0139^t)$ (taking into account the changes due to the reduction of the country's territory), where L_t and L_0 are the current number of labor resources in Russia and in 1960, respectively, in million people; t – calendar years; a, b and c are constant coefficients [Ibid]. The L curve is convex with the maximum number of labor resources in 1990.

Employment of labor resources is associated, first of all, with the volume of investments and their structure – extensive investments create additional jobs, and intensive investments 'destroy' them – and in secondly, with wages, or a consumption fund as a whole. Therefore, we will consider the mechanism for achieving the appropriate compromise proportions in the total product Q. Since in this mechanism, the fund for reimbursement of the total product is involved to the least extent, we will simplify somewhat for Luckily, focusing on optimizing the main part of Q – national income Y, as Keynes or Sraffa did.

Since the dynamics of capital return $\omega_{R(K)}$ is set exogenously in our model of economic development, according to the above empirical formula, adjusted for the indicator Y, the problem of optimizing development is reduced to the dynamics of the production apparatus of the country of the current period (K_t). The solution to this problem has the following steps (Fig. III.60).

Firstly, the minimum volume of national income (Y_{min}) is determined, which consists of the accumulation funds of the same name (I_{min}) and consumption funds (H_{min}). I_{min} provides an incremental shift in employment of the population: $I_{min} = K_{t-1} \cdot \omega_L = (K_{t-1}/L) \cdot \Delta L = E_{t-1} \cdot \Delta L$, where K_{t-1} – a set of capital goods of the previous change; ω_L is the growth rate of employment, taking into account the shift factor of the functioning of the economy; E_{t-1} is the capital-labor ratio of the previous period[1]. Based on these proportions, it turns out that the minimum growth rate of capital goods ($\omega_{K(min)}$) is equal to the growth rate of labor (ω_L): $\omega_{K(min)} = \omega_L$. The equation characterizes an extensive increase in capital goods, determined exogenously from the above forecasted data on the dynamics of the labor force. This dynamics in the form of a growth rate (λ_L, $\lambda_L = 1 + \omega_L$) also limits the minimum consumption fund (H_{min}): $H_{min} = H_{t-1} \cdot \lambda_L$, where H_{t-1} – the consumption fund of the previous period. H_{min} provides a constant level of consumption per one employed and the level of welfare of the entire population of the country, since the total wages are a source of support for young and elderly dependents. The minimum national income of the current period, therefore, is determined by the following equation: $Y_{min} = K_{t-1} \cdot \omega_L + H_{t-1} \cdot \lambda_L$.

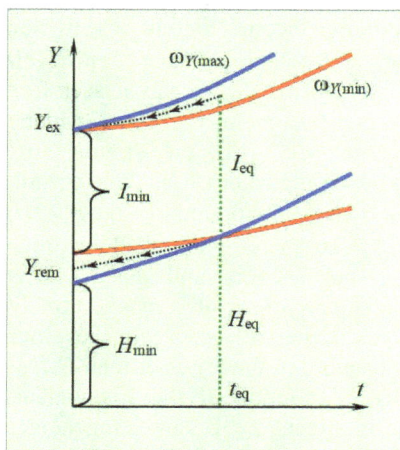

Fig. III.60

Secondly, the free, initially not distributed, remainder of the national income (Y_{rem}) is calculated as the difference between its expected (Y_{ex}) and the minimum values: $Y_{rem} = Y_{ex} - Y_{min}$. Subsequently, only Y_{rem} is subject to distribution for consumption and accumulation. Since it is about 18% of Y_{ex}, the problem of modeling economic development is conventionally simplified about six times.

---

[1] It should be emphasized that the expected increase in employment does not mean the elimination of unemployment, which, as shown in section 14 of the monograph, is inevitable in economic activity based on the criterion of maximum profit, as well as in the case of regulated profit.

Thirdly, two extreme variants of the use of Y_{rem} are considered: its full use either for consumption or for accumulation. Full consumption Y_{rem}, which makes it possible to significantly increase the current welfare of society, but in the long term gives only a minimum growth of the consumption fund and the national income as a whole ($\omega_{Y(min)}$), since in this case the minimum accumulation, being purely extensive, is carried out on the previous technical a basis that does not allow to increase the current capital return R_K in the economy. In this case, the value of $\omega_{Y(min)}$ will be entirely determined by the dynamics of the labor force: $\omega_{Y(min)} = \omega_{K(min)} + \omega_{R(K)} = \omega_L + 0 = \omega_L$. On the contrary, the full use of the free balance for accumulation allows, accordingly, to increase the efficiency of production by expanding the possibilities of using new equipment, technology, more qualified personnel and a high organization of production. All these innovations in our model of economic development will be expressed in an increase in the current level of capital return. It is logical to assume that the increase in capital return will be proportional to the share of innovative investments in their total volume. National income in this case will increase at the maximum possible rate ($\omega_{Y(max)}$). Economic long-term development according to these two options for the use of Y_{rem}, as can be seen from the figure, develops in such a way that during the period of time, which we call the "period of development equivalence" (t_{eq}), the volumes of the consumption fund are equalized, reaching the value of H_{eq}. The optimization parameter t_{eq} is determined by the following equation: $t_{eq} = \ln(H_{min}/H_{max})/\ln(\lambda_{Y(min)}/\lambda_{Y(max)})$, where $\lambda_{Y(min)}$ and $\lambda_{Y(max)}$ are the minimum and maximum rates of increase in Y, respectively.

The allocation and analysis of extreme development options show that under conditions of constancy of dynamic parameters during the period of equivalence of economic development, it is impossible to achieve a consumption fund greater than H_{eq}, since this level of consumption also gives any distribution of the free balance Y_{rem}. The period of equivalence of development t_{eq} is an endogenous variable of the model, but essentially depends on the predicted dynamics of the labor force and capital return. It is t_{eq}, in our opinion, that should be taken as the period of long-term modeling and forecasting of economic development, while other models and practice set it arbitrarily. Calculations show that t_{eq} is 15-17 years.

Fourth, the economic development model assumes finding the optimal parameters of the 'dichotomy' of the free balance of the national income Y_{rem} and the growth rate Y. The accumulation fund at the equivalence point (I_{eq}) is calculated based on the predicted capital return ($R_{K(eq)}$) and the difference in volumes national income ($Y_{max} - Y_{min}$) at this point according to the equation: $I_{eq} = (Y_{max} - Y_{min})_{eq}/R_{K(eq)}$. Discounting I_{eq}, H_{eq} and their sums (Y_{eq}) to the current year (dotted arrows in Fig. III.60), allow us to establish the optimal division of Y_{rem}, which ensures equilibrium employment, increasing the

246

efficiency of the economy and the welfare of society at the same time. Calculations show that the optimal division of Y_{rem} into investment and consumption is 70% by 30%, respectively. The optimal accumulation fund thus obtained determines the extensive ($\omega_{K(opt)}$) and intensive ($\omega_{R(K)(opt)}$) components of the optimal dynamics of the national income ($\omega_{Y(opt)}$) and the total aggregate product: $\omega_{Q(opt)} = \omega_{K(opt)} + \omega_{R(K)(opt)}$. The ratio of the intensive component $\omega_{R(K)(opt)}$ to $\omega_{Q(opt)}$, in turn, is an indicator of the quality of economic development (h): $h = \omega_{R(K)(opt)}/\omega_{Q(opt)}$.

The conducted modeling of economic growth and development makes it possible to clarify the relationship between micro- and macroeconomics. Microeconomics, which analyzes the system from the point of view of cybernetics, determines in its elements the direct cause-and-effect relationship 'capital – maximum profit'. Macroeconomics, which synthesizes the system, determines the optimal amount of total profit and, thereby, implements the feedback 'optimal profit – capital' of the system. Therefore, the norms of the relative efficiency of capital investments and the key rate of bank interest can be expressed in the form $\pi_{r(no)} = G_{b(no)} = (Q - B)/K$, and the total product Q will be determined by the formulas: $Q = B + \pi_{r(no)} \cdot K_{opt}$, $Q = B + G_{b(no)} \cdot K_{opt}$. But these macroeconomic formulas will also determine the price formulas in the markets for individual goods: $X_i = B_i + \pi_{r(no)} \cdot K_i$, $X_i = B_i + G_{b(no)} \cdot K_i$. Thus, we can talk about a single complex of 'micromacroeconomics'.

The demonstrated algorithm for optimizing the structure of the aggregate product and the key interest rate remains in force in the case when the minimum national income turns out to be greater than its expected value. In this case, the unallocated balance Y_{rem} turns into an unallocated inadequate (Y_{ina}), and the economy is in recession or protracted stagnation (Fig. III.61). Then the key interest rate characterizes the equilibrium values of indicators of the level of prices, employment, growth and balance of payments of the economy in the form of market defects functionally linked by us in a closed loop above: inflation, unemployment, recession and decapitalization.

In a private enterprise economy, the state is not in a position to directly regulate the commercial bank interest rate. But the optimal rate desirable for society can be realized due to the economic mechanism of penalizing overstated and subsidizing low interest rates of commercial banks by the Central Bank of the country in the process of regulating the norms for reserving their deposits.

The theory of general economic equilibrium is positive-normative in nature, assumes, based on certain social criteria, the replacement of maximum profit with optimal profit. Therefore, we must recognize the need for Keynes's non-laissez-faire principle, but its action in the macroeconomic study of the last phase of reproduction – the accumulation of goods.

Returning to the issue of the synthesis of the mainstream and 'neo-Ricardianism', it is necessary to conclude that Sraffa, like subsequent representatives of the direction, ignored the issues of economic growth, although, according to Kurz, they are considered 'long-term', which is evident from the title and content of their fundamental work *Theory of Production: Long-Term Analysis* (2004). But Sraffa's improved formula for 'production prices' can be successfully used in the theory of economic growth and make it more advanced – the theory of long-term development.

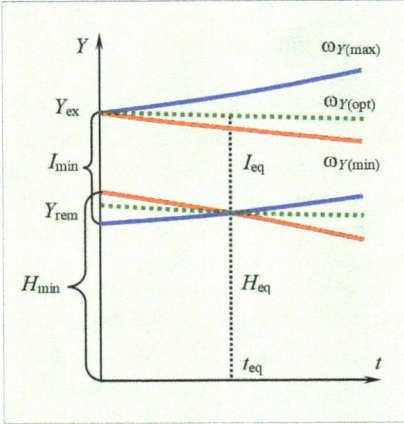

Fig. III.61

Sraffa in his early article *Laws of Return in Competitive Conditions* (1926), considering the process of formation of the average level of profitability of production, wrote that its "impact on the formation of prices of individual goods is insignificant, and their consideration therefore goes beyond the scope of this article" [111, p. 156]. Unfortunately, in his next work, he did not change his opinion about the really existing direct connection between the profitability of production and pricing.

Robinson, a well-known neo-Ricardian spokeswoman, wrote in the *Preface* to the collection of articles *A Guide to Post-Keynesian Economics* (1979): "While the switchback turned out to be an unnecessary distraction, Sraffa's revived classical theory of the rate of return provides the normal analysis of the long run that is required post-Keynesianism"[1]. But what this 'normal analysis' consisted of remained a mystery.

The remarkable book *Theory of Capital and Economic Growth* (2004) published in Russia by a team of post-Soviet economists who criticize the mainstream also speaks of the neo-Ricardian theory of economic growth, the beginnings of which are associated with Kaletsky (*Study of Economic Dynamics*, 1943). For Sraffa's study of a single rate of profitability of production, the next step was to develop a full-fledged theory of economic growth. Indeed, if, according to Roncaglia's figurative expression, the equilibrium in the Sraffa model is a "photograph" of the economy, then a number of such momentary equilibria should have been 'cinema'. But this did not happen and there is still no growth theory in 'neo-Ricardianism'.

---

[1] Cit. according to: [117, p. 152].

Modern neo-Ricardians speak of the 'organic' proximity of Keynes and Sraffa's theories. For example, Kurz writes, "that the analyzes of two of the most significant critics of orthodox economics in the XX century, Keynes and Sraffa ... complement each other ... The question is ... to bring together the theoretical alternatives to orthodox science developed by ... Keynes and Sraffa, that is, the theory of effective demand and the theory of normal prices and distribution" [63, p. 21]. We support this goal, but so far we see in the theories of meters only a few formal similarities: 1) the origin of Sraffa's theory as 'left Keynesianism'; 2) upholding by both economists of the principle of non-laissez-faire and the need for state regulation of market defects; 2) their search for the effective distribution of the same aggregate indicator – national income. The main divergence of teachings – the theory of value – does not allow us to talk about the 'organic' relationship of the teachings of Keynes and Sraffa. But these teachings belong to the controversial major scientific areas – macroeconomic mainst-rim and 'neo-Ricardianism'. Therefore, the interaction of methodologies and concepts of directions, the enrichment of the mainstream with certain theoretical achievements of neoricardians, shown in our monograph, undoubtedly lead them to the synthesis

CONCLUSION
IDEAS DETERMINING THE ECONOMICS
DEVELOPMENT AFTER THE 'DISPUTE OF
TWO CAMBRIDGES'

In general, the adjustments and shifts in the theories of 'neo-Ricardianism' and the mainstream, presented above, allow us to speak about the synthesis of directions in the modern phase of the history of world economic thought, which we called 'Unified socioeconomy'. This scientific formation has not been fully formed and the question of its further development arises in the conditions of exhaustion of the subject of the 'dispute of two Cambridges'.

To answer this question, it is necessary to turn to the study of the long-term prospects of the economy itself. This will help us 'metaeconomics', which at the beginning of the monograph was designated as a special section economics devoted to the laws of the historical development of public production.

Samuelson, in the *Conclusion of his Foundations of Economic Analysis* (1947), noted that from the point of view of the "mainstream of economic science" [97, p. X], "analytical economic theory" [Ibid, p. XV], there are six stages of its development: 1) the study of the static balance of the economy; 2) achieving comparative economic statics; 3) the theory of maximizing behavior of an economic entity; 4) introduction into the scientific circulation of the 'principle of correspondence' of comparative statics and dynamics; 5) the theory of economic dynamics; 6) the theory of "comparative economic dynamics" [Ibid, p. 355]. At the sixth stage, the theory "should include ... all the five subjects considered above, but at the same time should cover a wide 'territory'" [Ibid], where, in our opinion, there are nonequilibrium processes of self-organization in economics and society.

The last two chapters of the monograph mainly analyzed static models of markets and models using comparative statistics, and in the previous, tenth section, we considered theories of growth and development, that is, economic dynamics. In this *Conclusion*, let us turn to the kinetics of economic development as a synthesis of its statics and dynamics. In this form, as we noted above, the theory is close to synergetics, which studies open self-organizing systems, and to 'metaeconomics', which is what is called the cutting edge of science[1].

It is important to emphasize that the methodological basis of economic kinetics, synergetics or 'metaeconomics' is dialectics as a universal science

---

[1] See, for example: [45, 20, 72].

of development[1]. Since the dialectical method was used by Marx (*Capital: Critique of Political Economy. Vol. I*, 1867), then his ideas of the formational development of social production, in our opinion, did not exhaust their heuristic potential, at present they attract attention economists, but they need a certain development and improvement, supplemented by institutional elements. In an updated form, this model will be briefly examined by us below in order to give a reasonable idea of the prospects for the 'Unified socioeconomics' in the future.

It is necessary, first of all, to revise the system of generalized economic coordinates and indicators of Marx.

Marx's analysis of the "production process in general" in the form "in which it is characteristic of all social structures, that is, the production process outside its historical character" [69, v. 46, part I, p. 274] indicates its duality, its existence as labor and human cooperation at the same time. "Production ... manifests itself as a natural (labor) ... [and] social relation, social in the sense that it means the cooperation of many individuals, no matter what conditions, how and for what goals" [Ibid, v. 3, p. 28].

Means of labor and cooperation are "means of production" in the broad sense of this concept, characterize the level of development of all production relations. And this affects the concepts of "productive forces", "basis", "superstructure" and "socio-economic formation" considered by Marx. With the expansion of the concept of 'basis', the inclusion of production relations of labor in it, the concept of 'superstructure' is also transformed, since labor relations have their own 'superstructure', their material design in the form of means of labor. We call these means of labor in conjunction with the process of labor itself "technology of production" and consider this concept as the first universal, generalized coordinate of the metaekonomix.

Marx's 'superstructure' of society does not contain 'basic' institutions. In reality, the economic superstructure exists in the form of an 'economic mechanism' as a material substrate, means of realizing production relations of cooperation, that is, a system of informal customs, principles, norms, rules governing and ensuring the sustainability of the economic life of the society. The economic mechanism organizationally formalizes the existing system of production relations of cooperation and, in conjunction with all other institutions of society, can be called an 'extended economic mechanism', or "sociology of production."

Thus, the economic structure of society can be represented using the dualism 'technology – sociology of production', which can replace the triad 'productive forces – basis – superstructure' of society and become a more

---

[1] The substantiation of this fundamental theoretical position is contained in the works of the Russian philosopher and economist Georgy Ruzavin (1922-2012): [91. 92].

productive tool for understanding the dialectics of economics.

To introduce indicators for these coordinates, we will also use Marx's methodology for measuring the levels of development of industrial relations, who used the indicators 'organic structure of capital' and "rate of surplus value" in his analysis of the market economy. To give these indicators a general market character, let us express the structure of the aggregate product of society in the following form: $Q = C + V + M$, where C – the natural rent, which contains the overwhelming part of the material costs of production, V – the cost of living labor in monetary terms, and M – the total profit in the form of the so-called 'cash flow', which includes depreciation deductions and net profit. Let's call the ratio C/V "the level of development of production technology" (P), and the ratio M/V – "the level of development of the sociology of production" (S). Both indicators historically as a whole increase, the first – with the replacement of living labor with materialized, and the second – due to an increase in the amount of capital goods in the economy, their depreciation and net profit per unit of living labor. To characterize not only market, but also other historical forms of organization of the economy, the indicators under consideration can be presented in the form of indices. Indicators P and S are related to the indicator of production efficiency (R) in the equation of the economic state of society: $R = l \cdot P \cdot S$, or: $R = l \cdot J$, where: J – the level of technological-institutional culture of production, and l – a fundamental economic constant, $l = R/(P \cdot S) = R/J = \text{const}^{1}$.

Proportional-disproportionate superwave development of human civilization in the coordinates '$P – S$', shown in Fig. 1, corresponds to Smith's theory of natural-social continuum (continuity) and, at the same time, to Marx's theory of discrete social development, since the model reflects the possibility of rapid technological advances only with a certain stability of sociology production and vice versa. In addition, the model synthesizes the concept of development of society with an impulse from Marx's technology with the concept of development with an impulse from Weber's sociology of production (*Protestant Ethics and the Spirit of capitalism*, 1904).

For a relatively developed economy, the alternate cause-and-effect relationship between technologies and sociologies of production is obvious, while for the stage of the emergence of society and economic activity, the question of the root cause becomes important, fundamental. The explanation of the very fact of the periodicity of economic development, the understanding of the economic unity of the history of society, to which many economists-theorists aspired, the explanation of many complex historical phenomena of the economic life of society, as well as the quality of long-term forecasting of changes in production.

---

[1] For more details on the derivation and analysis of this equation, see our work: [39].

Economic literature usually simply states the cooperativeness and instrumentality of the activity of ancient man, while in reality anthropogenesis not only requires some explanations from the economic theory, but also has an economic essence, which, in our opinion, can to be recognized within the framework of the 'metaeconomics'.

First, anthropogenesis lends itself to explanation only from the standpoint of the natural-social continuum and for this, first of all, it must be divided into two parts – socio-and techno-genesis. The nature of the interaction between the natural environment and the society is described by the universal 'Le Chatelier principle' proposed by the French chemist Henri le Chatelier (1850-1936), according to which The thym influence, which unbalances the system, causes processes in it that seek to weaken this influence. A sharp deterioration in the habitat, associated with coldness due to the onset of the next geological ice age on the planet about a million years ago,

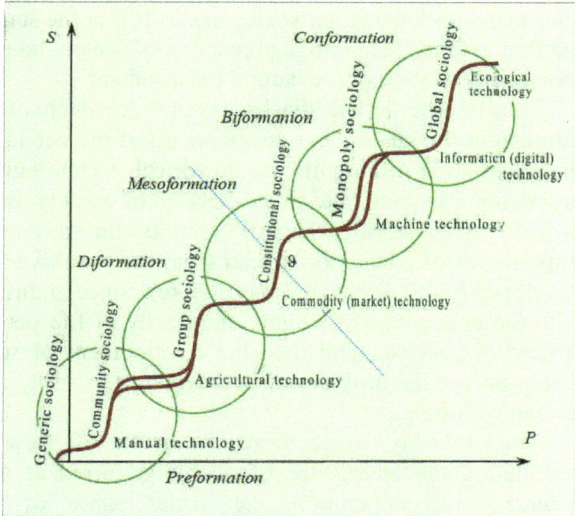

Fig. 1

caused such an internal restructuring in protosociety, which to a large extent compensated for the external catastrophic unfavorable environmental impact. The change in the internal structure of the system in this case could be reduced only to a closer contact of individuals, to their cooperation. The rupture of subjects with a familiar object – a useful nature for them – meant the establishment of additional intersubjective relationships. This cooperation of individuals has conditioned the formation of a primitive 'sociology of life' in the form of a set of certain rules, norms, taboos (prohibitions), traditions, language, mythological consciousness of people. Thus, it is sociogenesis that is primary in history. In Fig. 1 shows a socio-technological cycle with an initial deviation towards 'sociology', S. It is important to keep in mind that this beginning of history determines the entire subsequent cyclical evolution of society and the economy. The trend equation of economic development

$S = P$ in the second approximation of our model to reality, taking into account the frequency of movement of society, can be written in the following form: $S = P + \varepsilon \cdot \sin\sigma$, where ε – the amplitude indicator oscillations, σ – an indicator of the oscillation frequency.

Secondly, since the cooperation of individuals always has a downside – the specialization of their activities, the demographic expansion of the primitive cooperative genus meant the deepening of the specialization of individuals, and this, in turn, allowed them to some extent to use the moment for more successful fulfillment of certain roles in the cooperation of external objects as tools of labor. This significant event of technogenesis came only after many millennia after sociogenesis. It is at the stage of technogenesis that the first external technological reaction of society takes place in the form of a tool transformation of the natural environment.

Thirdly, the initial diachrony of socio-technological genesis persists throughout the subsequent development of the economy and is expressed in the alternation of significant historical technologies and sociologies of production. In fact, the entire history of society is a staged and cyclical process of restoring natural equilibrium through economic activity. Superwaves of adaptation spread from the primitive 'ecumene' to the future developed highly organized 'noosphere'. Since anthropogenesis is associated with the emergence of a significant rarity of life benefits, the economy is a system of survival, and then the development of society, while economic theory solves the problem of overcoming this rarity, ensuring the growth of human well-being.

And, fourthly, since from the point of view of the natural-social continuum, the emergence of people occurred at a certain level of their natural herd cooperation, the initial phase of the trajectory of the development of society somewhat goes beyond the frame of reference. The corresponding equation for the growth of civilization $S = f(P)$ in the third approximation of the model will already look like this: $S = P + \varepsilon \cdot \sin(k \cdot \sigma)$, where k under the sine sign – the proportionality coefficient characterizing the initial phase megacycle. The horizontal sections of the model, lying along the ascending abscissa 'P', correspond to the historical sequence of significant production technologies – manual, agricultural, commodity, machine, information and environmental, and the sections characterizing the progress along the ordinate 'S', represent, respectively, the tribal, communal, estate, constitutional, monopolistic and global sociology of production.

The change in technologies and sociologies of social production in its history occurs in such a way that each of them is not destroyed, but in a transformed form is included in the economic mechanism of a more developed society, that is, there is a process of 'removing' the simple from the complex as the cyclical development of the initial syncretic state of society. Transitions to higher levels of technology and sociology of production also mean the achievement of higher levels of production efficiency.

Specific historical forms of economic management represent the unity of significant technologies and sociologies of production. In the global wave process, it is possible to distinguish *Preformation, Diformation, Mesoformation, Biformation*, and *Conformation*, indicated in Fig. 1 circles, covering specific pairs 'technology – sociology'. Each socioeconomic formation is institutionally determined, has its own distinctive sociology of production, which formalizes its basic technology, but this sociology itself produces a new technology. Thus, all six historical significant technologies turn out to be connecting links of formations and are located in transition zones (in Fig. 1, these zones are located at the overlap of adjacent circles – 'formations').

The term 'preformation' (from the Latin 'prae' – in front) means social 'primary formation' containing in syncretic form the structures that predetermine the nature of all subsequent formations in history. The *Preformation* existed on the basis of clan-communal norms and hand-made tools.

The subsequent technological bifurcation of the trajectory of the development of society in antiquity on the line of extensive and intensive agriculture (hence the Greek prefix 'di-' in the name of the *Diformation*) led, respectively, to the slave system and feudalism, which turned out to be economically more efficient; in the Middle Ages it became dominant and became entrenched in a subordinated estate serf-sku system of lease and sublease of land.

Mesoformation (Greek 'mesos' means 'intermediate') corresponds to pre-industrial simple commodity production, constitutionally formalized by the institutions of private capital and free-hired labor.

The industrialization of market economies, which sharply increased the size of capital and rapidly changed their competitiveness, intensified the inter-sectoral outflow of capital, as a result of which competitive justice was established in society – obtaining the same profit (M) on capital (K), in whatever industry it is represented. Equal profitability of the spheres of capital investment testified to the completion of the process of formation of a harmoniously developed national economy, the technological basis of which was the aggregate industrial capital closely intertwined in the branches.

But industrialization also determined the general trend of lowering the average profitability of production (G_{mi}, $G_{mi} = M/(C + V)$) (Fig. 2, *a*). The essence of the trend was that, despite the aspiration of private business to increase the profitability of business through mechanization of production, at the macrolevel there was a gradual monotonous decrease in profitability.

This, at first glance, a paradoxical phenomenon reflected the internal crisis of the *Mesoformation*. If we divide the numerator and denominator of the fraction by the wage V in the indicator of the profitability of production and discard the resulting unit, we will find that the profit is proportional to the level of sociology production and back is proportional to the level of production technology: $G_{mi} = (M/V)/(C/V) + 1$, $G_{mi} \sim S/P$. Since the real economy is developing not synchronously, cyclically, and at this stage "machine technology" was growing, and classical market sociology was already quite stable, the average profitability G_{mi} of industrial production by

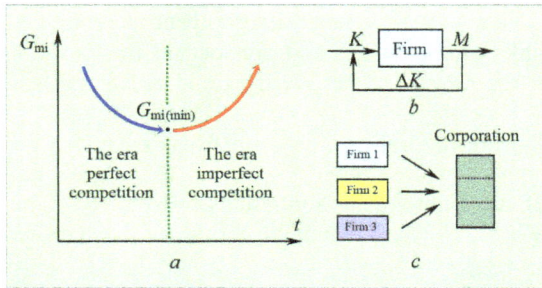

Fig. 2

the middle of the XIX century turned out to be minimal $(G_{mi(min)})$, which meant the onset of a systemic market crisis.

The market economy was able to acquire a 'second wind' in its further existence only with the transition from classical perfect competition to imperfect, monopolistic competition, which demanded a new institutional restructuring and, thus, the level of development of sociology of production to "monopolistic sociology". The 150-year-old modern strip of development of the corresponding *Biformation* (from the Latin 'bis' – twice) represents a monopoly of the first trade, and then the sphere of production of national economies. Having industrial technology as determinants, and the mechanism of implementation, corporatization of capital, that is, duplication of physical capital with financial capital (in the form of securities – stocks and bonds) and splitting the latter him on a part of an arbitrary denomination, monopolism ensured corporate control of sectoral markets and the possibility of obtaining super-profits due to the price dictate. And this superprofit was necessary not so much for additional incomes of entrepreneurs and capital owners as for reproduction in new competitive conditions of industrial capital itself and society as a whole.

The historical downward trend in profitability was replaced by a countertrend of its growth, the natural character of which was first shown by Sraffa (*Laws of Return in Competitive Conditions*, 1926), and then by the Americans Suizi and Baran *(Monopolistic Capital: an Outline of Americaan Economic and Social Order*, 1966). The classical method of 'internal' growth of enterprises by converting part of the profit into additional capital (ΔK), that is, by concentration of capital (Fig. 2, *b*), in the conditions of an industrial economy turns out to be inadequate and, when establishing a 'monopolistic sociology', is supplemented by the process of centralization of capital, which made it possible to quickly increase the size of the corporation due to its 'external' growth, that is, the absorption of small and medium-sized firms by large (Fig. 2, c).

However, with the formation of the corporate economy and the harmonization of sociology and production technology, a fundamental disproportion inevitably arises in the factor structure of the rapidly growing aggregate product (Fig. 3). Over a century of industrialization, from the middle of the XVIII to the middle of the XIX century, the share of costs for raw materials C and excess profits M in the total output of Q increased hypertrophied. Not only the deployment of machine technology in the economy had an effect, but also the redistribution of income in favor of capital, a part of the absolutely growing incomes of workers turned into a monopolistic excess profit of corporations.

Wages became inadequate for labor productivity and technological achievements of society, turned out to be incomplete and not sufficient for expanded reproduction of large-mass work power people of hired labor.

Thus, by the middle of the XIX century in the leading industrialized countries, such a production capacity of national economies was created, which, on the one hand, did not correspond to the narrow possibilities of marketing products due to

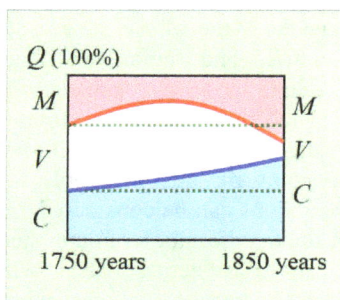

Fig. 3

the low effective demand of the population, and, on the other hand, On the other hand, it required additional sources of various raw materials. The accumulated industrial potential began to look for new resources and places for the sale of goods in the world periphery, the process of intensive internationalization of capital began. Relatively surplus national capital rushed on a large scale abroad and successfully consolidated in the economies of countries with cheap labor and natural resources necessary for industry. Since it was about interstate relations, not only economic methods of competition were used, but also diplomacy, political pressure, famously enslaving lending, concessions, bribery of the comprador bourgeoisie and direct military expansion.

During and as a result of World War I, in a number of underdeveloped countries, economic monopoly, due to various circumstances, combined with the monopoly of the state, which led to their transformation into the so-called 'socialist countries' and to the formation in them of centralized administrative command systems, which existed rather for a long time and allowed to systematically accelerate the process of industrialization of their economies. Thus, fourth stage of history *Biformation* was institutionally bifurcated, despite the preservation in it of the criterion of production profitability that is common for the two economic systems.

The presented formation model reflects the symmetry of history. The 'axis' of symmetry in the form of a dotted line passing in Fig. 1 through the *Mesoformation* and the dividing model into two parts, as well as the general diagonal trend in the development of society, show many similar and 'mirror' phenomena. In addition, the model shows that the technological dichotomy of the *Diformation* and the sociological dichotomy in the XX century *Biformations* are linked to each other. Countries that have gone through a slave-owning civilization in their development, created a mechanism of coercion to labor, institutions of public power and preserved democratic traditions, then, in the conditions of a monopolized industrial economy, they skip the stage of the state system planned economy. And on the contrary, countries and regions that have not gone through slavery subsequently gravitate towards 'socialism' and, under certain other circumstances, inevitably develop in this totalitarian form of industrial society. So, contrary to the theory of Marx, in *Biformation* there is no need for a transition to an economy of state monopoly for all countries. At the same time, and such transitions can be considered natural, and not just 'experiments of the chiefs' or the manifestation of other subjective factors of history.

From Western countries with corporate sociology, surplus capital in the form of cash loans and industrial investments was initially exported to underdeveloped countries, many of which turned into colonies and semi-colonies, and after World War II under conditions 'parade of sovereignty' of these countries and the lack of modern market infrastructure in them repatriated to the metropolis. The global migration of capital, which at first ensured a further increase in its profitability, as the levels of socio-economic development of the regions of the world economy approached, in the context of the transition to the market of former socialist countries and the advancement of the so-called 'new industries countries' Asia and South America, caused the general trend of falling profitability again.

The repeated decrease in the profitability of market production indicates that this main indicator of the business activity of capital in the process of historical development changes cyclically. This is a sign of not only the strengthening of the homogeneity of the world community, but also the crisis of the industry and the beginning of the transition to post-industrial, informational, technology, which becomes the basis of the *Conformation* (the Latin prefix 'con-' means 'together'), in which the "globall sociology", that is, the world system of universal institutions, which helps to implement the homogeneity of societies and their adaptation to the environment.

But, if the historical dynamics of profitability in the market is a cycle, then what is its trend and what are its origins and prospects?

Formation analysis of society shows that the trend of the cycle of profitability, as well as the entire history of social production, is the absolute constant of nature in its broad sense, that is, including society, the so-called 'golden proportion' of nature, which operates in all its specific formations of physical, chemical, biological, social origin and establishes balance and harmony in them.

Most simply, the 'golden ratio' is determined by dividing an ordinary straight line segment into two parts. If its length is denoted as a unit, its smaller part – for x, and the larger part – for $1 - x$, then the harmony of the segment will be observed when it is cut in the proportion: the ratio of the small part to the large is equal to the ratio of the latter to everything from cutting: $x/(1 - x) = (1 - x)/1$. From here we find x in the form of a square equation $x = 1 - 2x + x^2$, the solution of which gives us the numerical value of the 'golden proportion': $x = 0.382$. We designate this universal constant of harmony as G_Γ. In relation to society, G_H characterizes the harmony of net profitability for any method of production: $G = (A - B)/B$, where A and B are specific indicators of results and costs, respectively.

In Fig. 4 shows the general historical and prospective dynamics of the indicator G. The trajectory has a wave damping character and reflects the gradual, post-step compensation of the above-mentioned ecological catastrophe – a sharp cooling in the next 'ice age', which led to the appearance of in the biota of the Earth of the human population. The development of the arisen production activity will inevitably lead in the long run to stabilization of the disturbed 'golden proportion.' Separate cycles of the trajectory characterize the historical sequence of criteria for farming – the rentability of the agricultural (G_R), the

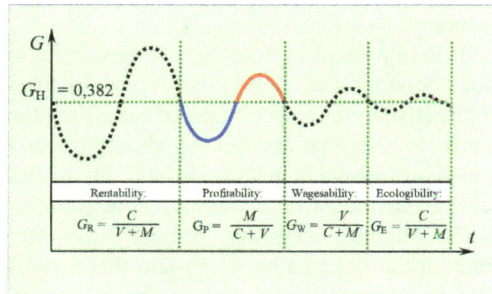

Fig. 4

profitability of the industrial (G_P), the 'wagesalary' of the information (G_W) and the 'ecologibility' of the global (G_E) society. The design of these four criteria is the same and is such that all three elements of the value of the produced product, that is, C, V and M, become the numerator of the total profitability indicator of production G as a residual target result, that is, C, V

and M, and they are also included in the denominator of the fraction in as a cost element.

So, since in primitive times the 'golden proportion' began to decrease, then in the criterion of rentability of management G_R introduced in a practical way, a natural rent C ($G_R = C/(V + M)$) appeared, which allowed people not only to successfully overcome the adverse consequences of an ecological catastrophe, but also to improve their well-being. The consequences of an environmental disaster, but also to improve their well-being. The growth of C also allowed the reproduction of land as the main factor of production and the development of agriculture. In the conditions of the industrial economy, the first historical criterion of production turned out to be ineffective and was replaced by profitability ($G_P = M/(C + V)$). And in this structure, the priority of profit was dictated by the task of growth and development of capital, that is, the very machine technology. The dynamics of G_P, like the dynamics of G_P, was cyclical (in Fig. 4, this cycle of the graph is drawn by a solid line), but the industrial cycle in amplitude turned out to be less than the agrarian cycle and thus significantly brought society closer to the indicator of absolute harmony G_H.

With the completion of the formation of industrial capital and the transition to a social market economy, the salary V becomes the residual income, and the profit M should be attributed to costs. The corresponding criterion of wagesalary production ($G_W = V/(C + M)$) – not the fruit of pure theory, it is predetermined by the logic of the historical development of public production and is adequate to modern information technology, the task development of 'human capital', the sphere of education and an innovative economy.

It is important to note that the new criterion is designed to achieve not so much economic as social goals, since for the first time in history it will allow to directly solve the problems of satisfying the whole complex plex of human needs. In fact, we are talking about 'effective socialism', and not 'formal' socialism, where a person is still an instrument for the functioning of a centralized industrial economy. That economic calculation, which was used in the planned economy, basically did not differ from the usual market commercial calculation. Here and there, profit was at the forefront. It is she who is primarily interested in the owner of capital goods, be it a private entrepreneur or a centralist state apparatus. The focus on the wages of production should sharply increase its overall efficiency and directly the welfare of workers.

The salary criterion was practically applied during the crisis of the planned economy in the USSR in the very economic practice of the so-called "team contract". The experience of its application in the 70s and 80s. in construction Nikolai Travkin (b. 1946) (now a political figure), healthcare surgeon Svyatoslav Fedorov (1927-2000) and other industries showed an explosive positive effect, but then he was subjected to severe attacks from the bureaucratic system and was curtailed in the course of further profitable market transformations in the country.

In our opinion, the so-called financial and economic crisis, in which the world community has been living since 2008, is associated with the need to move to a new criterion of production.

In Fig. 5 shows the proportions of the historical joint dynamics of agrarian (N), industrial (K) and informational (L) factors of production. The growth line of industrial capital goods is associated with the dynamics (dashed line) of financial capital (K_f), which, although it has its own market, is constantly adjusting to the volume of capital goods. In the conditions of the current stabilization of the world production apparatus, there is a separation from it that grows by inertia, that is, in the mode of not ordinary investment activities, but a monetary 'pyramid', a financial 'fictitious' capital. The restoration of normal operation of the financial sector will occur if it begins to invest in the growth of not the industry, but the service sector of

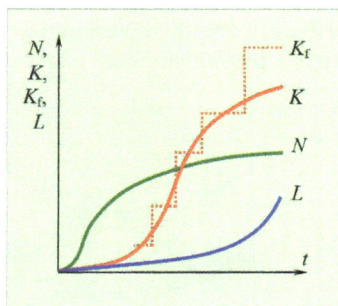

Fig. 5

the human factor, which is still relatively undeveloped. But the growth of the investment flow in the spheres of education and the formation of a modern mobile workforce in the conditions of preserving private property and the market, and requires the institution of wages, which creates a powerful fund for building a real socialism.

In modern conditions of falling profitability of market production, there are also facts of refusal of this criterion by entrepreneurs themselves. For example, the statement of the CEOs of 180 largest US companies (Business Roundtable Group) about the desire to work not for profit, but "for the good of all Americans" is indicative [145].

In the long-term historical perspective, after solving the main social problems of modernity with the help of the production wages criterion and in the conditions of the inevitable aggravation of environmental problems, society will have to introduce the fourth production criterion – the criterion of its ecologibility ($G_E = C/(V + M)$), which closes the reproductive circle of criteria and outwardly, in its design, coincides with the historically initial criterion of land profitability, but at a higher level of economic culture will allow residual formation of the "income of nature" C required for completion of the construction of an integral system 'nature – society'.

The need for the transition in the future to the criterion of environmental friendliness of production and the entire life of people is justified by an analysis of long-term forecasts of the development of the world economy, in particular the most famous forecast of Forrester (*World Dynamics*, 1971). In it, based on the method of 'system dynamics', which provides for the definition of not only direct, but also reverse causal relationships between social and natural phenomena, the author predicted an offensive in the middle of the XXI century the global crisis, consisting in a significant decrease in industrial capital, food production and the size of the world's population (Fig. 6).

As the causes of the disaster, Forrester names the depletion of natural resources and the deterioration of the human environment. The author made such a pessimistic conclusion after numerous variations of the variables of the model showed the fundamental impossibility of preventing a crisis. The chief developer of the first report to the Club of Rome (a non-governmental international organization established in 1968 and dealing with global problems) came to similar results, an American student of Forrester, Dennis Meadows (b. 1944) (*Growth Limits. The Report on the Project of the Club of Rome 'The Difficult Situation of Humanity'*, jointly with D. Medows, J. Randers and V. Behrens III, 1972), prepared on the basis of a more detailed model of the world economy. Moreover, both Forrester and Meadows found out that the indicator of quality of life, having reached the highest level in 1940, subsequently decreased and until 2100 would monotonically decrease due to deterioration in nutrition, material provision, high levels of population density and pollution. The introduction of the criterion of the ecological logic of production can prevent a crisis and improve the ecological global situation.

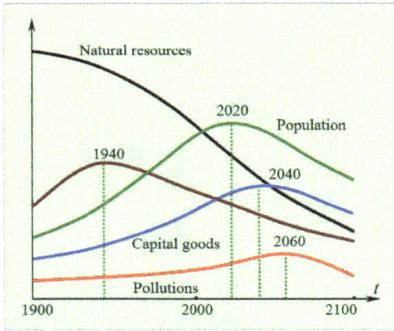

Fig. 6

Each of the first two indicated historical criteria ensured the predominant development of the corresponding production factor and introduced significant resource disharmony into the economy. The criteria for salary and environmental friendliness will behave similarly, but to a greater extent bring the world community closer to natural harmony.

The long-term forecast shown by us in the model of economic practice allows us to outline the prospects for the theory of economics itself – this is its adjustment to the criteria of wages and environmental friendliness of production. But what will the post-synthesis economic theory take on as a whole, and will it be 'economic'?

To answer these questions, let us turn to the complete retroeconomic model (Fig. 7), which, for special reasons, we presented in section 4 of the monograph in a truncated form, that is, with the beginning falling on Smith's synthesis theory. Recalling the symmetry inherent in the history of economic thought, as well as the manifestation of the action of sociogenetic law in it, it is necessary to repeat the position that the study of the more distant past expands the horizon and clarifies the knowledge of the future. Therefore, further in the model there will be two logically connected additional scientific formations. One of them precedes the 'Classical political economy' and the other follows the modern 'Unified socioeconomy'.

The ascent of economic knowledge to a market ideology was carried out in a rather complicated way. In ancient times, a person's ideas about economic activity were of a mythological-sacred nature and were simply merged with his other ideas-beliefs about himself and the surrounding reality. Such 'syncretic', embryonic, merged and undifferentiated economic knowledge, gradually filled with theology and then philosophy, was descriptive, descriptive, and existed for four and a half thousand years. This stage of knowledge, covering the transition from the 'state economy' of antiquity to natural, closed and self-sufficient economies of the Middle Ages, contained two directions: "phenomenolism", in which socially economic phenomena (in the figure it is depicted by a diagonal), and an alternative 'projection', notable for the far-fetched, unfeasibility of the projects of society restructuring already being developed at that time (depicted by the wave line).

The Ancient East (ancient Egypt, Mesopotamia, China and India) of the period of decomposition of the primitive system is the starting point of phenomenolism (3000 BC, in the figure this date and other dates BC are marked with a '−'), devoted mainly to the organization of the state economy kings (despots) and temple facilities.

Ancient Greek philosophers found ideas in Middle Eastern wisdom. Economic philosophy first appears in Socrates (430-399 BC), who moved from the natural philosophy of the ancients to the problem of self-knowledge and the study of man. His economic doctrine has come down to us in the exposition of the Socrates Xenophon (430-355 BC) (*Economy*, 400 BC) – the first 'sociologist-economist'. Xenophon outlined the subject of normative economic ethics, highlighted agriculture, investigated the social division of labor, spoke about the usefulness and mean value of the product of labor.

Normative-idealistic views on the economy and society were contained and developed in the philosophy of the Greek thinker Plato (437-347 BC) (*Politics, or the State*, 380 BC), which can be to be called the founder of the

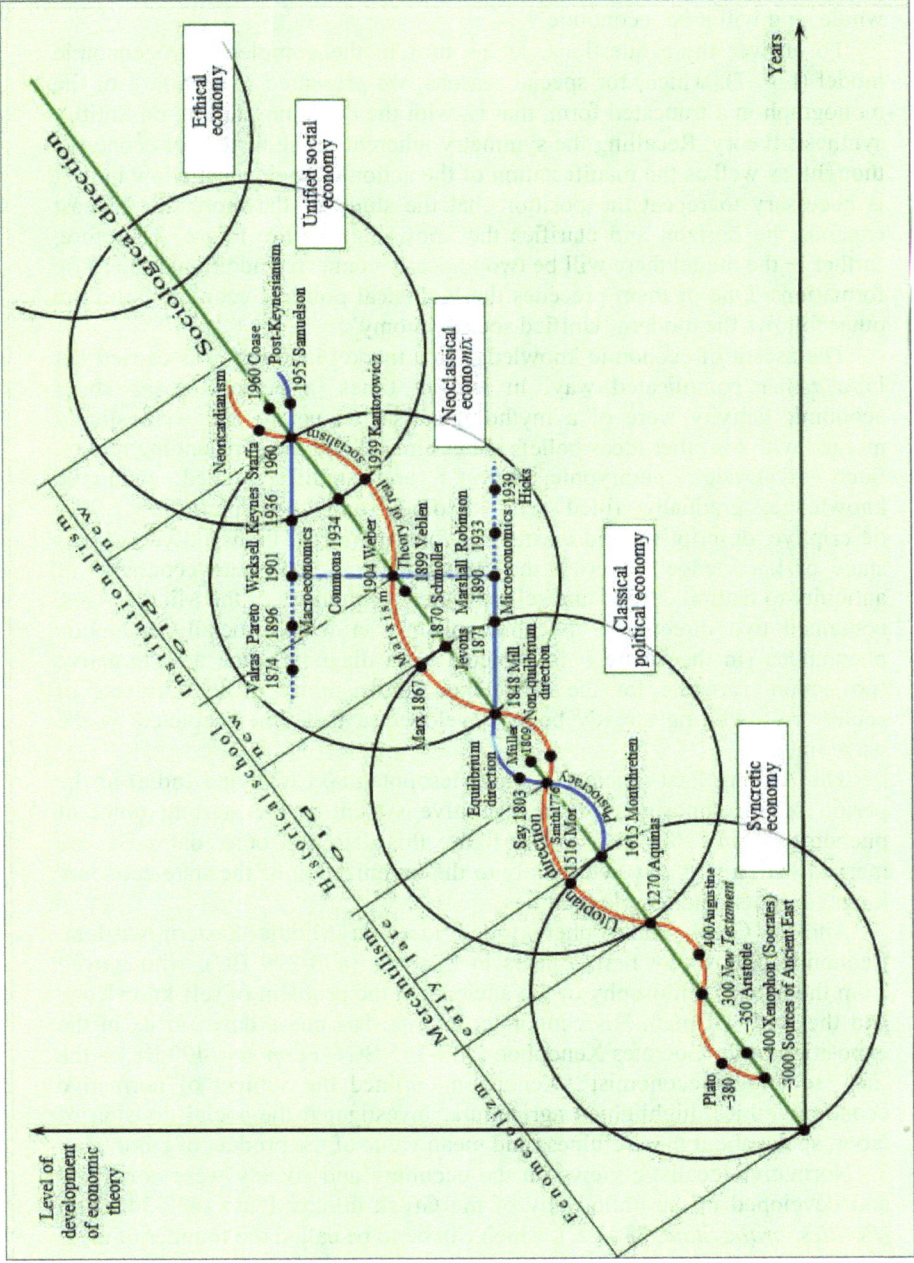

Fig. 7

ject direction of 'Syntetic economy'. He was not only a theoretician of the improvement of society, but also a failed reformer who tried unsuccessfully to transform the city of Syracuse into an 'ideal state'.

Aristotle (384-322 BC) (*Nicomachean Ethics*, 350 BC) was not a follower of the teachings of Plato and embodied in his scientific work the realistic positive direction of the philosophy of Socrates, as well as the tradition of naturalistic empiricism (materialism) pre-Socratic philosophy. Aristotle, unlike Plato, defended private property, which differentiates the well-being of people, and for the first time spoke of the 'middle class'. He divided wealth into natural (real, true) and artificial (monetary), and the science of wealth, respectively, into 'economy' and 'chrematistics', the object of which was negative.

The teachings of Plato and Aristotle were synthesized in the Christian composition *New Testament* (50) – 27 canonized works (4 *Gospels*: Matthew, Mark, Luke and John; *Acts of the Apostles*; and 22 *Epistles*). The canon affirmed the obligation of labor and distribution according to work, considered wealth as the 'root of all evil', prohibited usury interest, in one word, was a synthesis of economic knowledge of that time, relevant for institutional transformations in the period replacing the ancient economy with a feudal one.

But the *New Testament* not only synthesizes the theory of Hellenism, but, being a contradictory, dual doctrine about God-man and a programmatic work, becomes the source of two ideological directions – scholasticism and patristism. In general, scholasticism, based on neo-aristotelism and deployed throughout educational institutions, turned out to be an instrument of inclusion in the power of the church, which, declaring itself an intermediary between the haves and have-nots, took away the 'tithe' of land and products, waged a struggle against usury and interest, regulated trade. Neoplatonic patristics justified the replacement of the state by the church. The ideologist of patristics was the Italian of Algerian origin Aurelius Augustine (Blessed) (354-430) (*On the City of God*, 413-427). Proceeding from the primacy of faith over reason ("I believe in order to understand"), he develops Plato's ideas about a real and ideal state and opposes the sinful secular "earthly hail" a society with the all-round domination of the church is the "hail of God" based on man's love not for himself, but for God.

At the end of 'Syncretic economy', scholasticism and patristics are combined in the teachings of the Italian theologian and philosopher Thomas Aquinas (1225-1274) (*Summa Theology*, 1265-1273), in which he substantiates the naturalness of the estate-serf system. Aquinas can be considered the first theoretician of the commodity economy. Another Aristotelian question of 'fair price', Latinized by Catholics as justum pretium, is interpreted by Aquinas in a new way. For him, a "fair price" is a price that compensates not only the labor of the producer, but also the maintenance of the higher estates. His formula 'price = cost + rent' remains classic.

But at the beginning of Classical Political Economy, Aquinas' controversial doctrine of a 'fair price' split in two. 'Justice' entered the utopian direction of theory, and 'price' – into 'mercantilism'.

The utopian trend was a continuation of the idealistic systems of Plato, the *New Testament*, Augustine and Aquinas. It arose as a reaction to the spread of commodity-money relations, contrary to the 'biblical commandments', of the initial accumulation of capital and the strengthening of usury. The first systematized economic utopia was the theory of the English writer and theologian Thomas More (1478-1535) (*The Golden Book, as Useful as it is Funny, about the Best State Structure and the New Island of Utopia*, 1516), in which private property was declared unfair and state ownership of land and products was justified, labor was considered compulsory for everyone in the distribution of goods according to needs. Mora's teachings were continued by the Italian philosopher Tomaso Campanella (1568-1639), the Englishman Gerard Winstanley (1609-1652), the Frenchman Jean Mellier (1664-1729), Morelli (his name and dates of life are not known) and Gabriel Mably (1704-1785).

The historical boundaries of 'mercantilism' in economic literature are usually indicated by the period of the XVI-XVIII centuries inclusive. But, in our opinion, the birth of 'mercantilism' dates back to the XIV century, at the time of the completion of the crusades (1096-1270) in the Middle East (Syria, Palestine, North Africa), and its completion – in 1849, when it ceased act the *Navigation Act* of the English politician Thomas Cromwell (1485-1540) as an official instrument of the policy of replenishing the treasury with precious metals as monetary material. We also divide 'mercantilism' into early and late.

Early 'mercantilism', which existed until the end of the XVII century, represented the theory of trade and monetary circulation, and not just 'economic policy' as it is commonly believed. The first mercantilist should be considered the Frenchman Nicholas Orem (1323-1382) (*Treatise on the Origin, Nature, Law and Varieties of Money* (1360). The early mercantilists include the 'father of accounting' of the Italian Luca Pacioli (1445-1517) (*On Accounts and Records*, 1495) and Copernicus (*On the Evaluation of Coins*, 1519), as well as English William Stafford (1554-1612) and Man (1571-1641), Italians Gasparo Scaruffi (1519-1584), Bernardo Davanzatti (1529-1606) and Antonio Serra (XVI century), as well as the Frenchman Antoine Montchretien (1575-1621).

Late mercantilists, asking all the same questions of the origin and growth of monetary wealth, expanded their subject somewhat, since market relations had passed the period of initial capital accumulation. In general, as a descriptive and normative direction of the economic theory, 'mercantilism' acquired an institutionalist component – the theory of market ideology, which substantiates the transition from a dependent 'state-serf man' to a 'free economic individual'. Late mercantilists include the Englishmen William Petty (1623-1687), John Locke (1632-1704), Dudley North (1641-1691), John Law (1671-1729), Jacob Vanderlint (? -1740), David Hume (1711-1776) and James Stewart (1712-1780).

Montchretien (*Treatise on Political Economy, Dedicated to the King and Queen*, 1615) was at the beginning of his work a mercantilist, but then he changed his direction, and he can be considered the founder of 'physiocracy' in France. The development of the direction was promoted by the ideology of Enlightenment and the natural science of the Renaissance. The theory of "nature" included in the transfer of attention from trade to production, the absolutization of the productive forces of the land and agriculture, a reproductive approach in research, as well as the proclamation of the laissez-faire principle. In addition to

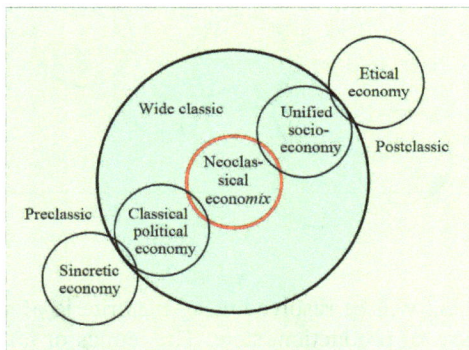

Fig. 8

Montchretien, we include Pierre Bois-Guillebert (1646-1714), Richard Cantillon (1680-1734), Quesnay, Vincent de Gournet (1712-1759), Pierre de la Riviera (1720-1793), Jacques Turgot (1727-1781), Victor Mirabeau (1715-1789) and Samuel Dupont de Nemour (1739-1817)

Despite the contrast between mature utopian, mercantilist and physiocratic theories from the middle of the XVIII century there was an intense convergent interaction between them (Fig. 7). The convergence of scientific positions was based on the acceptance of the market as the only efficient system of civil society functioning at that time and the understanding that the homo oeconomicus model with the laissez-faire principle is adequate to the free life of individuals. In that situation, Smith's teaching appeared, synthesizing the views of representatives of the corresponding directions. Therefore, in his *Wealth of Nations* (1776), we find a combination of elements of utopia and 'physiocracy', as well as a fundamental contradiction that determines the nature of all subsequent market theory.

The symmetry in the number and mutual arrangement of scientific formations, shown in our retroeconomic model, makes it possible to more clearly outline the content of the fifth, supposed formation. Since economic knowledge before Smith did not take shape in an independent science, developed in philosophy and theology, wore the general form of morality, then at the end of the entire cycle of its independent development it will go beyond the purely economic knowledge and will again become a moral science. This transformation will be facilitated by the phenomenon of 'economic imperialism', noted by us above. Therefore, we call the fifth, predictive formation, "Ethical economy", in which social issues of 'human capital' and environmental management will be resolved using the criteria of salary and environmental friendliness of production. state. The 'ethics of interest', attainable through government regulation in terms of the criterion of profitability, demonstrated by us above, under the new criteria will be extended to the whole complex of factors that determine the quality of life of people in the global community. And with the completion of the 'dispute of two Cambridges', the problematic nature of the 'Unified socioeconomy' and 'Ethical economy' will inevitably persist.

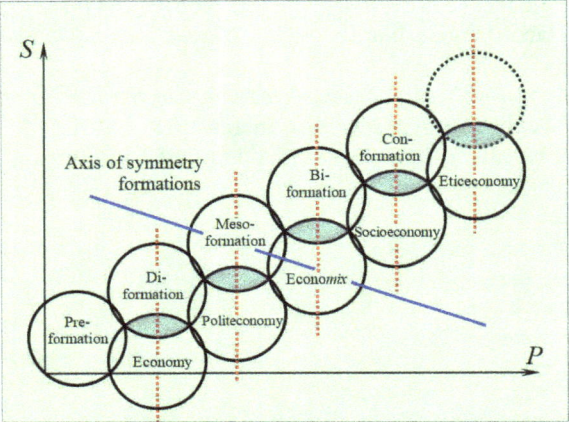

Fig. 9

'Syncretic economy', describing the natural economy from moral and religious positions, can be considered 'Preclassics', and the fifth scientific formation, with which people are connected, will hopefully implement The declaration of real equality of people, proclaimed back in the *New Testament*, and a fair solution to actual and specific socio-ecological problems, will be 'postclassics' (Fig. 8). Thus, the path from 'syncretika' to 'concretization' lies through the superformation, 'Wide classics', in which the formation took place, rather complex and dramatic development. tie, as well as unification of theories of market economics.

In Fig. 9 compares the metaeconomic model of the development of social production with the retromodel we have developed for the development of economic thought. The model shows that there is a certain mutual correspondence between the models, expressed in the fact that not only the theory as a

268

whole adequately reflects practice, but also practice realizes the ideas of the theory through the implementation of a specific economic policy. This correspondence between the formations in the figure is indicated by vertical dashed lines, and economic policy – by shaded areas of coincidence of formations, which line up in a row corresponding to the historical sequence of power systems: exocracy (coercion of a person by external nature), aristocracy (in the form of autocracy and theocracy), plutocracy, bureaucracy (in the form of technocracy and partocracy) and noocracy (the power of reason and knowledge).

Since 'Syncretic economy' describes the pre-market economy of *Preformation* and *Diformation*, political economy studies the pre-industrial market, 'Neoclassical econo*mix*' represents the theory of industrial society, and 'Unified socioeconomy' – the theory of post-industrial society, then the model a single 'axis of symmetry of formations' of practice and theory shows the possibilities of effective forecasting of the economy itself and advance theoretical elaboration and preparation for the solution of expected problems (indicated in the figure by a dotted outline).

Bibliogrphy

1. Avdasheva S.B., Rozanova N.M. The theory of the organization of industrial markets. M., 1998.

2. Aleskerov F.T. The history of collective choice in Russia and the Soviet Union // Arrow K. Collective choice and individual values. M., 2004.

3. Ananyin OI The economic theory of K. Marx // Economic theory in historical development: a view from France and Russia / under total. ed. A.G. Khudokormov, A. Lapidus. M., 2017.

4. Afanasyev V.S. The first systems of political economy (Method of economic duality). M., 2005.

5. Bartenev S.A. Economic theories and schools: history and modernity. M., 1996.

6. Barulin V.S. Social life. Methodological issues. M., 1987.

7. Bator F. Simple analytics of welfare maximization // Milestones of economic thought. Welfare Economics and Public Choice. T. 4. SPb., 2004.

8. Bentham I. Introduction to the foundations of morality and legislation. SPb., 1867.

9. Behrens V., Havranek P.M. Investment Performance Assessment Guide. M., 1995.

10. Business: Explanatory Dictionary: English-Russian. M., 1998.

11. Blanchard O. Macroeconomics. M., 2010.

12. Blaug M. 100 Great Economists before Keynes. SPb., 2005.

13. Blaug M. 100 Great Economists after Keynes. SPb., 2005.

14. Blaug M. Economic thought in retrospect. M., 1994.

15. Black J. Economics: Explanatory Dictionary: English-Russian. M., 2000.

16. Great Soviet Encyclopedia. In 30 volumes, M., 1970-1978.

17. Brodsky B.E. Macroeconomics: Advanced Level. M., 2012.

18. Bugayan I.R. Macroeconomics. Rostov-on-Don, 2000.

19. Buchanan J. The Constitution of Economic Policy // Buchanan J. Works. M., 1997.

20. Vasilkova V.V. Order and chaos in the development of social systems (Synergetics and the theory of social self-organization). SPb., 1999.

21. Introduction to the market economy / ed. I.J Livshits, I.N. Nikulina. M., 1994.

22. Vechkanov G.S., Vechkanova G.R. Micro- and macroeconomics. Encyclopedic Dictionary. SPb., 2000.

23. Vechkanov G.S., Vechkanova G.R. Economic theory. M., 2007.

24. World history of economic thought. In 5 volumes / ed. V. I. Cherkovets. M., 1987-1997.

25. Halperin V.M., Grebennikov P.I., Leussky A.I., Tarasevich L.S.

Macroeconomics. SPb., 1997.

26. Halperin V.M., Ignatiev S.M., Morgunov V.I. Microeconomics. In 2 volumes. SPb., 1994, 1998.

27. Hegel G.V.F. Compositions. In 14 t. M.-L., 1929-1959. T. 4, P. 130.

28. Gossen G.G. Development of the laws of public relations of exchange and the rules of human activity arising from it // World economic thought. Through the prism of centuries. In 5 volumes. M., 2004.

29. Grebnev L.S., Nureyev R.M. Economy. Basics course. M., 2000.

30. Grinberg R.S., Rubinstein A.Y. Economic sociodynamics. M., 2000.

31. Grodsky V.S. Interaction of demographic processes and economic growth // Economic sciences. 1976. No. 8.

32. Grodsky V.S. Laws of development of economic theory. M., 2004.

33. Grodsky V.S. Metaeconomics is a theory of technological and institutional changes in the evolution of social production. Samara, 2010.

34. Grodsky V.S. Development of the idea of state regulation of market defects by J.M. Keynes. M., 2013.

35. Grodsky V.S. Reconstruction of the Economies: A Neo-Cardinalist Approach. Samara, 2007.

36. Grodsky V.S. Retrokonomics, or Laws of the History of World Economic Thought. M., 2017.

37. Grodsky V.S. Retroeconomic theory. Samara, 2006.

38. Grodsky V.S. Modern problems of economics. M., 2011.

39. Grodsky V.S. The theory of transformation processes in the economy. Samara, 2016.

40. Grodsky V.S. What does the study of economic doctrines give. 10 Essays on Constructive Retroeconomics. Samara, 2009.

41. Galbraith J.K. The great crash of 1929. Minsk, 2009.

42. Jayley D.A., Reni F.J. Microeconomics: advanced level. M., 2011.

43. De Frey M. The history of macroeconomics: from Keynes to Lucas to the present. M., 2019.

44. Eliseeva I.I., Bykov V.V. Preface to the Russian edition // Kurtz H.D. Capital, distribution, effective demand. M., 1998.

45. Zang V.-B. Synergetic economy. Time and changes in nonlinear economic theory. M., 1999.

46. Ivashkovsky S.N. Macroeconomics. M., 2000.

47. From the manuscript of Karl Marx "Criticism of Political Economy (rough sketch 1857-1859)" // Problems of Philosophy. 1965. No. 8.

48. History of economic doctrines / ed. V. Avtonomova, O. Ananin, N. Makasheva. M., 2000.

49. The history of economic doctrines: (modern stage) / ed. A.G. Khudokormova. M., 1998.

50. Itwell J. Old and new controversy in the theory of surplus value //

Theory of capital and economic growth. M., 2004.

51. Keynes J.M. Selected works. M., 1993.

52. Keynes J.M. General theory of employment // Keynes J.M. General theory of employment, interest and money. Favorites. M., 2009.

53. Keynes J.M. General theory of employment, interest and money. Favorites. M., 2009.

54. Kendrick J. Aggregate capital of the United States and its formation. M., 1978.

55. Kindleberger Ch., Aliber R. World financial crises. Manias, panics and crashes. SPb., 2010.

56. Clarke J.B. Distribution of wealth. M., 1992.

57. Klauer R. Keynesian counterrevolution: a theoretical assessment // Keynes J.M. General theory of employment, interest and money. Favorites. M., 2009.

58. Kolemaev V.A. Economic and mathematical modeling. Modeling of macroeconomic processes and systems. M., 2005.

59. Krugman P. Return of the Great Depression? The world crisis through the eyes of a Nobel laureate. M., 2009.

60. Kuhn T. The structure of scientific revolutions. M., 1977.

61. The course of economic theory / ed. prof. M.N. Chepurin and prof. E.A. Kiseleva. Kirov, 2010.

62. Kurtz H.D. and Salvadori N. Theory of production: a long-term analysis. M., 2004.

63. Kurtz H.D. Capital, distribution, effective demand. M., 1998.

64. Lakatos I. Falsification and methodology of scientific research programs. M., 1995.

65. Lerner A.P. The concept of monopoly and the measurement of monopoly power // Milestones of economic thought. The theory of industrial markets. T. 5. SPb., 2003.

66. Lvov D.S., Rubinstein A.Ya. Measuring production efficiency. M., 1972.

67. Layard R. Macroeconomics. A course of lectures for Russian readers. M., 1994.

68. McConnell C.R., Bru C.L. Economics: principles, problems and politics. M., 1999.

69. Marx K. and Engels F. Works. In 50 volumes, M., 1955-1982.

70. Marx K. Capital: a criticism of political economy. In 3 volumes, M., 2011.

71. Marshall A. Fundamentals of economic science. M., 2008.

72. Milovanov V.P. Unbalanced socioeconomic systems: synergy and self-organization. M., 2001.

73. Mankiw P.G. Principles of Economics. SPb., 1999.

74. Nazar S. The path to the great goal: the history of one economic idea. M., 2013.

75. Nikiforov A.A., Antipina O.N., Miklashevskaya N.A. Macroeconomics: scientific schools, concepts, economic policy. M., 2008.

76. Nobel laureates of the XX century. Economy. Encyclopedic Dictionary. M., 2001.

77. Neumann E. Origin and development of consciousness. M., 1998.

78. Nureyev R. M. Course of microeconomics. M., 2007.

79. Olsevich Y.Y. The influence of economic reforms in Russia and China on the economic thought of the West. M., 2007.

80. Oreshin V.P. State regulation of the national economy. M., 1999.

81. Panorama of economic thought at the end of the twentieth century. In 2 volumes / ed. D. Greenaway, M. Blini, I. Stewart. SPb., 2002.

82. Patinkin D. Money, percent and prices. Combining the theory of money and the theory of value. M., 2004.

83. Pigou A. Economic theory of welfare. In 2 volumes. M., 1985.

84. Popper K. Logic and the growth of scientific knowledge. Selected works. M., 1983.

85. Reynolds M., Smolenskiy Y. Economic theory of welfare: the conditions under which change means improvement // Modern economic thought / ed. S. Weintraub. M., 1981.

86. Ricardo D. Principles of political economy and taxation. M., 2016.

87. Robinson J. The economic theory of imperfect competition. M., 1986.

88. Romer D. Higher macroeconomics. M., 2015.

89. Roncaglia A. Wealth of ideas: the history of economic thought. M., 2018.

90. Rothbard M. The Great Depression in America. M .; Chelyabinsk, 2016.

91. Ruzavin G.I.. Synergetics and the dialectical concept of development // Philosophical Sciences. 1984. No. 5.

92. Ruzavin G.I. Synergetics and systems approach // Philosophical Sciences. 1985. No. 5.

93. Rumyantseva E.E. New Economic Encyclopedia. M., 2005.

94. Sagradov A.A. Human Development Index: Application Experience. M., 2000.

95.Sachs J.D., Larren B.F. Macroeconomics. A global approach. M., 1996.

96. Samuelson P.A., Nordhaus V.D. Economy. M., 1997.

97. Samuelson P.A. Foundations of economic analysis. SPb., 2002.

98. Sandmo A. Economics: the history of ideas. M., 2019.

99. Sachko N.S. The time factor in the Soviet economy. M., 1976.

100. Seligman B. The main currents of modern economic thought. M.,

1968.

101. Selishchev A.S. Macroeconomics. SPb., 1997.

102. Selishchev A.S. Microeconomics. SPb., 2002.

103. Sen A. About ethics and economics. M., 1996.

104. Skidelsky R. Keynes. Return of the Master. M., 2011.

105. Macmillan's Dictionary of Modern Economic Theory. M., 2003.

106. Broken J. Economics. Express course. SPb., 2007.

107. Sludkovskaya M.A., Rozinskaya N.A. Development of Western economic thought in a socio-economic context. M., 2005.

108. Smirnov A.D. Lectures on Macroeconomic Modeling. M., 2000.

109. Smith A. Research on the nature and causes of the wealth of peoples. M., 2007.

110. Modern economic thought / under the editorship of S. Weintraub. M., 1981.

111. Sraffa P. Production of goods by means of goods. Prelude to the criticism of economic theory. M., 1999.

112. Stiglitz D., Sen A., Fitoussi J.-P. Misjudging Our Lives: Why Doesn't GDP Make Sense? Report of the Commission on Measuring Economic Performance and Social Progress. M., 2016.

113. Stoleru L. Equilibrium and economic growth. Principles of Macroeconomic Analysis. M., 1974.

114. Say J.-B. Treatise on Political Economy // Say J.-B. Treatise on Political Economy; Bastiat F. Economic sophisms. Economic harmony. M., 2000.

115. Tarasevich L.S., Grebennikov P.I., Leussky A.I. Macroeconomics. M., 2003.

116. Tarasevich L.S., Grebennikov P.I., Leussky A.I. Microeconomics. M., 2003.

117. The theory of capital and economic growth / ed. prof. S.S. Dzarasov. M., 2004.

118. Feldman A.M. Economic theory of welfare // Economic theory / ed. J. Itwell, M. Milgate, P. Newman. M., 2004.

119. Philosophical Encyclopedic Dictionary. M., 1983.

120. Fisher S., Dornbusch R., Schmalenzi R. Economics. M., 1993.

121. Frankfort G., Frankfort G.A., Wilson D., Jacobsen T.V. On the eve of philosophy. Spiritual quest of ancient man. M., 1984.

122. Harris L. Monetary theory. M., 1990.

123. Heilbroner R.L. Philosophers from this world. Life, time and ideas of great economic thinkers. M., 2008.

124. Hicks J.R. Cost and capital. M., 1998.

125. Hicks J.R. Gospolin Keynes and the "classics": an attempt at interpretation // Keynes J.M. General theory of employment, interest and

money. Favorites. M., 2009.

126. Hodgson D. Economic theory and institutions: Manifesto of modern institutional economic theory. M., 2003.

127. Khodov L. G. Fundamentals of State Economic Policy. M., 1997.

128. Khudokormov A.G. Economic Theory: The Newest Currents of the West. M., 2009.

129. Schumpeter J. The history of economic analysis. In 3 volumes. SPb., 2004.Vol. 3.

130. Schumpeter J. Capitalism, Socialism and Democracy. M., 1995.

131. Eggertsson T. Economic behavior and institutions. M., 2001.

132. Eichner A. Why is economics not yet a science? // Theory of capital and economic growth / ed. prof. S.S. Dzarasov. M., 2004.

133. Economic encyclopedia / ed. collegium, under the leadership of acad. RAS L.I. Abalkin. M., 1999.

134. Arrow K.J. Uncertainty and the economics of health care welfare // Vekhi ekonomicheskogo thoughta. Welfare Economics and Public Choice. T. 4. SPb., 2004.

135. Economics / ed. A.I. Arkhipova, A.N. Nesterenko, A.K. Bolshakov. M., 1998.

136. Economic theory / ed. D. Itwell, M. Milgate, P. Newman. M., 2004.

137. Economic Encyclopedia / Ch. ed. L.I. Abalkin. M., 1999.

138. Challenge. 1983. November / December.

139. Edgeworth F.Y. Mathematical Psychics: an Essey on Application of Mathematies to the Moral Sciences. L., 1888.

140. Fisher I. The nature of Capital and Income. N. Y., 1923.

141. Garegnani P. Heterogeneous Capital, the Production Function and the Theory of Distribution. Review of Economic Studies. 1970, № 37.

142. Hicks J. Crisis in Keynsian Economics. N. Y., 1974.

143. Hicks J. Revision of Demand Theory. Oxford, 1956.

144. Hicks J.R. Value and Capital. Oxford, 1939.

145.https://www.rbc.ru/business/20/08/019/5d5b40de9a7947f157ec8aa1?from=frommain.

146. Jevons W.S. Money and the Mechanism of Exchange. L., 1875.

147. Keynes and the Modern World. In 2 volumes, Cambridge, 1983.

148. Keynes, John Maynard / The New Polgrave: A Dictionary of Economics. Vol. 3. L., 1987.

149. Robinson J. Economic Heresies. N. Y., 1971.

150. Robinson J. Economic Philosophy. N. Y., 1962.

151. Robinson J. The Production Function and the Theory of Capital // Review of Economic Studies. 1953. XXI.

152. Romer J. New Direction in the Marxian Theory of Exploitation and Class // Analitical Marxism / ed. by J. Romer. Cambridge, 1986.

153. Skidelsky R. John Maynard Keynes. The Economist as Saviour, 1920-1937. L., 1994.

154. Samuelson P. Econmics. An Introductory Analisis. N. Y., 1955.

155. Samuelson P. A note on the Pure Theory of Consumer's Behavior // Economica, February. 1938.

156. Samuelson P.A. A Revisionist View of von Neumann's Grovth model // John von Neumann fnd Modern Economics / under eds. Dore M., Chakravarty S. and Goodvin R. Oxford, 1989.

157. Steedman I. Marx after Sraffa. L., 1977.